Insight Guides

Created and Directed by Hans Höfer

The Pacific Northwest

Project Editors: Janie Freeburg and Diana Ackland
Update Editor: John Wilcock
Managing Editor: Martha Ellen Zenfell

Editorial Director: Brian Bell

Houghton Mifflin

APA PUBLICATIONS

Höfer

Freeburg

Ackland

Abbott

Pierce

Pintarich

Covering the American northwestern states of Washington and Oregon, and bringing the work of 30-odd resident writers and photographers into one volume was never going to be an easy task. That said, the challenge seemed perfect for Insight Guides, the series founded by **Hans Höfer** over 25 years ago. The first title, *Insight Guide: Bali*, was published by Höfer's Apa Publications in 1970 and became the seminal work for this widely acclaimed series. With a formula that combines frank writing and bold photojournalism, the Insight series had the scope to do justice to both the task and the territory. Although over the years *Insight Guide; Pacific Northwest* has been updated, revised, reviewed and revamped, all in keeping with our changing times, the people who were involved in that first edition way back in the 1980s still deserve a bow. Thanks, first of all, then, to **Janie Freeburg** and **Diana Ackland**, the original project editors.

Freeburg has planned, edited and designed a number of publications in her job as a public relations specialist. A graduate of the University of California, Irvine, with a degree in comparative cultures, she also studied commercial art and graphic design.

Ackland was editor in the features and articles department of *Good Housekeeping* magazine and later the *Los Angeles Times* syndicate. When the book came out she was serving as vice-president of Sequoia Communications, the Santa Barbara publishing company she helped set up with her husband.

The task of researching and organizing the efforts of diverse writers and photographers went to the public relations manager of the Seattle Art Museum, our field editor **Helen Abbott**. A graduate of the University of Washington, she has lived on both coasts and traveled from Canada to Mexico. Abbott worked as an editor at Rosebud Books in Los Angeles where she guided *The Best of Los Angeles, The Best of San Diego* and *The Architecture of Los Angeles* to press.

J. Kingston Pierce and **Richard M. Pintarich** collaborated on the extensive first section of the book, covering geography, history, modern economy and the people of the Northwest. Pierce is a journalist with a special interest in Northwest history. His interests have taken him to writing and editing positions at newspapers and magazines in Seattle, Portland, Detroit and Boulder, Colorado.

Pintarich is an instructor of history at Portland Community College and holds an MA in history from Portland State University. A Portland native, he is also a contributing editor on *Oregon Magazine*.

Elizabeth Bailey Herman, an English/journalism graduate of the University of Washington, wrote about the Space Needle and other attractions of Seattle, while **Leslie Johnson**, a Seattle native, has traveled throughout Puget Sound and explored the beautiful, uninhabited isles amid the San Juans. **Marilyn McFarlane**, a Portland freelance writer, has traveled widely in the United States and much of Europe. Her work has been published in numerous magazines and travel publications, and she has written and collaborated on a number of books, as well as serving as correspondent for several regional newspapers.

When not pursuing her favorite

hobby, birdwatching in rural eastern Washington and exploring the back roads of that state, **Elizabeth DeFato** is Seattle Art Museum's librarian. To date, DeFato's peregrinations have taken her across the US and throughout western Europe.

Gerald Nelson, a native Northwesterner, has written several books, including *Seattle: The Life and Times of an American City*, which provided valuable insight. Travel writer **Lee Foster** has contributed to several Insight Guides in the past. He has also written extensively for numerous travel publications and published several books on travel, gardening and health. A few of his pictures can be seen in this book too.

Foster

Marnie McPhee has written about the Northwest for the last decade and contributed the section on Portland.

Warren

Long

Eugene resident **Stuart Warren** is a tour director for a major tour company and has guided tours through Yosemite and Yellowstone National Parks as well as throughout the United States and Canada. His collaborator **Ted Long** is a graduate in journalism from the University of Wisconsin. A travel writer and tour guide, Long has traveled extensively from Colombia to Canada. Freelance writer **Mark Hoy** has spent many years in the Northwest, writing of his concern for the region's ecology and future.

Writer, editor and former bookstore-owner **Charles Ackley** is a native of the Wallowa County in Oregon's northeast corner. His first-hand experience and enthusiasm make his contribution an integral part of the guide. Many thanks. **Elton Welke** is a writer and magazine editor with experience at *Sunset* and *Better Homes and Gardens*, with many books to his credit.

Marine biologist **David Gordon** writes extensively for local news magazines, hosts a monthly radio program on the rich marine resources of Washington, and has traveled along the coast as a collector of specimens for zoos and aquariums.

Also with a love of the outdoors is **Stephanie Irving**. Her writing has appeared in publications for the Seattle Art Museum and the University of Washington, and in *Puget Sound* magazine. **Patty Belmonte** is an Olympia freelance writer and marketing consultant with a special interest in natural resource and agriculture industries. **Suzanne Kotz** assembled the extensive array of information in the Travel Tips section. She is head of publications for the Seattle Art Museum.

Irving

Four people who have worked hard to keep this book updated over the years are **Giselle Smith**, editor of *Seattle Magazine*, **John Wilcock**, Apa Publications' West Coast editor, and the author of two of this book's essays, **Martha Ellen Zenfell**, Apa's Editor-in-Chief of North American titles, and **Susan Dumett**, also of Seattle.

Wilcock

One of the most outstanding features of this book is the work of principal photographer **Ed Cooper**. A native New Yorker, Cooper's affection for some of America's most dramatic landscapes is evident in many of the images that follow. His work has appeared in all the major US conservation and outdoor magazines. Thanks, too, to Oregon-based photographer **George Baetjer**, and Washington-based photographer **Joel Rogers**.

Cooper

CONTENTS

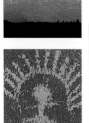

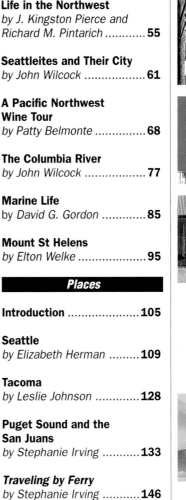

Introduction

A New Frontier
by J. Kingston Pierce and
Richard M. Pintarich **19**

History and People

Beginnings
by J. Kingston Pierce and
Richard M. Pintarich **20**

A Land of Plenty
by J. Kingston Pierce and
Richard M. Pintarich **25**

The Explorers Arrive
by J. Kingston Pierce and
Richard M. Pintarich **28**

The Boom Years
by J. Kingston Pierce and
Richard M. Pintarich **42**

Modern Times
by J. Kingston Pierce and
Richard M. Pintarich **49**

Features

Life in the Northwest
by J. Kingston Pierce and
Richard M. Pintarich **55**

Seattleites and Their City
by John Wilcock **61**

**A Pacific Northwest
Wine Tour**
by Patty Belmonte **68**

The Columbia River
by John Wilcock **77**

Marine Life
by David G. Gordon **85**

Mount St Helens
by Elton Welke **95**

Places

Introduction **105**

Seattle
by Elizabeth Herman **109**

Tacoma
by Leslie Johnson **128**

**Puget Sound and the
San Juans**
by Stephanie Irving **133**

Traveling by Ferry
by Stephanie Irving **146**

Sea Kayaking
by Leslie Johnson **148**

The Washington Coast
by Marilyn McFarlane **152**

CONTENTS

The Washington Mountains
by Stephanie Irving **168**

Central Washington
by Elizabeth DeFato **174**

Inland Washington
by Gerald B. Nelson **187**

The Columbia River Gorge
by Lee Foster.................... **194**

Portland, Oregon
by Marnie McPhee **202**

The Oregon Coast
by Lee Foster.................... **214**

Willamette River Valley
by Stuart Warren and
Ted Long **228**

The Rogue River
by Mark Hoy **239**

**Oregon Caves National
Monument**
by Mark Hoy **244**

Southern Oregon
by Stuart Warren and
Ted Long **249**

Bend and Central Oregon
by Stuart Warren and
Ted Long **258**

Lava and Lake Country, Oregon
by George Baetjer **268**

John Day Fossil Beds
by George Baetjer **279**

Northeast Oregon
by Charles Ackley.............. **285**

National Parks

Olympic National Park
by Elton Welke **297**

North Cascades National Park
by Elton Welke **300**

Mount Rainier National Park
by Lee Foster.................... **302**

Crater Lake National Park
by Lee Foster.................... **307**

Maps

Washington State **104**
Oregon State **104**
Heart of Seattle **110**
Greater Seattle **114**
Olympic Peninsula **158**
Downtown Portland **203**
Southwestern Oregon **240**
Oregon-Bend Area **260**
Crater Lake **307**

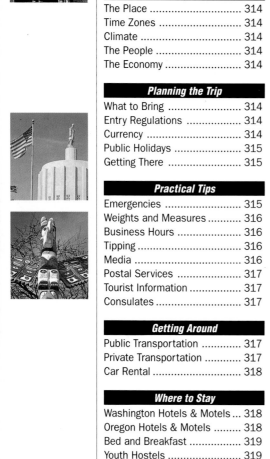

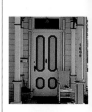

Getting Acquainted

The Place 314
Time Zones 314
Climate 314
The People 314
The Economy 314

Planning the Trip

What to Bring 314
Entry Regulations 314
Currency 314
Public Holidays 315
Getting There 315

Practical Tips

Emergencies 315
Weights and Measures 316
Business Hours 316
Tipping 316
Media 316
Postal Services 317
Tourist Information 317
Consulates 317

Getting Around

Public Transportation 317
Private Transportation 317
Car Rental 318

Where to Stay

Washington Hotels & Motels ... 318
Oregon Hotels & Motels 318
Bed and Breakfast 319
Youth Hostels 319

Eating Out

Where to Eat in Washington 319
Where to Eat in Oregon 319
Drinking Notes 320

Attractions

Museums 320
Art Galleries 320
Theaters 320
Movies 321
Libraries 321
Tourist Attractions 321
Tours 322

Festivals and Events

A Portland Calendar 323
A Seattle Calendar 324
Nightlife 324

Shopping

Sales Tax 325
Shopping Areas ....,... 325

Sports & Leisure

Participant Sports 325
Spectator Sports 325

Language

General 325
In the Airport 325
In Print 326
In Hotels 326

Further Reading

General 326
Other Insight Guides 326

Art/Photo Credits 327
Index 328

A NEW FRONTIER

Without question, water is the major factor affecting life in the Pacific Northwest – water in the form of rain (either too much or too little), snow, lakes, rivers, sounds, inlets and, of course, the ocean. This varied region is surrounded by water or the evidence of water's action on the landscape. And the effect is extraordinary.

Looking at Washington and Oregon from an imaginary vantage point high above the Cascade Mountains range, one cannot help noticing the differences in the landscapes and lifestyles that these craggy barriers to water create. The western portion of the region is green and fertile, lush with vegetation year-round. It is heavily populated by comparison to the east and, in the summertime, it is a gorgeous playground for the sportsminded with sailing, fishing, hiking, backpacking and all manner of outdoor activities. To the east, the arid stretches of land that lie in the rain shadow of the mountains are patchworked with irrigated agricultural riches. The east boasts lakes, rivers and miles of golden, waving wheatfields – as well as recreational wonders of its own.

For the visitor, the Pacific Northwest's ocean beaches, rain forests, pristine mountains and verdant valleys hold an obvious allure. The two largest cities, Seattle and Portland, feature sophisticated amenities, as well as mountain views. And the small-town friendliness of the rural regions is a boon to the traveler.

The Pacific Northwest offers miles of mountain vistas, ferryboat tours through emerald islands, the subtle beauty of the desert in springtime, the quiet pleasures of flycasting and birdwatching, and the exhilarating challenge of whitewater sports or cross-country skiing – all in a breathtakingly beautiful environment.

For once, the travel cliché is correct. This destination has something for everyone; it is truly a new frontier.

Preceding pages: face of the ages; Seattle skyline; misty forest at Cape Lookout State Park; Cascade Range volcanic peaks seen from the Middle Sister; Cannon Beach, Oregon; old farm buildings in winter dress, Lopez Island; fields of golden wheat near Pendleton, Oregon. **Left**, a pioneer village at Cashmere, Washington.

There were no curious tourists around to take snapshots of the Pacific Northwest's Paleozoic shoreline, but we know that some 200 million years ago Pacific Ocean waves lapped at beaches that today lie high and dry not far west of the Idaho border. There was no Pacific Northwest. In its place stood a mammoth bay, stretching from northern California into Canada.

But the continents were restless. The Americas were parting from Europe and Africa, and butting against the Pacific Ocean course of 100 million years they went their separate ways, with the Klamaths most likely standing for a time as a huge island in the blue Pacific.

When a descending basalt ocean floor slides 60 miles (96 km) into the bowels of the earth, as the Pacific floor did beneath the encroaching North American landmass, it melts and begins returning to the surface in fiery, liquid form. So about 100 miles (160 km) behind the westward edge of North America's steady march to the sea a chain of

floor. When the two plates collided, the heavier ocean bottom dove beneath roaming North America.

As the North American continent skidded over the hard bedrock seafloor, it scraped off the soft coastal plain and continental shelf, bulldozing these light materials ahead of it. The debris grew higher and wider until it formed a new range of coastal mountains along the western edge of North America. These mountains are today known as the Wallowas and the Blues.

The Klamath Mountains in southern Oregon and California's Sierras were also a part of this new coastal range, but in the ash and lava-spewing volcanoes emerged to further develop this edge of the continent.

The sun rose and set millions of times on this fair corner of the world before anything close to the present Northwest coastline was established. It was only 35 million years ago that the ocean bed of the Pacific finally cracked and began sinking many miles offshore, parallel to this coastline. Behind it emerged a straight north–south line of volcanoes in the bay, the predecessors of today's Cascade Range. These volcanoes stretched

Above, Mount Rainier seen shimmering through a field of beargrass.

across the mouth of the old bay to create an inland sea. This sea was slowly filled in by sediments sliding from the continent to the east and by violent volcanic activity that tossed more than 1,000 feet (300 meters) of molten rock and ash into the captured body of water over the course of the next 10 million years.

The coup de grace for this huge inland waterway came when the western Cascades abruptly ceased their incessant belching. Fissures opened up just east of the sea, spewing unparalleled quantities of molten basalt that covered hundreds of square miles of the sea bed to an average depth of 500 feet (150 meters). Today, this so-called Columbia Plateau covers about 225,000 sq miles (582,000 sq km) in eastern Oregon, eastern Washington and Idaho, and it ranks as one of the two largest basalt flows in the world.

Fifteen million years ago, at about the same time that basalt flows were covering the land in this area, the northern half of the Coast Range began to emerge. These mountains weren't built up from the muck piled against the continental plate by the descending Pacific Ocean floor. Instead, sediments that had accumulated beneath the part of the sunken floor nearest today's Oregon and Washington coastlines uplifted the stranded floor, bending it high enough to form the Coast Range and to expose the fossils of the former seabed.

A snake in hell: Rivers cut through all of this geological turmoil. The Snake, at the eastern edge of Oregon, fought a course over the new land, digging a deeper and deeper path, creating what we know today as Hell's Canyon. At more than a mile down from rim to river, this is the deepest canyon in North America. And then there is the mighty Columbia. For eons this river pushed relentlessly through the Coast Range and etched its way into the strata of what we recognize today as the Columbia Gorge, exposing thick layers of geology along the gorge's basalt walls that represent millions of years of geological development.

Ice ages have played their own games with the Columbia's course. Just a few million years ago, a long tongue of ice ground down the Okanogan Valley to block the river in what is today central Washington. It brought with it huge amounts of rock from Canada, liberally distributing that rock in the form of glacial moraine ridges and huge boulders called "haystacks," or glacial erratics. Some of the abducted boulders were set down on native stones by the marauding ice to become the "balanced rocks" of today.

The westward-flowing Columbia backed up behind this ice dam until it overflowed its banks to the south and gouged a 35-mile (56-km) long channel across the country in southern Oregon. The liberated river splashed over a basalt ledge to create a prehistoric cataract 40 times mightier than Niagara Falls. When the iceflow retreated, the Columbia returned to its old westward channel, leaving as evidence of its southern rampage Grand Coulee, a huge chasm at the head of which is Dry Falls, a ghost falls that, at 3 miles (5 km) across and 400 feet (120 meters) high, is one of the world's geological wonders.

Eruptions: Volcanoes have become an important, if sometimes neglected, aspect of the region's history. About 8,000 years ago, Native Americans were here to witness the explosive eruption of Mount Mazama, the large crater of which now holds Oregon's picturesque Crater Lake. And in May 1980, Washington's Mount St Helens gave Northwest residents an all-too-powerful demonstration of the forces that created this region. This was certainly not the first time that Mount St Helens had demonstrated its pyrotechnic capabilities – and it probably won't be the last.

The mountain's incontinence holds an important place in Klickitat Indian mythology. As the ancient Klickitat story goes, a pair of Indian warriors, Wyeast and Pahto, fought each other for the love of an enticing Indian maiden. This was no ordinary forest skirmish, but involved earthquakes as well as valleys of rock and fire exchange across the Columbia River. To once again settle the earth, the gods transformed Pahto and Wyeast into mountains along the Cascades chain: Wyeast became Mount Hood, while Pahto became Mount Rainier. The virtuous maiden who had captured the hearts of both warriors was, of course, changed into the once-graceful Mount St Helens. Perhaps the moral of the story is that even the most virtuous of maidens can blow their stacks at times.

But it isn't volcanoes that have made a name for the Northwest. Mostly it's the rain. Nineteenth-century explorers Meriwether Lewis and William Clark, sent into this part of the country by President Thomas Jefferson, were decidedly unhappy with the weather they encountered. "Eleven days rain and the most disagreeable time I have experienced," Captain Clark noted laconically in his journal on November 17, 1805. Even Clark's ecstasy some days later at finally catching sight of the grand Pacific Ocean was… well, dampened by the showers: "We spread our mats on the ground and spent the night in the rain." Supplies were wet. Clark was wet. Their Indian guide, Sacagawea, was wet.

In the east, those who read the expedition's journals sighed at the incessant dampness of the place. And yet they came to the Pacific Northwest anyway.

The Pacific Northwest has been given a bad name for its moist climate. Some folks find the dampness depressing, and there are psychologists who link the rain to high suicide rates in the region (the state average in Oregon for 1978 was 15.6 suicides per 100,000 people). More than a few people who move here from other parts of the country in search of the good life, move away again complaining that the number of dreary days each year is more than they can bear.

Not everyone is so critical. Some people actually *like* the rain, whether because it provides some climatic diversity (there's nothing worse than continual sunshine, right?) or because it nourishes a rich variety

By the middle of the 19th century, after the US government had claimed Oregon and Washington as its own, the extreme rainfall here had become well accepted. Folks back east joked about the precipitation. By the 1860s Californians – no doubt jealous of the climate here, as Californians are jealous of everything else about the Pacific Northwest – were calling Oregonians "webfeet."

Maybe H.L. Davis, in his novel of western Oregon pioneer life, *Honey in the Horn*, captured Northwest weather most artfully when he wrote that from November "until spring the rain never totally stopped and the light never entirely started."

of vegetation in the area. A reader poll published by the Portland *Oregonian* in the late 1970s showed that twice as many people in the Beaver State welcome seasonal rains as dread their onslaught.

Blame the land: Local topography, large-scale weather systems and bodies of water throughout the region are the keys to Pacific Northwest weather. Storms rolling in off the Pacific Ocean reach the Northwest fully charged with water vapor to pour buckets of rain on the coast and coastal mountains. Places in these verdant hills, such as Valsetz, Oregon, are said to be some of the wettest spots on earth. One hundred and forty-five to

180 inches (about 400 cm) of rain descend yearly on the Olympic Mountains. In January 1935, Washington's Quinault Ranger Station recorded 35 inches (90 cm) of rain in just *four days.*

In inland Oregon and Washington, the rain doesn't fall so heavily. Air blowing over coastal mountain ranges loses altitude and dries. Towns just east of these mountains sit in "rain shadows" of diminished precipitation. A huge rain shadow can be found just to the east of Oregon's Cascade Mountains, extending more than 150 miles (240 km) inland. Western Oregon and Washington host some smaller rain shadows and distinct micro-climates. Port Townsend, the small

northwest Washington town known for its Victorian architecture and affinity for the arts, sees something under 20 inches (50 cm) of rainfall a year, as does the Medford-Ashland area of Oregon, guarded from the coastal storms by the Siskiyous.

As air shoots farther east toward the Cascades, it again rises, condenses and picks up moisture, leaving downtown Seattle with an annual precipitation of about 35 inches (90 cm) and Oregon's Willamette Valley with

Left, Blue Glacier on Mount Olympus, Olympic National Park. **Above**, Captain's Rock overlooks the Columbia River near Wallula Gap.

40 inches. This is not exactly the sort of weather in which to wear designer open-toed sandals, but it is better than you'll find at seaside resorts. Each rise in topography captures some moisture from the air, so that Portland's West Hills, hangout for many of the city's wealthier residents, may be hit with 5 or 10 more inches of rain each year than those in the city's growing business core farther east.

People who have lived in both Portland and Seattle are struck by how different weather is from one city to the next. Blame much of that on the beautiful but wind-swept Columbia River Gorge. The gorge provides relief to northeastern Oregon and southeastern Washington, serving as a conduit through which moist Pacific winds can blow toward Idaho. But it also promotes the passage westward of chilly continental air. The number of freezing days in the City of Roses each winter averages 44, whereas Seattle has about 16. On the other hand, because east winds can reach the Cascade Range, they have again picked up moisture.

The Cascades divide the Pacific Northwest in a north–south line running from the Canadian border to the knot of peaks and precipices in southern Oregon. Two of its several majestic, snow-capped mountains – Mount Rainier (14,410 feet, 4,400 meters) and Mount Hood (11,245 feet, 3,400 meters) – provide dramatic backdrops to this region's largest metropolitan areas: Seattle-Tacoma and Portland-Vancouver.

The Cascades also divide the Northwest into wet and dry halves. To the west is wet. To the east, land is caught in the semi-arid rain shadow of the mountains. There are some huge stands of Douglas fir and ponderosa pine in the Blue, Wallowa, Ochoco and Selkirk Mountains, as well as magnificent mountain scenery, but much of eastern Washington and Oregon is dry land painted in shades of ochre. While Portland averages 152 days each year on which .01 inch or more of rain falls, the southern Washington town of Yakima counts only 68 such days.

This is a rugged, starkly romantic land. In many ways it's the quintessence of the American West, the old West painted so well by Frederick Remington, described with such poetry by novelist A.B. Guthrie, and scored by Aaron Copeland – the frontier West as portrayed on film.

A LAND OF PLENTY

Native Americans of the Pacific Northwest have long been regarded as the richest Indians in North America, their wealth supplied by nature. Coast Natives enjoyed a rich environment of food supplies, from game, berries and roots to fish and shelled sea animals. What nourishment the Natives couldn't capture from the sea, they could fish from coastal rivers, into which salmon and steelhead regularly swarmed to spawn. Food so easily obtained gave these Natives leisure time in which to develop a distinct culture.

Tribes: Unlike most North American Natives, these coastal peoples had scant understanding of the word "tribe." They tended to live in stable villages of extended families, groups that never adopted tribal names but simply spoke of each other as "of our people." And they lived well, residing in huge cedar-plank lodges or "long houses"; being 110-feet (35-meters) long, it's easy to figure how these structures came by this name. Canadian artist Paul Kane recorded some of these dwellings on canvas, and described others he saw as "the largest buildings of any description among Indians, divided in the interior into compartments to accommodate eight or ten families."

Like the white men who would eventually outnumber them in the Northwest, these coastal Natives were fiercely independent. Promotion to leadership positions within a village was more often than not based upon a man's capabilities, rather than upon his familial heritage or material wealth. It was expected that a leader would set a fine example to be followed. Historian Gordon B. Dodds explains further that "leaders would be followed, not obeyed, as each individual participated in warfare or the hunt on an individual basis, and if a man decided to return home he suffered no stigma for deserting the cause."

Warfare among these Native Americans, however, was rare. They were essentially contented, peaceful peoples, and most warfare they engaged in probably amounted to little more than brief raiding of other villages

to procure slaves. In a bountiful land there was little else worth fighting for.

Early white travelers, weaned on tales of rampaging red men of the Midwestern plains, were often perplexed by this different breed of Natives, and were befuddled by the myriad languages and dialects spoken along the coast. "The Northwest contained many mutually unintelligible language groupings," wrote the historian Dorothy Johansen. "In western Washington, the predominant tongue was Coast Salish. In Oregon from the mouth of the Columbia to Tillamook Bay and east to the Cascades, Chinookan languages were spoken. The Tillamooks belonged to the Coast Salish. The Klatskanie on the Columbia, a band on the Willapa River, and another on the Rogue River, were enclaves of Athabascan-speaking peoples.

"Within the major language groups so many different dialects were spoken that neighbors could not easily communicate verbally with one another."

Puzzle: To communicate in light of this linguistic jigsaw puzzle, the Natives developed something known as Chinook jargon, a curious amalgam of many Native tongues. With the incursion of white sea traders into the area, many French, English and Russian words were absorbed into this lingua franca of the Northwest coast. When explorer William Clark arrived in this area in the early 19th century, long after maritime trade had reached the region, he found that Northwest Natives were familiar with a somewhat unusual selection of words such as "musquets, powder, shot, knife, file, damned rascal, (and) son of a bitch" – words that were apparently used frequently in trading.

Natives of northwest Washington shared many of the customs familiar to their Canadian neighbors, the Kwakiutl. Leisure afforded them by the abundance of nature allowed them to become great sculptors of wood, a skill most apparent in the representation of family heraldic crests or totems carved on poles or painted on boards.

Large cedar trees, plentiful along the coast, were made not only into excellent canoes, but were also fashioned into chests and water-tight containers for cooking (the water

Left, ancient petroglyphs inscribed on a rock in Gingko State Park, Washington.

temperature was controlled by hot rocks pulled from the fire and dumped into the containers). Cedar was even used in clothes making. Clark noted that women often wore skirts made from strands of white cedar bark, "the whole being of sufficient thickness when the female stands erect to conceal those parts usually covered from familiar view, but when she stoops or places herself in any other attitude their battery of Venus is not altogether impervious to the penetrating eye of the amorite." It's little wonder that, in winter winds, these Native women preferred to be wrapped in furs.

Accumulation of wealth in materialistic Northwest Indian society gave rise to the

potlatch. This was a challenge, issued to a visiting leader by his host, to see who could summon the most "power" by giving away or burning belongings. If the guest couldn't give up as many worldly goods as the host, he and his group lost face. If nothing else, this sort of challenge ensured steady employment for Native artisans and traders.

Life on the dry side: Though coastal Natives lived among an embarrassment of natural riches, peoples east of the Cascade Mountains often suffered a shortage of supplies. Their population was scattered, concentrating where mighty runs of salmon, steelhead and eel coursed their ways up the Columbia

and its tributaries. Luckiest of these people, perhaps, were the Natives around Celilo Falls in the Columbia Gorge. Falls were among the greatest obstacles for spawning fish which had to leap high into the air while hurdling this surging barrier. Natives perched above the falls on fragile platforms could harvest 500 fish a day.

On the eastern plateaus of what are now Washington and Oregon, the diet of salmon had to be supplemented by mammal meat, fruit, roots and assorted nuts. Natives of the extreme southeastern section of the region were offered especially slim pickings as far as food went. In this arid environment, Indians such as the Paiutes were often forced to subsist on reptiles, rodents, grasshoppers and assorted common bugs. Ever the western wit, Mark Twain, once remarked that these Natives would eat "anything they can bite." The Klamaths and Modocs of southern Oregon were somewhat more fortunate, enhancing their diets with waterfowl captured from local lakes.

One trait shared among Northwest Natives, from whatever part of the land, was a rich oral tradition. They shared often ribald fireside tales of godlike creatures – Coyote, Blue Jay, Beaver, Raven and Otter. Antics of characters in Northwest Native mythology at first seem slapstick, but these lively tales tell how the world evolved as it did, and point out the importance of natural resources.

Northwest Native culture has, to a great extent, simply been subsumed beneath that of white American culture. Many of these Native Americans have found their future in liquor bottles in skid row districts of Portland and Seattle. Many others remain on reservations – including the Quinault Reservation of northwestern Washington and the Warm Springs Indian Reservation of central Oregon – where they try to preserve their culture. Only in the last few years have some Natives started to make a name for themselves in the white man's world.

The most lasting legacy of Northwest Native culture is the scattering of tongue-twisting names that can be found throughout the region, names like Skamokawa, Snoqualmie and Neakhanie. These make the region a richer place in which to live.

Left, Puget Sound Native chiefs included "Queen Victoria." Right, "The Duke of York."

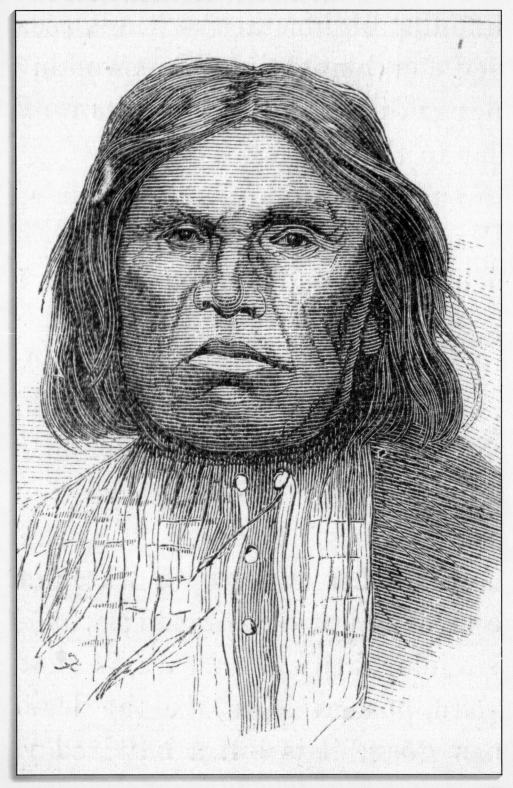

For almost a century, the Spanish viewed the Pacific Ocean as their private lake. But their smugness was shaken quite rudely in 1579 when British sea dog Francis Drake suddenly appeared off the west coast of South America. That he was one of the most notorious English pirates was cause enough for alarm, as he sailed his *Golden Hind* from port to port, plundering tons of Spanish gold, silver and other bounty. But of even greater concern was that Drake escaped north, rather than around the toe of South America.

and frozen substance," and an atmosphere of the "most vile, thicke and stinking fogges." He finally turned his *Golden Hind* south to cross the Pacific, stopping along the way in northern California, which, together with most of the West Coast, he dubbed "New Albion" in defiance of Spain's prior claims – a name which later appeared on maps charted by early maritime explorers.

But tales of the Northwest Passage lived on. It would take 150 years before lucre, legend and a liar would prompt thorough

To the Spanish, Drake's retreat was as mysterious as his arrival in the Pacific. And they were concerned: had Drake and the rival British finally discovered the fabled Strait of Anian, that legendary western gate of the long-sought-after Northwest Passage through the North American continent? If so, Spanish days of maritime supremacy might be winding down.

Drake hadn't discovered any Northwest Passage, of course. In fact, he had long ago stopped entertaining notions of its existence. Escaping from the Spanish, he had simply headed north to the Pacific Northwest, where he found the rain "an unnatural congealed

investigations and the beginning of the end for such romantic tales. In the meantime, they would help open up the land we now know as the Pacific Northwest.

The explorers arrive: Russians had begun searching for the Northwest Passage decades before Drake made his mysterious escape from the Spanish in the Pacific. The prospect of wealth had driven them to North America in the first place. They knew the value of furs in the markets of China, and their fur hunters, the *promyshlenniks*, had pushed relentlessly eastward across the frozen wastes of Siberia in search of more sable and sea otter pelts. From there these hunters had moved through Alaska and south into the Pacific Northwest. For many years, the Russians had a free hand in the exploitation of the Northwest sea otter.

Spain viewed every Russian foray as a threat to her claims in the Pacific. Spanish ships were sent far up the North American coast to investigate the Russian invasion. Their captains were greatly relieved to find that the fur thieves from Eastern Europe had established no permanent settlements in North America.

Though these voyages gave Spain the claim of original discovery of the Pacific Northwest Coast, it was never pursued. Spain never fully investigated its find. That would

have found the strait between 47 and 48 degrees north latitude, sailed for 20 days upon its glorious waters until he reached the North Sea, and then returned to Mexico. To enliven this deception, Valerianos said he had seen "some people on Land, clad in Beasts skins; and that the land is very fruitful, and rich of gold, Silver, Pearle, and other things, like Nova Spain."

The old Greek first spun his yarn to one Michael Lok, an armchair explorer and fortune hunter who whiled away many hours in English debtors' prisons drawing oddly contorted maps of the North American continent. The combination of the Greek mariner's fertile imagination and the bankrupt

be left to later explorers, many of whom would soon arrive in this part of the world, lured by a nifty piece of fiction cooked up by a 60-year-old Greek ship's pilot.

It was an eager world that seized upon the tale of Apostolos Valerianos, who claimed to have been a pilot for the Viceroy of Mexico – traveling under the pseudonym Juan de Fuca – when the viceroy came searching for the Strait of Anian in 1592. He claimed to

Explorers William Clark (far left) and Meriwether Lewis (left) traveled the length of the Columbia River. Above, the mighty Columbia during explorers' days.

visionary's frenzied quest for fame and fortune was an unfortunate thing for scientific advancement, but it spawned interest – lots of it. Lok wrote letters to everyone from Queen Elizabeth I to Sir Walter Raleigh, guaranteeing he could relocate this fabled continental shortcut, but it wasn't enough to spring him from gaol.

Yet the fanciful voyage of Juan de Fuca affixed itself in the minds of a wistful Europe. Explorers 200 years later still remembered the latitudinal directions the aging Greek had given.

In 1776 Captain James Cook undertook his third voyage of the world for the British

Royal Navy. There were several scientific reasons for the voyage, but one was a thorough search for the Northwest Passage – just to satisfy the public. The English government had even offered a £20,000 prize for discovery of the passage, though Cook himself saw not the "least probability that ever such a thing existed."

Cook cruised the Northwest coast, but because of bad weather missed the mouth of Columbia and headed north. While in the area, he and his crew traded metal to the Natives in exchange for furs, which the seamen used for bedding and clothes. Following Cook's murder in the Hawaiian Islands in 1779, his crew arrived in China, where they, as had the Russians before them, discovered their furs would fetch a pretty penny. Though Cook didn't live to see it, his name is associated today with the beginning of the Northwest fur trade. Had it not been for fables of a cross-continent passage, he might not have had such a place in history.

Fur brought British traders flocking to the Pacific Northwest. One trader, Charles Barkley, arrived at Nootka Sound on the west side of Vancouver Island in 1787. After exchanging goods with island Natives, he sailed south and, according to his wife's diary, "to our great astonishment, we arrived off a large opening extending to the eastward, the entrance to which appeared to be about four leagues wide, and remained about that width as far as the eye could see, with a clear westerly horizon, which my husband immediately recognized as the long lost strait of Juan de Fuca, and to which he gave the name of the original discoverer, my husband placing it on his chart."

So what if this wasn't really the beginning of the Northwest Passage, as Apostolos Valerianos claimed it to be? Nobody knew that yet, and it was close to the latitude Valerianos had plucked from the air. Thus the pseudonym of a man who sailed a fictitious voyage became a feature of the Northwest landscape.

The late 18th century marked the beginning of a new era – one of unprecedented commerce and development – for the Pacific Northwest area.

In the spring of 1792, two ships were sailing off the coasts of present-day Oregon and Washington, both of them intent on probing the craggy coastline. One ship was

the British sloop *Discovery*, accompanied by the armed tender *Chatham* and commanded by Captain George Vancouver, a man who, as a midshipman, had accompanied Captain Cook on his West Coast expedition of 1778. The other ship was the *Columbia*, flying the colors of the United States and captained by Yankee fur trader Robert Gray. Vancouver was interested in exploration, especially of the Strait of Juan de Fuca and any Northwest Passage into which it might lead; Gray had his eyes on lucrative furs. Their different interests would determine their actions and help shape the history of this region.

Gray and Vancouver met at sea and exchanged news on the successes and failures

of their respective voyages. Vancouver was happy to hear that Captain Gray had found little profit in the waters around what is today called Washington's Olympic Peninsula, and that Gray was planning to head south in search of what he had heard might be the mouth of a great river.

Vancouver went on to explore the Strait of Juan de Fuca and the Gulf of Georgia, and was the first to circumnavigate Vancouver Island, giving Great Britain a strong claim to the area. Perhaps most important of all, he and Second Lieutenant Peter Puget directed two separate explorations of what Vancouver labeled Puget Sound.

Gray continued south to where his fellow captain had reported that the sea changed "from its natural to river coloured water." He sailed his good ship *Columbia* through the breakers of a treacherous bar and discovered a spacious harbor at the mouth of what later would be recognized as the mightiest river in North America, next to the Mississippi. This great waterway of the West was named Columbia after Gray's trusty vessel. Yet the thrill of geographical discovery and the fact that it afforded the United States claim to the entire valley of the Columbia meant little to Captain Gray – he was far more interested in the stocks of furs he was able to collect from Natives of the area.

Both countries soon shored up their respective claims to the Northwest with overland exploration.

In 1793 Alexander McKenzie was dispatched by the Northwest Company, a British fur-trading enterprise, to cross Canada and explore the northern reaches of the Pacific Northwest, giving Great Britain its second claim to the area.

The Americans weren't far behind. In 1803 President Thomas Jefferson sent Captains Meriwether Lewis and William Clark to explore the essentially-unknown Louisiana Purchase, a piece of land the United States had acquired by treaty with France and that took in all of what is now the central United

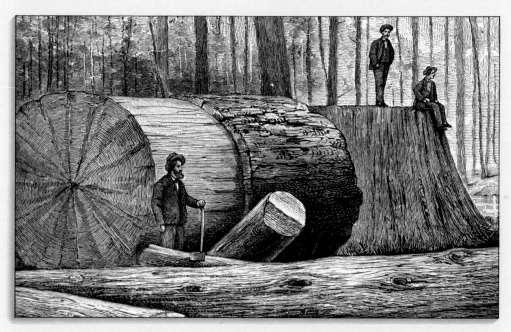

Though Vancouver and Gray had amicably divided their interests in the Pacific Northwest, their respective countries would do so less willingly.

After the claims of Spain were, by treaty, pushed below the latitude of 42 degrees in 1819, and after the vague claims of the Russians had been firmly established north of 54–40 in 1828, the United States and Great Britain would fight for control of the Oregon Country toe-to-toe.

Left, loggers fell trees in the lush Washington forests. Above, an illustration showing huge stumps of the primeval forest.

States. He followed this up in 1804 by ordering Lewis and Clark on a journey to the shores of the Pacific.

Jefferson didn't really believe the remote Pacific Northwest would ever become part of his United States. He viewed the Rocky Mountains as a natural western boundary for the country, and he worried that the only relationship possible between the United States and this far-off, wooded region of the North American continent might be colonial – a relationship that he, as a believer in democracy, found repugnant. But even more distasteful to him seems to have been the notion that the British would take control of the Northwest. This was behind his decision to send Lewis and Clark on their journey.

And what a journey it was. Following an arduous 4,000-mile (6,000-km) trek, the explorers finally glimpsed the Pacific Ocean on November 15, 1805, and they wintered near the mouth of the Columbia at Fort Clatsop. Disappointed to find no ship on the river that could cart them back to civilization, members of the group returned overland in 1806, bringing back carefully-composed maps, observations of animal life and valuable scientific collections.

Pure discovery wasn't foremost on the minds of the British. The Hudson's Bay Company, which for years was the dominant breaths something about the initials HBC standing for "Here Before Christ."

Thompson had still greater plans, of course. He wanted to establish British hegemony down to the lower Columbia River and thus ensure his position in history. How frustrated he must have been when he arrived at the river's mouth and found that the Yankee fur trader John Jacob Astor had established Fort Astoria there in 1811, on behalf of the Pacific Fur Company.

Looking back at those early decades of the 19th century, an observer might find much that was comical about relations between the Americans and the British in the Pacific Northwest. During the War of 1812, for

force in the Northwest, was interested primarily in the great fur resources of the area, and it established trading posts throughout present-day Oregon and Washington. Especially active in their establishment was David Thompson who, in 1807, not only explored northeastern Washington and northern Idaho, but busied himself setting up trading posts in the area as a barrier to American fur traders who would soon encroach upon the region from the east.

When American fur traders did begin to move in, they were confronted by so many Hudson's Bay Company flags waving over trading posts that they muttered under their instance, the crew from a British sloop-of-war planned to capture Fort Astoria, unaware that it had already been sold to the British Northwest Company. But at the time, no one saw much at which to laugh. Each side wanted total domination. It wasn't until 1818 that they agreed upon a joint occupation of the territory. And even then there were some who wanted to torpedo this delicate peace.

Dr John McLoughlin, the so-called White-headed Eagle and factor of the Hudson's Bay Company at Fort Vancouver, near where the city of Vancouver, Washington, now stands, was intent upon making matters as rough as possible for the many restless American beaver trappers who were pouring into "his" Oregon Country. He even went so far as to send an itinerant trapper called Peter Skene Ogden to the Northwest's eastern reaches, "a rich preserve of beaver." Ogden's sole purpose was to capture every fur-bearing rodent before those damn Yankee trappers came prowling further west. Ogden and his henchmen spent six years in the wilds, undiplomatically exterminating every beaver they could find.

But such acts didn't stem the westward movement of Americans. Ever since Lewis and Clark had returned from the Northwest and published their journals, the people of

enterprise and promote the propagation of Christianity in the dark and cruel places about the shores of the Pacific."

For several reasons Kelley was for a long time just too busy to devote himself to his dream. But then in 1829 he found himself both unemployed and the owner of a bankrupt textile mill. It was the break he needed. Suddenly bereft of responsibility, he organized the American Society for Encouraging the Settlement of the Oregon Territory. The society was incorporated by the Massachusetts Legislature, and Kelley was named general agent – a job which, among other things, promoted him to the position of the region's chief publicist.

the nascent United States were convinced that the Oregon Country belonged to them.

New Eden or bust: One day in 1817, a Boston educator named Hall Jackson Kelley picked up a copy of *The Journals of Lewis and Clark* and, like other Americans of his time, became obsessed with the potential of the Northwest. It was that year, he was to say later, that "the word came expressly to me to go and labor in the field of philanthropic

Left, **Fort Clatsop, near Astoria, Oregon, was once the resting place of the Lewis and Clark party.** **Above**, **a more modern log home in the Enchanted Valley, Olympic National Park.**

He began publishing pamphlets to let the world know the riches offered by the Pacific Northwest. Never having been to the area, Kelley borrowed liberally from the journals of early explorers and used his imagination to fill in the gaps. The result of his blending plagiarism and pure invention was, as one might expect from a publicist, a glowing report on this "New Eden."

In 1831, Kelley several times petitioned the US Congress for military aid and protection for a group of settlers heading to Oregon. Many people signed on for the adventure, but the whole thing fell apart when the federal government refused to underwrite the expedition. Never one to give up on a dream, in 1832 Hall Kelley launched his own small expedition.

His planned route would take settlers down the Mississippi River to New Orleans, where they would set sail for Vera Cruz, after that crossing Mexico and boarding a ship to the Columbia via the Hawaiian or Sandwich Islands. Things went fine until Kelley reached the bawdy town of New Orleans and was robbed by members of his own party. He gladly "dismissed them all." Kelley lost more property in New Orleans and on the ship to Mexico, with what was left going to insistent customs authorities. Alone and destitute, he finally made his way across Mexico and up

When partially cured, Kelley caught up with his party by taking a perilous ride in an Indian canoe down the Umpqua River.

If Hall Kelley expected a hero's welcome at Fort Vancouver, he was greatly disappointed. Charges had come from the governor of California that Kelley and his fellow travelers had stolen horses while in the Sacramento Valley. Hudson's Bay Company factor Dr John McLoughlin was cool to the "marauders" (certainly more likely horse thieves than was Kelley), but locked Kelley into an evil-smelling shed used for cleaning fish and game because he was the one responsible for leading all these American infiltrators into "British" territory. After

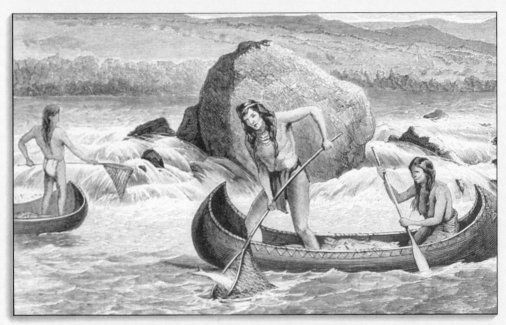

through California as far as Monterey. Kelley was having second thoughts about continuing north when he met a party of hunters and traders, and convinced them to accompany him to the Oregon Country. Their group was soon joined by a band of "marauders" also interested in the Northwest.

While the party was busy getting Mexican horses to sell up north, Kelley was catching malaria. By the time he and his compatriots reached southern Oregon, he was no longer fit enough to travel. Falling from his horse, he prepared to meet his maker. Just then, a Hudson's Bay Company physician came into their camp and tended to Kelley's illness.

spending a winter in the shed, Kelley was shipped off to Hawaii, where he fumed about his mistreatment and spread nasty rumors about the Fort Vancouver factor.

Despite his personal failures, Kelley's frenzied pamphleteering drew attention to the Oregon Country. Some members of his American Society for Encouraging the Settlement of the Oregon Territory – including Nathaniel Wyeth and Henry Spalding – would later become settlers and boosters of the region. But all Kelley's efforts to publicize the Oregon Country achieved little compared to publicity drawn from the story of "The Four Wise Men from the West."

These Wise Men who arrived in St Louis, Missouri, in 1832 were members of the Nez Perce tribe, who had learned from explorers Lewis and Clark that the white man had a "Book from Heaven" which described how to reach the happiest of all hunting grounds. The four journeyed to St Louis to discuss the matter with William Clark.

These Indians were looking for something more in the form of a road map than the enigmatic "Good Book," which was a source of disappointment to them. Worse, two of the four died in St Louis, about as far from heaven as one could find in those raw frontier days, and the others returned to tell their tribe the bad news.

FLATHEAD INDIANS.

But their departure didn't go unnoticed. At the time the wandering Nez Perce arrived in Missouri, America was experiencing an upsurge of evangelical enthusiasm. Missionaries were ready to go anywhere there were lost souls to be found.

One of these missionaries was Methodist Jason Lee, who headed west from Massachusetts, hoping to follow the godless Nez Perce as they returned to their Northwest homeland. But his momentum was so great that he shot right past the Nez Perce's dry

Left, netting salmon from a traditional canoe. **Above**, dressed for battle.

Palouse lands and settled in the fertile Willamette Valley where, unfortunately, epidemics of influenza, smallpox and measles had wiped out all but the heartiest of tribesmen. Discouraged by the lack of potential religious converts, Lee directed his preaching toward the smattering of white settlers in the area. A majority of these whites were Catholic French-Canadians who had formerly been engaged by the Hudson's Bay Company and had since settled in the area of French Prairie, with some Americans scattered around the vicinity of Fort Astoria. Wanting more of a flock, Lee also devoted a good deal of energy to attracting industrious, moral, American families to the Oregon Country through his writings and eastern lecture tours.

The Cayuse War: Lee was soon followed to the godless West by Marcus Whitman, who established his mission near Walla Walla, and by the Reverend Henry H. Spalding, who made his home farther north. Whitman was only slightly more successful than Lee in Christianizing the Natives; he was convinced that the only hope for their salvation was that they should be completely immersed in a "superior" (read "American") culture.

The Cayuse around the Whitman Mission were never immersed in Euro-American culture, but they were overwhelmed by the white man's diseases. During one especially severe outbreak of measles in 1847, Whitman, a practicing physician as well as a man of the Good Book, gave the suffering Natives medication to cure their ills. He completely ignored Dr McLoughlin's warning that the Cayuse had a nasty habit of killing medicine men that gave them bad medicine.

It didn't take the Native Americans long to realize that their tribesmen were perishing at alarming rates, but at the same time few whites seemed to fall victim to disease. Their conclusion? That Whitman had offered good medicine to whites and handed nothing but bad medicine to the Natives.

On November 29, 1847, the Cayuse stormed Whitman's mission, murdering not only the misguided proselytizer, but also his wife Narcissa and 12 mission residents. Others were held captive for weeks.

This incident touched off what was later labeled the Cayuse War. For two years, a not-always-competent contingent of Oregon volunteers chased the Cayuse around the upper Columbia River, until five of the Natives finally surrendered, "confessed" to the Whitman Massacre, and were hanged in a public ceremony at Oregon City.

The Methodists were followed to the Northwest by Father Francis N. Blanchet, who arrived in St Paul, Oregon, in 1838 to minister to the spiritual needs of a Catholic population. Blanchet also made a mighty effort to "re-Christianize" those Natives who had been persuaded to follow Methodist principles. This touched off a mild feud between Catholics and Methodists in the Willamette Valley, which confused local Natives even more about the meaning and intentions of the white man's religion.

An arduous journey: What with missionaries persuading their flocks to relocate in the Pacific Northwest, and a bevy of retired mountain men and scattered pioneers moving into the Willamette Valley and southwestern Washington, it's no wonder the British started to worry about their position and future in the region.

In 1839 a subsidiary group of the Hudson's Bay Company calling itself the Puget Sound Agricultural Company was organized to boost British settlement in the Oregon Country. The intention of the PSAC was to sell the New Eden idea to subjects of Her Majesty the Queen. In this way the PSAC company organizers hoped to "frustrate the settlers from the United States" who quite clearly had "designs on the area."

The PSAC effort was moderately successful in drawing settlers, and it strengthened the British presence north of the Columbia River. But it couldn't keep up with the migration of Americans.

Travel was no easy matter for pioneers heading for this New Eden. Not only was the cross-country journey fraught with river dangers, arduous mountain climbs and dry, dusty miles across the Midwest, but the Northwest presented its own hardships.

Prior to 1846, pioneers reaching the Columbia River town of The Dalles had only one way to get their wagons into the Willamette Valley: they had to float the wagons and their worldly belongings down the turbulent Columbia on a hired raft or boat. Problems were many. One, of course, was the exorbitant fee of $50 per wagon and $10 a person. Another was that boats were not always available, and when they were,

the pioneer diaries are replete with accounts of capsizings and drownings in icy rapids.

Pioneer Jesse Applegate witnessed the pathetic condition of the sick, exhausted, hungry and penniless immigrants waiting at The Dalles in the fall of 1845 for any sort of craft to take them on a perilous ride down the river. He succinctly described the last leg of their dust-eating, 2,000-mile (3,200-km) trek west, to the Oregon City *Spectator* in 1847: "A scene of human misery ensued which scarcely has a parallel in history – the loss of life and property was enormous…"

Another pioneer, Sam Barlow, reached The Dalles in 1845, and quickly decided that after six months of bumping across the plains,

his battered wagon wasn't even worth the $50 to float it down the Columbia. While at The Dalles Methodist Mission, Barlow heard rumors of a Native American trail that crossed the Cascade Mountain barrier just south of the snow-covered flank of towering Mount Hood. He decided to try a mountain crossing. "God never made a mountain but what he provided a place for man to go over or around it," Barlow insisted.

Though he didn't succeed in getting wagons over the mountains that year, in 1846 Barlow opened a land route into the Willamette Valley. Many people of the Oregon Country applauded his efforts, but most pioneers who traveled his steep, dangerous Barlow Road considered it the most grueling part of the entire Oregon Trail. Oxen and horses perished along the Barlow Road. Wagons were abandoned or their contents discarded, and some hills were so steep the wagons had to be lowered down by ropes – just a stone's throw from their Willamette Valley destination.

Overland travelers often had little to look forward to when they *did* reach the Willamette Valley. The journey may have been completed, but ahead of them could lay a cold winter as they tried to begin life anew with only what they could salvage from a grueling wagon ride. Pioneer E. W. Conyers lamented

rotted in unattended fields, as once-productive farms surrendered to weeds. The local legislature had to postpone its 1848 session, because only nine representatives were left in the territory. No one remained who could set type or run presses, causing two newspapers to fold and the Oregon City *Spectator* to suspend operation for nine months. An 1848 visitor to Oregon City, the first town incorporated west of the Rockies, said its population appeared to consist of "only a few women and children and some Indians." In all, in 1849 only 8,779 people were found living in what is now the state of Oregon.

Blame it all on California. Gold had been found there, and many believed the sudden

that, by the time members of his party had reached the valley, they were completely out of food. He prayed: "We live in the hope that there will be plenty for all when we arrive at our destination. My! Oh, my! What a hungry crowd the people of Oregon will have to feed during the coming winter, and the great majority of them have no money to buy with."

In gold we trust: Many Oregon pioneers of the late 1840s were surprised at how deserted they found the Willamette Valley. Crops

Left, the base of Snoqualmie Falls is the site for spear fishing. **Above**, teepees, sailing ships and the mountain vista across Puget Sound.

exodus of two-thirds of Oregon's male population spelled doom for settlement in the Willamette Valley. Instead, it was the best thing that ever happened to Oregon.

Trade was anything but brisk in 1848. The territory had so little money that its legislature made wheat legal tender, requiring merchants to accept it at one dollar a bushel. A farmer selling a wagon to his neighbor held an IOU for three harvests, and for legal services attorney Peter Burnett was once paid $49 in the form of a note good only for brown sugar at 12½ cents a pound. Territorial Governor George Abernethy doled out rocks for change at his store, and "Abernethy Rocks" became an accepted, albeit cumbersome, unit of exchange. Ironically enough, when a financially-strapped territorial legislature voted to make wheat, beef, and virtually any product legal payment for taxes, Abernethy vetoed the measure because he viewed it as "inconvenient."

It was gold that turned this pathetic economy around. Willamette Valley farmers mining in California prior to the big rush of 1849 found the pickings easy, gathering surface deposits as if they were part of some grand Easter egg hunt. When mining became too much like work, they returned to Oregon, bringing $2 million worth of gold with them. Oregon finally had some sort of currency

They returned knowing that 100,000 California miners would pay handsomely for Oregon products, and local farmers saw that they did. Warehouses were packed with surplus wheat, and the value of Oregon's former currency shot up 400 percent. The value of produce and lumber, the latter a long-established trade good, went up in proportion. Eggs were sold for a dollar a piece in gullible California. After 40 years of poverty, Oregon Territory was booming, and the visions of Eden were finally coming to fruition.

In search of untapped metal deposits, California prospectors ventured into the hills of southern Oregon, where nuggets were dug up in 1851. Thousands of shovels began

beyond wheat, spuds and Abernethy Rocks. Measuring gold dust, however, proved both woefully inaccurate and awkward, leading the legislature to mint standardized coins in 1849. It was, of course, unconstitutional for a state or territory to make its own currency, but that inconvenient section of the Constitution didn't prevent citizen William Rector from organizing the Oregon Exchange Company to mint so-called "Beaver Money," gold coins stamped in $5 and $10 denominations with the ubiquitous toothsome rodent on the obverse side.

Shrewd Oregon prospectors brought back more from California than gold, though.

turning up rich pockets throughout the hills – millions of dollars were extracted from places with names such as Rich Gulch and Sailors Diggings. Gold was found in ancient stream beds and on ledges high up in the hills. Miners even struck it rich in churning surf, working the sandy beach places of the Oregon coast around Whiskey Run, south of Coos Bay.

These discoveries amounted to the vanguard of Oregon settlement outside the Willamette Valley. Timing was propitious, coming as it did on the heels of the 1850 Donation Land Act, which stimulated settlement by giving each Oregon settler 320 acres

(130 hectares) and, as a bonus, an additional 320 acres (130 hectares) in his wife's name. With most of the choice and rich Willamette Valley lands rapidly being claimed, the gold rush to southern Oregon opened remote, fertile valleys to a ravenous market.

The wilderness soon sprouted bustling towns, with Jacksonville as the metropolis and Scottsburg as its transportation nexus. Mule trains soon shared trails with stagecoaches running from Jacksonville to notorious San Francisco and Portland, opening a route that would later become part of the Oregon and California Railroad land grant.

The more people who came to the Northwest, the more apparent it was that they the United States into the Oregon Country was fast becoming a torrent. In 1839, almost 1,500 immigrants arrived, and in 1845 the annual arrival count had reached 2,500. The Hudson's Bay Company and the British watched helplessly as these upstart Americans poured into the verdant Willamette Valley and, worse, began moving north of the Columbia.

"Fifty-four-forty or fight!": For the British, the writing on the wall was clear by 1846. Americans would continue to populate the Oregon Country at a steady rate. They were clamoring for "manifest destiny," something they interpreted as the United States' sacred right of possession over all lands between the

needed some sort of regional government. Some official body had to protect land claims and levy taxes. Meeting at Champoeg in 1843, settlers selected a committee to draw up codes for a provisional territorial government, which would exist "until such time as the United States of America extend their jurisdiction over us."

This call for local government came none too soon. The trickle of immigration from

Left, a wagon train following the Oregon Trail crosses the plains east of the Cascade Mountains. **Above,** horses and Conestoga wagons crowd the main street of Olympia, Washington, *circa* 1875.

Atlantic and Pacific oceans – including Canada, as far as many people were concerned. Many Americans were picking up the chant of "Fifty-Four Forty or Fight!" a message to Britain that the United States wanted all the land up to latitude 54 degrees, 40 minutes, and was willing to go to war in pursuit of such land.

This was mere rabble-rousing, not official US government policy, yet the sons and daughters of Great Britain certainly weren't willing to do battle over an area so remote from their homeland and largely occupied by foreigners. Their primary interest was in maintaining the business of the Hudson's

Bay Company, which, as it turned out, could fend for itself perfectly well.

So in 1846, Great Britain finally gave up joint occupation, ceding all properties south of the 49th parallel – which included the much-sought-after natural harbor of Puget Sound – to the feisty US government.

Two years later the Oregon Country had gained official US territorial status. Abraham Lincoln, an Illinois lawyer and later sixteenth president of the United States, was selected as the territory's first governor. However, he refused the offer because his wife, Mary Todd Lincoln, objected to moving to such a remote outpost as Oregon. It has been said that she felt her family would be safer in Washington, DC.

The position was filled instead by Joseph Lane, a pro-Southern slave owner who went on to oppose Lincoln in the election of 1860, running as the vice-presidential candidate on the Southern Democratic ticket with John Breckenridge. Republican Lincoln won only 36 percent of Oregon ballots cast in that election, but he carried the state due to a Stephen Douglas-Breckenridge split of the Democratic ticket in that year.

By 1860, though, the Northwest was not what it had been. After the British agreed to relinquish any rights to the land, Northwesterners were free either to maintain the area as it had been, or to reorganize territorial boundaries. The Oregon Territory, left at its original size – taking in not only present-day Oregon, but Washington, and most of Idaho – and governed from south of the Columbia, as it had been, might have been difficult to manage well. At least that's the way some residents living north of the river figured it, so they started agitating for a separate territory, perhaps called "Columbia."

In December 1852, a petition was submitted to Congress to recognize this new territory. When it came before the House two months later, Kentucky Representative Richard Stanton objected to the name as Columbia could be confused with District of Columbia – better known now as DC.

Stanton suggested the territory be renamed Washington, partly in honor of the first US president, George Washington. Other congressmen complained that this name would only confuse it with the city of Washington, DC, and at least one representative suggested it might be more fitting to give the territory an Indian name. However, the name Washington was decided upon, and on March 2, 1853 President Millard Fillmore signed a bill creating a "Territory of Washington." Just as predicted, the name has caused confusion ever since.

Oregon, at this time, was mulling over US statehood. In 1854, and twice thereafter, residents of the Oregon Territory rejected the idea of a constitutional convention to create a state. Some, in fact, wanted Oregon to follow the lead of Texas, which had separated from Mexico and formed the famous Lone Star Republic in 1836. But Oregonians remained stubbornly indecisive about their future, frustrating "Oregon Republic" advocates.

So why did Oregonians finally change their minds on statehood? Part of the reason lies with the 1857 US Supreme Court case, *Dred Scott v. Sandford*, which declared it illegal for a territorial legislature or the US Congress to prohibit slavery in any federal territory – only a sovereign state was allowed to do that.

At the time, pro-slavery sentiments ran hot and heavy in the veins of some prominent Oregonians, including territorial governor Lane who, by the way, refused to free his slaves until 1878, long after Lincoln's Emancipation Proclamation. But the pro-slavery camp was a minority – the majority were simply racists who wanted a white Oregon.

If Oregon were a state, they reasoned, it would allow them to legislate against slavery, and blacks, in general. So, when offered the option of Oregon statehood again in 1857, Oregonians voted by about seven-to-one for a constitutional convention. Fears that pro-slavery forces would ultimately push Oregon into the Union as a slave state were few and proved unfounded in 1858 when Oregonians voted by a comfortable two-to-one margin to introduce their wooded territory into the United States as a free state.

President James Buchanan laid his approving quill to the proclamation admitting Oregon as the thirty-third state on February 14, 1859, but the news didn't reach the Pacific Northwest until the steamer *Brother Jonathan,* sailing from San Francisco, docked at Portland a month later.

Right, gathering hops for Washington's new brewing industry.

Once Oregon became a state, the motive for increasing population became more frankly pecuniary. As railroad and shipping tycoon Henry Villard put it to his German investors in 1873: "The greatest assurance for improving the prospects of the bondholders lies in increasing the population."

Villard established an immigration bureau in Portland in conjunction with his land office and another in Boston to attract European immigrants and to encourage unhappy New England farmers to head west. He then set up agents working in Scandinavia, Germany and Russia. The world was soon swimming in Northwest promotional literature, pictures and stereopticon slides of the New Eden. This was all in Villard's best interests, of course.

In 1873, the Northern Pacific Railroad, under the financial control of New York banker Jay Cooke, discontinued its westward building spree at Bismark, South Dakota; the plan had been to build the railway east from Duluth, to join tracks laid eastward from Puget Sound. Cooke's banks were closing their doors, and the US financial panic of 1873 had begun.

Villard saw much potential in the coupling of this languishing railroad line and his Columbia shipping concern. So he approached some financier friends in New York, and borrowed enough money – $8 million – to entice NP directors to sell their company.

In 1876, Villard had extravagant Northwest exhibits sent to the Centennial Exposition in Philadelphia as promotions for this area, and, because people were still heading to California, promotional displays were shipped south as well to attract those errant homesteaders. Despite some immigrants thinking that the Pacific Northwest climate was too severe for agriculture, Villard's displays and a reported total failure of the crop in California soon combined to convince them otherwise.

This was much to the consternation of California leaders, who also recognized the value of population expansion. As the disgruntled editor of one Bear State newspaper complained: "It is not the blindness of the immigrants to the natural attractions of California, but the industry of Oregon agents that robs us of the laboring thousands that seek our shores."

The California editor did not exaggerate. In 1877, 18,000 people arrived in Oregon, and there were stories of successful Northwest promoters depopulating entire villages of Russians.

Although his personal empire crumbled in 1884, Henry Villard had helped populate Oregon and made Portland the hub of railway and steamboat traffic to the Northwest. Acerbic Portland newspaper publisher Harvey Scott boasted that, because his fair city was the Northern Pacific's western terminus, its destiny was as "the metropolis of the region." Within little more than two decades of gold having been discovered in Oregon, Portland had grown from a clearing in the woods called Stumptown into a city described by historian Dorothy Johansen as "the web of commerce and culture," and it stood unchallenged as the San Francisco of the Pacific Northwest.

Neither Tacoma nor Seattle on Puget Sound was much enamored of Villard, however. Both towns smarted at the preferential treatment Portland had received at their expense. Though Villard had promised to build a spur off his rail line through Tacoma and Seattle, he had gone broke before it could be completed. It wasn't until 1887 that the Northern Pacific, under different management, completed its Cascade Division through the Yakima Valley and Stampede Pass to Tacoma. Seattle had to wait until the completion of James J. Hill's Great Northern Railroad in 1892. Subsequent railroad and Puget Sound boosterism lured immigrants to northwestern Washington.

The population of the Pacific Northwest increased by almost half a million in the 1880s. Washington figures jumped by 275,000, and Governor Miles C. Moore proudly reported an influx of more than 95,000 newcomers between 1887 and 1889, a figure greater than the entire population of the Washington Territory in 1880.

Logging and lumbering: The more people in the region, the more opportunity for its financial development. Even the eastern halves of Oregon and Washington, which were sparsely populated before the Oregon gold rush and some unspectacular searches for metals in northeastern Washington, were now bustling with businessmen – and loggers.

It was natural that the Northwest – crowded as it was with huge evergreen trees – should develop as a center for logging. But it wasn't until gold and nationwide publicity began attracting folks to the area that there were enough people to support the industry here. Many men were just as happy to stay back in Maine or Michigan, where the cutting was still good and entertainments (much needed after weeks or months of living in the woods) were more accessible.

of felled timber in 1890: more than 1 billion board feet. Reports are that only half of the native timber in what is now Washington's Thurston County was left standing in 1890.

Railroads helped expand the market for Northwest lumber. Montana, Colorado and Iowa all wanted some of it. Oregon did rather better than Washington when it came to cross-country lumber shipping, as railroad freight rates in the state were more favorable than those up north.

But most of the lumber was still carried by sea craft. Lumber was in great demand in California, which took 200 million board feet in 1883 and 1884, and 323 million in 1889, the year that Washington became a

The lumber industry grew quickly in the Northwest. By about 1884, sawmills around Puget Sound consumed 1 million board feet of wood a day. Rafts of logs from around Hood Canal and the western shore of the Sound floated to mills at Port Gamble and Port Ludlow. Seattle and Tacoma profited as ports for loading both local lumber and logs from outlying areas. In 1880, 160 million board feet of timber were felled, which seems like nothing when compared to the quantity

The Pacific Northwest's early wealth was founded in large part on timber. <u>Above</u>, the University of Washington's Forestry Building, Seattle.

state. Much of the lumber was also shipped to foreign markets. Puget Sound was crowded with vessels arriving empty and leaving loaded with cut timber bound for Australia, Chile, Buenos Aires and Shanghai. Cargoes might be as large as 1 million board feet of lumber, valued as high as $20,000. Residents of Seattle were more than ready to accept the income from the shipping of the valuable lumber.

Klondike fever: Seattle had always been something of an upstart, as cities go. The fact that some early settlers called their town-site "New York-Alki," which meant "New York by-and-by," illustrates very well the sort of pretension that has always characterized the Emerald City.

That Seattle is the Northwest's largest metropolis today is a matter not only of industriousness, but also of good fortune. Portland seemed early on to be the city with the best hopes of economic success. Even Tacoma appeared to have a better chance than did the little town on Elliott Bay.

Seattle had been settled in 1851, and named after Salish Indian chief Sealth, who had befriended some of the town's earliest residents, been converted to the Catholic faith, and was ultimately removed with his people from the Elliott Bay area to a Port Madison reservation. Residents of Seattle had big

Women who worked as prostitutes read it, packed their bags, and set off for the fields in hopes that they could turn a pretty penny out of the pockets of avaricious goldseekers. No wonder that when the Portland set sail on its return voyage to Alaska, it went with a full complement of passengers.

Seattle became the jumping-off point for later prospectors, or "sourdoughs" as they were called, heading for Alaska and the Yukon. Ships of every configuration and size sailed down Puget Sound to Elliott Bay, where their captains knew there would be eager men waiting for the passage north. There were always more men wanting to go than there were ships to carry them.

dreams for their town, but there never seemed enough capital to lend them reality.

And then gold was discovered in Alaska. A breathless July 17, 1897 telegram announced that "The steamship Portland has just arrived in Seattle with a ton of gold on board." Men who had put in so much time sifting river gravel or wielding pickaxes in California, Oregon and Colorado read it with hope that the Alaska rush might provide them with the fortunes that they had failed to find earlier in the century.

Other men who had missed the previous rushes decided this telegram gave them their own chance to fulfill their mining dreams.

Females were in great demand up north, and Seattle became a center for traffic in white slaves. Women were coaxed aboard ships bound for the Northwest with promises of "the good life," only to spend the following years being pawed for money by dirt-caked miners. A shipload of 500 people, mostly widows, set off from New York to Alaska, where the women hoped to capture rich husbands. Unfortunately, their vessel ran into trouble rounding Cape Horn, and legend has it that a cannibal chieftain tried taking one of the women as his bride. From this whole shipload of people, only one woman was fortunate enough to reach Alaska.

Seattle was doing its very best to take advantage of the Alaska strike. A failed newspaper editor named Erastus Brainerd was appointed as publicity man for the city. He printed advertisements of Seattle's virtues and its link to Alaska in magazines all over the world.

A government assay office was finally established in Seattle in 1898. During its first four years in business, the office counted more than $174 million on its scales. The little city on Elliott Bay grew rich from sourdough profits spent at its stores and houses of entertainment.

By the time the Alaska and Yukon gold rushes had lost their vitality in the diapered would mark the hundredth anniversary of the explorers Lewis and Clark visiting the Northwest. However, the basic reason was stated by Portland fair promoter Henry Dosch. "In the first place," he said, "it means money – lots of money… I know that such expositions pay – pay immensely."

Visitors to the Lewis and Clark Exposition couldn't help but be impressed. Designed by John Olmsted, successor to famous city planner Frederick Law Olmsted, it was as beautiful as any 385 acres (156 hectares) in the nation.

Its stately exhibit halls were surrounded by rose-lined walks and carefully manicured terraces. At its northern end, the mammoth Spanish Renaissance Government Building

days of the 20th century, Seattle was starting to challenge Portland as the great metropolis of the Northwest.

"The iron is hot": This didn't sit easily with Portland businessmen. They didn't want to see their industry and shipping business drained off by Seattle. Something had to be done, they thought, but what? And that's when they decided it was about time for the Northwest to hold a world's fair.

There were many lofty reasons for holding such a fair – for one, its 1905 opening date

Left, the Oregon State Seal. **Above**, steamships ply Puget Sound and Seattle's busy harbor.

reflected its grandeur in the waters of Guild's Lake, framed by the white peaks of the Cascade Mountains. The Forestry Building – "the largest log cabin in the world" – honored Oregon's relationship to its woods. Gondolas bobbed on the lake, their courses interrupted every now and then by a "diving elk," one of the most peculiar attractions. At night the buildings and lakeside walks were outlined with lights. Every Oregon county, most states and several nations had exhibits at the exposition, contributing to the total construction expenditure of $25 million.

The fair and its publicity paid off for the City of Roses. Not only did investors realize a 21 percent return on their dollars, but in the five years following the fair, the population of the Portland area doubled, reaching 270,000 in 1910.

Such success convinced the Seattle city fathers that they were about due for a fair, as well. It started out with the manageable name "Alaska Exposition." But as its scope became wider, so its moniker became longer. By the time the fair finally opened in 1909, its promotional banners had to be stretched to accommodate the name "Alaska-Yukon-Pacific Exposition." In the end, though, everyone just called it the A-Y-P).

The A-Y-P proved as prosperous as the Lewis and Clark Exposition, drawing 3,740,551 visitors over its 138-day schedule and convincing many people who had visited Seattle from other parts of the country to remain. In 1910 the population of Seattle for the first time exceeded that of Portland – surpassing it by 30,000.

These expositions and accompanying bombast put Portland and Seattle on the map, and there was great demand for information on the rest of New Eden, as well. The Pacific Northwest had become a very saleable item.

Racial hatred: It was perhaps less attractive a proposition, though, if your skin didn't happen to be white.

Both Oregon and Washington had pushed for the riddance of the Chinese from their shores. In November 1885, sinophobes in Tacoma marched through the rain to roust Chinese residents of the city from their homes and load them onto a train bound for Portland. A year later, Washington Territory passed a law forbidding Chinese from owning property in the state.

Men of Seattle were not happy with the Asian influence in their town, and in early 1886 many knocked on the doors of Chinese homes, told the occupants that the building was condemnable, and said that the Chinese should leave town immediately unless they wanted to face trouble. Three hundred and fifty Chinese were "escorted" to the city's waterfront, where they were scheduled to be shipped off to San Francisco. A writ of *habeas corpus* stopped such expulsions, but it didn't calm the town. Anti-Chinese groups were popping up all over. Militiamen finally had to be called in to keep the peace.

In February of that year, most of Seattle's Chinese, convinced that persecution would be inevitable if they remained in town, left aboard the steamer *George W. Edler*, bound for California.

Oregon was more notorious for its racist behavior toward blacks than Chinese. Though its citizens had, just after the Civil War, passed the 13th Amendment to the US Constitution to abolish slavery, the 14th Amendment, guaranteeing citizenship to blacks, barely passed the Oregon Legislature, which voted to rescind its ratification – twice. The governor at the time didn't even bother to call a legislative session to vote on the 15th Amendment – black suffrage. Oregon didn't get around to approving the amendment until 1959 – 89 years after the US Secretary of State had declared it ratified.

Railroad boom: It wasn't until transcontinental railroads came to Oregon in the late 1880s that there was a significant increase in the state's black population. Many came with the railroads as porters and waiters, and a host of others sought employment in railroad-related capacities. It was tough for blacks to get any jobs except for menial labor, and a good number of black men turned toward work in the underworld.

The effectiveness of black political groups was growing, albeit ever so slowly. A branch of the National Association for the Advancement of Colored People (NAACP) was organized in Portland not long after the movement was founded in 1909.

One of the early campaigns of the Oregon NAACP was to protest the showing of D.W. Griffith's *Birth of a Nation* in 1915. Griffith's version of post-Civil War Reconstruction had Southern audiences shooting up the screen when a freed black man was shown seducing a white girl. The film drew wild applause when the white-hooded heroes of the film – members of the Ku Klux Klan – rode up to save the day.

Small wonder then, that alongside advertisements for *Nation* was displayed the Imperial Wizard's invitation to come join the newly disinterred KKK, which billed itself as "a high class order for men of intelligence and character."

By 1921, the so-called Invisible Empire was in full swing in Oregon, complete with white robes, hoods, King Kleagles and all the other fancy-dress trappings associated with the struggle against what the KKK defined as "Koons, Kikes and Katholics." It has been estimated that by 1922 there were 25,000 active Klan members in Oregon.

The Klan collapsed as suddenly as it had sprung to life. Rank-and-file Klansmen began to notice their dues rising sharply – was someone in charge lining his pockets? Dissatisfaction increased when some Klansmen pushed to recall Governor Pierce, who the Klan had almost single-handedly elected to office, but who appeared totally indifferent to Klan wishes once he was installed in Salem. Other Kluxers argued that it wouldn't look good to recall a man they'd worked hard to elect. The resulting power struggle tore what was left of the Klan apart. By 1924 it was finished in Oregon.

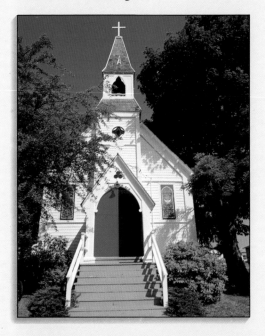

While the Ku Klux Klan was singing its swan song, the labor movement in the Pacific Northwest was becoming a political force of significance.

Commies and Wobblies: On February 6, 1919, Seattle became the site of the nation's first general strike. Sixty thousand organized workers walked off their jobs that day in a move that many people were calling a "revolution." The causes of the strike were complex. These were unsettled times, when men were desperately trying to recapture some

<u>Above</u>, **St Paul's Church presents a pristine exterior in Port Townsend, Washington.**

normality into their lives again after World War I. The 1918–19 influenza epidemic had forced people to wear protective masks and avoid public assemblies, and these measures had put the Pacific Northwest on edge. An estimated 20 million people worldwide died of the viral disease, 548,000 of whom lived in the United States.

The revolutions in Hungary and Russia were watched with suspicion, and there were fears that similar events might be sparked off in the United States. Already there had been serious confrontations between American businessmen and labor leaders.

Wary eyes were focused on members of the Industrial Workers of the World, or "Wobblies." Founded in 1905 by a coterie of "radicals," the IWW had opposed the role of the United States in World War I (which it dubbed the Capitalist War). The IWW had not only been criticized for its anti-war sentiments, but had been infiltrated by agents ostensibly guarding the country against "anarchy, sedition, and sabotage." IWW members were arrested for distributing anti-war literature, and some were even deported. Seven men died and another 31 people were injured at Everett, Washington, in 1916 as lumber company representatives and IWW members clashed.

Another confrontation seemed inevitable. It came when the Emergency Fleet Corporation in Washington, DC, refused to settle a threatened shipyard strike. On January 21, 1919, union leaders announced that shipyards would be struck. Other workers joined the shipyard action in sympathy.

When sawmill and ship whistles rang through Seattle on February 6, signaling the beginning of the strike, most civil services shut down until further notice. Four days later the strike was settled. Workers went back to their jobs after Lincoln's Birthday.

But the relationship between industry workers and their employers was never the same again. The idea of unionization became very popular, particularly in the Seattle area, and it didn't seem to wither despite economic hardships faced during the country's Great Depression of the 1930s. Workers believed unionization could help restore the foundations of US industry after the Depression. But it wasn't until the United States entered World War II that industry again felt really secure.

As America geared up for World War II, increased job opportunities and high wages for defense work encouraged many people to migrate to the Northwest, where the shortage of workers was so acute that Portland's Kaiser Company was running trains from the east and south to transport shipyard recruits. The September 30, 1942 edition of the *Oregonian* included a front-page photo of 500 happy New Yorkers arriving in Portland on the "Magic Carpet Special" en route to the Kaiser shipyards.

Immigrants: Long-time residents of Portland expressed disgust when over 100,000 wartime immigrants came pouring into the city. Some were concerned that there wasn't enough housing in the city, or that there weren't enough services to both support and control this new population. Others were unhappy that so many of these newcomers were black. "New Negro Migrants Worry City," the *Oregonian* headlined in 1942.

Yet things overall seemed to be looking up for the region. The number of manufacturing companies around Portland doubled between 1940 and 1946. Large war machinery plants around Puget Sound – including the Boeing Aircraft Company and the Puget Sound Navy Yard at Bremerton – were starved for help. Lumber companies, mining concerns and agricultural industries were frantically producing goods to keep up with demand. The population of the entire Northwest leapt by about 30 percent during the early 1940s.

But the outlook wasn't so rosy for the Japanese who had made their homes in Oregon and Washington. Like the Chinese before them, the Japanese (who by 1941 constituted the region's largest minority population) had met with discrimination in the two states. Washington had passed laws in 1921 and 1923 prohibiting the ownership of land by aliens. Many Oregon farmers resented the industrious Japanese, whom they saw as homing in on a good American industry.

After the Japanese bombing of Hawaii's Pearl Harbor in 1941 and the United States entering World War II, President Franklin D.

Roosevelt instructed military commanders nationwide to remove any persons of Japanese ancestry from areas that might be considered militarily significant. In March 1942, Washington, Oregon and California were designated as a military area in which all Japanese might be confined. Stockades were built at The Dalles, Oregon, and at other locations around the region to house the Japanese. Their land was confiscated, much to the delight of the Americans who had envied their farming abilities. There was widespread fear that, on the loose, Japanese might somehow turn up government secrets and alert enemy agents, or act as spotters for industrial installations of significance to the US war effort.

It certainly didn't help to quell such fears when, in June of 1942, a Japanese submarine surfaced near the mouth of the Columbia River and lobbed a 5½-inch shell at Fort Stevens, a Civil War-era installation. The shell missed, but it left Oregon with the distinction of being the only one of the 48 states attacked during World War II.

The war brought millions of dollars to fill Northwest coffers, but it also stimulated a change in the local economy. No longer would it be exclusively based on natural resources – trees, fish and agricultural goods. Demand for war machinery had stimulated the expansion of manufacturing companies, concerns much less vulnerable to economic fluctuations. The electro-chemical and electro-metallurgy industries boomed between the mid-1940s and early 1950s, with more than 600 outfits of this kind locating around Portland during that period.

Trees and fish were still important to the areas; they had, after all, helped build the two states. But post-war population and industrial growth were shaping a new profile for Oregon and Washington. The Northwest was trying to shed its backwoods image in favor of one more in keeping with the 20th century – or even the 21st.

The Northwest republic: Standing at the base of Seattle's 605-foot (185-meter) Space Needle, and looking up its spidery legs to the saucer-like top, one can't help but be impressed. This isn't the tallest structure in the

Left, Boeing's plant in Everett, Washington, is one of the largest employers on the West Coast.

city (the new Columbia Seafirst Center – 76 stories – claims that title), nor is it the most architecturally significant (the 42-story Smith Tower, completed in 1914 and for years the tallest building west of the Mississippi, is more enduring in its attraction). But the Space Needle has become a symbol for Seattle – maybe for the entire Pacific Northwest.

Seattle booster Joe Gandy explained the significance of the Needle to *The New York Times* when the structure and the surrounding Century 21 Exposition were being planned more than 30 years ago: "Back when we were in school, if you wanted attention, you put up your hand. That is what the Space Needle will do for the Fair and Seattle."

New England and the Midwest saw the Northwest as a pristine, enriching place.

This image of the Northwest as a pragmatic, environmentally-sound place seemed every bit as attractive to various disillusioned Americans as had its much earlier image as a rough-and-tumble stomping ground for pioneers.

But it wasn't only people from Tuskaloosa and Detroit who were swept away by this image of the Northwest. Northwesterners themselves revelled in the romantic picture of their land and promoted the region as an exclusive place fit only for a chosen few. They didn't want either Oregon or Washington to be thought of as just another state.

As Portland's Lewis and Clark Exhibition and Seattle's Alaska-Yukon-Pacific Exposition ushered in the 20th century, so the Space Needle and Seattle's world's fair of 1962 tried to introduce the Northwest to the future.

The era they ushered in was certainly one of dramatic change. The 1960s and early 1970s brought violence to the Northwest, as it did to all parts of the country. Students demonstrated on campuses around the region, decrying US involvement in the Vietnam War. But it was also during this period that the Pacific Northwest developed a great deal of pride in itself and accrued a certain cachet in the US. Suddenly everybody in

They loved it when Oregon Governor Tom McCall announced in the 1970s that the world could "visit our state of enchantment – but, for heaven's sake, don't stay," and even publicized such sentiments on billboards around the state. This is God's country, they boasted, and it's ours.

The new Northwest: The Pacific Northwest of today is a combination of past and present. If you roll through the dust of eastern Oregon, you can see old stagecoach stops and abandoned mining operations. Walk along certain sidewalks and it's possible to find hitching rings in the concrete, embedded there in days when no one had heard of

Henry Ford, but everybody knew the price of a saddle and a good horse. Seattle still boasts Native American totems and hidden, rotting docks where sailing ships loaded lumber.

But today you can also see a new Northwest, born out of the suffering of recent years. This new Northwest is striving to meet a future that is more complicated than anything it has ever faced before.

Traditional Northwest industries – lumber, agriculture, and fishing – haven't fared well over the last few years. In the early 1980s, newspapers were full of stories about sawmills closing down and laying off workers. Between just three years, Oregon's wood industry lost almost 20,000 employees.

process making Gates one of the richest men in the United States. But computer and software manufacturers were not the only industries with a canny eye on the future.

While the 1960s and 1970s called for Northwest isolationism, the 1980s and 1990s encouraged business cooperation – especially as regards the so-called Pacific Rim, an area taking in the West Coast, those parts of Asia bordering the Pacific Ocean, and both Australia and New Zealand. Roughly half the world's population lives within this rim area. Selling to this population means money – lots of it. And Northwest business wanted a piece of the action. Governors from the region set off touring in the Far East,

Instead, all business eyes are now turned firmly towards high technology. Tax breaks in the state were planned to keep such industries here, and here they have settled. Bill Gates' billion-dollar company, Microsoft, attracted thousands of young, bright and talented newcomers to the area, professionals from all over the world. His and other software industries have in themselves spawned dozens of other companies, in the

talking to foreign trade ministers to build up future business contacts. The significance of the Pacific connection is undeniable: each $42,000 in export creates a job in Oregon, and over 15 percent of manufacturing positions in the state are dependent upon exporting. Judging by Seattle, the nearest port to the lucrative Asian market, the work has paid off. The port of Seattle now does 95 percent of its business with Asian countries.

Tourism, too, has finally been recognized as an important industry, and both Oregon and Washington have established state travel promotion budgets in the hope of attracting visitors. "Come but don't stay" is passé.

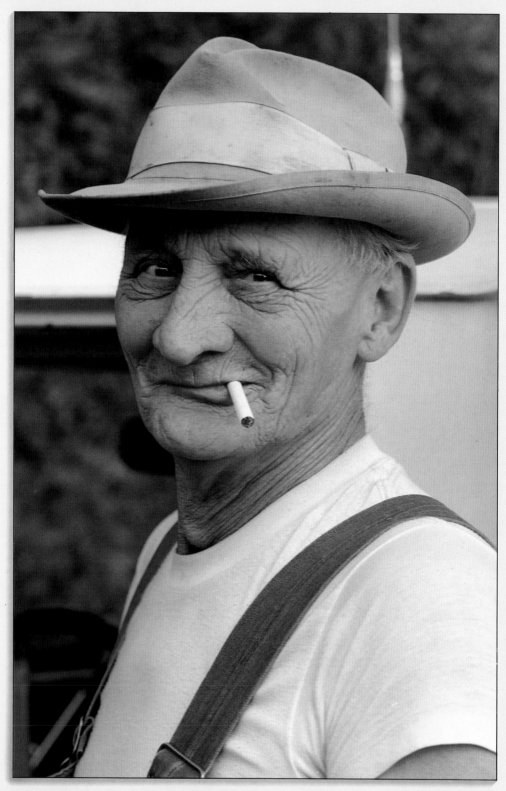

It may be a misnomer to label all residents of Washington and Oregon "Northwesterners," as if all are of the same ilk and conviction. Yet a single common quality might be the shared fierce pride in the land, as if the opening stanza of *America the Beautiful* (you know, amber waves of grain, spacious skies, and fruited plains) must have been written with the Northwest in mind.

Do something as seemingly minor as mispronounce the name Oregon (correct: Orygun) or Klatskanie (Klat-skuh-neye) and expect to be politely but insistently corrected. In many ways, Northwesterners think of their region as distinct from the rest of the country and ahead of its time.

As *The Atlantic* stated in a 1976 cover story on the Pacific Northwest, "Some northwesterners even fancy themselves as offering the nation an alternative future – one that is open to change and modernity, but insistent on testing these blessings against agreed values and ways that the Northwest wants to hang on to. The future that the Pacific Northwest would like to enjoy is so clearly recognizable to it – more recognizable than the future seems to be to the rest of the nation – because that future looks so much like the Northwest to be seen today."

To which the *Atlantic* writer added, "If only everyone is lucky."

But beyond sharing a geographical location and a love for the region, it would be grossly unfair to lump Oregonians and Washingtonians under a common label. The Northwest is a region of individualists, of many races and creeds, and of philosophical, occasionally even political, opposites.

No matter how guarded Northwesterners have been over the last two decades in extolling the virtues of this region, thousands of new residents have come here to live. So many people have come, in fact, that this growth is having a dramatic effect on the population profile.

Twenty years ago, the campuses of Reed

College, the University of Washington, Lewis and Clark College and Whitman College were predominantly white. Today the faces in the crowd are not only those of African Americans, but of Africans, Arabs, Hispanics and Southeast Asians. Hispanics are the fastest growing ethnic group in the United States, numbering at least 20 million: there are upwards of 100,000 Hispanics in Oregon now, surpassing Asians, Native Americans and blacks as the largest minority group in the state. The increase of Hispanics in Wash-

ington has been similarly dramatic.

Since the end of US military involvement in Southeast Asia, thousands of people who once lived in that corner of the world have relocated to Washington and Oregon. They have set up sub-communities in Seattle and Portland, there to try rebuilding their war-torn lives. They wander through city streets in small, quiet groups, often in fine robes that stand out in seas of gray three-piece suits and tank tops.

In areas where these new Northwesterners live, their Caucasian neighbors turn from their midday soap operas to watch them head for market, and wonder all the while what

Preceding pages: an outdoor pastime – picking arrowleaf balsamroot in the Washington Mountains. **Left**, a Hood River apple farmer. **Right**, a rock climber on belay.

these strangers in a strange land think of their new home. The Southeast Asians have come to the United States looking for a New Eden.

But it isn't only along ethnic lines that Northwesterners can be divided. Culture, attitudes and lifestyles differ dramatically even between residents living west of the Cascade Mountains and those who call the east their home.

"Wet-siders" and "Dry-siders": There's a long-standing snobbery among both "wet-siders" (as those folk living in the Northwest's western half are called) and their eastern or "dry-sider" brethren. If you're a wet-sider, you look at eastern Oregon and Washington as running rampant with cattle and rattle-

traffic jams and something chic that won't keep a body going called nouvelle cuisine. The west has long been considered politically liberal, the east ultra-conservative.

Simply put, neither side really knows what the other is like. Yet they're happy with their misconceptions, and frequently unhappy with each other. More than once, this unhappiness has led to efforts to reshape state boundaries, to separate east from west. As the tale goes, master orator Stephen A. Douglas foresaw such troubles when Congress was considering Oregon statehood in the mid-19th century. At one point it's said that Douglas, then chairman of the United States Senate Committee on boundaries, stood before a large

snakes, its cities little more than pioneer forts on alkali flats, its population made up largely of rednecked hicks who spend a lot of time polishing their saddles and buying garish steer horns to mount above the grills of gas-guzzling Cadillacs.

The snobbish dry-sider has an equally bogus image of life on the other side of the "Cascade Curtain." For him, the west is a haughty playground for money-grubbing "yuppies," a place made dangerous by the presence of Mount St Helens and the Green River Killer, and made unhealthy by air pollution. From the east the cities of Seattle and Portland represent nothing but noise,

map of the proposed state and, as his fellow committee-men watched in surprise, raised his cane and dragged its foot down the line of the Cascade Range.

"This is your natural boundary!" Douglas exclaimed. "There is the line marked by nature as the eastern boundary of your state. Oregon should lie wholly west of the Cascade Mountains."

A land of individuals: Mavericks and maverick movements of one sort or another are hardly new to the Northwest. Politicians in this area have long pushed for populist reforms, even when they were unpopular. Over the last 20 years, the Northwest has sought to set a pace for reforms and environmental conservation that might be followed by the rest of the country. It has made concerted efforts at revitalizing the historic districts of major Oregon and Washington cities, and has likewise invested in inner city and highway beautification programs which have pumped life into the region.

It is told that, in the mid-1930s, US Postmaster General James A. Farley raised his drinking glass at a formal dinner in Seattle and offered up a toast to "the forty-seven states and the soviet of Washington." The toast referred directly to the rise at that time of labor unions in the Evergreen State. But to some people at that dinner, it alluded also to

Washington's history as a hotbed for communitarian experimentation.

No fewer than a half-dozen utopian communities had sprung up in the state of Washington since the late 19th century, including colonies in Lewis and Skagit counties and on the Kitsap County peninsula. The Puget Sound Cooperative Colony, founded at Port Angeles in 1887, helped establish that town on the Strait of Juan de Fuca as a viable commercial center. Other colonies came and

Left, Oregon's coastal sand dunes provide for an exuberant leap. **Above**, a tulip-picker from Mount Vernon, Washington.

went, their members initially attracted by ideas of sharing goods unselfishly with others but discouraged by such basic things as insufficient building materials and even the lack of local entertainment.

Idealistic communities still pop up today. Most people who visit the Northwest arrive with some knowledge of Bhagwan Shree Rajneesh, bearded leader of a large group of red-clad disciples who arrived in the state from India in 1981. Although no longer around, the original Rajneeshees said they were merely seeking the right to practice their religion. However, they stirred concern among state residents by allegedly purchasing assault weapons and were accused of drug smuggling and prostitution on behalf of their guru. For their part, the Rajneeshees wished to remain on their central Oregon property. The Beaver State was adopted as their own little park – a place of refuge, they believed, for when the rest of the world perished in a nuclear holocaust. But the Bhagwan was deported in the late 1980s and high-level group members were later convicted of poisoning townspeople.

The Northwest's so-called "survivalists" hope to wait out an uncertain future. Most of these people have sought refuge around Grants Pass, Oregon. Like other small groups of survivalists in Oklahoma, northern California and Arkansas, these people are expecting a collapse of society as we know it. Maybe the end will come as a result of nuclear war, rampant inflation that produces uncontrollable food riots, or a breakdown of government systems. In any case, these folks want to be ready. They've come to southern Oregon because they believe it an unlikely target for bombing in the event that war should come to the shores of the United States. And they've stocked up on guns – rifles, handguns – just in case they need to defend themselves from less far-sighted neighbors who haven't prepared adequately for the end of civilization.

Are these people paranoid? Or are they more far-sighted than the rest of us? Either way, it's a commentary on the tolerance of Pacific Northwesterners for people who might be classified as "different" or "unusual." If this tolerance has invited a certain amount of controversy into their midst, it has also made the Northwest a colorful place in which to live.

Seattle – and the Pacific Northwest in general – is known as the place to be. In the 1980s, newspapers and magazines began to run cover stories about how its beautiful surroundings, superior lifestyle and booming economy made a little-known earthly paradise. People are pouring in, and many of the locals hate it.

The influx is nothing new – the same thing was happening a century ago. In September 1870 *Harper's Weekly* ran a story extolling Seattle as the Mediterranean of the Pacific and the future Queen City of the Pacific. Within a few years Seattle's population exceeded 43,000, fueled by rumors that it would be the terminus for the transcontinental railroad. Tacoma became the western terminus of Henry Villard's Northern Pacific railroad in 1883, but a decade later James R. Hill, a one-eyed Canadian visionary, brought in his Great Northern Line.

Pleasure place: The railroad companies worked hard to promote the Pacific Northwest. At one time the Northern Pacific Railroad employed almost 1,000 agents in Europe distributing pamphlets extolling the joys of farming in the West. And a promotion booklet by the Oregon, Washington Railway and Navigation Co. raved about "this place where pleasures abound." Perhaps they were telling it like it was, because Collier Cobb, who claimed to be one of the nation's foremost economists, wrote: "Nature must have ordained that Puget Sound should be the trade center of the Pacific."

The turn of the century saw brochures with titles like *Seattle: Seaport of Success*. One flyer was headed "The State of Washington Calls You to the Land of Larger Chance Where Life Is Still in the Making, First in Opportunity."

In 1928 the *Seattle Star* insisted that "Population is still the big need of Seattle and the Pacific Northwest," although later that year the city's Chamber of Commerce was able to boast that its boosterism was paying off and

that the past seven years had seen an increase in automobiles from California from 8,000 to 50,000 and visitors to Mount Rainier National Park had increased by almost 400 percent to 219,000 a year.

What a difference in attitude today when a popular bumper sticker reads HAVE A GOOD TRIP – BACK TO CALIFORNIA. Writer Jonathan Raban says locals choose to believe that most of the newcomers are Californians "who bring with them escalating real estate prices and demands for first class food and deferential service." Anti-California jokes, Raban wrote in his *Hunting Mister Heartbreak: A Discovery of America*, allowed Seattleites to vent their disquiet and anger at the effects of mass immigration without being tagged as racist. "You could happily jeer at a Californian in a way that you would not dream of jeering at a Black or an Asian." Soon to spring up was a group called UCLA – United Californians Looking for Acceptance in Seattle.

Some of the recent influx is merely trendy. *Rolling Stone* called Seattle "America's premier haven for eccentrics," saying it had "developed an image as the new center of groovy, unmotivated slackerdom…Seattle is the place to go not to find out who you are but to postpone finding out who you are… True Seattleites, ones that came here independent of the hype, know that eventually the scene will burn itself out and Seattle will go back to being its normal weird self."

Still they come: Despite popular belief, the big changes of recent years are not just down to the influx of Californians (who account for less than one-quarter of the city's population) but an invasion by settlers from almost everywhere. About 11 percent of Seattle's residents are Asian. Americans of Asian descent make up 17 percent of the enrolment at the University of Washington where 62 professors specialize in East Asian studies. The Port of Seattle does 95 percent of its business with Asian countries. This connection dates back to the 1860s when the Chinese came to build railroads.

Seattle's Office for Long Range Planning forecast that the city's population would increase by 28,000 (5.5 percent) between

Preceding pages: the Pacific Northwest remains the undisputed hub of micro-brewing. Left, Seattleites refresh themselves with healthy, outdoor pursuits like rowing.

1980 and 2020 with surrounding King County growing by an astonishing 67 percent, adding one million new residents. Growth has since slowed but with a percentage increase of around 2 percent a year, Washington still has one of the fastest-growing populations.

Washington's two biggest companies remain dominant in their fields and are still growing. Boeing recently signed a huge contract to supply aircraft to China, and this will keep it busy into the new century. Microsoft, the $4.5 billion software giant on a 265-acre (107-hectare) campus in Redmond across Lake Washington, has drawn hundreds of programming whiz kids to the area to start up or work in multi-media companies making

Shadowcatcher. Incidentally, both Allen and his better-known Microsoft co-founder Bill Gates, are building $30-million homes that have theaters, entertainment centers and – in Gates' case – an electronic delivery system that can display the 100,000 paintings to which he owns the rights.

Seattle's innovative art scene includes Northwest CyberArtists, whose members combine experimental music, art, dance and technology in such avant garde shows as a water fountain controlled by music or data gloves that can point to a spot and make sound come from it. "These things wouldn't happen in the Bay Area or LA because there's no economic incentive to them," says Marc

CD-ROMs. *The Washington Post* bought 80 percent of Mammoth Micro Productions; Meredith Corp. (*Better Homes & Gardens*) bought into Multicom Publishing, another CD-ROM maker. Microsoft co-founder Paul G. Allen's Starwave Corp. is producing CD-ROMs in collaboration with big names like Clint Eastwood and Peter Gabriel. Sega chose Seattle to host the first of its 150 Interactive Entertainment Centers, featuring a package of virtual reality attractions, motion simulators and high-tech gimmickry.

"Seattle is becoming a hotbed of people who came from film, TV, games, computers and music," says Lucie Fjeldstad, who chairs

Lucas, founder of Lone Wolf and writer of software for professional audio equipment. "The Northwest has a better ethic for the creation of new media."

Naturally, there are naysayers. Sherman Alexie, a local writer who recently moved back to the city, thinks the city is self-impressed. "Seattle pretends to be this huge multicultural city, but it's not. Mostly it's a liberal enclave of middle-class white people who can afford to pick and choose what other cultures they want to dabble in."

Impact of success: Pulitzer prize-winning author William Dietrich writes about the environment for the *Seattle Times*, and he pulls together some interesting statistics. The Census Bureau forecast that by 2020 Washington would gain 2.7 million people; the Seattle-area population grew 38 percent between 1970 and 1990, but developed land increased by 87 percent; and the miles each household drives have risen more than three times faster than the population.

Washington and Oregon lose 75,000 acres (33,000 hectares) of commercial land each year to development, says Dietrich. This is land permanently lost, as the clear cuts of timber companies are not replaced. At the turn of the century, when paved highways were still non-existent, Seattle had just 50,000 people and rivers were still undammed.

People in Snohomish County noted that the statistics were predicting the adjoining areas would absorb most of the predicted influx. In response, the county voted to create "urban growth" areas to accommodate the increased population. This latest example of what is known as "rural rebound" didn't sit well with local environmentalists.

"It's coming down to a battle between the ruralness of Snohomish County and giving in to the forces of sprawl driven by greed," retorted Ellen Gray of the local Audubon Society. The ripple effects of rezoning 8,000 acres (3,200 hectares) of agricultural land puts pressure on beleagured farmers to sell out to developers, encroaches on Native American tribal lands and fishing rights, and makes flooding more likely by altering a water shed that absorbs heavy rains.

Dr Delton W. Young, a psychologist who acts as consultant to juvenile courts in the region, goes beyond environmentalism and declares that the new suburbs are changing society for the worse, and as such they are a public-health issue. "The configuration of our suburbs is defined by grids of five-lane highways that are needed to feed the malls and superstores. Everyone is forced into cars to meet every need, and casual contact among neighbors disappears.

"Residential areas have been fragmented into odd clusters of houses and apartment complexes crowded on every side by highways, car lots and billboards. Neighborhoods are seldom allowed to be well insulated from the clatter of commercialism and the din of heavy traffic.

"Where human needs have been put aside in favor of the short-term interests of growth and construction, we can witness a couple of decades later many of the most obvious signs of social instability – youth violence, school failure and substance abuse."

Public spirited: Nevertheless, one of Seattle's less tangible assets is the undeniable public spiritedness of its citizens. More than eight out of ten residents participate in curbside recycling, the highest rate in the country (although the city still ships 400,000 tons of garbage to Oregon each year). In

Fortune magazine's recent rating of the best US cities to work in, Seattle dropped a few pegs to sixth place but was still described as "relaxed, forward-looking, environmentally sensitive and passionately involved when debating the city's continuing growth."

The King County Council still funds local culture with grants to everything from local theaters to the Seattle Opera, but the public kicks in generously. Seattle Symphony chairman Ronald B. Woodard cited "heroic efforts" by more than 10,000 donors in balancing the symphony's annual budget, and the ongoing regional arts boom has seen almost every art museum in the area undergoing

Left, *The Nutcracker Suite,* **performed by the Pacific Northwest Ballet, part of a cultural explosion. Right, a large percentage of the city's population originally came from Asia.**

expansion or renovation. This is evidence that people are moving to the area at least partly because of its vigorous cultural life.

Bicycle commuting seems to have made greater headway here than in most American cities. The city's traffic department, after surveying 13 major bicycle entryways into downtown, reported a 28 percent increase in morning cyclists since 1992. Typically around 1,100 cyclists per day clocked on in those streets alone.

Local environmentalist Alan Thein Durning thinks Seattleites can build on their good works and set an example for the rest of the country. "If we can't make the economy work with nature here, then where else can

we?" he asks, pointing out that high education levels, a tradition of innovative policies and a global outlook fostered by Pacific Rim connections give Seattle a headstart.

Durning is director of Northwest Environment Watch (NEW), a think tank whose mandate is to track the region's trends (population, timber jobs, gas emissions) and survey such ecological disruptions as the effects of radiation leakage. He is also writing a sequel to his ground-breaking *How Much Is Enough? The Consumer Society and the Future of the Earth* (W.W. Norton, 1992).

Washington State's Growth Management Act is judged one of the most progressive pieces of legislation of its kind in the country, but NEW's agenda calls for redirected taxes and subsidies to trigger catalytic reforms. One example is pollution tax at the gas pump and perhaps replacing payroll tax.

It's the big picture that counts, Durning says, arguing that a list of things to save the earth just makes people feel guilty. NEW says "You're worse off than you ought to be because the system just isn't set up right."

Open-mindedness: New ideas usually get a positive response in Seattle. Starbucks may have over 600 branches turning Americans into espresso fiends, but it still serves 1,000 cups a day at its original spot in the downtown Westlake Center. And when Seattle launched micro-brewed beer a decade ago the trend spread quickly on the West Coast. The Pacific Northwest remains the hub of micro-brewing, with the highest per capita draught beer consumption in the US.

One of the city's most successful exports has been Nordstrom's, a popular store whose amiable style is quintessential Seattle. Founded as a shoe store by Swedish-born John Nordstrom who made a fortune in the Alaska goldfields, it is still family-owned and is famous for its politeness and caring attitude toward its customers.

Grandchildren of the family say they were raised "kneeling in front of the customer." Staff are free to find and bond with customers according to the Nordstrom Rules: Rule No.1: *Use your good judgement in all situations. There will be no additional rules.* Nordstrom spread into California in the late 1970s, and a competitor said it changed the face of retailing in a place where everybody was just trying to sell things. The chain expanded into the Midwest in 1991, retaining its legendary politesse. There is some talk of future expansion into Europe.

Somehow even Big City Seattle seems to mind its manners more than most. Margaret Larsen, who left New York City to work as a TV anchorwoman couldn't agree more. "Seattle has a very different rhythm," she says, "and it lacks the frantic qualities that some big cities have. There are a lot of diverse groups and ethnic contributions and it just seems to have gelled effortlessly."

Left, Seattle's fondness for espresso spawned Starbucks coffee houses, now nationwide. **Right**, cyber art is everywhere in Space City.

The Pacific Northwest is known for its pioneering spirit, as is its wine industry. Meeting the many challenges inherent in a young, rapidly growing industry, the Northwest's winemakers have established themselves among the best in the world in around two decades of production.

The region had less than 10 wineries in 1975; today the industry boasts about 200. The Pacific Northwest is now the nation's second largest producer of *vitis vinifera* grapes – the premium European wine varieties – including Cabernet Sauvignon, Pinot Noir, Chardonnay and Riesling.

Northwest wineries are primarily small, family-owned operations, tucked into a land of many contrasts, traversing farmland, hillsides, lush fir forests and sagebrush-dotted deserts. Divided by the great Cascade Mountain range, the wine grape-growing regions of the Pacific Northwest are as diverse as the wines they produce.

Washington grapes are almost exclusively grown on the eastern side of the Cascade range in an arid environment featuring long, warm, sunny days and cool nights.

Oregon's grapes are grown on the west side of the mountains in the marine-influenced Willamette Valley, which has been likened to a "cooler, wetter Napa Valley." Yet despite its diversity, the Northwest is the only region in the country, outside of the state of California, where growing conditions are considered ideal for premium wine grape varieties.

Wine in Washington: Washington leads the Northwest region in wine and grape production with 11,000 acres (4,000 hectares) in premium vinifera vineyards. Experts estimate that as much as 150,000 acres (60,000 hectares) in the state are suitable for vineyards. If just one-third of the potential acreage is planted, Washington's premium wine industry would be the equivalent of California's well-known Napa/Sonoma wine region in size.

Washington's potential for premium wine production was officially "discovered" in 1966 when renowned wine critic Andre Tchelistcheff first sampled a homemade Gewurztraminer made from Yakima Valley

grapes and called it the "best Gewurztraminer produced in the US." In 1974 a 1972 Chateau Ste Michelle Johannisberg Riesling won first place in a blind tasting organized by the *Los Angeles Times*. Washington State wines continue to receive widespread respect and recognition, winning prestigious honors in many major competitions.

Washington State has long had potential as a great wine-producing region. Eastern Washington's two fertile river valleys, the Yakima and the Columbia basins, lie just

north of the 46th degree latitude, similar to the Bordeaux and Burgundy regions of France. The area's sandy loam soil over volcanic rock base yields moisture easily and provides good heat retention.

This, along with the Cascade Mountains, which create an arid, semi-desert climate, results in a region with near-perfect growing conditions for producing classic European vine types. Long warm days and cool nights create ideal conditions for grapes with excellent balance – heavy with sugar yet still high in natural acid.

Although most of Washington's wine grape-growing activity takes place east of the Cascades, the majority of wineries are located near the metropolitan centers of the west. This means grapes must travel an average of 200 miles (320 km) from vineyard to winery. It also means that a day's wine touring from downtown Seattle is not too difficult an accomplishment.

Oregon's outcrop: Oregon's vineyards are primarily found on the cool, moist west side of the Cascade range that is nearer the coast. Family-owned cottage wineries, with vineyards situated on 5–20-acre (2–8-hectare) plots, are common here. This also means visitors are likely to meet the person whose name is on the bottle. Look for Oregon's wineries in rural or semi-rural areas – to the

the University of California, Davis, impetuously announced his intention to produce the exceptional – but difficult to grow – Pinot Noir grape in Oregon's fertile Willamette Valley. On Lett's heels came a host of nearly 40 pioneering winemakers.

Oregon's primary growing areas are concentrated in the western part of the state on hillsides overlooking the fertile Willamette, Rogue and Umpqua river valleys. Like Washington, which is experimenting with cool weather grape varieties west of the mountains, Oregon is just beginning to develop a new wine region in the irrigated agricultural district located along the Columbia River in east central Oregon.

east and west of the Interstate 5 corridor from Portland to Grants Pass.

Oregon had its viticultural beginnings in the early 1960s when Richard Sommer, now hailed as the father of Oregon's table wine industry, began growing the first premium wine grapes in Oregon and established Hillcrest Vineyard near Eugene. In 1965, David Lett, a young viticulture graduate of

Preceding pages: Pacific Northwest wines, around since the early 1960s, are gaining in reputation every year. Left, Preston Cellars owner surveys the Riesling harvest. Above, harvesters pick the grapes with care.

Oregon's premier varieties include Pinot Noir, Chardonnay, White Riesling, Gewurztraminer, Pinot Gris and a host of fruit and berry wines. Sparkling wines, produced in the traditional French champagne method, are an important fairly new addition. Of interest is Oregon's Truth in Labeling law, which is the strictest consumer-oriented wine labeling regulation in the entire country. Oregon-produced wines must contain at least 90 percent of the grape named on the bottle; federal regulation requires only 75 percent.

Idaho has recently joined larger producers Washington and Oregon with a handful of small wineries and a few larger ones. In fact, Ste Chappelle Vineyards, located in Caldwell, 35 miles (56 km) west of Boise, is the second-largest winery in the entire region. Designed after a Paris chapel, Ste Chapelle's stunning winery and tasting room feature 24-foot (7-meter) cathedral windows overlooking the vineyards.

Touring northwest wineries: Visiting hours of the many cottage wineries of Washington and Oregon vary – some are open by appointment only and others are not open to visitors. Several books, available in local bookstores, offer extensive touring information as well as information on where to stay, where to eat, and what to see. *Northwest*

young professionals. This establishment produces in excess of 1½ million gallons (6.75 million litres) a year.

Fashioned after a French country manor, complete with pastoral setting, the winery is one of the state's leading attractions with over 150,000 visitors each year. Chateau Ste Michelle has expanded to open two other production and tasting facilities, Chateau Ste Michelle in the Yakima Valley and Columbia Crest Winery at Paterson along the Columbia River Gorge.

Columbia Winery was formerly Associated Vintners, and it is one of the oldest wineries in the state. It sits just across the street from Ste Michelle in Woodinville, and

Wines by Paul Gregutt and Jeff Prather, *Touring the Washington Wine Country* by Chuck Hill, *Northwest Wine* by Ted Meridith, *Touring the Wine Country of Washington* and *Touring the Wine Country of Oregon*, both by Ronald and Glenda Holden, will enhance an excursion into the Pacific Northwest wine country.

Several wineries or tasting rooms are to be found conveniently close to the city of Seattle. Chateau Ste Michelle, the largest winery in the Pacific Northwest, has its headquarters in Woodinville, which is located just east of Seattle and within convenient reach of that city's many wealthy (and thirsty)

it also owns the Paul Thomas Winery in Bellevue. French Creek Cellars is also located in Woodinville and is open daily. It has a shaded salmon creek out back and a small picnic area for relaxing. Situated in Seattle's south end is the small E.B. Foote Winery. Tastings tend to be on Saturdays only or by appointment.

Puget Sound wineries: A bit farther from Seattle, Puget Sound area wineries are still within an hour or two of the city and offer a look at Western Washington's unique and beautiful landscape as well.

Just off the scenic State Highway 410 at El-Hi Hill is found the Manfred Vierthaler

Winery. Vierthaler is a German native and adheres to German ecological practices. An immense Bavarian-style chalet houses his winery, tasting room, gift shop and Royal Bavarian Restaurant, as well as his family's living quarters.

Snoqualmie Winery is located within a mile of the magnificent Snoqualmie Falls, an attraction that draws one and a half million tourists annually. Quilceda Creek Vintners, just 3 miles (5 km) from the quaint, rural Snohomish community of Quilceda, is open by appointment only. Owner Alex Golitzen's winemaking talents were nurtured by his uncle, the world famous winemaker Andre Tchelistcheff.

Bainbridge Island Winery, located on one of the main ferry routes to the Olympic Peninsula, is open for tastings Wednesday to Sunday. In the vacation community of Sequim, a refashioned 60-year-old dairy barn is the quaint new home for the Neuharth Winery and tasting room, open Wednesday through Sunday. Down the road is Lost Mountain Winery, open during the last week of June and the first week of July or by appointment.

In the Nooksak Valley, near Deming, is Mount Baker Vineyards. This pleasant little winery on the Mt Baker Highway makes varietal wines.

Along the Columbia River: Named after the Salish Indians of Oregon's rugged coast, Salishan Vineyards is located above the Lewis River in the town of LaCenter near the Oregon border. Salishan's 1978 Pinot Noir is widely acclaimed as one of the best in the region. Salishan Vineyards is open weekends and by appointment. A cherry-grower turned winemaker, Chuck Henderson planted some experimental vines on his 300-acre (120-hectare) orchard near Bingen over 20 years ago. His efforts led to the development of Mont Elise Vineyard, which is now open to tasters daily.

Arbor Crest Winery in Spokane is the project of third-generation farmers, David and Harold Mielke. The brothers have opened their winery on the banks of the Spokane River where picnic tables overlook the river. Tasting is available daily.

Situated just 6 miles (10 km) from down-

town Spokane, Latah Creek Winery includes a tasting room, picnic area, gift shop and arts and crafts studio. In an A-frame cabin lodged between tall evergreens, Worden's Washington Winery is Spokane's oldest. Originally an apple grower, owner Jack Worden has produced a number of award-winning varieties. Chinook Wines in Prosser makes Semillon, Sauvignon blanc, Chardonnay, Merlot and Cabernet Sauvignon and is open for tours Friday through Sunday or at other times by appointment.

Known in the Northwest for its deliciously sweet onions, Washington's southeast corner near Walla Walla is now gaining recognition as a wine producing region as well and currently has several wineries in production. The appropriately named L'Ecole No. 41 is housed in an early-1900s frame schoolhouse. The elegant tasting room is open Wednesday through Sunday and by appointment. Nearby is Woodward Canyon Winery, another small facility open daily.

Every year, during the second week in May, Gary and Nancy Figgins open Leonetti Cellar for public tastings. Housed in an attractive building constructed of native stone in Walla Walla, the Figgins' winery has produced some fine, award-winning Cabernet Sauvignons.

Yakima Valley producers: The Yakima Valley is the viticultural center of the state and hosts Washington's largest group of wineries. The valley is rich agriculturally and its crops include fruit, hops and grapes. The Yakima area's more than 25 wineries are located along the I-82 corridor nestled among farmlands and orchards.

Covey Run Wines, designed as a showcase of the Yakima Valley growing region, features first-class tasting and visitor facilities. The Hogue Cellars is one of the largest wineries in the region; public tastings are available daily. Not far away, Hinzerling Winery specializes in red wines and sweet dessert wines perfect for after dinner. The winery is open daily for tastings.

Yakima River Winery, at the edge of the Horse Heaven Hills, is the home of John and Louise Rauner, two transplanted New Yorkers who have immersed themselves in their art to create a host of award-winning wines. The Rauners founded the Yakima Valley Wine Growers' Association and are working to put the Yakima Valley on the nation's

Oregon has over 100 wineries. Left, savoring the tastes in a tasting room.

wine maps. Kiona Vineyards, at the eastern end of the Yakima River Valley near Benton City, is open to visitors daily.

Stewart Vineyards, in Granger, makes a wonderful late-harvest Riesling and is open daily for tastings. In the small town of Zillah, near Yakima, is Portteus Winery, which makes a good Cabernet Sauvignon and Merlot. Not far away is Hyatt Cellars, which is open daily except in January, and Zillah Oakes Winery, which is open to the public every day.

Several wineries are clustered in the Tri-Cities, an area comprised of Pasco, Richland and Kennewick. The largest family-owned winery in the Northwest, Preston Premium Wines produces some 100,000 gallons annually. Located 5 miles (8 km) north of Pasco, the winery has 16 wines along with a rustic tasting room and picnic park that overlook the vineyards. Gordon Brothers Cellars, outside Pasco, makes excellent Cabernets and Merlots and is open weekends in summer or by appointment.

A tour of Oregon wineries: Located within an hour's driving time from Portland, wineries are attractively stretched across the fertile Tualatin Valley.

Award-winning Oak Knoll Winery, southwest of Beaverton, was founded in 1970 by the Ron Vuylsteke family. Oak Knoll produces its quality wines from Oregon-grown fruits, berries and varietal grapes and is open for tastings daily.

Ponzi Vineyards is the closest winery to Portland, nestled into rolling farmland just 15 miles (24 km) southwest of the city. Ponzi produces fine dry table wines and features a large stone and timber tasting room open every day except during January.

Touted as one of Oregon's most attractive wineries, Shafer Vineyard Cellars is a small winery located in the beautiful Gales Creek Valley. Picnic lovers can enjoy some of Shafer's award-winning white wines beneath a small oak grove adjacent to the winery – open daily during the summer and on weekends most of the year.

Bill and Virginia Fuller boast a spectacular view of Tualatin Lake as well as premium estate-bottled wines at their Tualatin Vineyards winery, which is open to visitors daily except in January.

Nearly half of all Oregon's wine grapes are grown in the fertile Yamhill County region. Yamhill County is host to more than a dozen Oregon wineries, as well as many fruit and nut orchards, farms and small down-home country towns.

With a reputation for producing some of Oregon's best wines, Adelsheim Winery opens during two events each year, one in the spring and one at Thanksgiving. However, entrance is by invitation only.

In the north end of the county on State Highway 47 and south to State 99 are several small family-owned and operated wineries. Elk Cove Vineyards, named for the magnificent Roosevelt Elk, features a tasting room open daily. Chateau Benoit offers a spectacular view and also encourages picnickers

to visit for daily tastings. Arterberry Winery is known for its sparkling ciders and is open for tastings on weekends. The nearby Amity Vineyards specializes in wines made from the Pinot Noir variety and is open daily from May to November. Oregon's premier wine estate, Montinore Vineyards, is open daily for tastings and tours.

Rex Hill Vineyards, outside Newburg, makes Chardonnays and a good Pinot Noir that ages beautifully. The winery features spectacular grounds and a beautiful Northwest art collection open daily February through December.

One of the oldest and probably most celebrated premium wine grape vineyards in Oregon is Eyrie Vineyards, which was established in 1966 by the pioneering winemaker David Lett and his wife Diana. The vineyard is in the Red Hills of Dundee and the winery, which is best known for award-winning Pinot Noir and Chardonnay wines, is in nearby McMinnville. Knudsen Erath Winery, situated on 265 acres (105 hectares) outside Dundee, is one of the state's top three producers.

Another of Oregon's "big three" wineries, Sokol Blosser, is a short drive from Knudsen Erath in the south end of Dundee. As well as having been bestowed with both regional and international awards for its wines, Sokol

Blosser has also garnered major honors for the architectural design of its tasting room.

Willamette Valley wines: Oregon's capital city Salem is home to some of Oregon's newest wineries. In the heart of downtown Salem, Honeywood Winery, the oldest producing winery in the state, offers a full line of fruit wines. Orchard Heights Winery, nearby, is open Tuesday through Sunday, except in January and February. Silver Falls Winery,

Left, the Chateau Ste Michelle Winery, just east of Seattle and one of the area's largest, attracts many visitors. Above, a vintner displays his own personal product.

on the East side of the Willamette Valley near Silver Falls State Park, specializes in red wines and is open daily, June through September.

Oregon's second largest city, Eugene, makes an ideal base for touring. Alpine Vineyards, nestled in the spectacular foothills of the Coast Range Mountains southwest of Corvallis, is open daily in summer. Highlighted by European architecture, the Hinman Vineyards Winery is located in the foothills of the Oregon Coast Range, about a 25 minute-drive from Eugene. It is open for tastings daily.

Along the Umpqua: Phillippe Girardet established Girardet Wine Cellars in 1971 in the picturesque Umpqua Valley, reminiscent of his native Switzerland: he is now experimenting with red and white French cultivars new to Oregon winemaking. The winery is open for tastings daily from May through September and on Saturdays during the remainder of the year.

The Henry Estate Winery, located on the scenic Umpqua River near Roseburg, produces high quality dry varietal wines from Gewurztraminer, Chardonnay and Pinot Noir grapes. Considered the father of Oregon's table wine industry, Richard Sommer established Hillcrest Vineyard in 1961 and was the first Oregon vintner to grow vinifera grapes. The winery specializes in late harvest White Riesling and offers daily tours, a tasting room and wine sales.

The Mount Hood Loop is one of Oregon's favorite visitor attractions. Several wineries are located east of Portland, on or near scenic Mount Hood Loop, and specialize in fruit and berry wines. Hood River Vineyards and the Mount Hood Winery are both open daily in the summer. The Wasson Brothers Winery is also known for its fruit and berry wines; it is open daily for tastings. St Josef's Weinkeller in Canby features varietal wines and is also open daily to the public.

Home to the famous Shakespeare Festival in Ashland, which attracts thousands of people annually, Southern Oregon also hosts Valley View Vineyard near historic Jacksonville, Siskiyou Vineyards with its picnic facilities, trout lake and nature trails, in Cave Junction, and Bridgeview Vineyards Winery, also situated in Cave Junction. Along Oregon's majestic and rugged coast is the Nehalem Bay Wine Company.

Some 300,000 pioneers left Independence, Missouri, and trekked 2,000 miles (3,200 km) on the Oregon Trail to begin a new life out west. Those who survived drought, Indian attacks, and cholera faced one last obstacle before reaching the fertile Willamette Valley – the vast Cascade Mountains.

In the entire 700 miles (1,120 km) of the Cascades Mountains there are only three places where the pent up waters can escape to the sea: the Klamath and Pitt valleys and the deadly Celilo Falls through which the Columbia River rages. From being 1 mile (2 km) wide and 50 feet (15 meters) deep for much of its 1,200-mile (1,320-km) length, the Columbia River here is channeled through a gorge only 100 yards (90 meters) wide. Charles Nordhoff wrote: "Of course water is not subject to compression… the volume of the river is not diminished… the river is suddenly turned on its edge."

For many thousands of travelers to the Pacific Northwest, the turbulent Columbia and its tributary the Snake eased their journey – until they reached the Celilo Falls. There they would have to load their wagons onto makeshift craft and take their chance with the rapids. Only after 1845 did it become possible to avoid the rapids by taking Sam Barlow's precipitous and expensive toll road that skirted the slopes of Mount Hood. The road led directly to Oregon City, the first incorporated city west of the Rockies, which was founded around the flour mill built earlier by John McLoughlin, a manager with the Hudson's Bay Company. Indians burned his first three houses, but the fourth has survived. With its ancient furnishings, it is still the most-visited local landmark.

Wheat and wine: Mostly by happenstance the early pioneers stumbled up the Willamette River, a tributary of the Columbia, and settled the Willamette Valley. It proved to be one of the most fertile regions on the American continent, and by the beginning of this century it took more than 150 ships to transport

the region's wheat. Today more than half of Oregon's population lives within 10 miles (16 km) of the river in this 100-mile (160-km) valley between Portland and Eugene, a region renowned for its 50 wineries.

East of Mount Hood (11,245 feet/3,428 meters) and 26 miles (40 km) south of the Columbia is the Hood River Valley, which is almost as productive as the Willamette Valley. It produces annual harvests of 185,000 tons of apples, pears, and cherries.

Before World War II the area was given

over mostly to asparagus farmed by Japanese, who had arrived in the 19th century to work on the railroad. First the Japanese had to contend with the Anti-Alien Association, which tried to stop them buying land. Then, after the attack on Pearl Harbor in 1941, the Japanese were interned. Most did not return. Hood River is today a pleasantly old-fashioned American town on the riverbank at the mid-point of the gorge. The US ski team trains on the slopes of Mount Hood, which is a popular skiing area. Fishermen and river runners fill the town's hotels, and board sailing, white water rafting and mountain biking are popular occupations.

Preceding pages: sea kayaking below Priest Rapids Dam, Hanford Reach. **Left**, the Astoria Bridge. **Right**, salmon fisherman. Sources says stocks have been depleted by up to 85 percent.

The very same year that Sam Barlow was contemplating his trail around Mount Hood, a couple of other pioneers – Amos Lovejoy from Boston and Francis Pettygrove from Portland, Maine – were busy founding another community on the Willamette River. Tossing a coin to decide on a name brought victory to Pettygrove, and Portland was named. The coin can still be inspected in one of the city's museums.

Portland was nearer the ocean than Oregon City, and was destined to be a major port. What started out as the Great Plank Road – 6 miles (9 km) of planks side by side in the mud by the river – had by 1854 become the terminus for ships coming around Cape

Horn from the east. Eventually more than 50 shipping lines were using the Portland docks.

Henry Weinhard moved his brewery from Fort Vancouver, across the river, in part to satisfy the thirsty prospectors who transferred here from sailing ships to river boats en route to the Idaho gold rush. His offer to pump beer into the Skidmore Fountain on opening day was reluctantly turned down by city officials. In 1869 the Californian and Oregon Railway, later to be the Southern Pacific, arrived at Portland.

The river is dammed: As early as 1889 a pair of visionary entrepreneurs in Oregon City had visions of converting the power of the Willamette Falls into electricity and sending it along 14 miles (24 km) of wires for use in Portland. It was a revolutionary concept which no one in America had achieved before, and it changed Oregon life for ever. Electric trolley lines soon replaced horse-drawn carriages; houses, shops and businesses blossomed with light (Portland's 400 saloons stayed open all night); and freight transportation boomed on the new electric railways. For the first time in a century, farmers had the prospect of some relief from their drudgery.

Once hydro-electricity had proved itself, construction of the dams became inevitable. By the early 1930s over-grazing and drought – less than 10 inches (25 cm) of annual rainfall – had substantially depopulated much of the Columbia Plateau. More than half the rural households of Washington and Oregon were still without electricity half a century after Thomas Edison's light bulb had been invented. A dam that would plug the country's second biggest river, water an area twice the size of Rhode Island and provide a virtually unlimited supply of electric power was almost everybody's dream.

Although the average density of the US is around 41 persons to the square mile, Washington, Oregon, Idaho and Montana together average only one-fifth of that density. Yet, as Richard L. Neuberger wrote in his 1938 book *Our Promised Land*, the Columbia basin has about 4 percent of the population of England, France and Germany combined, and it can generate more hydro electricity, grow more wheat and cut more timber than all of them together.

Dams are condemned: And so, as William Dietrich writes in *Northwest Passage*, "the mighty Columbia was not just harnessed, it was utterly transformed from an unruly river into a series of placid pools: the most heavily damned river system and the greatest producer of hydroelectricity in the world." Only in retrospect can it be seen that this progress has been a mixed blessing. "Two centuries of abuse have left the Columbia River Basin with severe problems of pollution and environmental degradation," says RiverWatch, an organization which for 25 years has been trying to spread awareness about what it calls "the most radioactive river in the world."

The fact that its waters were used to cool reactors at the Hanford Nuclear Reservation between 1944 and 1971 (with the contaminated water flowing directly into the river) is only one of the Columbia's problems, but it's a good place to start. At one time as much as eight billion gallons of this radioactive water per year were flowing unrestricted, affecting shellfish as far away as San Francisco Bay. Even today, nuclear waste from Navy submarine reactors is being barged up to Hanford for burial.

Forestry is the most widespread activity in the Columbia River Basin, and the destruction is such that less than 10 percent of the region's ancient forests are still intact. Modern forestry practices, with their extensive road building and clear-cutting, cause exten-

sive water pollution that threatens fish and wildlife. The US Forest Service, the world's largest road builder, is also one of the world's biggest polluters, having built at least 100,000 miles (160,000 km) of road through a region that a century ago was virtually untouched wilderness.

Also high on the hit list of RiverWatch are the industrial polluters, 29 of which it names on a map that is widely sold throughout the Northwest. The offenders include pulp and

Left, studying the eco-system. **Above**, two centuries of abuse have left the beautiful Columbia River Basin with serious problems.

paper mills, aluminum production plants, ore refineries, lumber mills and food processors in addition to mines and smelters of lead, cadmium and zinc whose wastes poison the water and kill wildlife.

"Federal regulation of mining is archaic," RiverWatch says. "The Mining Law of 1872 still guarantees miners the right to purchase public lands at $5 per acre, virtually free of environmental legislation." As for dioxin, the major by-product of pulp mills using chlorine to bleach their paper products, a few years back it reached dangerous levels in bald eagles and other fish-eating birds.

The system must change: This situation continues, a frustrated RiverWatch says, because powerful industry is left to regulate itself, a status it has achieved "by bullying state and federal agencies, manipulating scientific data… and buying political clout."

RiverWatch pinpoints other enemies, too. Sewage discharges and industrial wastes from communities by the river; the diking and draining of estuary wetlands induced by large-scale farming; even the regular dredging carried out by the US Army Corps of Engineers, whose methods stir up and redistribute muddy, toxic sediment.

Perhaps surprisingly, the engineers have become the major target for today's environmentalists for exactly the same reason they were widely admired for so much of this century – they build dams. In the 1930s construction began on the Bonneville Dam, and it created a 48-mile (77-km) lake on the Columbia River, 40 miles (64 km) east of Portland. Since then, another dozen or so dams have been built, transforming a free-flowing torrent into what RiverWatch describes as "a series of stairstep, slackwater, computer-controlled reservoirs." Pulitzer prize-winning author William Dietrich uses more colorful language. To him, it is "like an anaconda that has swallowed 14 rabbits."

Studies show that dams are disastrous for river ecosystems. From the Canadian border to the last dam before the ocean, the Columbia River stretches 600 miles (960 km). All but 47 of them (74 km) have been transformed from healthy ecosystems to impoverished reservoirs, wrote Robert S. Devine in *The Atlantic Monthly*. Dams once epitomized progress and Yankee ingenuity. Then came public resistance to what Devine describes as "the enormous cost and pork barrel smell of many dams and a developing public understanding of the profound environmental degradation that building dams can cause."

Devine writes about watching a lone 14-foot (4-meter) pleasure craft negotiating one of the locks at the Lower Granite dam. It cost 43 million gallons of water to raise it to the lake, water that could have generated about $700 worth electricity – a year's supply for an average house. The water could also have saved dying salmon. Smolts (baby salmon) need to run the river from Idaho to the sea in 6–20 days, during which time their bodies change in expectation of salt water. Now that dams have reduced the river flow, the journey takes 60–90 days. Few of the young

salmon reach salt water in time, says Devine.

Indians and salmon: When the white man arrived, the Native Americans faced competition for once-abundant salmon. In her 1872 book *All Over Oregon & Washington*, Mrs Frances Fuller Victor wrote that as late as 1849 hundreds of Chinook fishermen filled the bay but "not a canoe is now in sight. The white race are to the red as sun to snow, as silently and surely the red men disappear, dissipated by the beams of civilization."

There were 30,000 Indians in the river tribes when the whites arrived, Mrs Victor wrote, adding: "The immense numbers of all kinds of salmon which ascend the Columbia

annually is something wonderful. They seem to be seeking quiet and safe places to deposit their spawn and thousands of them never stop until they can reach the great falls of the Snake River, more than 600 miles from the sea." When her book appeared, seven fisheries employing 300 men and packing almost 15,000 48-lb (22-kg) cases of salmon a year were operating within 3 miles (5 km) of Cathlamet, which offered views of St Helen's (9,677feet/2,950 meters) 80 miles (130 km) to the south. A few miles upriver another 18 canneries were working year-round, making cans and barrels when the fish were not running. One salmon fills about ten cans.

Cayuse Indians protested that the dams would be the last straw, eliminating most of the salmon that remained and making their rights to the salmon worthless. Under the 1855 Treaty of Walla Walla they had relinquished much of their land in return for the rights to fish for ever. "These rights were given us for as long as the river flows, the sun sets and the grass grows on nearby hills," one of their chiefs had said at the time.

Some estimate that today's salmon runs have declined 85 percent from earliest records. This is despite the 170 million fish artificially hatched each year and the 5,900-foot (1,800-meter) stairway pools, which cost $7 million and pass 100,000 Chinook salmon a day.

There's only one place the Columbia River is unchanged – at its mouth. At its most powerful, it thrusts 150 billion gallons of water a day through the sandbars into the Pacific. The torrent has capsized 2,000 boats in the 185 years since John Jacob Astor's Pacific Fur Company created the first American settlement on the Pacific Coast at Astoria. Now cruise boats stop here 200 times a year, depositing 23,000 passengers at the 17th Street Dock regularly used by Coast Guard cutters. A bridge over the 4-mile (7-km) wide river connects Washington and Oregon.

Constant dredging has failed to tame the river; it is still one of the most dangerous places in the world. Stormy seas are so frequent that the Coast Guard set up its National Motor Lifeboat School just at the tip of Cape Disappointment.

Left, new construction has taken its toll on the river basin. **Right**, "an unruly river [turned] into a series of placid pools."

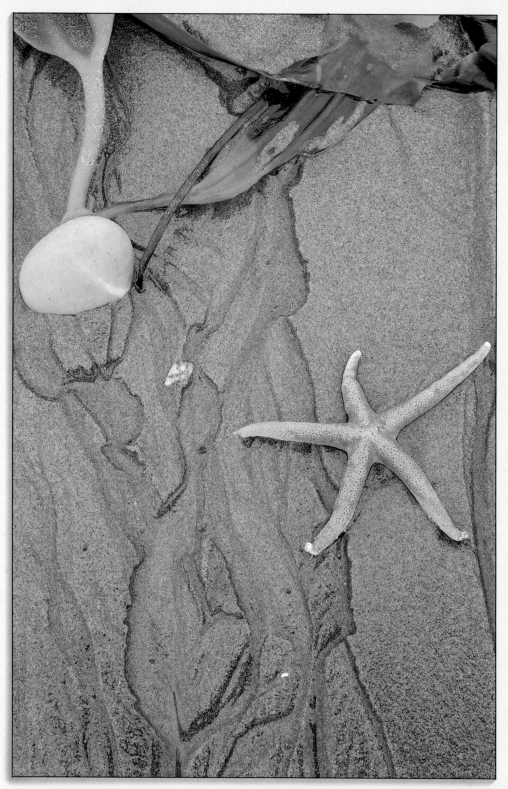

"Bold shafts of light race across the pinks and purples of the irregular substrate... twisted bullwhips embrace the tangled masses of bladderwrack and laver...highlights of red and orange life forms...grinding rocks...groaning timber..."

A commentary on Picasso's last canvas? A transmission from the *Voyager* space probe? No, just a page from a Northwest tidepooler's notebook. Other entries penciled in this weather-beaten book describe days spent stalking razor clams on a sandy beach in Puget Sound, watching gray whales from a windswept overlook on the Pacific Ocean, and launching a kite from a rolling Oregon sand dune.

Outdoor lovers escape to the unrestricted, unchanged splendor of the thousands of miles of wild aquatic habitats along the beaches, preserves, bays and estuaries that line Puget Sound, the San Juan Islands and the open coasts of both Oregon and Washington. Here, an unrivaled abundance of birds, mammals, fish and invertebrates populate the shore.

Seashore habitats: The shores here are new ones. As the glaciers receded and revealed virgin stretches of land, seawater moved in and gradually sculpted the volcanic rock and cobbled till into notched fjords, buttresses and spires. Rocky shores, placid sandy strips, and mixed beaches of stones, sand and silt developed between these prominent glacial sculptures. Each beach type supports its own wildlife community – plants and animals specifically adapted to thrive in their own eco-niche. Beachwalkers can discover several distinctive habitats and identify hundreds of plants and animals between the tidemarks of a 50-mile (80-km) section of Northwest seashore.

Rocky habitats are common to the northern shores of Washington's Olympic Peninsula and the Strait of Juan de Fuca, and they continue at regular intervals down the Oregon coast. Composed of jagged granite boulders, eroded sandstone pillars, blowholes and arches, these stunning beach vistas have

been the mainstay of countless color calendars. Crashing waves pound the cliffs in a continuous state of war, regaining the very fortresses that once sprung from the ocean during the post-glacial epochs. The craggy northern beaches are often lined with forests of evergreen, spruce, cedar, hemlock and fir. The trees cling in perilous positions to the eroded cliffs, while far below lie the casualties of the never ending struggle – bleached tangles of driftwood, heaped together at the water's edge.

The interior beaches of southern Puget Sound are peaceful reminders of passive resistance as sand and mud, slowly deposited by a network of rivers and streams, reclaim the bays and inlets through the process of siltification. A characteristic aroma pervades the scene – it is the smell of intertidal life, much of it concealed below the layer of silt.

Under such nurturing conditions, regional aquaculturists have honed the science of shellfish production, yielding the Quilcene oyster and, more recently, a tasty but diminutive Olympic cousin. When tidal conditions and the harvest quotas permit, these calm bays are the best place to search for clams or mussels.

Throughout the year, birdwatchers tally a full roster of gulls, sandpipers, plovers and ducks. Coarse-grained coastal sand beaches of southern Washington and central Oregon may be slim on sealife but are rich in rolling dunes, flowering dune grasses and unparalleled photographic rewards.

Mixed, or cobbled, beaches are transition zones giving shoreline explorers the best of both worlds. These mini habitats, a mosaic of smooth stones interspaced with a grout of sand and silt, can reveal a metropolis of crabs, sea anemones and clams. This is the domain of the Northwest's "State Invertebrate," the geoduck clam, a seafood delicacy and one of the largest burrowing clams anywhere in the world.

Exploring seashore gardens: At low tide visitors to the Northwest can stroll down beach paths that rival English country lanes. Where the 40–50°F (4–10°C) Japanese current bathes the shore in nutrients from offshore upwelling, the sea has blossomed in a wealth of strange and beautiful life forms. This nurturing environment literally stacks animal upon animal, color upon texture in a subtle gradient of life that occupies every available seaside niche.

Pastel pinks: On rocky shores, beachwalkers are quick to find pastel pinks and violet hues coating the surfaces of partially submerged rocks. Hardly the result of a paint spill at sea, it's really the work of coralline algae, small crusty aquatic plants rich in calcium carbonate. Adding to the other-worldly feel of the tide line are the vibrant splotches of yellow, orange, pale blue or red of still other encrusting forms. These are the sponges, bryozoans, ascidians and sea squirts – primitive animals, plant-like in appearance, that form dense colonies on hard surfaces and feed directly on the water-borne nutrients. Farther along the shore are the more recognizable plant species – bladelets of red algae, leatherlike mats of green fucus, sargassum, and a few waving sea palms. Their name suggests they are the weeds of the sea, but the harvesters of dulce, sea lettuce, porphyra and kelp (delicacies in many Asian societies) think of them as sea vegetables.

Browsing merrily amidst this sea salad are small black turban snails and clusters of checkered and Sitka periwinkles. They share this feast with the limpets, small flattened relatives of the snail that cling tightly to rock faces, awaiting the turn of the tide. Their strength is surprising; don't even bother trying to peel one off. The chiton, another curious snail relative, has evolved its external shell into eight internal plates – collectors call these butterfly shells – visible as a ridge along its back. Most chitons are small, a mere 2 to 3 inches (5 to 8 cm). However, the featureless, reddish brown gumboot chiton, an 8-inch (20-cm) lumbering "mega-mollusc," can be a stumper to novice tidepoolers. Seaside explorers struggle to place this creature in the appropriate animal, vegetable or mineral kingdom. Northwest coastal Natives chose to forgo any attempts at classification but elected to incorporate the gumboot in their stews.

Sea flowers, stars and pincushions: Sea anemones are called the flowers of the sea. Strikingly colored relatives of the jellyfish and corals, they use harpoonlike threads on their radially arranged tentacles to ensnare floating prey. Pink and green aggregate anemones resemble faded zinnias. They cover the cobbled rocks of mixed beaches and can divide like an amoeba to form countless clones. A favorite of tidepoolers, the green anemone is a true sea farmer. It gets its luminescent body cast from zoochlorelle, a microscopic algae cultivated within the anemone's tissues. But the real flowers in this aquatic garden are the red headed and red and green anemones, the largest and most brilliantly colored deepwater blossoms, seen only during extremely low tides.

Still another pigment from nature's palette is carried by the purple or ochre sea star, a five-rayed, rough-skinned hunter of shellfish. Other stars contribute equally vibrant hues – the bright-red blood star, dusky rose star, and the safety-orange and blue-streaked sun star are all frequently found by walkers along the beach. A colossus among Pacific sea stars, the twenty-rayed star attains a length of 3 feet (1 meter) and may possess as many as 24 arms.

The thorns in this rose garden are red, purple and green sea urchins – bristling pincushions that are related to the sea stars. Urchins thrive in a variety of habitats, from surging surf-swept beaches to the calmer kelp-forested inlets. Huge red urchins prefer deep water lairs and congregate in prickly mats at the bottom of tidepools.

Scrambling through the surreal seascape are the crabs, small-scale armored tanks, oblivious to the ravages of storm or swell. They range in size from a tiny secretive pea crab to the 2-lb (1-kg) Dungeness crab, an epicurean delight and the main attraction at Northwest fishmarkets. Oceanic tidepools teem with small hermit crabs. They find shelter in abandoned snail shells. When the need for a roomier "mobile home" arises, a bigger shell is carefully selected and the trade-in is completed.

On cobbled beaches, lifting a rock will produce several dozen scurrying purple or green shore crabs, caught waiting out the tide, shaded from the ravages of the sun and the beaks of predatory sea birds. Decorator crabs take a more creative tack in concealment – they attach sponges, weeds and debris to their bodies to blend effectively with the shoreline flora.

Like a fish out of water: A number of fishes are in fact capable of withstanding routine drydocking at low tide. Tidepool sculpins dart about in their natural aquariums, Northern clingfish stubbornly hold fast to the undersides of rocks, and bright orange or green penpoint gunnels keep the lowest of profiles in the moist recesses of cracks and crevices. The Pacific spiny lumpsucker must be seen to be believed. This Northwest oddity resembles a warty olive tennis ball with eyes. It's a deepwater fish that invades the intertidal zones in winter to spawn.

A feeding ground for shorebirds: As beachwalkers progress down the shore, they become aware of other eyes inspecting the pools and cobbles. As the tide moves out, the shorebirds move in to seek a midday snack

root about in the bottom sediment. A large silvery-backed Arctic loon interrupts its fishing to emit a long, yodeling cry. Many waterfowl arrive from the far north in autumn; their numbers increase as handsome canvasbacks, widgeons and harlequin ducks join the offshore flotilla.

Perennial favorites on the remote outer shores, black oyster-catchers use their chisel-shaped beaks to pry limpets from rocks or to chip away the shells of mussels. Tufted puffins dive through the waves and fill their brilliantly banded beaks with herring and surf smelt, then alight beside stately rhinoceros auklets in their island rookeries.

Few hikers will forget the stately elegance

from the litter of live and dead beach animals. The tranquility is shattered by the clamor of herring, mew and glaucous winged gulls, disputing each other's claim to the leftovers. In the mudflats, dunlins, whimbrels, plovers and killdeers use their slender legs and long beaks to gingerly negotiate the exposed bottom in search of shellfish, crabs and worms.

Further from shore, the waterfowl – coots, scaups and buffleheads – tread water, passively feeding on floating plants, or diving to

Above, purple starfish in a tidal zone at Patos Island State Park, the San Juan Islands.

of a great blue heron as it silently stalks through the grasses that line a salt marsh. Nor are they likely to forget sighting their first bald eagle surveying the unbroken shoreline panorama from an aerie high atop a sturdy cedar tree.

Planning a beachwalk: Beachwalkers unfamiliar with the area should first consult a tide table or graph. These indispensable charts, available at boating or fishing supply stores, detail the time of day and magnitude of the two daily high and low tides.

Northwest tides can vary by over 10 feet (3 meters). At certain times, stretches of shoreline will be exposed to hikers and tidepoolers;

six hours later, these same stretches will be covered over by several feet of seawater. By picking the lowest tides, beachwalkers can see habitats and shorelife that might be exposed to daylight only a few times each year. Misjudging the time of tidal change could result in a cancelled trip or, worse yet, an unfortunate shoreline stranding, as tidal waters silently sneak in to fill the beach route behind an unwary hiker.

Cloud-free days: The easiest beachwalks are in the summer months. Coastal weather is predictably mild and midday tides are at their lowest, favoring more extensive beach hikes and back-packing trips. In winter, dedicated beachcombers take advantage of the holes between maritime squalls. Armed with flashlights and lanterns, they use the low nighttime tides for some exotic midnight rambling. Of course, even during the sunniest, cloud-free days, coastal weather can change abruptly. It's best to phone the weather service for an extended regional forecast before heading out on an important trip.

Purchasing a good field identification guide to Northwest marine life will add to the enjoyment of any shorewalk. University of Washington biologist Dr Eugene Kozloff's *Seashore Life of the Northern Pacific Coast* and *Exploring the Seashore in British Columbia, Washington and Oregon* by Gloria Snively, are both inexpensive, readable overviews of this region's flora and fauna. However nothing approaches a glimpse of the real thing; visiting the Seattle, Tacoma or Newport Aquarium, or any of the smaller regional interpretive nature centers along the coast, beachwalkers can get an eye-to-eye preview of some of the animals they'll encounter in the field.

Beachwalking *haute couture* should include protective clothing, foul weather gear, or the more adaptable Gore-Tex wear. Most hikers prefer the layered look – a hooded jacket, thick wool sweater, and T-shirt – allowing for quick changes to accompany quirks of weather. Waterproof footwear with good traction for rock hopping is essential. So is a good pair of garden gloves to prevent scratches from barnacle covered boulders. On the open coast it's hard not to get a little wet even with the utmost care, so a spare pair of socks, even a full change of clothes, is not such a bad idea. Hikers might want to include a lightweight pair of binoculars and, of course,

their camera. A shovel and bucket for clamming, a picnic lunch or a kite to fly while the tide level drops can round out a rewarding day trip to the beach.

Despite its rugged appearance, the sea beach, like any natural system, is a delicate balance of many individual environmental factors. As intruders in this frail ecosystem, we should adhere to a unique etiquette in order to preserve this harmony for future explorers. Visitors should follow strictly the state Fish and Game Department rules that limit harvests of fish or shellfish and respect the protected status given to posted sanctuaries and parks.

They must strive to minimize their impact on the intertidal communities – filling holes and returning upturned rocks to their proper places. Beach animals seldom survive once removed from their habitats, so taking "pets" is unwise. An updated Native American proverb suggests that when visiting the seashore, one should take only photographs and leave only footprints.

Marine mammals: At the top of the food chain are the marine mammals: sea otters; the cetaceans (whales, dolphins and porpoises); and the pinnipeds (seals and sea lions). All of these animals, by evolutionary standards, are recent invaders of the ocean coast, yet they show a mastery of the aquatic realm. They, like us, enjoy the diversity of sealife along the broad stretches of unoccupied coast that characterize the Northwest. Unlike their human counterparts, who must dress up in neoprene suits, cumbersome harness and tank, face masks and fins in order to explore the briny deep, these great mammals display an enviable ease as they negotiate the emerald green seas.

To spy the sleek black dorsal fin of a speeding orca whale or catch a glimpse of a lone sea lion peering out from between the waves – these are the unforgettable high points of a beachwalk or ferry ride. While many of these animals were once ruthlessly slaughtered for the short term economic gains of whaling and the fur trade, they now receive rigorous federal protection that prevents additional exploitation. Some, like the Washington sea otter, maintain only token populations.

However, several Northwest species are staging dramatic comebacks. Both humans and the marine mammals have another chance. The marine mammals are in a better position to strengthen in numbers and thrive unmolested in their habitat along Pacific shores. The people can try again to learn from and appreciate the thrilling and educational sight of a breaching gray whale, an orca spyhopping, or a teeming seal rookery.

Seals and sea lions: The most commonly sighted marine mammal is the harbor seal, year round resident of Puget Sound and coastal Washington and Oregon. The mottled gray or bluish dappled adults may reach a length of over 6 feet (2 meters) and are abundant on haul-out areas and breeding rookeries. During summer months, mothers can be seen tending young pups or just doz-

lions employ their broad flat front flippers to propel themselves, often with show off acrobatics, through the water. Harbor seals, equally at home in the water, choose to scull conservatively with their hind flippers.

California sea lions entertain shoreline visitors in much the same fashion that their domesticated cousins enthrall circus crowds. They bark, argue, waddle about and cavort with great boisterousness. Tawny brown males attain lengths of 6½ feet (2 meters) and may weigh 600 pounds (270 kg). Females are smaller, seldom exceeding 6 feet (2 meters) and 200 pounds (90 kg). Steller's sea lions migrate from both California and British Columbia breeding grounds to share the

ing and digesting a meal. Like many marine mammal species, harbor seals are understandably wary of human contact. They are more often viewed with binoculars from afar. When surprised by hikers, they scramble en masse into the water, swiftly disappearing.

A close examination of the Northwest's two sea lion species will reveal the primary identification trait: ears. California and Steller's sea lions both possess small rolled up ear flaps; harbor seals don't. Other differences become apparent underwater. The sea

Above, *epiactis prolifera,* **the flower-like brooding anemone native to Washington.**

Northwest with their California relatives. They are easily recognized by size alone. Bull males approach a bulky 10 feet (3 meters) and 2,000 pounds (900 kg). When spotted from a boat, their heads look like huge cardboard boxes adrift upon the sea.

Home to dolphins: Washington State Ferry riders and San Juan Island boaters often spy what appear to be auto tires bobbing on the surface. Then, a small triangular dorsal fin breaks the water. This runaway radial is actually the rounded back of the harbor porpoise, the smallest oceanic cetacean. These shy, gray creatures are common residents of the shallows of straits and inlets. They are not gregarious like their bottle-nosed cousins of oceanarium fame and are usually glimpsed from a distance.

If the race is truly to the swift, the Dall porpoise is sure to capture the prize at the next marine mammal marathon. Dalls surprise boaters by displaying great speed (up to 30 knots), producing roostertails of spray well ahead of slow moving vessels. Another spirited daredevil is the Pacific whitesided dolphin. Well established in large schools (50–100) up and down the coast, the gray, black and white markings of this species give it an elegant, tuxedoed appearance. Pacific whitesides are often seen racing in harmony, sometimes as escorts for larger, fast moving cetaceans – the minke and pilot whales. But it is their acrobatic prowess – astonishing leaps of some 20 feet (6 meters) into the air, complete with aerial somersaults – that have endeared them to Northwest nature lovers.

Celebrity dolphins: By far the largest and most impressive member of the dolphin family is the orca, commonly called the killer whale. These strikingly marked glossy black-and-white predators were once harpooned and shot at by mistrusting fishermen. Their mistrust was unwarranted – while the 30-foot (9-meter) orcas presented some competition as unsurpassed hunters of salmon, cod, sharks, seals and even other dolphins, no evidence links them to assaults on humans. Today, now we have shed our misconceptions about these animals, orca whales have been escalated to near celebrity status. They are models for plush stuffed toys, T-shirts, mugs and bumper-stickers. Their voices, a mixture of clicks, whistles and screams, have appeared on several record albums. And the sighting of a 6-foot (2-meter) tall orca dorsal fin cutting through the waters will bring cheers from observers.

Orcas travel in family groups called pods; three such groups are year-round residents of Puget Sound. Individuals have been identified by subtle differences in fin and body markings, and a whale museum at Friday Harbor on San Juan Island has been established to share research and observational data on these inspiring Washington residents. In late spring and summer several companies in Friday Harbor lead boat tours to view orcas in the Strait of Juan de Fuca and Haro Strait, giving people a close-up appreciation of the formidable cetaceans.

One of nature's greatest spectacles takes place a few miles off the Washington and Oregon coast. In spring and late fall, hikers of the coastal headlands can witness the longest migration of any mammal – the 12,000-mile (19,000-km) voyage of the Pacific gray whale. Anyone lucky enough to see the migration is watching more than a journey between northern feeding and southern breeding grounds. They are seeing the remarkable return of a species reduced to a few hundred animals less than a century ago. Current populations number close to 15,000. The excitement of this comeback is shared by hundreds of avid whalewatchers, who fill charter vessels and small boats and set out to join the migration in progress.

Up close the gray whale's head presents a broad shaggy mass of barnacles and short bristling hairs. It lacks a dorsal fin but displays a series of 10–14 "knuckles" along the ridge of its 40–50-foot (13–16-meter) back, distinguishing it from other Pacific whales. Whale-watchers are likely to see flukes and flippers, perhaps a mother escorting her calf. Charter boats leave the fishing centers of Westport, Washington, or Newport, Oregon, and usually offer pre-trip slide-illustrated lectures. Some boats are staffed by on-board cetologists to further enhance the cruise.

Beachwalk destinations: Marine scientist Edward F. Ricketts, the visionary "Doc" of Steinbeck's novel *Cannery Row*, once remarked: "It is advisable to look from the tide pool to the stars and then back to the tide pool again." Visitors to the Northwest need not look far to experience this oneness with the cosmos. Native Northwesterners all seem to accumulate a list of their favorite strolls, and some of them are willing to share their finds.

In Washington most of the prized spots are in state parks or county owned lands, with easy beach access, campsites, clearly marked trails, even ranger staffed programs. One trek begins at Rialto Beach, 6 miles (9.5 km) north of the Quileute Indian Reservation at La Push on the Olympic coast. Travelers reach the shore at Rialto by crossing an austere latticework of enormous felled trees. Here they find a seascape of rock outcroppings, headlands and craggy islands stretching 22 miles (35 km) north to Cape Alava. The northward journey begins at the fantastic portals of Hole-In-The-Wall Rock, negotiable only at low tide. Once through, hikers are treated to an unsullied world of anemone fringed tidepools, mussel covered boulders and driftwood shrines.

For the less intrepid, Tongue Point at the Salt Creek Recreation Area (State Highway 112 west of Port Angeles), affords much of the rugged splendor of the open coast. This dramatic promontory in the Strait of Juan de Fuca, the connecting channel between Puget Sound and the Pacific Ocean, harbors animals representative of both waters. Here red, purple and green sea urchins intermingle in the tidal pools. Great strands of bullwhip kelp undulate in the strong currents, imparting a feeling of remoteness and isolation that belies the proximity of the city of Port Ange-

Cascadian and Olympic forests to create teeming deltas and estuaries full of life.

One such intertidal hot spot is the Nisqually National Wildlife Refuge, midway between Tacoma and Olympia on Interstate 5. This region combines salt marsh, mudflat, grassland and forest habitats. Mud shrimps, juvenile salmon, hawks and ducks share the banks of the Nisqually River and the McAllister Creek. Also at the refuge is a rookery for hundreds of great blue heron, which nest in the surrounding deciduous forest. At sunset, they take to the air and fill the sky with their haunting silhouettes.

Oregonians claim to have the best beach sites in the Northwest. They may be right.

les, just 13 miles (21 km) to the east.

Continuing on US 101 towards Sequim, travelers find the Dungeness National Wildlife Refuge and the longest natural sandspit in the United States – 5 miles (8 km) long and growing each year. The spit creates a quiet bay that has become one of Washington's favored havens for sea birds.

Puget Sound's best shore walks are southern wanderings where the Deschutes, Puyallup, Chehalis and Skokomish rivers transport the fertile soil from Washington's

Above, orca and a small boat enjoy a day out in Puget Sound.

The Oregon coast is a checkerboard of sandy beaches, rocky headlands and transitional zones, all just minutes from US 101. Often, the elements combine within a few miles of each other, as at Coos Bay, where Cape Arago State Park, the Charleston lighthouse, and the Oregon Dunes National Recreation Area (literally taking over stretches of US 101) are all within a 10-mile (16-km) drive. An Oregon road map reads like an intertidal telephone directory: Cannon Beach, Cape Foulweather, Cape Perpetual, Oceanside, Sea Lion Caves and Sunset Bay. These are all picturesque places to begin collecting your beachwalking memories.

MOUNT ST HELENS

"The moon looks like a golf course compared to what's up there."
—*President Jimmy Carter*

The countryside around Mount St Helens has changed in recent years. But even forewarned that the cataclysmic May 18, 1980, eruption altered the mountain and landscapes surrounding it, the words and pictures do not prepare one for the extent of devastation wrought by the explosion and subsequent mud slides down the mountain. Driving through mile after mile of uprooted forests, landscapes of kindling wood covered with basalt ash, all the hyperbole that has been written about the mountain in the past few years somehow seems pale.

Describing the volcano's impact on the countryside around it is a task imbued with humility. After all, what can be said about the most enormous geological eruption of the century, a volcanic spasm more violent than 300 Hiroshima-size nuclear weapons?

The May 18 explosion blew away a cubic mile of the summit, reducing its elevation from 9,677 feet (2,950 meters) to 8,364 feet (2,550 meters) and flattening 230 sq. miles (595 sq. km) of forest. Afterwards, 771 million board feet of lumber were salvaged from downed trees on 90 sq. miles (230 sq. km), enough wood to build 77,100 three-bedroom houses. Another 140 sq. miles (360 sq. km) of devastated forested land is preserved in the monument's interpretive area.

In the wake of the blast, nearly 70 people perished under ash and mud slides. The toll on the wildlife was estimated at 5,000 black-tailed deer, 1,500 elk, 200 black bears, 15 mountain goats, together with unknown numbers of mountain lions, bobcats, small rodents, birds, fish and insects. According to biologists, the region's rare spotted owl population was wiped out.

A favorite view of the mountain, especially among painters and photographers

throughout the past century, had been from the northeast side of the mountain with serene Spirit Lake in the foreground. What is left of Spirit Lake today is more a reminder of Dante's *Inferno* than forest tranquility, and for miles around the mountain landscapes are more disquieting than any filmmaker could achieve with all the special effects and glee men in his trick bag. The mountain's "big blow" leaves no doubt that we are no more than precarious visitors on a global space ship with a direction of its own.

Eight hundred and fifty active volcanoes currently form a ring of fire in mountain ranges around the Pacific Rim, any of them capable of heroic pyrotechnics. The biggest eruption in recent history exploded on the Pacific Island of Krakatau in 1883. Ash and fallout from the blowup colored sunsets around the world for two years, and a tidal wave generated by the blast killed 36,000 people in nearby Java and Sumatra.

Before St Helens, the last similar explosion in the Cascade Range was approximately 7,000 years ago when Mazama, a 9,900-foot (3,020-meter) volcano in southern Oregon, exploded, spreading ash across today's entire northwestern United States. The top of the mountain collapsed forming today's world famous Crater Lake, a caldera 6 miles (10 km) across and a half mile deep in Crater Lake National Park.

The 700-mile (1,100-km) long chain of mountains that forms the Cascades extends from Northern California to southern British Columbia. They contain many volcanoes that have significantly shaped the Pacific Northwest. Most of the volcanoes are bigger than St Helens, and their histories have all been violent, with potential for more.

In May 1914, Northern California's Lassen Peak resumed eruptions and explosions that continued for almost seven years. In 1975

Scientists with the US Geological Survey have been monitoring Cascade volcanoes in their Volcanic Hazards Project since 1967, and their seismometers warned of Mount St Helens' reawakening well in advance of the 1980 eruption.

Volcano hazard watchers will not predict which of the range's volcanoes will next erupt, but USGS studies list Mount Hood and Mount Shasta as top candidates. On the other hand, say scientists, it could be any of the hundreds of lesser volcanoes and cinder cones that run the length of the Cascades.

Certainly a characteristic shared by all the major Cascades volcano peaks is that they are strikingly beautiful, usually snow and ice

Mount Baker, near the Canadian border in Washington, belched steam for several weeks. These activities, and the explosion of St Helens, have geologists pondering whether the Cascades are entering a period of increasing volcanic activity.

The major danger from even modest volcanic activity in the Cascade Range is snow melt and mud flows. For instance, several communities are built on the ancient mudflow paths of 14,410-foot (4,400-meter) Mount Rainier. There were some steam explosions on Rainier in the mid-1800s. In the same period volcanic activity was reported on Mount Baker and Oregon's Mount Hood.

covered, ever beckoning and often luring climbers and hikers to their slopes and wonders. Several – Lassen, Crater Lake, Mount Rainier – are contained in national parks.

All the volcano summits loom, sometimes unexpectedly, from green forests that frame and punctuate their size and beauty. The largest of the volcano peaks – Mount Rainier, for example – are virtually continents unto themselves with forested slopes rising to alpine meadows capped by glaciated arctic-alpine summits. The larger peaks create their own mountain-top climates.

It is the goal of many climbers, and the achievement of a few, to scale all of the

Cascades' major volcano peaks. The glaciers and ice fields of these mountain tops are the training grounds for most of the American expeditionary climbers active in the Himalayas during recent years.

Exploring St Helens: From Interstate Highway 5 – the route a majority of visitors follow to Mount St Helens – it is a short drive to the Visitors' Center via exit 49, then 5 miles (8 km) east on State 504. The area is now designated the Mount St Helens National Historic Monument. It's easy to obtain national forest maps, literature and information at the center, and see an extraordinary 22-minute film of the volcano and its 1980 eruption, compiled partially from news film.

engines stalled, computers stopped, the grit was in everything. The mountain's ash was to contribute to the globe's sunsets for many years to come.

Those visiting Mount St Helens for a day or more can approach the mountain from several sides. The most interesting places to view the mountain and its landscaping work are along the North Fork of the Toutle River, where mud slides and floods covered miles of watershed; Forest Service Road 26 to Windy Ridge which was in the blast path of the volcano; and from Ape Cave near the town of Cougar. Besides the main Visitors' Center, there are information centers at Iron Creek, near Randle, Yale, Cougar and Pine

Being only minutes by air from the Northwest's major cities, the volcano received almost as much media coverage as the first moon landing.

Sending clouds 60,000 feet (18,290 meters) into the air, St Helens exploded with the force of 400 million tons of TNT and dumped volcanic ash across the US all the way to Maine and around the world. Immediately after the explosion, Yakima, a city of 50,000, floundered under 800,000 tons (812,800 metric tons) of ash from the volcano. Car

<u>Left</u>, before the big blast: **Mount St Helens and Spirit Lake**. <u>Above</u>, post-eruption destruction.

Creek. Around the mountain, the Forest Service has designated a few dozen viewpoints, all of which are good photography sites. There are several fine national forest campgrounds near and around St Helens.

Mount St Helens National Geological Area is in Gifford Pinchot National Forest – the entire region a forested green pedestal for snowy volcano peaks. Until the recent eruption, Mount St Helens was the loveliest of them all, but from many vantage points, as you drive on roads in the region, you can see not-too-distant Mount Adams, as well as gigantic Mount Rainier to the north and Mount Hood to the south.

WEL
WIN

HERB H&J's H
FISHING, HUNTING

NORTH
CASCADES
HIWAY

PEARRYGIN LAKE
STATE PARK

BARB
SHO

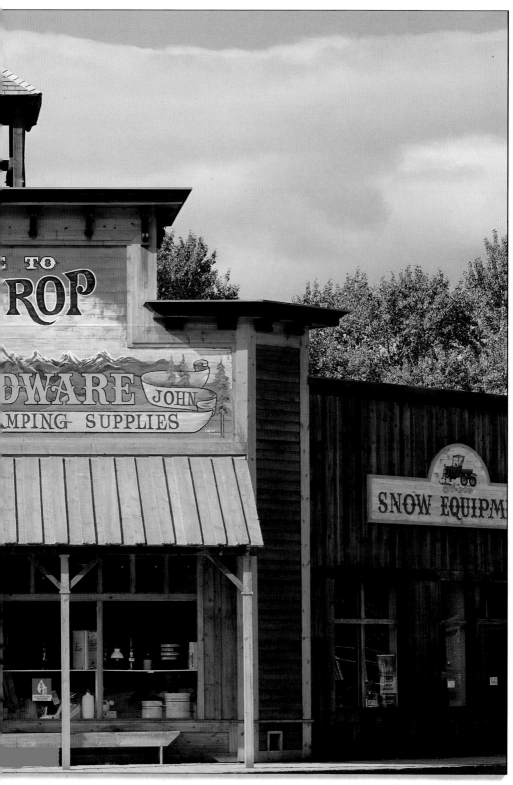

101

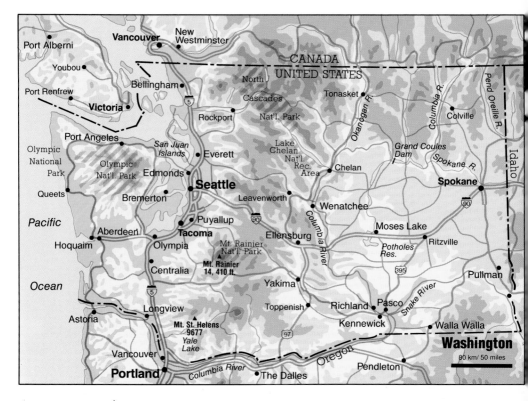

Port Alberni
Youbou
Port Renfrew
Victoria
Vancouver
New Westminster
Bellingham
Port Angeles
Olympic National Park
San Juan Islands
Rockport
Everett
Edmonds
Seattle
Queets
Olympic Nat'l. Park
Bremerton
Puyallup
Tacoma
Pacific
Aberdeen
Olympia
Hoquaim
Centralia
Mt. Rainier Nat'l. Park
Mt. Rainier 14, 410 ft.
Ocean
Longview
Mt. St. Helens 9677
Yale Lake
Astoria
Vancouver
Portland
Columbia River
The Dalles
CANADA
UNITED STATES
North Cascades Nat'l. Park
Tonasket
Okanogan R.
Colville
Columbia R.
Pend Oreille R.
Lake Chelan Nat'l. Rec. Area
Chelan
Grand Coulee Dam
Spokane R.
Spokane
Leavenworth
Wenatchee
Columbia River
Ellensburg
Moses Lake
Potholes Res.
Ritzville
Yakima
Toppenish
Richland
Pasco
Snake River
Kennewick
Walla Walla
Pullman
Oregon
Pendleton
Idaho
Washington
80 km/ 50 miles

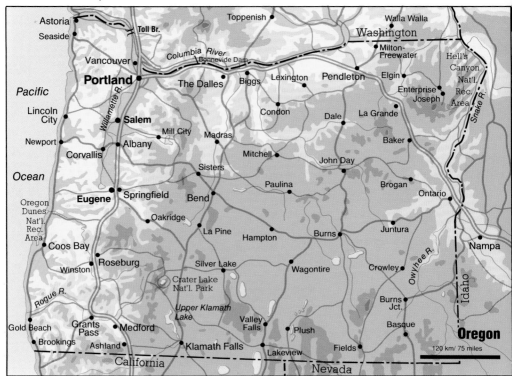

Astoria
Seaside
Toll Br.
Toppenish
Walla Walla
Washington
Vancouver
Columbia River
Bonnevide Dam
Milton-Freewater
Portland
The Dalles
Biggs
Lexington
Pendleton
Elgin
Hell's Canyon Nat'l. Rec. Area
Pacific
Lincoln City
Willamette R.
Condon
Enterprise
Joseph
Newport
Salem
Mill City
Madras
Dale
La Grande
Corvallis
Albany
Mitchell
Baker
Ocean
Sisters
John Day
Brogan
Oregon Dunes Nat'l. Rec. Area
Eugene
Springfield
Bend
Paulina
Ontario
Oakridge
La Pine
Hampton
Burns
Juntura
Nampa
Coos Bay
Winston
Roseburg
Silver Lake
Wagontire
Crowley
Owyhee R.
Rogue R.
Crater Lake Nat'l. Park
Burns Jct.
Gold Beach
Grants Pass
Medford
Upper Klamath Lake
Valley Falls
Plush
Basque
Idaho
Oregon
Brookings
Ashland
Klamath Falls
Lakeview
Fields
California
Nevada
120 km/ 75 miles

104

PLACES

The Pacific Northwest: two scenic states straddled by the ridge of the Cascade Mountain range. The west side beckons with the region's two major cities, its miles of coastline and its verdant river valleys. The east boasts lakes and rivers, dramatic geologic wonders and the subtle colors of fertile plains.

Insight Guide: The Pacific Northwest takes you on a tour of Washington and Oregon, beginning with Seattle, the Pacific Northwest's largest metropolis. Seattle offers preserved historic districts, a bustling waterfront, modern architecture and countless parks – all against the backdrop of snow-covered Mount Rainier. Then take a ferry tour of Puget Sound, its charming harbors and villages, and the gem-like San Juan Islands. The itinerary then jumps to the state border to work northward along Washington's coast, a collection of rustic seaports, beachwalks and sea life.

Within a few hours of Seattle, the Cascades offer year-round recreation. Just over the crest is another world for the outdoor enthusiast: central Washington's lakes and rivers. Further east, growing Spokane and its neighbors are covered in "The Inland Empire" chapter. The mighty Columbia River, now defining much of the Washington/Oregon border, has a character and legacy of its own – appropriately, the chapter "Columbia River Gorge" is sandwiched between our tour of the two states.

This Insight Guide takes the traveler through Oregon, beginning with Portland, a big city with a small-town welcome. Follow your instincts – and the Columbia River – to the sea, and join us on a journey down the Oregon Coast. The great Willamette River also suggests a southward exploration, and the chapter covering the Willamette River Valley brings this site of pioneers and settlers to life. Southern Oregon, from Grants Pass and the rafter's haven, Rogue River, to historic Jacksonville and the Ashland Shakespearean Festival, invites a visit as well.

Central Oregon, using the city of Bend as a base, offers still more delightful mountain wilderness and recreation areas. Further east, Lava and Lake Country has unequaled geologic and archaeological features, including the surprising John Day Fossil Beds. Northeast Oregon's pleasures range from wildlife refuges to the deepest gorge in North America – the dramatic Hell's Canyon.

A special feature section outlines the attractions of the Northwest's four magnificent – and varied – national parks. Additional features include an in-depth look at the region's wealth of marine life; the story of Mount St Helens' volcanic eruption; and a survey of the Northwest's flourishing wine industry.

Preceding pages: daffodils flank Mount Rainier; western-style store-front in Winthrop, Washington; flowers in Oregon's Shore Acres State Park.

SEATTLE

Off in the northwest corner of the map, Washington State has often been dismissed by easterners as a forested wilderness where only lumberjacks, cowboys and Indians roam. A cosmopolitan city with a small-town atmosphere, Seattle has managed to change all that – to both its delight and dismay. The emergence from international obscurity may be traced from the successful 1962 World's Fair at Seattle Center.

Located in the center of western Washington on eastern Puget Sound, Seattle's spectacular environs of mountains and lakes make it a city that people choose to live in for its geographic characteristics alone. Little more than 140 years old, it has had no time to develop Boston's ostentatious history, or the frantic enterprise of New York. Seattle is a new migration mecca where tired Easterners find relaxed, friendly residents, accessible sights and rain-scrubbed greenery in place of big city smog, crime and slums. No urban sprawl is even possible there because hills and waterways serve as natural barriers.

Seattle was founded on contrasts. It is high peaks and lowlands, dry in late summer and damp the rest of the time. Black tie sits with beards and Birkenstocks at the opera, financiers swap summit stories with the mountain climbing elite, and the city proper pokes fun at its suburban eastside.

While Seattle's population is generally well educated and white (75 percent), the poorer Central District settles against the stately Broadmoor neighborhood. The enormous variety of nationalities living together in this port city make up a peacefully intermingled community of Europeans, blacks, Indians, Scandinavians and Asians.

With a population of just over 500,000, Seattle has been called the smallest major league city in the nation, a title symbolic of inherent contradictions. A rampant "catch up" mentality is marked by the construction of the Kingdome for major league sports, the multiplication of skyscrapers in a thriving office core, and a $160 million convention center. Tourism offices broadcast the "Emerald City, Jewel of the Northwest" and "America's most Livable City" in an effort to bring in a larger tax base. But Seattle has avoided becoming a tourist trap where visitors are shuffled off to "attractions" that most residents never bother to visit.

To balance Seattle's big-city urges is a sense of small-town caring and a fierce civic pride. The drunk and homeless are treated with well-known leniency, and people speak to strangers at bus stops. Sensitive, humanistic development in areas like Pioneer Square and the Pike Place Market has been encouraged by dedicated citizens' groups. The fear that a tourism heyday will change the city's pleasant character have given rise to the tongue-in-cheek "Lesser Seattle" citizens' group which tries to discourage potential immigrants.

People with BAs and MAs drive taxis or wait tables to stay here, and everyone knows how to have fun. Five thousand

Preceding pages: despite a fast-changing scene, the Space Needle remains the symbol of Seattle. **Left,** Pioneer Square. **Right,** Seattleites snacking.

acres of city parks are well used and big celebrations like the Seafair tradition and various street fairs can be found in most neighborhoods at some time during the year.

Recreation choices in Seattle range from cross-country and downhill skiing, hiking, and camping in the nearby Cascade and Olympic mountains to swimming, fishing, waterskiing and sailing on the numerous lakes and inlets that pepper the region.

Rainfall in Seattle is less than in any of the major eastern seaboard cities, but the general cloudiness and light mists make it seem wetter than it really is. While the worrisome weather factor has never stopped outdoor sports, it has nurtured a profusion of bookstores, and according to *Publishers' Weekly* they are frequented by the nation's most avid book buyers and borrowers.

Also encouraged by the weather is a repertory theater community of international acclaim that is second only to New York City's in relative size. Unusual art-house movies premiere here.

The cost of living in Seattle is roughly the same as the national average, and the quality is just slightly higher. As it welcomes new visitors (the ones who don't want to stay), this compact city with so much to see keeps a close guard on its charming and ingenuous ways.

Downtown Seattle: With shiny glass towers and low older buildings climbing the hill from the harbor, downtown Seattle is exciting to look at and interesting to explore. The retail core is a bustling area with a good quality department store within walking distance of most major hotels. **The Bon Marche** is a full-scale retailer, stocking a wide selection of clothing and gifts.

Nordstrom's service-first policy makes its mostly apparel arrangement successful. **Westlake Mall**, near Nordstrom, a complex of office and retail space, located between Pine and Olive, is a focus for downtown activity.

A few blocks west on First Avenue, **Labuznik** is a fine Eastern European restaurant that features fine al fresco dining, perfect in warm weather.

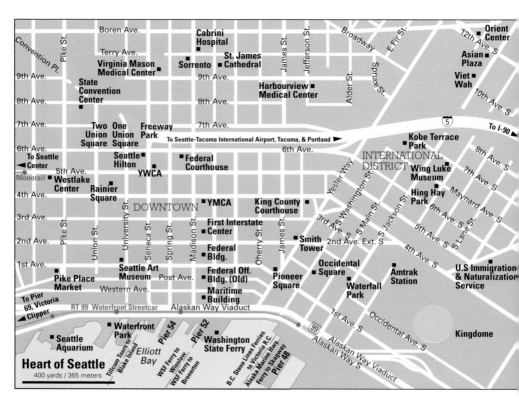

Heart of Seattle
400 yards / 365 meters

South of the larger stores at Fifth and Union is Minoru Yamasaki's striking and controversial **Rainier Tower**, balancing on a pencil point and filled with three stories of elegant shops around a beautiful atrium. A carpeted underground concourse leads directly to **Eddie Bauer**, a fairly fancy recreational outfitter whose enormous success bespeaks Seattle's open-air bent.

Additional shops on the block form the retail district's second shopping center, and the grand Chinese-style **5th Avenue Theater** is also worth a look. On the southern edge of the retail center is the princely old **Four Seasons Olympic Hotel**, a piece of 1920s class luxuriously restored with an ornate Spanish Ballroom and Garden Court.

The commercial sector of town between Pioneer Square and the retail core consists mostly of office towers, some startling in design. The 1960s and 1970s saw the arrival of such behemoths as the **1001 Fourth Avenue Building** on Fourth Avenue, whose courtyard is graced by Henry Moore's notable bronze sculpture, *Vertabrae*, as well as a wealth of other public art pieces. On Fifth and Columbia local developer Martin Selig's sleek, Darth Vaderesque **Columbia Seafirst Center** looms over the city with 76 stories of office space. The **Seattle Trust Court** two blocks west is a low profile contrast with its two courtyards of lunch spots and shops. The **Washington Mutual Tower**, completed in 1988, is the most strikingly handsome building in the city.

Breathing spaces in the midst of the high-rise setting of career activity are few and welcome. On Fourth Avenue between Spring and Madison, the **Seattle Public Library** is a murmuring haven for researchers and browsers alike. Nearby, **Freeway Park** is the ingenuous creation of a civic-minded group called Forward Thrust. Built over 12 lanes of the Interstate Highway 5 between Hubble and Spring streets, it is a lovely setting for free lunchtime concerts in spring and summer. The greenery and man-made waterfalls drown traffic noise and city tension.

Lake Union and Lake Washington from Queen Anne Hill.

Abutting Freeway Park is the mammoth multi-level convention center with plentiful exhibition space and meeting rooms. An exciting new development is architect Robert Venturi's downtown branch of the **Seattle Art Museum** with a floorspace of 44,000 sq. feet (4,000 sq. meters) which opened in the fall of 1991 close to the waterfront between First and Second, University and Union.

For a young city, Seattle has surprisingly varied architecture, many examples of which have been lovingly restored. The **Seattle Tower** is a beautiful example of art deco style, as is the **Washington Athletic Club** at 1325 Sixth Avenue.

Along with obvious landmarks like the Smith Tower in Pioneer Square and the nearby King Street railroad station, downtown Seattle has a wealth of low old buildings with extensive terra-cotta molding and decoration. Horses' heads and gargoyles can be found on more than one building, as well as a striking set of walrus heads on the nicely restored and domed **Arctic Building**.

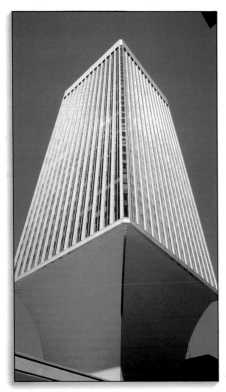

Seattle's waterfront: Part of what makes Seattle unique is its fine, deep harbor. Its piers were once the busy home of working cargo and fishing vessels. Some such activity remains but the bulk of the industrial functions moved to the Duwamish Waterway and Lake Union long ago, leaving a long waterfront promenade with a great deal of largely untapped potential. Tourist attractions – some junky, a few marvelous – and restaurants have taken over the piers, and many different plans, exciting if unconfirmed, have been proposed for a more pedestrian-oriented future.

Starting from the south end near Pioneer Square, the first stop on the waterfront is **Pier 48**. Periscopes here provide an excellent view of Puget Sound and the Olympic Mountains. Moving north, a public boat landing precedes the old Seattle landmark, **Ye Olde Curiosity Shoppe**, at the foot of Spring. Many items are on display including fleas in dresses, mummies and a wide array of inexpensive souvenirs. The Bremerton and Winslow ferries leave from the Seattle Ferry Terminal at **Pier 52**.

Next to the Fireboat Station at Madison, munch some fish and chips from **Ivar's Acres of Clams**, first in a chain developed by the late Ivar Haglund, long known as Seattle's premier prankster, promoter and restaurateur. The next stretch of walkway features tourist shops offering souvenirs of the area. From **Pier 56**, tours of the harbor and a Native village on **Blake Island** round out the visitor's choice of activities.

The more unusual features of the waterfront begin with **Waterfront Park**, a true city park that extends from piers 57 to 59 with no grass but picnic spots aplenty, an angular bronze fountain and a great view. The **Seattle Aquarium** at the foot of the Pike Place Hillclimb on **Pier 59** exhibits a great variety of salt and freshwater creatures and plants in their natural setting.

Piers 65 through 69 house fish packers and Port of Seattle offices. **Pier 70** is a return to the average boardwalk fare with live music, seafood and crafts shops in a rustic building. **Myrtle Edwards Park** completes the waterfront tour at

The Rainier Bank Building.

the north end, where it joins with the **Elliott Bay Bikeway** for 1¼ miles (2 km) of green promenade to a new public fishing pier at the far end.

Seeing the waterfront, downtown and outlying areas is made easy by the City of Seattle's efficient **Metro Transit** system. Metro runs two beautifully restored 1927 Australian streetcars up and down the waterfront past piers, parks and ferry terminals seven days a week. A 30-minute round trip takes you from piers 48 to 70 with five stops along the way. From the streetcar you can transfer easily to the regular Metro coaches that canvass the city. In addition to an excellent county-wide service, Metro provides the convenience of a ride-free zone in the core of downtown between Jackson Street on the south and Battery Street on the north, and the Alaskan Way waterfront on the west and Sixth Avenue on the east.

The single most animated place in the city is also exceptional because it gives one a feel for every walk of life. This is the **Pike Place Market**, built on stilts on the headland overlooking Elliott Bay between Western and First avenues. This old-world, open-air market is the oldest continuously active market of its kind in the United States. Started in 1907 as a place for local farmers to sell their produce, the original arcade ambled and spread into a maze of corridors, stairwells and hidden shops on several levels, which today are a haven for some 230 small businesses of all types.

The floors on the mezzanine level are wavy because the structure is a combination of 14 different buildings constructed at different times. The market had reached such chaos and disrepair by the 1960s that it was threatened by high-rise condominium development. But Seattle's unquenchable preservationists, led by a local architect, the late Victor Steinbrueck, succeeded in their fight to give the market back to the people. Now a 7-acre (3-hectare) historical district surrounded by urban renewal plans, the market remains a busy place where gourmets can select live lobsters, and pensioners buy crisp lettuce for small

Sailboats in Shilshole Marina.

change, from the producers who sell their fresh goods to the buyer first hand.

The market's primary occupation is food. Over 50 restaurants, from the funky **Pink Door** lounge to the tiny **Emmett Watson's Oyster Bar**, serve up any type of dish, especially seafood, from early breakfast to midnight snack. A few favorites are the **Athenian**, with its expansive view of the bay and extensive food and beer selection; **Maximilien-in-the Market**, a cozy French cafe; **Il Bistro** on the lower level, catering to the upwardly mobile crowd; and **Place Pigalle**, a bistro overlooking the bay.

At **City Fish** is a ramp leading to the lower levels of the market, where a great jumble of odd shops vie for the wanderer's attention. Among the wares are vintage clothing, music boxes, fresh Market Spice orange tea and exotic herbs. Farther north on the arcade the craftspeople, outnumbering the farmers twofold, sell handmade jewelry, gift items and leather goods. Street musicians play for loose change at several designated spots around the market.

A postage-stamp-like park with benches, a Quinault totem pole and a spectacular view of the bay mark the end of the historical district at the foot of steep Virginia Street. **Steinbrueck Park** is a fine place to watch the soapbox derby that rollicks down Virginia each Memorial Day as the highlight of the Pike Place Market Street Fair.

A collection of chic businesses and condos aimed at downtown Seattle's expanding junior executive crowd is growing on the fringes of the market. Across First Avenue from the arcade, gourmet coffee and kitchenware shops, design stores and clothing boutiques have gradually transformed the area's flavor. Townhouses and studios bringing outrageous rents perch on the Pike Place Hillclimb down to Western Avenue. More highbrow residential construction is in the works, as cheap hotels and apartments disappear.

Belltown: City fathers came up with a great idea in the early 1900s to allow downtown activity to spread north to where Seattle Center is now. One entire hill of the original seven, named Denny Hill after a prominent founder, was removed to improve access to the city core. The west side of Denny Hill was sluiced into the bay, making the waterfront tideflats much larger. The resulting flat **Denny Regrade** is an area of condominiums, neighborhood bars and movie theaters.

As Pioneer Square was upgraded, many artists moved uptown to cheaper studios in the Regrade's south section, dubbed **Belltown**, around Bell Street. Now in the early stages of redevelopment itself with public funds going for middle- and low-income housing renovation, Belltown is vying for attention with its nightlife.

The **Virginia Inn** on First Avenue is the common starting point on tavern-hopping nights for fraternity boys and trendies of all kinds. One of the most popular stops is the **Crocodile Cafe** which offers a lively bar, a separate live music area and a cafe area that serves good food.

A few restaurants, all with exhibitions of paintings on their walls, com-

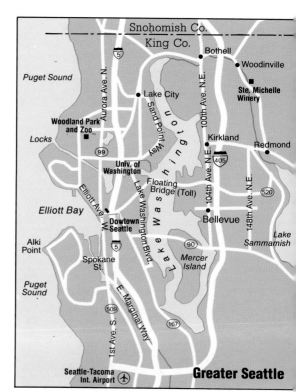

Greater Seattle

plete Belltown's identity as a place for artists. Most unusual is the **Gravity Bar** on Virginia Street where espresso, pastries and fashionable meals are served in rather startling surroundings. The **Two Bells Tavern** is one of the best spots in this still-slightly-seedy part of town.

A 90-second monorail trip above the Denny Regrade streets connects the retail core of the city to a people watcher's paradise – **Seattle Center**, recreational hub and home base for the performing arts. Designed for the 1962 World's Fair, this 74-acre (30-hectare) urban park brings together everyone in the city with a diversity of facilities and events that include basketball games, trade shows, concerts, restaurants and an amusement park. The graceful landscaping, plentiful public art, fountains, and large open spaces make the park an ideal site for summer festivals like Bumbershoot (over the Labor Day weekend), a four-day program covering all of the arts, and a Folklife Festival (Memorial Day weekend) featuring a wide array of Northwest performers.

The **Space Needle** is Seattle's most famous landmark, and views of mountains, city and water from the 500-foot (152-meter) level are unmatched. The restaurant revolves a full 360 degrees in an hour, but prices are high. The same view can be had from the observation deck for a minimal elevator fee.

Precursor of the Washington State Convention Center downtown, the Seattle Center has long been a host for conventions and trade shows. A 40,000-sq.-foot (12,000-sq.-meter) **Exhibition Hall**, 6,000-seat **Arena** and ample meeting rooms are complemented by the enormous **Center House**, formerly an armory and now alive with 50 shops and a wide variety of restaurants. The Center's **Coliseum**, with a capacity of 15,000, provides a fine setup for big league sports, as well as a good site for rowdy rock concerts.

Foremost with children of all ages is the **Pacific Science Center**, the focal point of the World's Fair. Over 200 hands-on exhibits that "show how our world really works" are housed in six buildings gracefully ornamented with lacy high arches and reflecting pools. Natural history films on a giant screen, computer displays, a planetarium, volcano simulator and laser light shows are permanent attractions complemented by fascinating traveling exhibitions.

The Seattle Center is primarily a playground for the arts. A crafts gallery selling Northwest art is located by the colorful **International Fountain Court**. The north edge of the center houses the city's professional performing companies. The **Opera House** hosts a year-round variety of cultural events. The top-notch Seattle Youth Symphony and the Seattle Symphony Orchestra offer regular subscription concerts and special pop concert events. The Opera Association, founded in 1964, produces five operas during its regular season from September to May and an additional one in summer.

The **Pacific Northwest Ballet**, a classical company that has won national recognition for its December performances of the *Nutcracker Suite*, has a five-month season in the Opera House

Chief Seattle, named local Indian leader.

and occasional smaller-scale shows are held at the University of Washington.

Most lively of all the arts in Seattle is theater. With over 40 separate theater companies and several more loosely formed dramatic associations, this rainy town is second only to the Big Apple for live theatrical performances. The varied range includes classical and contemporary plays, comedy and lively musical productions.

The **Seattle Center Playhouse**, former home of the Seattle Repertory Theater ("The Rep"), is now the home of **Intiman Theater**. The Rep's new residence is the flashy 860-seat **Bagley Wright Theater**, an investment that reflects the city's devotion to dramatics. The Rep's season is six plays strong, stressing the contemporary, but including well-produced classics. From the lofty Bagley Wright to the smaller, 174-seat **Bathhouse Theater** at Greenlake, from established professional companies to workshops for amateurs, this diverse theater community is one of Emerald City's brightest jewels.

Pioneer Square: The traditional district for less formal Seattle nightlife, **Pioneer Square** is also a premier locale for tourism by day. Nowhere is the city's past more beautifully and consistently displayed than in this 20-square-block historical district in south downtown. Now the center for Seattle's visual arts scene, the restored buildings of Pioneer Square house the city's highest concentration of galleries as well as stylish restaurants, gift shops, bookstores and many bars that feature a variety of live entertainment.

Pioneer Square was the founding site the settlers chose when they left Alki Point in 1852 for a superior harbor on Elliott Bay. Steep Yesler Way was once the Skid Road that sent logs rolling down to the town's first mill. The area's low, ornate brick and stone buildings do not represent the original architecture; they were built according to an orderly plan after the Great Fire of 1889 destroyed most of First Avenue from University to King streets.

The business center of Seattle moved uptown in the early 20th century, and so the Skid Road area declined. The majestic, 42-story **Smith Tower** went up in 1914 at the corner of Second Avenue and Yesler in an attempt to anchor business to the south. The tower was the pride of Seattle, and for many years it was the tallest building west of the Mississippi. A look at the city from the observation floor shows the pleasing contrast of the small, colorful old buildings with the sleek skyscrapers that lie toward the northeast.

After World War II, Skid Road was a forgotten home of cheap hotels and winos. In the 1960s, artists began to move their studios into the low-rent lofts, and the same civic pride that later saved the market defeated an urban renewal plan that would replace old structures with parking lots and office towers. Prevented from rebuilding, property owners invested great sums of money to remodel building interiors in wood and brass. High-priced condominiums and the urban chic set have moved in beside the rescue missions and pensioners that are still a part of the square. Artists and transients coexist and can be found partying together during their district's Fat Tuesday block party each winter.

Pioneer Square can be explored from the bottom in the **Underground Tours**. (Poor drainage after the 1889 fire necessitated raising the streetline one level.) Guides describe life in old Seattle while leading the way through a maze of old shopfronts, dimly skylit beneath the streets and shops.

Pioneer Place Park is the heart of Pioneer Square. The great pergola of ornate ironwork and glass shades curved wooden benches from sun or rain. A 60-foot (18-meter) Tlingit Indian totem pole and bronze bust of Chief Seattle, the city's humanistic forefather, are displayed to remind Seattle of her roots.

Fronting onto the square is the elaborate Romanesque-style **Pioneer Building**, which has a spacious courtyard interior. Close by are the two restaurants that vie for status as the oldest eating establishment in Seattle: the **Merchant's Cafe** and the **J & M Cafe**. Both feature long mahogany bars and other 1880s decor, and Merchant's has live lounge acts most nights. On Yesler Way, toward the water, **Trattoria Mitchelli** is a popular spot. It is a favorite late-night breakfast haven with excellent espresso and a cozy mood.

With a tree-studded median and old-fashioned globe streetlights, First Avenue is a lovely promenade with many attractions. **Silver Image Gallery** features fine-art photography and other galleries show a wide variety of local artists. Also exceptional are the **Northwest Gallery of Fine Woodworking**, with furniture by regional woodworkers, and the **Flying Shuttle**, a crafts gallery featuring the work of Northwest fiber artists. The **Elliott Bay Book Company** on First Avenue is a fine place to browse, with a wide selection and a cozy basement cafe that attracts a quiet, intellectual crowd.

A primary landmark in Pioneer Square restoration, the **Grand Central Arcade** was once a hotel. It has two levels of book and gift shops surrounding a chandeliered brick courtyard, as well as

The lion's share of fame goes to this Seattle museum.

the Bakery, which offers a likely candidate for the best cinnamon roll in Seattle. In the Arcade visitors can watch artisans, including ivory carvers, glassblowers and silversmiths perform their intricate crafts.

The rear of the Arcade opens onto **Occidental Park**, a mall with benches for a breathing space away from traffic. In a second floor shop on brick paved Occidental mall, **Foster/White Gallery** is Seattle's largest fine arts dealer. Featured are items from the renowned Pilchuck Glass Center and the works of contemporary painters and sculptors of high reputation. Only a short walk away, **Waterfall Gardens** is a private oasis of rushing water and sculptured rock, donated to the city of Seattle by the United Parcel Service.

A final amenity of Pioneer Square is that it has become a music and entertainment hub. **Doc Maynard's** and the **Central Tavern** feature rhythm and blues or rock bands brimming with home-grown enthusiasm. **Swannie's** is a comedy club underground.

That giant round slab of concrete on the southern end of the city skyline has been called an orange juicer, a pillbox, or the generous half of a sliced basketball. It is the **King County Domed Stadium** (**Kingdome**), built in 1976 to bring major league sports to Seattle.

The largest of Seattle's sports facilities, the Kingdome symbolizes Seattle's avid pursuit of big-league city status. The stadium capacity swells from 40,000 for basketball games up to 70,000 for rock concerts and other stage events. The Seahawks play NFL football here, and the Mariners take on other American League baseball teams, playing games under the world's largest self-supporting roof.

Tours of the Kingdome from astroturf to grandstands include a look at the history of sports in the **Royal Brougham Collection**. Tours begin three times a day at the D Gate. Calling ahead for confirmation is advised.

The International District: Kingdome events are numerous and big enough to affect its neighbors by bringing shoppers, hungry restaurant hunters and the threat of encroaching parking lots to Pioneer Square and the Dome's eastern neighbor, the **International District**.

Seattle is a leader in Asian shipping and cultural connections. The fourth-largest Chinese population in the US makes the International District (ID) the third-largest Chinatown in North America. But don't let these facts fool you. It's not called Chinatown (you'll be corrected if you use the term), and it's not the glitzy tourist production found in San Francisco or in Vancouver, BC. Marvel instead at the unparalleled racial diversity in the International District, almost a city in itself with its own social and political organizations.

Isolated by the West Seattle Freeway and the Kingdome, the ID was once the point of arrival for immigrants from all over the world. A large concentration of blacks, some whites and a number of Native Americans share the district with the two major groups. Chinese and Japanese, Filipinos, Koreans and Thais live, work and socialize here with Hawaiians, Samoans, Mien, Hmong, and the more recent arrivals, the Vietnamese, Laotians and Cambodians.

Originally a refuge for Chinese laborers released after the completion of the Transcontinental Railroad, the ID survived the depletions of the 1880s anti-Chinese riots and World War II internment of Japanese-Americans to become a unified, active community. Nearly 30 clubs for gambling and general socializing are scattered throughout the district. Meeting halls like the refurbished **Nippon Kan** in old Japan-town under the freeway still thrive.

While the ID is small, there is a bounty of ethnic restaurants to choose from (about 40, half of which are Chinese owned) and authentic groceries and shops. Strolling down the streets of the ID you will find herbalists, massage parlors and acupuncturists, exotic pets and the notorious **Wah Mee Club**, site of a 1983 multiple murder linked to youth gangs and gambling activities that had all Seattle abuzz for months.

The **Mikado**, a Japanese restaurant on Jackson, is frequently given rave

Left, Smith Tower in Pioneer Square. Right, the Pacific Science Center.

reviews, and the **House of Dumplings** on King Street serves excellent *dim sum*. King Street is the center of Chinese shop activity, with shark fins, trussed poultry, pungent herbs and secret ingredients sold with a pinch of advice by shopkeepers. **Sea Garden**, on Seventh, is a popular Chinese eatery in the area. Also located on King Street is **Uwajimaya**, the biggest Japanese supermarket in the West.

Seattle's Asian history is preserved in the small but excellent **Wing Luke Asian Museum** on Seventh Avenue South, dedicated to the first person of Asian ancestry to be elected to office in Seattle, and dedicated also to Asians in the Northwest. Among the exhibitions are historical photos and herbal medicines. **Hing Hay Park**'s dragon mural is a larger-than life depiction of local Asian events. The park is also the setting for martial arts exhibitions and Chinese folk dancing. A giant brass dragon graces the nearby **Children's Park**, and the ID's last park, named **Kobe** after Seattle's Japanese sister city,

is a quiet place to contemplate the meeting of Western and Eastern cultures.

Seattle Hills: Six of Seattle's original seven hills form a protective cluster around downtown and **Elliott Bay**. Rising as distinct neighborhoods between the bay and **Lake Washington**, these areas afford Seattleites a rare choice of spectacular city skyline views and cultural flavors. The West Seattle neighborhood, connected to southern industrial Seattle by a bridge over the Duwamish Waterway, juts its nose well into Elliott Bay.

Alki Point, the westernmost tip of this promontory and Seattle's founding point, is the site of a 1918 working light station and a wonderful place to view the snowclad Olympic Mountains across Puget Sound. A cruise along Marine View Drive features lovely windswept homes overlooking the bay. Singular, clear nights occur when one can see the lights of **Magnolia** from Duwamish Head twinkling across the bay.

Only three streets and a bridge connect the hamlet of Magnolia to the rest

The University of Washington.

of the city via Queen Anne Hill. From this isolation, a separate suburb, with orderly streets and well-tended houses perched above the water, has grown up close to the city center. A circle of the spectacular bluff is made from the east (downtown) corner along West Galer Street and Magnolia Boulevard.

At the Boulevard's northern end is 520-acre (210-hectare) **Discovery Park**, the largest and most naturally varied of all Seattle parks. A former army base, the park features woods, sandy dunes, picnic grounds, bicycle paths, a museum and the **Daybreak Star Indian Center**, an educational and cultural haven for the United Indians of All Tribes.

Completing the loop above Salmon Bay on the North brings the tourist to Seattle's steepest streets. One of the first areas settled, **Queen Anne Hill** is largely residential with a small commercial village and Seattle Center at its base. The north and top sides consist of cozy family dwellings interspersed with narrow cobblestone streets. A long, skinny shopping area runs the length of Queen Anne Avenue North.

Capitol Hill is the vibrant star of the parade of hills, with a blending of youthful spirit and mature grace that no single part of downtown can match. Capitol Hill has the highest population density, and the largest concentration of gays in the city. Its streets, bars and cafes host a lively mix of rich, poor, gay, straight, married, single, young and old. Students from Seattle Central Community College on Broadway, nearby Seattle University, and the Cornish College of the Arts bring youthful enthusiasm to the streets of a neighborhood that has more public housing for seniors than anywhere in the city.

Broadway is the heartbeat of the district with its glamorous furniture, clothing and gift stores and its flashy cafes and bars. An ideal place to watch fashion and trends on display, the mood of the street is set by a series of lifesize, numbered bronze footsteps in the sidewalk that teach strollers the mambo, rhumba, waltz and other dance moves.

Many pleasant restaurants are found on and just off Broadway. At the north end of the hill is the **Rain City Grill**, serving elegant Northwest cuisine, and farther south is **Mamounia**, an authentic Moroccan experience. Greek food, glorified burgers and designer dessert spots round out the fare on the hill. The favorite sugar and caffeine havens are the trusty **B & O Espresso**, the **Pacific Dessert Company** cafe and Seattle's favorite chocolate bar, the **Dilettante**.

At Broadway's north end, the Harvard Exit's old-style movie theaters: the colonial, pillared **DAR Hall** and **Cornish South Campus** mark the transition to the hill's stately older section. Old homes with leaded glass windows and manicured lawns line 15th Avenue East, home of the countercultural **Cause Celebre** cafe. **St Mark's Cathedral** on 10th Avenue East is a spacious retreat that resounds to the tones of a famous tracker organ. From the cathedral grounds you can see most of the city across the freeway that cuts into the hill's western edge. The Cornish College of the Arts next door is the Northwest's only college of visual and performing arts.

Vendor at the Seattle Center.

The connoisseur's eye will be satisfied at **Volunteer Park**, a luxurious 40 acres (16 hectares) on Capitol Hill's northern crest. Circling drives and manicured lawns lead to a conservatory and an old water tower with a 75-foot (20-meter) vantage point.

The park was home to the Seattle Art Museum for more than 50 years and now hosts the newly renovated Seattle Asian Art Museum. The artistic bent suggested on glittering Broadway is fulfilled by this old neighborhood's quiet grandeur. A leisurely walk through the area adjacent to and just east of Volunteer Park is a good way to see a cross-section of Seattle's older residential architecture, much of which is well-preserved and renovated.

Slow placed and less affluent, **First Hill** (more often called "Pill Hill") towers due east of Seattle's business district. It is the home of six hospitals, numerous clinics, several churches and a vast expanse of low income residences on the east slope called the Central District. Many blacks and Indo-Chinese

have made their home here. The impressive **Sorrento Hotel** on Madison is well-known for its mahogany-paneled Hunt Club Lounge, and the **Frye Art Museum** on Terry and Cherry houses a collection of 19th-century American and European paintings.

Southernmost in the chain of hills between downtown and the lake is **Beacon Hill**, yet another area of racial admixture. Only 30 percent of the residents are white and the rest are Japanese, Chinese, Korean, Filipino, Chicano, Italian, Native American and black. Ethnic markets abound on the south hill, where the noise level is already high from the proximity to Boeing Field. Desirable for its contrasting quiet atmosphere, the north hill has rock gardens, condos, a few mansions and the one thing all these hills share – million-dollar views.

Trucks rumble across a plain of warehouses and factories in Seattle's south end, west of Interstate-5. Here the **Rainier Brewery** gives tours of the plant, and **Oberto Sausage** is ground up

The Japanese tea garden in the University of Washington Arboretum.

and packed. Close by is **Boeing Field International**, a busy cargo and private plane airport. The stunning **Museum of Flight** at the south edge traces the history of aviation and highlights the remarkable success of the Boeing Company – Seattle's leading exporter and largest employer.

Begun in 1916, the Boeing Company has five plants stretching north to south from Everett to Renton. Tours are led through the Everett Plant, a roofed space so large that its temperature conditions must be controlled to prevent rain clouds from forming. It is the assembly site of 747 and 767 jumbo jets. Seattle's economy has diversified over the years, allowing less dependence on Boeing, but it is still the largest industry, bringing in more than $25 billion a year from the sale of jetliners and helicopters, aerospace and computer technology.

The **Duwamish Waterway** between South and West Seattle is lined with fish canneries and flows in two channels around man-made Harbor Island into Elliott Bay. The shift in location of container and shipping activity to this island has opened up the downtown waterfront for more picturesque uses. Through a series of bays, channels and a small lake, Puget Sound is joined to freshwater Lake Washington. Pleasure and working boats follow this salmon migration path, leaving salt water behind at the **Chittenden Locks**.

The locks are an engineering feat that provide Seattle with a 25,000-acre (10,000-hectare) inland freshwater harbor. It's quite fun in the spring to watch the boats jam up (some 80,000 to 100,000 boats pass through each year) in a rush to be raised 21 feet (6 meters) from saltwater Puget Sound to freshwater Salmon Bay. At the locks, you can also take a stroll through 7 acres (3 hectares) of botanical gardens and watch the salmon and steelhead go past the locks in the summer via a fish ladder.

Salmon Bay is the center for much maritime activity and home to boats that fish for halibut, cod, salmon and herring. **Fisherman's Terminal** on its south shore is the headquarters of the Northwest's largest fishing fleet. The

docks house a full range of boats from the smallest trawler to the largest ships that traverse the Pacific from California to Alaska. Early morning finds the wharf awakening to business as fishermen arrive from their homes in **Ballard**, the town built on the bay.

The Ballard community's livelihood and recreation are centered on Salmon Bay and the Ship Canal. It is a stolid, conservative community whose large Scandinavian population makes it a unique ethnic enclave. Fishing, sawmills and the lumber industry have always kept Ballard running.

A streetcar used to carry the workers to the mills and the Fisherman's Terminal, and a historical district has been preserved along the old route. The bricked streets and old granary are well worth a stroll. The best time to visit Ballard is during one of several Scandinavian holidays and food fests in August and October, when the streets lined with Scandinavian and Norwegian delis and shops come alive.

The bright orange **Fremont Drawbridge**, built in 1916, ushers tallmasted sailboats through a scenic section of canal to Lake Union. **Fremont** is a well-kept hamlet with restored shops and strong community feeling. The beloved, sturdy *Waiting for the Interurban* sculpture at the base of the bridge has average, solid citizens standing together at a bus stop. The statues are often "dressed" in old clothes and bedecked with banners for holidays such as St Patrick's Day or locals' birthdays.

On the lake's northern shore, a piece of old working Seattle has undergone a dramatic change in direction at **Gasworks Park**, the only industrial site conversion park in existence. From 1906 to 1956, the black monstrosity of refining towers and twisting pipes belched smoke and polluted Lake Union, as it made natural gas from coal. The local architect Richard Haag figured that such an unusual structure on a prime piece of property looking into the very center of downtown should somehow be properly humanified.

By 1976, what were once slag heaps had become sculpted, green, kite-flying mounds, and photographers crowded in to capture the stark beauty of a former eyesore. As children watch the ducks from the edge of the playbarn, the distinctively shaped towers stand as a nagging reminder of yet another generation of industry.

Northern neighborhoods: Seattle's northern reaches have a more relaxed, family feel that tends to quicken to a faster pace around the University of Washington campus.

The **Woodland Park Zoo** in the north end of Fremont began as a family estate in 1889. Strong bond support and inventive management have made it one of the nation's most original zoos, where animals have room to roam in natural settings and visitors unobtrusively blend in with the local habitat.

The most outstanding attractions at the zoo are the gorillas' lush tropical rain forest, the desert and nocturnal house, and the 5-acre (2-hectare) African savannah, where lions, hippos, giraffes, zebras and elephants are subtly separated by hidden barriers.

Also on the grounds is the estate's original formal rose garden. Outside the zoo, wooded picnic areas abound. The east side of the park has tennis courts, pitch and putt golf, and the remains of an old buggy road tracing over to Greenlake, a mecca for the summer sun and fitness crowd.

On the east shore, skate and bicycle rentals, sports stores, a gym and two ice cream shops blend with small, older businesses. **Saleh Al Lago** is a consistently high quality, high priced cafe in the neighborhood and **Spud Fish and Chips** is a to-go favorite. Comely Ravenna Boulevard, once a creek bed that fed into Greenlake, connects this neighborhood to the **University District** (U District).

The **University of Washington**, founded in 1861, is 35,000 students strong and the nation's largest holder of federal medical research grants. Its beautifully landscaped, gracious campus awes one with an air of timeless intellectual refuge. Yet its museums, lecture series, concerts, arboretum and high powered Husky football team invite the city in to participate.

The **Thomas Burke Memorial Washington State Museum** at the north entrance to the campus has an excellent collection of art and artifacts of Northwest Coast Indian and Pacific Rim cultures. Also on campus is the **Henry Art Gallery**, which displays 19th- and 20th-century paintings and hosts big-name traveling exhibitions, as well as lectures and workshops.

"The Ave": A plethora of commuter students has helped make the University District a thriving, colorful nucleus for shopping and socializing, centered on University Way. "The Ave," as it is often called, is a cornucopia of coffeehouses, used book shops and second-hand record stores, and ethnic (especially Asian) fast food spots, all geared to cosmopolitan student life.

According to a recent survey, the **University Bookstore** is the largest American bookstore under one roof, with enormous commercial and textbook selections as well as gifts, luggage and camera supplies. Other favorite

The University District from Queen Anne Hill.

places to visit are the resplendent **La Tienda Folk Arts Gallery**, the **House of Rice** oriental grocery and gift shop, and any number of smoky espresso houses where budding Baudelaires gossip, drink coffee and write masterpieces.

One mile from campus the **Washington Park Arboretum** meanders southeast toward Lake Washington. Since 1934, the vast, wooded arboretum has doubled as a botanical research center for the university and as a peaceful park where the public can observe the good effects of Seattle rain. A vast array of plant families, from rhododendrons to birches to roses to sequoias, are cultivated in groupings like Azalea Way and the Rhododendron Glen, and discreetly labeled with Latin names. Greenhouses and a visitors' center are found at the park's north end.

Also to the north, **Foster Island Wildlife Sanctuary** is a marshy area where the concrete pillars of I-520 stand amongst the grasses and ducks. Canoes rented from the UW's **Waterfront Activity Center** are a good way to explore the area. A trail connects it to **Marsh Island** in Union Bay and to the **Museum of History and Industry** on Montlake "Cut." Home of state historical mementos and marine artifacts, this small museum also has an aerospace wing. An authentic **Japanese Garden** with a teahouse and small, restful lake lies near the south entrance to the park.

The **Leschi Marina**, popular **Leschi Lakecafe** and **Mount Baker Park** face the brilliance of Lake Washington. Green parks line the shore, allowing a clear view of the lake and Mount Rainier all the way to **Seward Park** at the southernmost end. Seward is a lovely wilderness peninsula with numerous ponds where gamefish are raised. The park's 2-mile (4-km) lakeside trail and hilly loop road form the finale of this popular tour for bicyclists, who are given right of way by signs along the whole route.

The growing network of planned scenic drives that are also marked as bike routes runs through the Seattle neighborhoods. Many visitors are astounded at the popularity of bicycling in Seattle,

Maples in Woodland Park.

given the inhospitable wetness and extreme topography of the place, but thrive this sport does. The 1,300-strong membership of the **Cascade Bicycle Club** organizes year-round group rides (open to all) that connect official bike-ways like those on North Lake Union or Elliot Bay to obscure back roads and parks all over the area.

The **Burke-Gilman Trail** is the primary bike path, an old railroad bed that stretches 12 miles (20 km) from Gasworks Park along the UW campus and the shore to the lake's northern tip. The trail is a gathering place for cyclists and a jumping-off spot for extended tours to the lake's east side. (The 40-mile/64-km round trip to the **Ste Michelle Winery** in Woodinville is a time-tested favorite.) The Seattle Engineering Department has worked closely with the bike club to design detailed maps of scenic routes for those who enjoy beautiful views while they are keeping fit.

Eastside: Navigating the waterways and highways of the Eastside requires a few main reference points. The bridges that run east and west across Lake Washington are the **Evergreen Point Floating Bridge** (SR-520) that connects downtown Seattle, just south of the University District, to Kirkland and continues on to Redmond.

The **Mercer Island Floating Bridge** (Interstate 90) connects southern Seattle with south Bellevue via Mercer Island, a residential community about midway across Lake Washington. The main north–south route on the east side of the lake is Interstate 405 which runs the length of Washington State and goes directly through Bellevue, Kirkland and north on to Bothell and Woodinville. The road eventually ends up in Vancouver, about three hours north across the US–Canadian border.

While traffic jams on the floating bridges during rush hours attest to the Eastside's primacy as a suburb, a boom in hi-tech industry and other business is creating free-standing **Bellevue**, Washington's fourth largest city. This fast-growing city demands notice with its businesses, parks and growing concern

Mount Rainier seen behind smooth-barked madrona trees.

for cultural amenities. The phenomenally fast growth of employment, offices and retailing in Bellevue demonstrate its race for urban status. Outside the downtown area, single family residences blend with new industrial and office parks to attract new companies.

Incorporated in 1953, Bellevue has grown rapidly from 5,900 to 90,000 residents in 25 sq. miles (64 sq. km). Bellevue and nearby **Kirkland** began as rural communities of summer homes; they changed with the construction of two floating bridges to Seattle. When the freeway project into Seattle failed, Eastsiders established their own businesses as alternatives to the tiresome daily commute.

With fewer zoning restrictions than Seattle, Bellevue's central business district is a sprawling, thriving retail center with over 8,000 active businesses. Over a dozen motels offer accommodation. **Spazzo Mediterranean Grill** restaurant at the top of the Key Bank Building has good food and the best view in town. **Domani** has the downtown section's classiest menu, noted for its many pasta variations. A sea of free parking lots is the first sign that this is primarily a shopper's downtown.

The focal point is **Bellevue Square**, the largest shopping center in the state. This mammoth mall, done up in a rich forest green, has a dazzling array of shops and department stores. The showpiece of the mall and the city is the **Bellevue Art Museum**, ingenuously placed atop all the activity in a third floor atrium. The museum also offers lectures, films and workshops.

Also in the square is the **PANACA Gallery** of regional arts and crafts, a partner in the museum's new growth. Each year this organization sponsors Bellevue's crowning cultural achievement: the Pacific Northwest Arts and Crafts Fair.

Largest of its kind in the Northwest, the fair has a juried selection of quality works by regional artists. The Bellevue Jazz Festival is another regional exclusive, held on the **Bellevue Community College** campus. Three outdoor stages host professional jazz musicians from the Northwest and other parts of the US. But jazz is not the only music on offer: the campus auditorium, with its superb acoustics, is the only home for the Eastside's theater company and rising star Philharmonic Orchestra, which will achieve its ambition of becoming fully professional within the next few years. The Eastside Youth Symphony, which gives many talented young musicians an early platform, is also based here and is well worth a visit.

A physical breather from the fervent activity and exhaust fumes of the central business district can be had in Bellevue's excellent network of parks. Three tiny plots of picnic areas and trees brighten the downtown area. Bellevue is also graced with several greenbelts and community centers, boat ramp sites, nature study parks and five developed beachfront parks, the largest and most popular of which is **Chism Beach**. Here you can take time off from culture, commerce and consumerism to enjoy the open air and pleasant surroundings. The rural **Kelsey Creek Park** preserves a glimpse of Bellevue's peaceful past with a working animal farm and several jogging trails that wind through a lightly wooded hillside.

Main Street, west of Bellevue Way, is another enclave from the past where over 90 shops have retained the flavor of Old Bellevue on bricked streets. Flower baskets hang from streetlamps and visitors will find antiques, clothing, home furnishings and a few restaurants to while away shopping time. To the northeast is **Paul Thomas Wines**, makers of vinifera wines and superb original blends of fruit and vegetables, which attract visitors who are interested in something out of the ordinary.

An interesting sidetrip to the southeast of Bellevue along I-90 brings the visitor to the quaint town of **Issaquah**, surrounded by the gentle humps of the "Issaquah Alps." Year-round community theater, a candy factory, a shopping village of old, former dwellings connected by board sidewalks, and a salmon hatchery attract sight-seers.

Hugging Lake Washington's easternmost shore is another picturesque, if somewhat larger, Bellevue neighbor that has managed to preserve the peaceful feel of a summer resort.

Kirkland's founder had big plans to make it a booming steel town, but this did not happen, which must have been a great disappointment for him and perhaps for those who would have worked there or profited from it, but for the visitor it is a great blessing. Instead, big business passed the town by and its newly renovated, charming downtown has been left to prosper slowly with galleries and shops taking over the Victorian buildings.

The highlight of a series of eight beaches and landscaped parks along Lake Street is **Marina Park** in the core of the village. Shops that open onto the waterfront, and an open sided hexagonal pavilion where free concerts are held all through the summer, make this a wonderful place to stroll.

More than 80 restaurants can be found in Kirkland, and several of them make good use of their spots on the bays. **Anthony's Home Port** is a Moss Bay favorite for eating, drinking and being seen. **DaVinci's Flying Pizza**, on the commercial strip parallel to the shore, is a fun, trendy place for pizza and pasta. The small **Cafe Juanita**, just north in the Juanita neighborhood, fully earns its rave reviews with an excellent Italian menu and wine actually produced on the property.

Several galleries of note blend with the antique shops to give Kirkland its character. The historic **Peter Kirk Building**, with its distinctive cupola, is the home of a fine gallery and the Creative Arts center, a studio school of design, painting and pottery.

Nearby in town are the **Lakeshore Gallery** of pottery, clothing and metalwork; and the **Foster/White Gallery**, featuring local artists' work. The town's custom cannery, just east of downtown, sells assorted canned and frozen seafood. If you are fond of seafood some of the canned varieties may be worth buying to take home, to give you a nostalgic taste of the Emerald City when your holiday is only a memory.

The "floating bridge" across Lake Washington.

TACOMA

Overlooking **Commencement Bay**, one of the best harbors in the world, **Tacoma** is the shipping, distributing and industrial center of the state. It is Washington's third largest city, after Seattle and Spokane, with a growing population of almost 180,000. Named after the local Native American word for Mount Rainier, Tacoma began in 1868 as two separate communities on the southwest shore of the bay. Rivalry for the name "Tacoma" was fierce between the two settlements until 1883 when a merger was granted by the state legislature. Lumber, railroads and copper-smelting companies made the city grow quickly. Tacoma's economic base today is founded on wood products, overseas shipping and the military.

Tacoma is currently experiencing a renaissance of civic pride and involvement. Renovations of historic structures, as well as new projects, are underway throughout the city. This can best be seen downtown at the six-block outdoor mall, the **Broadway Plaza**.

Handsome older buildings intermixed with architecturally up-to-the-minute shops surround the mall and make it historically fascinating as well as visually exciting. Sprinkled throughout the plaza are fountains, glass canopies and a children's play area.

The jewel of the plaza is the renovated **Pantages Center**. Originally designed in 1918 for traveling vaudeville shows, the theater seats 1,100 and is the center for Tacoma's performing arts. The city's residential districts contain many original Victorian homes from the turn of the century, with turrets, gables and beautifully leaded windows.

Tacoma's two museums are within walking distance from the plaza, and are definitely worth a visit. The **Tacoma Art Museum** features a design research center, fine traveling exhibits and a children's gallery; a great place to take the kids on a rainy afternoon. Exhibitions of Native American artifacts,

Left, Viking explorer Leif Erickson. **Right**, historic Fort Nisqually in Tacoma.

handiwork, old photos and American silver can be viewed at the **Washington State Historical Society Museum**, three blocks north of downtown.

Another source of pride for the city is its arena and convention center, the **Tacoma Dome**. It is the largest wood-domed structure in the world, and can seat up to 30,000. Popular entertainers, spectator sports and exhibitions are the usual fare. Much to Tacoma's delight, the Dome is getting a lot of the business that used to go to Seattle. Big-name performers now choose the Dome over Seattle's arenas for its superior acoustics and comfort, so watch the local papers for possible star attractions.

Lobster shops and espresso bars: Some of Tacoma's best restaurants are located on the bayside drive out to Point Defiance, Ruston Way. Overlooking Commencement Bay, the **Lobster Shop South** offers a waterfront deck, superb seafood and unbeatable views of the water and Olympic Mountains. (The Original Lobster Shop is located across the bay at Dash Point, and is equally recommended.) Also on Ruston Way is **Old Town**, Tacoma's birthplace. A few early buildings remain, along with a few new shops and restaurants. **Grazie** is an espresso bar, a delicatessen and a good restaurant rolled into one.

Tacoma is well-known for its beautiful and versatile parks, and **Point Defiance Park** is undoubtedly the best of them all. A zoo, an aquarium, hiking trails, beaches, gardens, a reconstructed fort and more are contained in its 500 acres (200 hectares). Peaceful green forests make up the majority of the park, and are a soothing remedy for the "industrial blues" one can experience in Tacoma.

For those with an afternoon to spend, the aquarium and newly remodeled zoo offer exhibits of Pacific Rim wildlife in its natural surroundings. A traditional Japanese garden and botanical gardens will satisfy the landscape enthusiast, and a variety of boating facilities should keep the sports-minded busy. Point Defiance has something for everyone, and is without question one of the best parks on Puget Sound.

Seattle night scene on Interstate 5.

PUGET SOUND AND THE SAN JUANS

For the first-time visitor to the Puget Sound area, it may be difficult to escape a sense of giddy disorientation. From the deck of a ferryboat one can shift gears from a bustling cosmopolitan atmosphere to timeless rural tranquility in the space of an hour. With the further aid of a bicycle or an automobile, the explorer can travel from a traditional fishing village of seafaring folk; through verdant farms that would bring a lump to the throat of the most hardbitten New Englander; to one of the most lush primeval rain forests in the world.

Begin a Puget Sound exploration at Port Townsend on the northeastern corner of the Olympic Peninsula, and continue south. (Note the many finger-like coves and inlets; Hood Canal to the south makes navigation somewhat tricky.) From Olympia, skip north to Edmonds, north of Seattle (Seattle is covered elsewhere, pages 109-27) and conclude with a visit to the San Juan Islands at the Canadian border.

Port Townsend: Perched on the northeastern corner of the Olympic Peninsula, where the waters of the Strait of Juan de Fuca and Puget Sound create muscle-bound riptides, is the brightly colored Victorian town of **Port Townsend**. Today the town is a haven for artists, writers, families seeking serenity – and tourists wishing they could stay forever.

Perhaps people have always dreamed they could stay forever in this geographical paradise. Balmy weather, jagged Olympic peaks standing guard to the south, views of cliffs on nearby Whidbey Island and the elusive "Great White Father" (Skagit Indian name for Mount Baker) shadowing the horizon, once assured pioneers Alfred Plummer and George Bachelder of the town's prosperous future. In the mid-19th century, they believed Port Townsend would become the great port of the Sound. But when Union Pacific's trans-continental railroad failed to connect to the Port

Townsend Southern Railroad, Seattle emerged as the port of entry for Puget Sound. Overnight, a town designed to hold 20,000 inhabitants was left with a mere 3,500.

Seventy years later, in 1961, Port Townsend residents, working under their own initiative, refurbished not only the Victorian homes of the years past but also restored the town's long dormant sense of civic pride.

The best way to visit this picturesque town, designated a National Historic District in 1976, is to stroll. The downtown district, centered on **Water Street**, is about four blocks of turn-of-the-century brick buildings. Here, in between glimpses of the Strait of Juan de Fuca and nearby islands, are fine Northwest art galleries, craft shops, antique stores and an impressive collection of delis and restaurants.

Thousands of photographs and other relics of bygone years fill **Jefferson County Historical Museum** at the end of Water Street. The museum, located in the City Hall (1891), is a relic itself.

The 1892 **Jefferson County Court-house**, an 1890 **Bell Tower**, and the stately **Customs House** all add to the rich and visible history of this fascinating, isolated town.

Climb the hill to "uptown" and walk among the multicolored restored Victorian homes. Determined to snoop? Hold off your visit until September when there is a Historic Homes Tour, for the **Rothschild House** (1868) is the only one that is a public museum.

However, there are a number of warm and quietly elegant bed-and-breakfast inns in and around Port Townsend. The **Ann Starrett Mansion** (744 Clay Street), **Hastings House** (313 Walker Street), **Heritage House** (305 Pierce Street), **James House** (1238 Washington Street), and **Lizzie's** (731 Pierce Street) are among a few of them.

If sightseeing and history become overwhelming, do what most residents would choose to do: walk down to one of the four city parks and savor the view. A nice beach walk begins at **Chetzemoka Park** and heads north towards

Fort Worden, which was originally constructed for coastal defense. It is one of three that made up a triangle of forts protecting Puget Sound. (The fort was the setting of the film, *An Officer and A Gentleman*.) Aside from beachcombing, you can tour Officers' Row and the Commanding Officer's quarters, climb through remaining bunkers, and visit the **Point Wilson Lighthouse**.

At certain times of the year, this fort is more than a military relic. Fort Worden is the home of popular summer arts programs including the Festival of American Fiddle Tunes (early July), the Port Townsend Jazz Festivals (February and June) and the International Folk Dance Music Festival (August). In the spring, rhododendron blossoms dress Port Townsend in a festive mood, giving rise to the charming and popular Rhododendron Festival.

There are two ways to leave this cultural oasis – that is, if you decide to leave. Hop on the ferry to Whidbey Island, or drive south, continuing your loop around the Olympic Peninsula. The

Port Townsend's Hastings House, *circa* **1890.**

drive will take you past the Chevy Chase Country Club with a magnificent view of Discovery Bay, south of Port Townsend. Here you'll catch glimpses of the Olympic Mountains through the smooth, red-trunked madronas which trim this windy road.

Indian Island to the east is the site of the US Navy ammunition station for ships entering Puget Sound. The public is not allowed on the northern end of the island, for obvious security reasons, but on the southern end, along the highway to **Marrowstone Island**, where there is access, there are fertile beaches for collecting clams.

Cross Indian Island to Marrowstone Island early in the morning and you are likely to see deer grazing. Coyotes and foxes are also a familiar sight here. **Fort Flagler**, on Marrowstone, is the second of the three forts forming the triangular Puget Sound defense; it closed shortly after World War I. Camping is welcomed at Fort Flagler.

The **Resort at Port Ludlow** is a luxurious and expensive condominium recreational complex with an intimate view of Mats Harbor on Hood Canal and the Cascade Mountains.

North Kitsap Peninsula: The **Hood Canal Bridge**, which connects the Olympic Peninsula to one of its fingers, the Kitsap Peninsula, floats on the water to the north. It is one of the three longest floating, or pontoon, bridges in the world. (The other two cross Seattle's Lake Washington.)

The Hood Canal Bridge is a vital link between Jefferson County (the northern Olympic Peninsula) and Kitsap County. Without it, residents and visitors would have to drive for at least an hour in order to circumvent Hood Canal. The new home of the controversial Trident Submarines is tucked away to the south on the canal at Bangor.

If you like views and beaches – and who does not – wander along the beach just north of the west side of the Hood Canal Bridge. There is a spit a few miles up. You can then walk to **Hood Head**, a former island with a man-made walkway to the mainland, offering views of

The marina at Brownsville, Kitsap County.

the Hood Canal Bridge, Mount Rainier, Foulweather Bluff and Port Gamble.

When you first spy **Port Gamble** on Kitsap Peninsula you may think you are touring the northeastern corner of the United States. Elm trees in Washington? Port Gamble, sitting in the rain-shadow of the Olympic Mountains, is actually America's oldest continuously operating lumber community. The town's founder, Captain William Talbot from East Machias, Maine, longed for a bit of his home town. The elm trees that line the street of New England-style clapboard houses were brought as seed-lings from Maine and around Cape Horn.

Port Gamble's sawmill and one store are still owned and run by the Pope and Talbot Lumber Company, the largest holders of timberland in western Washington since the mid-19th century. The **General Store** sells a little bit of every-thing, and though most locals don't do their regular shopping there any more, it has become a permanent fixture in the town. The upstairs of the store displays, allegedly, the largest collection of shells in the world.

In a museum just behind the General Store, Pope and Talbot preserves a vital chapter in Pacific Northwest history – the evolution of the Pope and Talbot Lumber Company and a history of lumber mills in the Northwest.

Just outside of town is the **Cyrus T. Walker Nursery and Forest Research Center**, established in 1976, for devel-oping the "super" seedling – trees that could potentially grow 50 percent faster than normal. Tours available Monday through Friday.

A short jaunt east of Port Gamble drops you into **Kingston**. (The ferry to Edmonds leaves from the end of Main Street.) From Kingston take Miller Bay Road to **Suquamish**.

Suquamish Indians: With both pain and pride Native Americans share the rich history of the region with each other – and visitors. While white men boast of settlers' homes dating to the 1850s, In-dian footprints have marked this region for more than 5,000 years.

The Suquamish tribe used to summer on Bainbridge Island. Camping on its shores, they picked and dried berries, caught and smoked fish, and dug clams. In 1855, loggers and homesteaders "bought" Bainbridge from the Suqua-mish. Though Chief Seattle signed the agreement, his tribe was not paid until a few years before his death in 1866.

Victorian homes and churches are left behind in Port Townsend and Port Gamble to tell the stories of the white settlers. Words, unknown symbols and silent stares of the elders are the power-ful substance of the **Suquamish Mu-seum**, off State 305 near Agate Passage. Here, there are Indian photographs and artifacts on display in an elegant sim-plicity. The taped words of Chief Sealth (Seattle) in an exhibition, "The Eyes of Chief Seattle," bring to life the tribe's turbulent past. The show won interna-tional recognition when it traveled to Nantes, in France, as part of Seattle's Sister City exchange.

The beach in front of downtown Suquamish is a good place to stroll and contemplate the past and future of these enduring people. You might want to visit Chief Seattle's grave, the **Old Man House** and the **Suquamish Fish Hatchery** in Suquamish. Chief Seattle Days, honoring the man who appeased relations between Indians and non-Indians, are celebrated during the warm days of August.

Bainbridge Island: Just across Agate Passage on State 305 is **Bainbridge Island**. Bainbridge Islanders consider themselves to be neither of the Navy genre of Kitsap Peninsula nor of the urban mentality of Seattle to which they are so closely knit.

Bainbridge is predominantly a "bed-room" community due to the large num-ber of Seattle commuters. The city is only a half-hour ferry ride away. The island, however, remains primarily ru-ral with quiet communities maintaining their own personalities.

Bainbridge Island is peppered with homes ranging from neatly kept up farm-houses and beach-with-a-view mansions to half-way-finished renovations. The only incorporated community is **Winslow**, with shops adorned with the work of local artisans.

If you don't mind a few hills, bicycling is the best way to poke around the numerous communities on the island. You may bring bikes on the ferry or rent old ones in Winslow. The Chilly Hilly Bike Ride on the last weekend in February marks the official opening day of bicycle riding in Seattle. To celebrate, over a thousand bikers spin, grunt and push their winter-weak bodies around the island. But there are a number of shorter, less demanding rides on Bainbridge. Just pick up a map of the island at the Chamber of Commerce located on Winslow Way.

Fay Bainbridge State Park is the only island park with campsites. With its expansive view of Seattle, the park is a wonderful place to stop for a picnic. On the opposite end of the island is **Fort Ward**, which was established during World War I to protect Bremerton Navy Yard. There aren't any campsites, but the rocky beach at sunset shows off the island's treasure – the views. The Olympic Mountains cast their silhouettes against a deep-purple sky, and the lights of Washington State Ferries reflect across the darkened water.

Make a point of stopping at the galleries and showcases of Bainbridge Island artists. Many of their showrooms are tucked away on back roads without much advertising until you're right there.

Cross back over Agate Pass from Bainbridge Island to the peninsula and you will soon be in **Poulsbo**, dubbed "little Norway." Seated at the tip of **Liberty Bay**, the town and the region strongly resemble the fjords of Norway. A white-spired Lutheran church looks down over the bay, and a wooden breakwater shelters a fleet of fishing boats. Colorful murals painted in the "rosemaling" technique depict Norwegian lifestyles.

Scandinavian crafts, jewelry and collectibles, as well as a variety of Norwegian-style food, are sold in Poulsbo and there are two waterfront parks, **Liberty Bay Park** and the **American Legion Park**, which add to the Norwegian flavor and nautical charm of the town. The Viking Fest in May and the Skandia

Lake Campbell and Simlik Bay from Mount Erie on Fidalgo Island.

Midsommarfest to mark midsummer in June are two popular celebrations.

Central Kitsap: Poulsbo's southern neighbor, unincorporated **Silverdale**, is a growing area. A population growth of around 50 percent from 1982 to 1992 was projected because of the expansion of the much-debated Navy Trident Submarine Base in **Bangor**. (Bangor plans to be home to 10 Tridents.)

Continue south to **Bremerton**. On Bremerton's First Avenue, it is difficult not to find someone involved in the Navy. There is no question that the Puget Sound Naval Shipyard is the county's largest employer. Mothballed and to-be-overhauled Navy vessels of all sizes loom along the shore of **Sinclair Inlet**. Ferries to Seattle leave from Bremerton and nearby Port Orchard (Southworth).

Blake Island just off Southworth is a park that you can get to only by boat. Hiking trails and campsites scattered around the island make it a popular destination for an afternoon sail. **Tillicum Village**, a tourist attraction on the island, features a longhouse replica, salmon barbecue and Native dancing.

The Southernmost Sound: The mainly residential **Vashon Island** offers some delightful walks along its beaches. From **Inspiration Point** there is a powerful view of Mount Rainier. Skiers might be interested to know that K-2 skis are made on Vashon Island. The island is just south of Bainbridge Island, and it is completely dependent on the ferry system. And the islanders plan to keep it that way, even though a bridge has been suggested many times.

Ferries head in three directions from Vashon Island: west to Southworth, east to Fauntleroy, and south to Tacoma. **Gig Harbor**, just west of the Tacoma Narrows Bridge, is a charming, yet unpretentious fishing community an easy one-hour drive from Seattle. While the town offers a wealth of galleries, shops and restaurants, it has avoided the cuteness of tourist-oriented communities. Local sailors have placed this harbor on their charts as one of the most beautiful harbors in the world.

The Gig Harbor Summer Arts Festival, featuring Northwest artists, is held in July. Also during July, the Performancer Circle puts on open-air plays. Go early and bring a picnic (don't forget a sweater). Contact the local Chamber of Commerce for specific dates.

Clams, crab and oysters abound in **Kopachuck State Park** a few miles south of Gig Harbor. Summers are a fun time to scuttle about the low tides. **Raft Island** is within swimming distance; **Deadman's Island** is not (perhaps some have tried?). The undeveloped island is a favorite picnic spot for boaters.

Washington's Capital: Olympia rests at the end of the Sound. What a surprising number of visitors don't know is that Olympia – not Seattle – is the Washington State Capital. When most westerners think of Olympia, they think of beer. Statistically speaking, the Pabst Brewing Company is the most visited attraction in the area.

But Olympia has some other impressive sights. Tours of the **Legislative Building** on Capital Way, which peak during House and Senate sessions, are

Squalicum Harbor, Bellingham.

on weekdays only. On a clear day a climb to the acoustically perfect dome offers spectacular views of Mount Rainier and Mount St Helens.

A wide variety of musical performances and art shows can be found at **Evergreen State College**. Founded in 1971, the college is beautifully designed on rolling hills, natural forests and a salt-water beach. The **State Capital Museum** commemorates Olympia's vicious local struggle to retain the site of the state capital.

The **Pabst Brewery**, off Interstate 5 at exit 103, offers tours during regular working hours, seven days a week. You can watch production on weekdays, when you can actually look in the huge vats and see the beer brewing. On weekends films tell the story. There is always free beer at the end of the tour.

The **Nisqually Delta**, not far from Olympia, is the only delta on the west coast that has not been developed or polluted. Great blue herons, golden eagles and hawks are frequently seen soaring overhead. There are walking trails through meadows and woods. But the best spots are discovered if you can bring a canoe or kayak and explore the many inlets and islands.

The Northeastern Sound: Much of **Edmonds'** heavy traffic is due to the Edmonds-Kingston ferry terminal, an important link to the mainland for residents of the northern Olympic Peninsula. A drive down Sunset Avenue provides a grand opening to Edmonds, with a view of downtown, Puget Sound and the Olympics. North of Edmonds is **Mukilteo**, where the ferry to the southern end of Whidbey Island leaves.

Just north of Mukilteo on I-5, take exit 189 west to **Everett**, the home of the Boeing Company's facility with the largest building in the world by volume. Boeing is the leading commercial and military aircraft manufacturer in the country, and makes for fascinating viewing. Tours are twice a day.

Everett, situated between Whidbey Island and the sharp Cascade peaks, is a premier mill town which contains the area's greatest concentration of mills

Snow blankets Friday Harbor, San Juan Island.

for wood processing, and has miles of smokestacks and floating logs.

Whidbey Island: Consider **Whidbey Island** for a quiet weekend getaway. The island's atmosphere encourages visitors and residents to slow down and savor its delights: its isolated beaches for easy morning walks, wooded trails leading to untouchable views, country roads through farmlands and forests, and many bed-and-breakfast inns.

There are three ways to approach Whidbey Island, the longest island in the lower 48 states. The simplest from Seattle is the Mukilteo–Clinton ferry or from Port Townsend via ferry to Keystone. Both of these rides offer a relaxed and inspiring introduction to the island. From the north, you can drive on to the island past the intimidating cliffs of **Deception Pass**.

Orcas, gray whales and porpoises play in Saratoga Passage off Clinton and Langley, while above, eagles, great blue heron and other birds fly. **Holmes Harbor**, with **Freeland** at its apex, treats marine-hungry appetites to fine sailing, boating and fishing. The vast rolling hills in the center of Whidbey augment the already breathtaking view of the Strait of Juan de Fuca. Once part of the triangle of forts established in 1890 to protect the sound, **Fort Casey** is now a favorite campsite and picnic area.

At least a dozen inns are scattered through the center and south end of Whidbey Island. You can pick from a choice of charming old farmhouses, glass and cedar mansions by the sea, and restored Victorians. The **Inn at Langley** (Langley), **Home by the Sea** (Clinton), **Cliff House** (Freeland) and **The Victorian House** (Coupeville) are only a few.

Coupeville (1892) belongs to the National Historic District, and it is one of the largest such districts in the state. The restored town with its Victorian homes is alive with maritime lore from the days of sea captains and smugglers. The **Captain Whidbey Inn** is a favorite weekend getaway for Seattleites.

Oak Harbor is the busiest town on the island. Just north of the town is

Restored cabin at Spencer Spit State Park, Lopez Island.

Whidbey's largest industry, the **Naval Air Station**, built in 1942. Group tours are by appointment. Two main attractions are the combat conditioning tank (like the one used in the film *An Officer and A Gentleman*), and the squadrons based at Whidbey. A Naval Air Show is presented annually in August.

A magnificent bridge at the rock cliffs of Deception Pass connects Whidbey to **Fidalgo Island** near **Anacortes**, the passageway to the San Juans.

Adjacent to the forest of refineries near Anacortes is the **Padilla Bay National Estuarine Sanctuary** for birds, animals and plants. Bald eagles, blue herons, Dungeness crab, otter and harbor seal are some of its residents. Large beds of eelgrass, the staple food for black brant geese, host 8 percent of the west coast's migratory population.

Anacortes is the front door to the San Juan Islands. It is a good place to pick up groceries if you are going to be camping on the islands. There are many charter companies based in Anacortes. A fine book on cruising the San Juans, *Gunkholing in the San Juans*, by Al Cummings and Jo Bailey-Cummings, describes some of the best waters and coves to explore.

The San Juan Islands: The San Juan Islands are the jewels of Puget Sound. These emerald islands nestle in the intersection of three waterways: Strait of Juan de Fuca, Puget Sound and Strait of Georgia. Whether your first glimpse is by ferry, canoe or sailboat, there is always something compelling about these islands. They have a way of casting a blissful spell over everyone who enters their realm.

The Washington State Ferries stop at four of the 172 islands: Lopez, Shaw, Orcas and San Juan. (Most of the other islands, residential and often privately owned, must be reached by private crafts.) Homes built in secluded coves beckon you to lay claim to a small corner of paradise. In the rain-shadow of the Olympic Peninsula, the islands absorb more sunshine than Seattle. The climate in winter, therefore, is pleasant and in summer it is magnificent.

Washington State Capitol at Olympia.

Musicians and writers, boat builders and fishermen, sewer diggers and potters, corporate retirees and cannabis growers are said to be a few of the odd assortment of Lopez Islanders.

Lopez, the first ferry stop, is a favorite island for many Northwest bicyclists. Not only is everybody friendly – waving is common courtesy on the island – but the island has relatively few hills. So riding can be a pleasure, not just a workout. You can camp on the north end of Lopez at **Odlin County Park** or **Spencer Spit State Park**.

Shark Reef Park has 40 acres (16 hectares) of beautiful but fragile forest to roam. The **Islander Lopez Resort** is a local hot spot during the off seasons; **Bay Cafe** serves wholesome eclectic ethnic food. Other dining choices include **Gina's**, a seafood market and restaurant, and **Gail's**, a deli-cum-restaurant. **MacKaye Harbor Inn**, a bed-and-breakfast inn where you can also get a home-cooked dinner in summer and the **Inn At Swift Bay** are part of the livelihood of this sleepy, pastoral island.

Shaw Island: A habit-clad Franciscan nun operates the ferry dock on **Shaw Island**. Nuns also run "The Little Portion" named after Saint Francis of Assisi's Chapel in Italy. Shaw is mostly a residential island and a gas stop for boaters, so few visitors ever see past the ferry dock nun. **Shaw Island County Park** is the only public beach on the island with eight campsites, picnic facilities and a great rope-swing.

Orcas Island: The early morning fog that often blankets the San Juan Islands is pierced by the tallest mountain in the San Juans – **Mount Constitution** in **Moran State Park** on **Orcas Island**. From the peak, which you can hike, bike, horseback ride or drive to, there is a spectacular panoramic view – 360 degrees of the Canadian mountains, the Cascades, the Olympic Peninsula, the San Juan Islands and Vancouver Island, Canada. Bald eagles often soar above – and below – you.

Moran State Park is a good place to hike even if you are not going to the top of Mount Constitution. There are sev-

Hotel de Haro at Roche Harbor, San Juan Island.

eral lakes and campsites – but if you want to stay, reservations should be made before you arrive on the islands. **Rosario Resort**, near the entrance to Moran State Park, offers impressive accommodation for anyone who prefers luxury to roughing it.

Orcas Island is the biggest and the most mountainous island of the San Juans. **Eastsound**, at mid-point, is also the heart of the island. There are galleries and shops to browse, with items from the island's multitude of cottage industries such as pottery, jewelry, weaving and even boatbuilding. **Bilbo's Festivo** in Eastsound is a favorite Mexican restaurant for locals and visitors. **Christina's**, also in Eastsound, has a more elegant atmosphere and sophisticated menu. On North Beach Road there is a bed-and-breakfast inn called the **Kangaroo House**.

Olga and **Deer Harbor** are two Orcas Island villages with picturesque marinas and select shops. The **Deer Harbor Lodge and Inn** combines a locally popular restaurant and a newly-built inn.

San Juan Island: The commercial center for the entire archipelago is **Friday Harbor** on **San Juan Island**. The marina and village are interesting and fun to wander through. The **San Juan Island Historical Society**, harboring relics of the island's past, and the **Whale Museum** are two fascinating museums in Friday Harbor.

Located in the heart of whale country, the Whale Museum is the only one in the United States that concentrates on the whale, rather than the fast-vanishing practice of whaling.

Orcas, or killer whales, are regular visitors to the waters around San Juan in summer. Watch them from the newly designated whalewatching park – **Lime Kiln Park**.

The hostel-style **Elite Hotel** on First Street in Friday Harbor is a favorite for bicyclists. The **San Juan Inn** is a simple place, just a few blocks from the ferry terminal. Reservations for accommodations on the island, except for the Elite Hotel, should be made well in advance for summer.

The music room of the Robert Moran House, Rosario Resort on Orcas Island.

On either end of the island are the camps from the "famous" Pig War, which actually is neither famous nor is it a war. Briefly, it went like this: in 1839, Lyman Cutlar, a Yank, killed a pig that belonged to an Englishman. At that time both British and Americans inhabited the island. This incident sparked a conflict that had been ready to start for a long time. Both countries sent troops in to decide the fate of the island. After a summer of soldiers, cannons and warships, without a bullet being shot, the bored countries flipped a penny. The San Juans became a part of the United States. Both the English Camp and the American Camp still exist, now popular areas to visit.

On the northwest end of the island, **Roche Harbor** is an elegant harbor complete with cobblestone roads and rose bushes. It can be enjoyed on a brief stroll or savored during a stay at the historic **Hotel de Haro**.

Duck Soup Inn on Roche Harbor Road has an adventurous and tasty Mediterranean menu that changes daily. Even if you can't stay longer, at least wait for the sunset, for it is always spectacular.

The lush tidal flats of the Skagit River are renowned as one of the largest flower bulb-producing areas in the world. An easy spring bike trip – the **Skagit Flats** are really flat – is the best way to see the flower-laden area. Yellow daffodils bloom in March. Tulips are best in April, but check a local paper, for the peak day varies annually.

Pry yourself off your bike in **La Conner** for a look around. Although this used to be a major trading center now it is just home to people who love to live there. Northwest artists like Mark Tobey, Morris Graves and Guy Anderson have captured the pastoral landscapes of La Conner. The **Black Swan** restaurant on First and Washington, well-known from Seattle to Vancouver, specializes in seafood.

From January to April, thousands of snow geese from Siberia winter in the **Skagit Wildlife Recreational Area**. When they leave, all 24,000 of them fly off within a span of 24 hours. (Take-off is no earlier than April 17 and no later than May 5.) Bald eagles also gather here during the cold months, one of the largest gatherings of eagles in the contiguous 48 states. Visitors are asked to use binoculars and remain on the roadside turn-offs.

The well-known Chuckanut Drive to **Bellingham** hugs the coastline, offering spectacular views of the San Juan Islands and **Samish Bay**. The **Oyster Creek Inn** and **The Oyster Bar**, with a view of Samish Bay, are two good stops along the drive. Bellingham is home to **Western Washington State University**. The school is located on **Sehome Hill**, and not only is the campus itself beautiful, but the hill it's perched on offers a panoramic view.

During June the Lummi Indians celebrate the Lummi Indian Stommish, which is similar to the potlatch. It is held on Lummi Island, a seven-minute ferry ride from **Gooseberry Point** in the Lummi Indian Reservation. A 7-mile (11-km) road travels the perimeter of the island, making an easy bike ride through serene countryside.

Left, totem pole carved by Paul N. Luvera Jr of Anacortes. **Right,** Victorian home in Bellingham.

As the sun warms the air from spring through the summer, the ferry riders gradually migrate to the upper deck. The sun softens the cool sea breeze, while hands grasp a well-worn novel and eyes follow the flight of a seagull. The sharp peaks of the Olympic Mountains glisten in the ferry's wake. The Cascade Mountains sink behind the approaching Seattle skyline.

Huge container ships from the Orient unload and load, in the city's port, as the ferry docks at Colman Dock in downtown Seattle.

boat to return. The importance of the missed hour quietly dissolves into a fine cup of early-morning coffee.

The Washington State Ferry System is a vital link for both native Northwesterners and visitors to the Olympic Peninsula and Pacific Coast. A glance at a map of Puget Sound will show you why ferries are an important mode of travel around the Sound. Thousands of inlets wrinkle its jagged coastline, making travel, other than by sea, not only costly but also time-consuming.

Some inhabitants of the Pacific Northwest make this trip twice a day.

Commuters rushing to the ferry with unbrushed hair and teeth in the early morning are a common sight at the Bainbridge Island ferry terminal. The minute the ferry departs, leaving behind the one sweaty body who did not run quite fast enough – or wake up early enough – the hurried pace is immediately slowed to the lull of the boat cradled in the waves.

Ferry commuters are a rare breed with a gentle perspective on life. The stranded person still on the ferry dock turns to the nearest cafe and settles behind a paper to wait for the

Ferries come in all sizes, depending on the route. Many of them are small, carrying just 55–65 cars with limited passenger seats on the main deck.

However, the ferries from downtown Seattle to Bainbridge Island and Bremerton seat 2,000 and carry 206 cars. The main cabin has a large, comfortable lounge area and a fast-food restaurant offering beer, wine and coffee. Directly above the passenger cabin is a sundeck, which is equipped with a solarium for riders who want to enjoy the fresh air during winter.

Most of the ferries – except the boats to the San Juan Islands – leave every hour during the day, but less frequently at night. However, you should check ferry schedules at one of the 20 terminals or call the Washington State Ferry System for information. The ferry to the San Juan Islands leaves five times a day during winter and more often in summer. Rates on all ferries increase slightly during the summer months.

The most convenient ferry terminal is Colman Dock on Seattle's waterfront where ferries leave to Bremerton on the Olympic Peninsula and Winslow on Bainbridge Island. The Bainbridge route is the most direct way to the northern end of the Olympic Peninsula. State Highway 305 crosses over to the peninsula at Agate Passage on the

Victoria, British Columbia. Two and a half hours on the jetfoil takes you past snowcapped mountains to elegant Victoria.

The ferry to the San Juan Islands from Anacortes, an hour and a half north of Seattle, is another special trip. Floating through the San Juan Islands is like sifting emeralds through your fingers. Each island touches you as if it were paradise regained. The ferry weaves through the labyrinth of 172 forested islands, past unpretentious homes hidden in coves, perhaps too close to civilization to be paradise, but still too far to touch.

The ferry landings on Lopez, Shaw and Orcas Island have few if any tourist facilities. On San Juan Island, the ferry docks at Friday

western side of the island. On clear, warm days, ferry travelers often spend the entire day basking in the sun on the upper deck, enjoying the views. Jump ship in Winslow, and spend an hour in the waterfront park, or try Pegasus, a comfortable coffee house which roasts a variety of beans on the premises. The Streamliner Diner, something of a Bainbridge institution, is regarded by locals as the only place for breakfast.

Even better than a short hop across the Sound is a trip on the *Victoria Clipper* to

Above, the Washington State Ferry and a cruise boat cross routes in busy Puget Sound.

Harbor, a small village of quaint restaurants, hotels and shops. (Reservations for accommodations, particularly during the summer, must be made months in advance.)

The Washington State Ferry System is continuing to grow. It is now using a few passenger-only catamarans which are smoother, faster, and more efficient in fuel consumption than the ferries that already skim across Puget Sound. The ferry system's search for better, faster boats is indicative of the increasing growth on the west side of the Sound and the concern to improve what is already one of the best water-transportation systems in the world.

SEA KAYAKING

Sea kayaking is an ideal way to experience the Northwest's abundance of marine life. When you are out in your kayak, you are sitting down in the water, not on it. You are at eye level and arm's length from the sea creatures. You can explore secluded coves and cliffs populated by a vast array of wildlife, a world inaccessible to the larger boats speeding by.

The Puget Sound area and its adjacent waters are a mecca of gulfs, bays, coves, straits, sounds, channels, passes, passages, inlets, arms and river deltas. In short, this is a sea kayaker's paradise.

Sea kayaking is both a historically significant and technologically appropriate method of transportation in the Pacific Northwest. The first sea kayaks were built by the Northwest's first human inhabitants about 10,000 years ago. Aleuts and Eskimos traveled as far south as San Diego in their slender craft made of waterproofed animal skins stretched over light wood frames.

Although the essence of kayaking remains unchanged, the technology has improved the kayaks themselves. Today's sea-touring kayaks are made from fiberglass and other plastics. A technique known as "vacuum bagging" allows fiberglass kayaks to be sea kayaks – extremely light, durable, self-propelled, non-polluting, efficient, economical and beautiful.

Sea kayaking is not just a sport for daring young adventurers. The ease and comfort of paddling these boats makes it possible for anyone in average physical condition to enjoy an hour-, day-, or even a week-long trip. Sea kayaks are sturdy and stable, and are designed to carry up to 200 pounds of gear and provisions.

There are kayaks that can seat one, two, or three kayakers, depending on the model. And they are unequalled in making the waters accessible. A sea kayak can launch or go ashore anywhere there are 2 inches (6 cm) of water. They are inexpensive, easily carried by hand and on car racks, and require no trailer, moorage, taxes, license, or fuel.

Right, a traditional canoe in use, precursor of the light modern sea kayak.

Sea kayak tours: The Puget Sound is home to a number of sea kayak tour companies. Each offers a variety of affordable trips, designed for both the novice and experienced kayaker.

Most trips are geared toward the beginner; the guides give full instruction before the journey begins and make sure that all participants are comfortable at handling the boats. Excursions range from one-day tours around Seattle's Lake Union to week-long adventures in the San Juan Islands, Washington's

interior waterways, Canada, and southwest Alaska. The San Juans are a popular destination for many kayakers.

The Northwest Outdoor Center, on Lake Union, is a great starting point for day-long excursions. Just rent a boat, launch it off the center's dock, and off you go. Rental kayaks and equipment such as life jackets, paddles and car racks are inexpensive and available by the hour, day, weekend, or week.

An urban day tour offered by the center is a great way to learn the basics of sea kayaking and see Seattle from a unique point of view. The Lake Union tour circumnavigates this diverse city lake and includes a stop for refreshments and a history lesson. There are also moonlight tours around Lake Union and dinner tours to lakeside restaurants.

Trips in the San Juan Islands are a specialty of three companies: Northern Lights Expeditions, Northwest Sea Ventures and Outdoor Odysseys.

All three companies tailor their trips to accommodate the predicted weather and sea-currents and to maximize seasonal opportunities to see wildlife. Camping and kayaking equipment, meals and full instructions are provided, and no experience is necessary. Trips require pre-registration; call or write a few months in advance. Sea kayaking in the San Juans will give you a taste of the best the Northwest has to offer.

THE WASHINGTON COAST

The Olympic Peninsula juts out like an oversized thumb from the fist of Washington State as if it were hitching west. But there's no further west to go; this is the frontier's end. From here, America looks out across the Pacific Ocean toward Asia.

Along the outer length of the thumb, the wilderness meets the sea in a jumble of coves and bays, beaches and foaming breakers. Some of this remote, storm-swept shoreline is Native American land where travel is restricted, and 50 miles (80 km) of the coast is national park, accessible only on foot. The rest is beach and bay. In summer, it's a paradise beyond compare.

Vacationers flock to the coast to admire the snow-crowned Olympic Mountains standing against blue sky on the east and the sparkling Pacific Ocean reaching to the horizon on the west. In winter, it's a different story, when rain, the main feature of the region, falls down from the sky relentlessly and constantly. The hardy locals settle in to wait out the gray, bleak months, knowing spring will bring some of the most beauteous of nature's bounty. The snow-melt will cascade in falls down steep cliffs, the tree-blanketed hills will glow emerald-green, the rivers will leap with fish, and the sea will dance in several benign shades of blue.

The upper edge of the peninsula-thumb, protected by vast Vancouver Island, is tamer. Here the waters of the Strait of Juan de Fuca roll gently to rocky shores and quiet fishing resorts. Despite change and development, much of this Olympic-shadowed region looks just as it did when early explorers claimed it for Spain or for England, depending upon who was doing the discovering. That was two centuries ago, when sailing ships sought routes to the region's wealth of resources.

Cape Disappointment: In 1788, a British fur trader named John Meares, after

Preceding pages: **Point-No-Point** **on the Kitsap Peninsula.** **Below, Cape Disappointment**

many attempts to pilot his ship across the treacherous Columbia River, gave up and, looking across the tossing surf at the rain-lashed, gloomy headland north of the river, named it **Cape Disappointment**. The name still seems appropriate to those visitors who seek balmy weather and discover only endless, bone-chilling rain. However, even the storms have their attractions here. Watching the wind-whipped waves from one of several overlooks or from the **Lewis and Clark Interpretive Center** gives a certain kind of thrill of its own.

The center, perched on a cliff in **Fort Canby State Park**, exhibits actual journal entries and displays that explain the secrets of the expedition of 1804–6. The intrepid explorers ended their historic and adventure-filled journey at this spot. Also in the state park are two lighthouses, one on North Head and one on Cape Disappointment. The latter, built in 1856, is the oldest in the Pacific Northwest. It can be reached by a short, woodsy path leading from the **Coast Guard Lifeboat Station and Surf**

Mussel shells in a Washington Coast tidal zone.

School, the only one of its kind in the world, which teaches boat handling and rescue operations in the rough surf.

North of the Cape is the village of **Ilwaco**, where there is no question about the purpose of life – fishing. And salmon fishing represents life at its fullest. Visitors swarm to quiet Ilwaco in season, although it is much calmer now than it was at the turn of the century when knives and rifles often had the last word about who owned the rights to fishing grounds. Today's tourists find charter services like Pacific Salmon and Tidewind Charters eager to take them out to sea in search of the elusive silver and king salmon.

There aren't as many charter crafts bobbing at the harbor wharves as there used to be in the unregulated days of a sea that swarmed with salmon, but sports fishermen usually catch their limits. They also turn to the challenge of hooking the hefty halibut, tuna or sturgeon. After proudly posing for a trophy photo, the satisfied fisherman heads for the **Portside Cafe** to drink coffee with the regulars, brag about the day's catch, and gaze at the harbor through steamy windows while dreaming of what might end up on the end of his line tomorrow.

When the seas are rough or fishing palls, a dry-land attraction is the **Ilwaco Heritage Museum**, which has exhibitions illustrating the history of fish, forests, oysters and clams in the area.

Long Beach Peninsula: The due-north road from Ilwaco, State Highway 103, runs up a long, skinny strip of land called the **Long Beach Peninsula**. In the late 19th century, the peninsula was a summer playground for Portlanders. They would ride a steamer down the Columbia river and then board a train that ran to **Seaview**, at the peninsula's base, on a narrow-gauge track.

In 1881, Seaview's original promoter, Jonathan Stout, had big plans for the little town, but during the depression of 1893, his hotel was destroyed by fire and his real estate sales to Portland speculators fell through.

However, Seaview is still a favored holiday destination. It has an historic inn, old-fashioned cottages and a wistful hint of halcyon summers gone by. It also has some of the best clam chowder in the west, served at **My Mom's Pies**. (The pies are fine, too.)

Seaside attractions: The economy of Long Beach Peninsula is based on three industries: tourism, cranberries and oysters. Like many seaside communities, the town of **Long Beach**, just north of Seaview, leans heavily on tourism with a carnival touch. It has go-carts and bumper cars, kiddy rides, miniature golf and a bizarre museum that displays an unlikely assortment of shells, antiques and sideshow creatures.

In Long Beach, visitors can see the "world's largest frying pan," rent mopeds, drive on the beach, play golf, and participate in one of the biggest kite festivals in the country. The August festival includes competitive events for handcrafted kites, children's kites, stunt kites and illuminated kites, all of them soaring above the sea during a week-long celebration. The major attraction, though, is the beach itself. A wide stretch of uninterrupted sand extends the full 28-mile (45-km) length of the peninsula; it's claimed to be the "world's longest beach."

Backed by rolling, grass-covered dunes, the hard-packed sand is open to vehicles; fortunately, there is room for all on this shoreline. Boating, beach-combing and surf-fishing, with clam necks as bait, are popular pastimes, but when freshwater fish is the only kind that will satisfy, anglers head for **Loomis Lake** and its tasty rainbow trout.

Blooms and berries: Flower lovers seek out **Clarke's Rhododendron Nursery** on Sandridge Road. The 15-acre (6-hectare) nursery is one of the largest in the country specializing in rhododendrons; in spring and summer, it's a rainbow-like forest of colorful blossoms.

North of town on Pioneer Road, a research station, jointly supported by the US Department of Agriculture and Washington State University, studies cranberries. Since 1883, when newcomers from Massachusetts noticed the area's strong resemblance to Cape Cod, cranberries have been grown commercially in the area.

About 550 acres (223 hectares), yielding about 40 percent of the statewide total of berries, are now under cultivation on the peninsula. That's a lot of cranberry sauce. Because of it, there are cranberry festivals, a flag (the Banner of the Bogs) and guided tours of the research center that show how the tart red berry is grown and harvested.

Oyster harvest: The region's best-known product, however, is the oyster, as the mounds of shell piled near wharves would indicate. Oystering on **Willapa Bay** is a $20 million-a-year industry that began in the mid-1800s with the discovery of the delicate *ostrea lurida*.

The small, native oyster was in great demand, especially in San Francisco during gold rush days, and the beds were soon depleted. An observer at the time wrote that "I have seen forty sailing boats at one time loaded with oysters…two and three schooners loading at one time, each of which would carry from 4,000 to 5,000 bushels of oysters." Japanese oyster larvae were imported to save the industry.

Today the larvae are still shipped in, planted and harvested as the superbly flavorful Willapa Bay oyster. Canneries, a hatchery and shippers are located at the protected harbor of **Nahcotta**, and tours of the plants may be arranged. All oyster beds on the Willapa Bay tidelands are privately owned; oysters may not be collected by the public.

Across the bay from Nahcotta is the largest estuarine island on the Pacific Coast. Heavily forested, home to bears and elk, the **Willapa National Wildlife Refuge** can be reached only by boat. Information on getting to the island, where there are a few camping sites, may be obtained from the refuge's headquarters, 12 miles (19 km) north of Ilwaco on US Highway 101.

The Long Beach Peninsula's north-ernmost settlement is **Oysterville**, a drowsy village on the marshlands of the bay. The once-booming oyster center has long since been bypassed by change, though it has gained recent renown through the writings of historian and wordsmith Willard Espy, a descendant of the town's early settlers.

To take a walking tour of Oysterville's historic homes and churches is to step into another century. The quiet streets, the sighing trees and the handsome structures still standing seem to whisper of a livelier day, when a plate of oysters from this tranquil bay sold in San Francisco for a coin worth two and a half $20 gold pieces.

Free concerts are given on Sunday afternoons during the summer at the church in the National Historic District.

The flocks at Leadbetter Point: Finally, Long Beach Peninsula is tipped by **Leadbetter Point**, where a hundred species of birds have been sighted during migratory periods. Part of the point is closed to all entry from April through August, to protect the nesting snowy plover. **Leadbetter Point State Park Natural Area**, on the bay side of the tip, is open to visitors, however. Located 3 miles (5 km) north of **Oysterville**, at the end of Stackpole Road, the grassland, marshes, low forest and sand are particularly popular in the summer with beachcombers, hikers and birdwatchers.

Long Beach Peninsula forms the western shore of Willapa Bay. The eastern side has its own peaceful appeal, with sheltered waters for small boats and good fishing in the creeks and rivers that run into the bay here. Steelhead, sea cutthroat and salmon swim the **Naselle River**, whose quiet waters make pleasant kayaking and canoeing.

US 101 turns east where the Willapa River joins the bay, wending toward the shipping and mill towns of **South Bend** and **Raymond**. The main attraction for visitors to South Bend is the impressive **Pacific County Courthouse**. The courthouse, dubbed a "gilded palace of extravagance" when it was built in 1911, contains artful carvings and murals and an illuminated stained glass dome of green, lavender and gold.

Visitors to South Bend may also tour the modern **Coast Oyster Company**. The Visitors' Center in the heart of town supplies information. Four miles away, the lumber mills of Raymond process timber as they have done since the town's inception. But times have changed;

From the lumber-boom years: the sawmill at Port Gamble.

where there were once 20 mills in a once-booming port, only two are now in operation. Timber is still the economic backbone of the community, as it is in many parts of the northwest, but with decreasing prices and demand, the industry no longer reigns supreme.

The sad tale of Willie Keil: Most highway maps show "Willie Keil's Grave" near Raymond, and many a traveler has wondered who Willie was and why he's mentioned on the map. The answer is a sad tale. In 1855, 19-year-old Willie Keil, about to head west from Missouri, died of malaria. His distraught father, having promised his son he could lead a wagon train, built a tin-lined coffin, filled it with whiskey, and carried his son's body across the plains to be buried at the family's new homestead. The grave is a historical site.

State Highway 105 travels west, paralleling Willapa Bay to the coast, and **Shoalwater Indian Reservation**. A sliver of a finger of land that pokes way out into the bay is called **Toke Point**, named after a local Indian chief.

The Shoalwater Indians who lived on Toke Point were a peaceable group, who had easy access to a rich bounty of seafood and game. These Native Americans, like so many before and after them, were virtually destroyed by smallpox when the white man's disease moved in with the settlers.

The town of **Tokeland** remains close to its 19th-century roots. Little changes in the drowsy, picturesque village on the point. It's a good spot for the gentle sports of birdwatching, canoeing and crabbing from the dock. The town has an RV park, an antique shop and a bakery. A museum that displayed fine Indian artifacts for a time has turned to bingo, but the building's carved facade and adjacent totem still merit a look.

The old **Tokeland Hotel**, built in 1885 and listed on the National Register of Historic Sites, is open for both dining and lodging.

Cranberries along the coast: There's no avoiding cranberries in this part of the world. For 12 miles (19 km) along State 105, from Tokeland to Westport, the

The village of La Conner, shadowed by snow-covered Mount Baker.

cranberry is grown, harvested, processed and honored with special events. In June, the Cranberry Blossom Festival celebrates the shrub's pink blossoms, and growers choose a King of the Bog. Visitors may see exhibitions on the industry's history, buy artwork from sidewalk booths, and watch athletic contests. In July, the Grayland Beach and Bog Jog takes runners on a winding course along roads lined with cranberry bogs, and thence to the beach.

Large state parks with excellent camping facilities flank the town of **Grayland** (a lot of places in the Pacific Northwest are named Gray, not for the weather but for Robert Gray, the British sea captain who explored the region in the late 1700s). On the south is **Grayland Beach State Park**, which has 60 campsites, a self-guided nature trail and 4,000 feet (1,220 meters) of ocean frontage.

A few miles north of town is **Twin Harbors State Park**, with 332 campsites among the salal and ferns. The **Shifting Sands Nature Trail** meanders through this woodsy area over the dunes and onto the beach.

Visitors who continue on to **Westport**, at the end of a short arm of land that marks the entrance to **Grays Harbor**, are rewarded with a view of a marina filled with colorful fishing boats, both sport and commercial.

This is the newest part of the town; 50 years ago, the dock area and the land on which it stands did not exist. It was created gradually by nature and by the dredging done by the Port of Grays Harbor. It's a busy place now. Westport calls itself the salmon capital of the world, a title that is disputed by Ilwaco and by Waukegan, Illinois, but is indicative of the thousands of fish that are caught here every season

Charter boats are available to fish for tuna, halibut, ling cod, red snapper, sea bass and, from May to September, salmon. Commercial trawlers and crabbers also work out of Westport basin.

Salmon fishing: A 1,000-foot (305-meter) walking pier was recently built at Westport which allows the non-boater an opportunity to fish, and the stroller to enjoy the view. Every spring, Westport's fishing community rears tiny salmon (fingerlings), obtained from a state hatchery, in a net pen in the boat basin. The fish are fed by hand for two months and then released to the ocean. Two years later, those fish return to the boat basin, seeking a place to spawn. Since spawning must take place in freshwater, they soon leave the salty basin, but before they swim out in search of a freshwater stream, some are caught by people fishing from the pier.

A blue steel observation tower stands at one end of the boat basin, on Westhaven Drive. Visitors may climb it for views of boats at sea, freighters carrying cargo, and whales during their migration periods. Several charter companies feature half-day whale watching trips that allow their passengers to see the 40-ton mammals at close range.

Splashing out: Since Westport's main attraction is its fishing, the splashing, lively marina is lined with motels and restaurants and charter companies. However, non-fishers find plenty to do. At **Westhaven State Park**, also known as **Agate Beach**, collecting shells, driftwood and agates is, as they say locally, "nature's own tranquilizer." Tours of the Westport Lighthouse may be arranged through the Coast Guard.

Observing offshore birds such as the pink-footed shearwater and the arctic tern has been a popular pastime since the Audubon Society began field trips here 20 years ago. Birdwatchers climb into boats and head for the birds' resting and feeding spots. Following commercial fishing vessels assures success, for clouds of birds circle them in search of tasty scraps.

The old **Westport Coast Guard Station** has been refurbished as a historic maritime museum, preserving mementoes of Westport's past. Old photographs and fishing gear, shipwreck remnants and Indian artifacts are displayed in the white, Nantucket-style station that faces the harbor.

Westporters and Graylanders are festive folk, seemingly ready to celebrate almost anything – even orthopedics. There's an annual Seafood Bash, a Saltwater Festival, the Blessing of the Fleet, a Driftwood Show, Salmon and Bottom Fishing Derbies, Glass Ball Month, Fabulous Fourth Fireworks, and, yes, an Orthopedic Bazaar.

During the summer months, a passenger ferry runs between Westport and **Hoquiam**, on the northeast side of the harbor, and negotiations are underway to establish a ferry service to Ocean Shores. It's a short journey as the crow flies, but a long one (50 miles/80 km) on the road all the way around the harbor.

Those driving up the coast take State 105 east toward the twin cities of Aberdeen and Hoquiam, shipping and milling ports at the eastern tip of triangular Grays Harbor.

Aberdeen, home of the clamburger and the Chokers (the Grays Harbor Community College team), is a sizable city with numerous waterways and a pioneer museum in the old armory. At **Bowerman Basin**, adjacent to the Hoquiam-Aberdeen Airport, birdwatchers enjoy the spectacle of thousands of resting and feeding birds during their annual migrations. **Hoquiam's Castle**,

built in 1897 by a local lumber baron, is a historic attraction that is open to visitors for tours in the summer. A 600-piece crystal chandelier and a rosewood grand piano are among the elegant furnishings in the red mansion on a hill above town.

Another notable Hoquiam landmark is **Polson's Museum** located on US 101. Once a 26-room mansion, it now houses historic memorabilia of the Grays Harbor area.

An Eden for slugs: A side excursion on this coastal trip is a visit to the hamlet of **Elma**, about 20 miles (32 km) east of the harbor on US 12. Site of the annual Grays Harbor County Fair, Elma is even more renowned for its unique July festival – the Annual Elma Slug Festival. With parades, slug races and booths, the event draws thousands to the spoof in a climate that is Eden for slugs.

Back at Grays Harbor, State 115 curves around the northern rim of the bay, through heavily logged and replanted forest, ending at the coast and a wide, flat peninsula running southward.

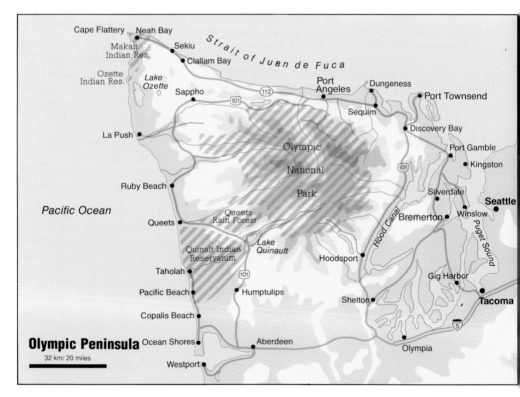

Ocean Shores, begun in the 1960s as a sprawling resort development with nightclubs and wide boulevards, has backed away from that ambitious approach and is now an area of summer homes scattered over the dunes. There are several motels and restaurants, an 18-hole golf course and opportunities to fish, clam and beachcomb.

At the end of the peninsula, on the bay side, is the **Ocean City State Park Marine Interpretive Center**, which describes and displays the local area's marine life.

North of Ocean Shores and close to the highway is pretty, 112-acre (45-hectare) **Ocean City State Park**. The forested park has numerous campsites and trailer hookups, and it's full of waterways for canoeing and kayaking.

North into wilderness: The drive north, up State 109, heads for the more remote portion of the coastline, and wilderness draws closer. The sand on the beaches is a fine, dark gray, piled with driftwood and alive with seagulls. Fog and mist drift through the landscape, muting the sky, the dark green forests and any pretense of civilization.

Pacific Beach, a rundown village off the highway, offers camping facilities in a state park; otherwise it is mostly a naval facility and center for oceanographic research. Its northern neighbor, **Moclips**, has a more prosperous appearance, with homes and resorts and restaurants on cliffs overlooking the sea.

Eleven miles (18 km) beyond Moclips on the coast is **Taholah**, an Indian village, that is the last settlement accessible by car. Beyond it lies the **Quinault Indian Reservation**, where travel is restricted. Some maps show a coastal road through the reservation, but it is not passable. Visitors may fish on the reservation with a permit from the tribe, and sometimes the Indians, expert fishermen and boaters themselves, will take interested tourists for canoe trips up the **Quinault River**.

Crystal Sampson, great-granddaughter of a Quinault chief, was one of ten born in her grandmother's cabin in Taholah. At the age of 19, she left the

The coast at
Long Beach.

reservation and moved to Portland to attend business school. Now she's back in Taholah as health manager at the Human Resources Center. "We have problems here," she says. "It's a matter of self-esteem, not money. As wards of the government, Indians lose pride in themselves and their culture. Some want to make dugout canoes, yes, but most of the young are more interested in fiberglass racers." She smiles and shrugs. "I don't know what the answer is, but we're working on it."

To continue up the coast, travelers must retrace their route to Moclips and head northeast on the partially-paved Moclips/Olympic Highway, or go further south to Pacific Beach and drive the longer, but fully paved, route to US 101.

On its way north, 101 passes by **Lake Quinault**, a lovely, cold blue lake with handsome **Lake Quinault Lodge** at its edge. In this rain forest, tree limbs are thick with dripping moss and ferns, and groves of cedar, fir and hemlock are so dense they appear as a bright wall of green. A short distance from the lodge

and ranger station, one may see bald eagles, wild swans and Roosevelt elk.

Where highway meets coast: Then the highway angles west again, toward the mouth of the **Queets River** and the long strip of national park that borders the coast. This short segment is the only place where US 101 touches the coast in Washington.

At **Kalaloch** (pronounced Klay-lock), a lodge with cabins and a restaurant overlooks Kalaloch Creek and the sea. It's a popular destination. **Kalaloch Lodge** is booked months in advance by vacationers eager to hit the beaches in search of razor clams, surf smelt, perch and summer sea cutthroat. There's also a campground nearby.

Seven beaches, each a short hike from the highway, are within 6 miles (10 km) of Kalaloch. It's easy to walk from one to the next, but visitors should first obtain a tide table, available free at information centers and businesses, which tells the daily lows and highs of the surf. Tide tables are advisable before spending time on any Washington

Rosario Straits and the Deception Pass Bridge.

160

beaches. Outgoing tides are dangerous for swimmers, and incoming tides have caused more than one explorer to be marooned on a rock.

Shipwrecked sailors: Off the coast lies **Destruction Island**, so named because sailors were massacred by Indians near here in the 19th century. The history of this wild shoreline is full of harrowing tales. At times, especially when spruces creak in the wind and waves resound on the rocks, the entire coast seems haunted by ghosts of shipwrecked sailors and warring Indians and settlers.

At **Ruby Beach**, famed for its spectacular ocean views, US 101 again turns inland. The next place the traveler can drive toward the coast is just past Forks, where a 15-mile (24-km) road follows the Soleduck and Quillayute rivers to diminutive **LaPush**.

The village is friendly, pretty and quiet, even when jammed with summer tourists. It fronts a lovely charcoal gray beach strewn with driftwood – the "bones of the forest, picked clean by the sea," as the descriptive panels say. High breakers roll in from the northwest, and the mournful moan of warning buoys is constant. Tall offshore rocks, known as seastacks, form wildlife refuges, sanctuary for puffins, murres, guillemots and auklets.

Thomas ("Ribs") Penn, last of the dugout canoe masters, lives in LaPush. A member of the Quileute tribe, he builds dugouts of red and yellow cedar for the love of it. Penn learned the traditional craft from his grandfather and father. " I still talk to them," he says. "If I have a problem building, I take a walk and I ask my father in the Indian way. When I come back, I always know." His dark brown eyes are fathomless. "My people were so talented. Give them a piece of wood, they could do anything with it. But now, no one's interested. Maybe my grandson. He watches. If he comes back from California, maybe he'll build, too."

LaPush is busy and festive in August, with its **Quileute Days** celebration that features, among other attractions, dugout canoe races and a parade. Folks

"Seastacks," natural architecture of the coast, near Rialto Beach.

come from miles around, although in the evening, places to eat, much less what might pass as nightlife, can be fairly hard to come by. Across the mouth of the Quileute River from the town is **Rialto Beach**, a noted camping and fishing area.

Just south of LaPush is a beach that is one of the most picturesque among numerous scenic spots. It can be reached by a 1-mile (2-km) trail which has a long series of angled wooden steps where the path is most steep and muddy. A seastack and rugged **Teawhit Head** are landmarks that make the beach especially popular with photographers.

Lake Ozette: The next accessible part of the coast (other than by foot) is at **Lake Ozette**. To reach the lake from LaPush, travelers must drive back to US 101, north to **Sappho**, and take an unpaved road for 10 miles (16 km) to State 112. At Sekiu, another gravel road runs south toward Ozette.

The lake, one of Washington's largest, is one point of a three-path trail triangle. Each of the two trails to the shore is 3 miles (5 km) long, and each is cedar boardwalk all the way. Tennis shoes are preferable to vibram-soled hiking boots on these slick plank paths. The third trail borders the sea between Cape Alava and Sand Point. **Cape Alava** is the westernmost point in the 48 connected states and is the site of an important archaeological dig. A 500-year-old Makah Indian village, inundated and preserved by an ancient mudflow, has been partially resurrected under the supervision of Washington State University. The dig is now closed, but artifacts removed from the site are on display in a Neah Bay museum.

Sand Point, at the end of another of the triangle of trails, has a shore with teeming tidepools and superb scenery. If the hike is made as a loop, it's a 9-mile (14-km) venture that demands exertion. The ranger station at Ozette has detailed information.

The return to State 112 is a half-hour drive; from there it's 13 miles (20 km), west to **Neah Bay**, home of the Makah Indian tribe. One of the best museums in

Old shipwreck along a wilderness beach.

the Northwest is located on the east edge of town: the **Makah Research and Cultural Center**. It contains well-displayed artifacts from the dig at Lake Ozette and some replicas made by local craftspeople. There's a whaling canoe with harpoons and details on the methods Makah hunters used. There are baskets, clothing, implements, hooks and tools, and intricate weavings of cedar, bird feathers and animal hair. Totem poles include a Thunderbird with eyes and beak that could be moved by manipulating strings.

Neah Bay itself is a noted fishing center and has several motels, boat launchings and charter fishing companies. The town, which is a part of the Makah Indian Reservation, devotes the last weekend in August to Makah traditions. Salmon bakes, costumed dances, canoe races and parades are held in honor of the culture that has changed but still lives.

The most northwestern point: By following the signs to **Cape Flattery**, the determined traveler can stand on the northwesternmost point of the contiguous United States. It's a muddy hike to the tip of the cape, but the view is magnificent. Great waves crash deep into cliff caves that have been carved by centuries of such action. The cape was named in 1778 by the British explorer James Cook, who spied "a small opening which flattered us with the hopes of finding an harbour…On this account I called the point of land to the north of it Cape Flattery."

Tatoosh Island, directly off the cape, has a picturesque lighthouse. The island is presently owned by the US Geological Survey and is used for oceanographic studies. Once it was the home and burial ground of Makah Indians.

South of Cape Flattery, another of the state's scenic wonders borders national park land. **Shi-Shi** (pronounced Shy Shy) **Beach**, 3 miles (5 km) of sand between **Portage Head** and **Point of Arches**, is considered Washington's true wilderness beach. Getting there demands a rugged walk, but the hiker is rewarded with a dramatic spectacle. Great jagged, offshore rocks and a smooth beach with myriad tidepools make this spot a superb destination for the visitor seeking unspoiled beauty.

The peninsula's upper rim: The drive back from Neah Bay, east on State 112, passes close to the gentler waters of the Strait of Juan de Fuca.

Protected by the huge landmass of Vancouver Island, the surf crawls to shore, rather than crashing, as it does on the western side. Eagles are often seen on tree branches or soaring above the water. Smoke from woodstoves drifts through the air over every village. Farms and cattle dot the peaceful landscape, and the Canadian island across the strait looms hazily green and peaked with frost on the horizon.

At **Sekiu**, a harbor-facing community nestled against a hill, visitors may see scuba divers looking for abalone and octopus. The village has more boats than houses, as this is fishing country, and a base where vacationers return year after year.

There are numerous spots along the shore road to stop for fishing, camping,

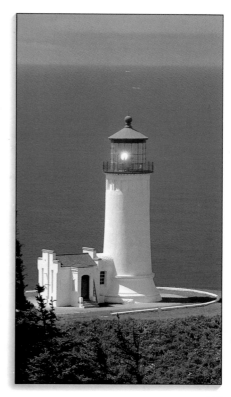

North Head Lighthouse, near Ilwaco.

picnicking and scenery-admiring. Their names tell their stories: **Pysht** (a Clallam Indian term meaning "wind from all directions"), **Pillar Point**, **Jimmy-Come-Lately**. With a more prosaic name, the county park at **Salt Creek** is one of the main recreational areas along the peninsula's upper rim. The park's 196 acres (79 hectares) were originally used as a World War II harbor defense site. Called **Fort Hayden**, the military reservation concealed heavily camouflaged, bomb-proofed batteries.

After the war, Clallam County purchased the military reservation and created a campground with picnic tables and shelters, a marine life sanctuary, hiking trails, horseshoe courts and a children's playground.

Another 2 miles (3.5 km) up a steep, potholed road leads to **Striped Peak**, where the only human touch is a picnic table. The drive is worth the effort, for the view is magnificent, with the Olympic Mountains to the south, Vancouver Island north across the strait, and coastal vistas east and west as far as you can see.

Fourteen miles (22 km) further east on the highway takes the traveler to **Port Angeles**, the largest city in this part of the state. It bustles with ferry traffic going across the Canadian border to and from Victoria, BC. An observation tower at City Pier provides a good vantage point for watching the ferries, freighters and pleasure boats sailing the strait.

A short walk from City Pier is the **Clallam County Museum**, in the County Courthouse. Changing exhibitions, showing various aspects of the region's history, are displayed beneath the art glass rotunda window of the building, which is on the State Register of Historic Places.

Port Angeles is not only a gateway to Canada; it also provides an entrance to the beautiful Hurricane Ridge area of **Olympic National Park**. Signs point the way to the Visitors' Center, where maps and brochures are available.

Oddities at Sequim and Dungeness: Seventeen miles (27 km) east of Port Angeles is the town of **Sequim** (pronounced

Coastline at Rialto Beach, Olympic National Park.

Skwim), which has some of Washington state's more unusual features. One is its sunshine. Because the area is in the rain-shadow of the Olympic Mountains, Sequim has an annual rainfall of under 17 inches (43 cm). To say that so little precipitation is rare in the coastal areas of the Pacific Northwest is to understate the situation. Sequimites enjoy the fact that because the weather is so dry, their farmlands require irrigation.

The rich dairyland in the Sequim valley creates a bucolic setting of rich green pastures and browsing cattle at the feet of the towering, craggy snowcapped Olympic Mountains.

Dungeness Spit, 5 miles (8 km) northwest, is one of nature's oddities. Wind, waves and erosion have created a sandy hook 6 miles (11 km) long, laden with driftwood and rocks. Now a wildlife refuge, it shelters thousands of birds during their migrations, and walkers often see other marine life, such as seals and sea lions, at close range.

An easy 10-minute walk on a salal-fringed trail goes from the bluff above the spit through the woods and onto the beach. The path is accessible by wheelchair to a viewpoint. The park on the bluff, **Dungeness Recreation Area**, has camping and picnic sites.

Wineries and herb farms: Also in this area is an oyster farm that offers U-Pick oysters when the tide is low. For further taste thrills, Sequim boasts two hospitable wineries, both of which offer tours, tasting rooms and sales: **Neuharth** and **Lost Mountain**.

Cedarbrook Herb Farm, open all year round except for winter Sundays and holidays, is a pleasant diversion full of spicy scents. It has herbs and gifts offered for sale at an old-fashioned white farmhouse. Cedarbrook is on Sequim Avenue, approximately a mile south of the center of town.

Finally, as if to prove how unusual Sequim is, there's a game farm north of town that is home to animal movie stars and to several endangered species. Visitors can see the animals at **Olympic Game Farm** by driving through or taking an escorted tour. Zebras and guanaco will trot up to the car window and press their noses against it, looking for bread handouts if the car stops, and the huge bears will sit back on their haunches and beg for food.

A film star even more famous than Ben the Bear left a legacy of land to Sequim. That's why the boat basin at Sequim Bay is called **John Wayne Marina**. The actor often vacationed on the property he owned here.

Steaks, seafood and sautés: Fishing and crabbing and clamming are important activities at Sequim and Dungeness. Good seafood is available at **The Three Crabs** restaurant and **Casoni's** serves Italian food.

Sequim Bay State Park, east of town, is a typical Northwestern campsite, all rustic wood benches and moss in a lush green setting of cedars and ferns. Trails lead among the trees to a pebbly beach and boat launch.

As State 112 curves away from the bay, it crosses a point of land and meets another larger bay named **Discovery** by George Vancouver in 1792, although it had already been charted and named by Spanish explorers who arrived two years earlier. He was enthusiastic about the natural beauty and spent two weeks in the bay, repairing ships and brewing spruce beer, which supposedly tasted like champagne.

At this point, US 101 heads south down **Hood Canal** toward **Olympia**. Travelers who wish to see a final stretch of Washington coastline should turn east instead, on State 20, and angle across the peninsula to **Port Townsend**, a historic city that is steeped in a Victorian past. Old hopes of becoming the state's major metropolis faded long ago, but Port Townsend has attained new status as a picturesque example of life in the 1890s. The homes of leading citizens of an earlier day have become bed-and-breakfast inns, antique shops line the streets, and grand old mansions are open for viewing.

Strolling through a town where time stands still seems a fitting end to a journey through a coastal wilderness where time, as humans reckon it, has little meaning and where pockets of the legendary past are alive today.

THE WASHINGTON MOUNTAINS

There are few places in the world where you can ski in the morning and sail in the afternoon, where you can attend a world class play or symphony and walk out to an unpolluted view of snowcapped mountains, where you can be an engineer during the week and a ski instructor on the weekends, where you can hike to alpine lakes one day and bike to vineyards the next. Washington is an Eden where dreams of escaping into the mountains, sailing into a deep purple sunset and skiing down challenging slopes come true every weekend within a short distance from home.

When the warm months replace the gray clouds, the entire State of Washington heads for a favorite fishing hole, campsite, river or lake – and there are always enough of them to go around.

Rather than hibernating throughout the notoriously wet months, the active Northwesterners wring excitement from the environment in all sorts of ways. Within one to two hours from Seattle – in all directions – there are peaks to conquer, rivers to run, slopes to ski, wildlife to watch, and even natural hotsprings to soak in. Even during the winter there are places in the state with sunny skies – the eastern side of the mountains is generally more arid than the western side.

The two primary mountain ranges in Washington are the Olympics and the Cascades. The Olympic Peninsula is the first to greet water-logged clouds after their long uninterrupted journey across the Pacific Ocean, resulting in moss-draped rain forest. The Cascades, just east of Seattle, catch the last drops from the once full clouds. But by the time they crest the mountains, the water supply – to the dismay of the farmers and to the glee of hikers and skiers – has been depleted. Consequently, the west side of the Cascades (appropriately labeled the "wet side" by author Bill Speidel) warrants layers of rain gear, while the east side calls for suntan oil.

Preceding pages: the craggy peaks of Mount Index. Below, Mount Adams.

Mountain views are a constant reminder to Seattlelites that the white wonders of winter are only an hour away. On winter evenings and weekends damp city dwellers burst out of the concrete walls with a craving to attack the slopes.

Variations on the slopes: At the top of **Snoqualmie Pass**, 47 miles (75 km) east of Seattle on Interstate 90, are four ski areas: **Snoqualmie, Ski Acres, Alpental** and **Hyak/Pacific West.** They do not always have the best snow in Washington, but the convenient drive and night skiing assure their popularity. It also guarantees crowds on the weekends. Three of the areas – Snoqualmie, Ski Acres and Alpental – are now jointly owned and offer one ticket for all three areas. Clustered on the verge of the snow level, the snow conditions are often what is called "Seattle Cement."

Snoqualmie is more of a hill than a mountain. But the slopes are always busy. Though the hill may not be challenging for the advanced skier, it is fine to learn on. **Snoqualmie Ski School** is one of the biggest in the country and offers excellent instruction.

Just across the highway is Alpental, where Olympic Gold Medalist Debbie Armstrong began racing. Alpental is perhaps one of the most challenging areas in the state. The relatively small hill is steep and full of moguls.

Ski Acres shoulders Snoqualmie. As an intermediary between Snoqualmie and Alpental, the terrain is for everyone from beginner to expert.

Hyak/Pacific West, a half-mile east of the first three areas, picks up the leftovers – and gives them a decent hill for a cheaper price.

Three hours either side of Seattle are Washington's best known slopes: **Crystal Mountain** to the south and **Mount Baker** to the north. Higher elevation means more plentiful, lighter snow. When the clouds are off the top of Crystal Mountain, you are face to face with **Mount Rainier**, and spectacular views of the many other volcanic cones in the Cascade chain: **Mount Hood, Mount St Helens** and **Mount Baker**. Hotel and condominium accommodations are available in Crystal's village, complete with restaurants, bars, swimming pool and saunas.

Mount Baker, the start of the Sea to Ski Race on Memorial Day, is only open on the weekends. But it usually operates through mid-May, while most Washington ski areas shut down lifts in April. The nearest accommodations to Mount Baker are available in **Glacier**, 17 miles (27 km) down the mountain.

Located between Mount Baker and Snoqualmie, an hour and a half north of Seattle on US Highway 2, stashed in the middle of the North Cascades spires, is **Stevens Pass**. Built in 1936, the area has aged like a fine bottle of wine. New lodges and lifts do not detract from the friendly home-town atmosphere. Variety tempts every appetite here: from a triple chair on the beginners' slope to some of the best expert runs in the country. A large variety of slopes are lit until 10pm for night skiing.

Noses sporting zinc oxide and sunglasses are more common on the east side of the mountains. The sunbathed

Winter cabin in the Mount Baker National Forest.

slopes are just far enough from Seattle to discourage the crowds. Ticket prices are lower here, and the snow billows like powdered sugar instead of slumping like cement.

Mission Ridge in **Wenatchee** (east of Seattle on I-90) is the most diverse of these areas with groomed intermediate runs to bowls of untouched powder. Smaller areas that are fun for both the downhiller and the cross-country skier include **White Pass** (south of Mount Rainier on US 12), **Loup Loup** between Twisp and Okanogan (east on State 20; the road is closed in winter, so use alternative routes), and **49 Degrees North** tucked away in the northeastern corner of the state. All offer accommodations in nearby towns.

Puddles and paradise: Cross-country skiing is a sport that one can enjoy without being confined to certain boundaries. But in the past it also meant that skiers had to be adventurous enough to break their own trails, often through unknown territory. Recently in the Cascades there has been an organized effort to make cross-country ski trails more accessible to all levels of nordic skiers. Most ski areas now offer cross-country equipment, lessons, and, in some cases, prepared tracks. At the east side of Snoqualmie parking lot is the **Ski Acres Cross-Country Center**, with about 34 miles (55 km) of tracks. Lessons and rentals are also available.

For the slightly more adventurous, the Washington State Parks and Recreation Committee has designated many Sno-Park areas at trail heads. Sno-Park permits can be obtained at the Parks and Recreation Committee in Olympia or from any National Forest or Parks Service. However, before heading into the backcountry, call the Avalanche Warning Hotline (tel: (206) 976-ROAD), during winter. The snow conditions in the Cascades are frequently conducive to avalanches. If the hazard is high, pick a different area.

A couple of the Sno-Park novice areas are below 3,000 feet (910 meters), so snow may be scarce. Call to check snow and weather conditions (tel: (206) 976-ROAD), during winter.

Leavenworth, directly east of Stevens Pass, and a good 3-hour drive from Seattle, is a village sugarcoated in Bavarian cream. The surrounding area is spectacular for skiing, ice climbing and hiking and rock climbing in the summer. The **Bavarian Nordic Club** maintains three cross-country tracks just outside the town, at the **Golf Course**, **Fish Hatchery** and **Ski Hill**. The Forest Service has marked the roads and trails open to skiers. Inquire at the office in Leavenworth. The **Edel Haus Inn** bed-and-breakfast and **Haus Rohrbach Pension** are two elegantly rustic places to stay, both offering ski packages.

To the south, Mount Rainier is a magnet for dedicated cross-country skiers and mountaineers of the highest technical abilities; it also draws casual hikers and skiers who can explore the path at its base. (See the *National Parks* chapter on pages 258–9 for more information about **Mount Rainier**.)

The enchanting Methow Valley in **Okanogan County**, located 5 hours northeast of Seattle, also offers superb skiing. The **Methow Valley Ski Touring Association** provides over 60 miles (100 km) of tracked and untracked trails following rivers and ridges. **Liberty Bell Alpine Tours** will helicopter you into the mountains, drop you off on a peak and promise a full day of bliss. Heli-skiing (not for beginners) is based at the **Mazama Country Inn** (Mazama Junction and North Cascades Highway). In addition to the WVSTA trails, the inn maintains 19 miles (30 km) of groomed trails that begin at its front door. Ski rentals are available.

Climbing to the peaks: In 1883, I.C. Russell wrote in a report on existing glaciers, "That the mountains of the Northwest will win worldwide renown for the beauty and interest of their glaciers, as well as for the magnificence of their scenery, is predicted by all who have scaled their dizzy heights."

Climbing, perhaps more than any other sport, is a very personal experience. There is an intimacy with fear inherent in the challenge of perching on the edge of oblivion. The serrated peaks, the chain of massive volcanoes, and the smooth rounded foothills of the Cascades all contribute to the staggering variety of walls to scale.

Although it is almost ridiculous to generalize about anything in the Cascades – the weather, terrain, or the vegetation – generally speaking, the North Cascades are composed of more stable granite and metamorphic rock types, while the less jagged mountains south of Snoqualmie consist of more fragile sedimentary and volcanic rock, which tend to make climbing much more hazardous.

Leavenworth and Wenatchee, both east of the mountains, are popular spots for climbing enthusiasts. The generous number of nearby peaks and cliffs offers a variety of exciting routes.

Whitewater thrills: Kayaking Washington's whitewater is not a sport for beginners. Rivers in the Cascades run in a boiling rampage at one time of the year, and a bottom-scraping trickle at another. *Washington Whitewater*, by Douglas and Lynn Conant, is a thorough book mapping many of the area's finest runs. The authors move swiftly from the intermediate rivers like the **Cowlitz** and the **Skagit**, to the Class III expert rivers such as the **Wenatchee, Green River Gorge** and **Skykomish**.

While getting used to the conditions, paddlers should choose a river in keeping with their level of experience. The **National Oceanic and Atmospheric Administration** (NOAA) lists current water levels and updates them twice a week during peak seasons from April to November; call NOAA for information. Wet-suits in western Washington's glacial melt waters are a must.

If you are not yet a paddler, but would like to get a feeling of what river running is all about, this is the place to do it. There are many river raft companies that would love to get your feet wet and make your heart beat faster. Located in Seattle are: Blue Sky Outfitters, Downstream River Runners, Northern Wilderness River Riders, Orion River Expeditions, River Recreation Inc., Wildwater River Tours and last but not least, Zig Zag Expeditions.

Lush rain forests on the west side, North Cascade Mountains.

CENTRAL WASHINGTON

The "Evergreen State" becomes almost lost to memory once the east-bound traveler crosses the Cascade Mountains at any one of the several passes within one or two hours of Seattle. This once arduous journey is now a scenic drive. Gone are the green valleys and Douglas-fir forests, the dampness and the blue cast to the landscape present even on the sunniest of days.

The steady descent from the Cascades unfolds increasingly beautiful vistas – first ponderosa pine forests on gently sloping hills, which from early spring well into summer are dotted with wildflowers like the bright yellow balsamroot and varieties of blue lupine. Here the early morning traveler may see white-tailed deer or an occasional elk grazing near the roadside: the coyote, too, makes sudden appearances and then disappears into the woods.

Wide sky: Gradually, lovely valleys emerge, some with weathered farmhouses, and glimpses of rivers and lakes are caught from the main highways. The forested areas slip away, and stands of trees become fewer. The sky widens and the earth spreads forth as far as the eye can see, at first in colors and patterns formed by cultivated crops, and then into the brown and silvery green semi-arid sagebrush steppe of the vast Columbia Basin. Far more than a flat steppe land, here are coulees, buttes, dry falls and scablands and an array of wildlife and recreational facilities that would take a naturalist or sportsman a lifetime to explore in depth.

For the visitor new to the region, perhaps the biggest thrill will come with the first sighting of the great Columbia River. Three hours east from Seattle on Interstate 90, the river comes into view at the crest of rolling hills near **Vantage**. The road then drops down swiftly to cross the river over a graceful bridge and then climbs again. High above are paved viewing areas for gazing at the river as it passes beneath spectacular basalt cliffs.

Evidence of ancient life: Millions of years ago, before the Cascade Mountains were formed, the climate of eastern Washington was far different from what it is today. Moist air from the Pacific Ocean fell on huge forests and swamps, sustaining an amazing variety of plant life. Petrified wood fossils from more than two hundred species of trees once growing in eastern Washington have been identified in one area alone, the Gingko Petrified Forest State Park near Vantage.

Numerous gigantic lava flows of unbelievable force engulfed the landscape over a period of several million years, covering much of eastern Washington and parts of Idaho and Oregon with black basalt. One of the deepest areas of basalt in the world, it is known to geologists as the Columbia Basin basalt field. In the intervening years between flows, soils developed and supported plant life. Even an untrained observer can see these soil layers sandwiched in between lava flows and note the evidence of life millions of years ago.

Striking columns of basalt, formed as lava cooled and contracted, rise sentinel-like from the earth in various parts of central and eastern Washington. One of the most arresting is found along the south side of **Frenchman Coulee**, a few miles east of Vantage. The view in all directions is spectacular. Continuing down to the coulee floor, the road passes through sagebrush country to the banks of the Columbia River – and ends. Here one can stop to fish or perhaps just reach down to touch the great river.

In some parts of central Washington, layers of basalt buckled to form ridges, plateaus, gentle valleys and broad, shallow basins. The Umtanum and Menashtash ridges and the Saddle Mountains south of Ellensburg were formed in this way. The accumulation of various sediments in the basin soils at the foot of these uprisings has helped to make these areas the rich agricultural regions they are today.

During the Ice Age, a great ice sheet covered much of this part of the state. Huge basaltic rocks were torn from the earth and carried great distances, then left behind as the glacier retreated. Channeled scablands, a distinctive feature of the area around the **Columbia Wildlife Refuge** near **Moses Lake**, are stark expanses of flat lands marked by rock basins, coulees and buttes formed by the furious action of an ancient flood. Seepage from irrigation and nearby **O'Sullivan Dam** has created many small ponds in the scablands that are now host to several species of ducks.

The Columbia River: The **Columbia River** flows 1,270 miles (2,040 km) from its source in British Columbia to the Pacific Ocean. For the first 150 miles (240 km) of its course toward **Grand Coulee Dam**, the river is now called **Franklin D. Roosevelt Lake**, a vast reservoir for waters controlled by the dam. The Columbia was once formidable and swift flowing, with many treacherous rapids. Diverted from its path by a huge ice dam millions of years ago, the river was forced to find new channels. In this way a huge coulee was formed, nearly 50 miles (80 km) long, 900 feet (270 meters) deep in parts, and

up to 4 miles (6 km) wide. The coulee became dry as the ice melted and the river reverted to its original course. Man has made use of this natural phenomenon – the huge dam that bears its name was built on part of the coulee. Gigantic pump-generators at the dam move water into Banks Lake; from there it moves through a complex system of waterways to irrigate 500,000 acres (202,000 hectares) of formerly dry lands.

One of the great wonders of the west, Grand Coulee Dam attracts thousands of visitors each year. Endorsed by President Roosevelt as a Works Progress Administration project, construction of the dam began in 1933 and provided thousands of jobs before it was completed in 1941. Twice as tall as Niagara Falls and 5,233 feet (1,590 meters) long, the dam is the largest concrete structure in the world. The United States Bureau of Reclamation staffs an excellent Visitors' Center which offers guided tours of various parts of the structure. Self-guided tours and a wealth of fascinating information about the history, functioning and effect of the dam are available. Each night during the summer a bureau employee gives a lecture about the dam near the parking area.

Grand Coulee Dam was built to do more than provide irrigation waters for the parched lands of eastern Washington – it was designed to supply hydroelectric power as well. Available by 1941, the power was used to support wartime industry, particularly for aluminum and atomic energy plants in southeastern Washington. It was not until 1951 that water from the dam began to be used for irrigation.

The effect of the Columbia Basin Irrigation Project has been dramatic. Production of apples, potatoes, wheat and, more recently, wine grapes has increased greatly. The potential for apple production in this area rivals that of the Wenatchee Valley and Yakima County, the top apple producing regions in the country. As originally planned, the Columbia Basin Irrigation Project was to serve 1,095,000 acres (43,000 hectares). Slightly less than half of that area is still without water from the project. Rising costs of extending the equipment, controversy over developing alternative sources of water, the impact of rapid population growth on the environment and other issues have made the future of the project uncertain.

The Okanogan River Valley: One of the most picturesque areas in Washington is the lovely **Okanogan River Valley** in north central Washington. Situated in the midst of the **Okanogan National Forest**, the valley extends from the Canadian border south to **Brewster**, where the Okanogan River flows into the Columbia. Dry and rolling pine-forested hills climb to almost a mile in elevation in the upper reaches of the area known as the **Okanogan Highlands**. Numerous lonesome valleys eventually give way to the larger valley of the Okanogan River. Here the traveler can drive for miles on country roads on a summer day before seeing another car or signs of human habitation. Quietly beautiful views in every direction are the reward for a stop; the silence is broken only by an occasional bird call.

A late 19th-century gold rush brought miners and settlers to this remote land, and in **Molson**, near the Canadian border, buildings from that period can still be found, along with a pioneer museum with old mining equipment and other artifacts from the past. Side trips from US Highway 97 at **Ellisford** on narrow country roads, sometimes unpaved, provide access to numerous small lakes that are excellent for trout and bass fishing: **Whitestone**, **Spectacle** and **Wannacut Lakes** to the west and **Palmer Lake** to the north of Loomis. South of Loomis the partly unpaved road winds to **Conconully** and **Conconully State Park** with 81 campsites to attract boaters and fishermen. In the surrounding area numerous primitive campsites, with latrines but no water, are maintained by the Department of Game. Wildflowers common to the dry forest are abundant in the spring and early summer, and the patient bird-watcher will be rewarded with sightings of pine forest species like the red crossbill and pygmy owl. Higher elevations are home to the mountain bluebird and

the goshawk and other species common to the high country. The valley between Conconully and **Blue Lake** and the **Sinlahekin Wildlife Refuge** is range for wild turkeys and introduced bighorn sheep; mule deer, beaver, coyote and smaller mammals also live here. A perfect spot for a quiet vacation, this lovely area has much to occupy the contemplative traveler for days on end.

Cattle ranching and fruit production are the principal occupations in the Okanogan Valley. Along US 97, **Oroville**, **Omak** and **Okanogan** are the largest towns. Omak attracts large numbers of visitors during the second week of August for the annual Omak Stampede and Suicide Race, during which horses and riders charge down a steep hill, cross the Okanogan River and dash for the rodeo arena. Other rodeos are staged in nearby towns throughout the spring and summer.

A museum by the river: The **Okanogan County Historical Museum** sits on the banks of the Okanogan River in the town of Okanogan offering interesting

Fields of flowers contrast with hills beyond.

historical exhibitions. Another museum, the **Fort Okanogan Interpretive Center** at Brewster, offers a broad historical survey of the area, including information about fur trading and riverboats. North of Brewster is a COMSAT earth station for satellite communication. The Visitors' Center at the station provides fascinating explanations of how satellite communication works.

Chief Joseph Dam at **Bridgeport** is part of the chain of dams harnessing the power of the Columbia River from Grand Coulee Dam to the Columbia Gorge. There are boat launching ramps above and below the dam, and **Bridgeport State Park** is a pleasant place to have a picnic lunch.

West of US 97 is the **Methow Valley**, a favorite recreational site for hikers and cross-country ski enthusiasts; one can also take a scenic river raft trip on the swiftly flowing **Methow River** in spring and summer with experienced rafting companies. The town of **Winthrop** is a favorite stop for many travelers unable to resist the chance to walk the boardwalks past false-front stores resembling a set from a western movie. Winthrop is also headquarters for pack-train operators during the summer months and for visitors who come to fish, hunt and camp. Overnight facilities range from National Forest Service campgrounds to **Sun Mountain Lodge**, perched on top of Sun Mountain 10 miles (16 km) from State Highway 20, with panoramic views of the North Cascades and trails for hiking and horseback riding.

From **Tonasket** the curious traveler can explore along State 20 which winds through valleys in parts of the **Colville National Forest**. Side roads, not always paved, lead to small lakes, like **Bonaparte Lake**, **Beaver Lake** and **Lake Bath**. Farther south, at Omak, State 155 meanders to the southeast, past a trunk road to Omak Lake, to **Nespelem** on the Colville Indian Reservation. The grave of the great Chief Joseph of the Nez Perce tribe is close by. From Nespelem the road goes south to emerge at Grand Coulee Dam.

Wheat-fields near Douglas, Washington.

East of the dam is the **Coulee Dam National Recreational Area**, which encompasses Franklin D. Roosevelt Lake. Extending for 130 miles (210 km) all the way to the Canadian border, this huge area is one of the largest and least used recreation areas in Washington. With summer temperatures ranging from 75–100°F (24–38°C) during the day, it is an ideal place for boaters and fishermen. Twenty-two campgrounds offering 524 sites dot the area: some are open all year long and most have boat launching facilities. Visitors should consult maps for access to the lake, or check with the area headquarters in the town of Coulee Dam. Many species of waterfowl are attracted to this region, and a wide array of birds and mammals make it a rewarding stop for nature lovers.

Lake Chelan: Stretching fjord-like into the remote northwest end of the North Cascade mountains, **Lake Chelan** is 55 miles (90 km) long and at 1,500 feet (450 meters) deep, is one of the deepest lakes in North America. At some points it is a narrow 1.5 mile (2 km) wide, at others it is 2 miles (3.5 km) from one shore to the other. At its northern end it lies at the foot of peaks up to 8,000 feet (2,400 meters) high. Farther to the south, it is surrounded by gently mounded pine forested hills.

Visitors arriving by car can reach the town of **Chelan** at the south end of the lake by US 97. A favorite vacation spot for sun seekers from other parts of the state, Chelan offers almost every kind of facility for overnight stops and water recreation. **Lakeside Park** at the west end of town and **Lakeshore Park** in the center of town are popular recreation spots for family picnics, swimming, sun bathing and boat launching.

A recent addition to the south side of the lake is **Slidewaters**, a commercial waterslide park which includes a picnic area, an arcade and a hot tub big enough for 60 people!

Reservations for overnight stays at Chelan are essential during peak season. The ever-popular **Campbell's Lodge** is the largest of many motels in the town. The dining room is justifiably well-known for its good food and friendly service; however, there is no lack of opportunity to eat elsewhere. **Wapato Point** in **Manson**, 13 miles (21 km) from Chelan on State 150, is a condominium complex which rents to visitors year round. Cross-country skiing is a popular winter sport near Chelan.

Two state parks on the south shore of the lake outside of Chelan provide more than 200 overnight camping sites. The larger of the two, **Lake Chelan State Park**, requires reservations and first night camping fees in advance. Happily, it is open for swimming and picnics for day users. **Twenty-Five Mile Creek State Park** offers campsites on a first-come, first-served basis; however, visitors can call ahead between 8 and 9pm the evening before to reserve a space. Beyond Twenty-Five Mile Creek the lakeshore is inaccessible by car.

Sail the lake: Once settled for a stay of at least one or two nights, no visitor to Chelan should miss the voyage to **Stehekin** at the north end of the lake. Take an excursion boat which leaves daily each morning during the summer months from the Lake Chelan Boat Company dock. There is a somewhat dreamlike quality to the trip by boat.

At first mostly residences and apple orchards, the landscape gradually gives way to dry forested hills and tall peaks on either side of the lake. Bears and mountain goats are occasionally seen on the slopes as the boat makes its way to flag stops for hikers and a scheduled stop at **Lucerne**, which serves **Holden Village**, 12 miles (20 km) into the interior. Once a mining center and now a Lutheran retreat, Holden is a jumping-off place for hikers headed to the **Glacier Peak Wilderness**.

At the head of the lake, Stehekin serves as a base for campers and hikers in the **North Cascades National Park**. Here also is the **North Cascades Lodge**, operated as a park concession, a restaurant and a park ranger station. Short nature talks are given by the ranger staff, and a shuttle bus takes visitors sightseeing in the **Stehekin Valley**. Another bus makes daily runs deep into the valley to various camps and resort and recreation areas. Horseback riding, backcountry pack trips, river rafting, bicycling and canoeing are just some of the activities available to those who stay. Day visitors can return on the *Lady of the Lake* after a leisurely lunch. An exhilarating alternative is to spend the afternoon and arrange to fly back to Chelan on a floatplane, thus experiencing the magnificent scenery from above.

A drive along State 155, between **Coulee City** and Grand Coulee Dam, is a trip of exceptional beauty. Here is the landscape imprinted on the memory from countless western movies – big, blue sky, starkly dramatic basalt cliffs, and still water lined with tule marshes. For most of the drive the two-lane highway hugs the eastern side of **Banks Lake**; usually there is little traffic. The 27-mile (43-km) lake is an equalizing reservoir for Grand Coulee Dam, but to the visitor it appears as a serene natural wonder lying between ancient cliffs. Public access is limited, thus preserving the illusion.

The chief exception is **Steamboat Rock State Park**, near the mid-point of the lake. Visible for several miles, Steamboat Rock looms grandly 1,000 feet (300 meters) above the lake and was a well-known landmark to Indians and early fur traders. A side road from the highway leads to the 900-acre (360-hectare) park, where there are picnic areas on a watered green lawn, a boat launch, boat moorage and 100 campsites. A hiking trail leads to the top of the butte which is also a wildflower preserve. The lake is the summer home of western grebes and various ducks and gulls, and is a popular hunting and fishing area in the appropriate seasons.

From Coulee City, at the south end of Banks Lake, State 17 heads south through Grant County on its way to southeastern Washington. **Dry Falls**, a registered national landmark, is an extraordinary reminder of nature's terrible force. Four miles (6 km) wide and 400 feet (120 meters) deep, the falls were once fed by the Columbia River on its way to the coulee floor below. The course of the river changed, leaving the coulee dry and the falls silent. It is an

Apple orchards near Cashmere.

awesome sight. High above the coulee on the east side of the road, the Visitors' Center provides breathtaking views of the falls and an abundance of interpretive information.

Sun Lakes State Park: Encompassing a series of small lakes below Dry Falls is **Sun Lakes State Park**, one of the most popular state parks in Washington during the summer months. **Park Lake**, accessible from State 17, offers rental cabins, trailer hookups and campsites, a nine-hole golf course, rental boats and even horses for hire. At **Lenore Lake**, a marked trail leads to the **Lenore Caves**, thought to have sheltered Indians passing through the area thousands of years ago. Farther to the south, **Soap Lake**, with its high mineral content, is another popular spot for summer visitors.

Much of the large area to the south of Soap Lake is changing from flat sagebrush country to fertile fields and orchards because of irrigation water made available from the Columbia River Irrigation Project. Often the dramatic before-and-after contrast can be seen on either side of the road: newly planted fruit orchards or grass crops on one side; sagebrush, tumbleweed and related plants on the other. Small ponds and lakes formed by the rising water table exist where once there was no water, and wildlife and recreation areas are scattered throughout the landscape.

The Columbia Basin has become one of the most important waterfowl breeding grounds in Washington and is an excellent place for hunting and fishing. Millions of other birds make use of the marshes, lakes, potholes and puddles for feeding and resting on their annual migration along the Pacific Flyway. During spring and summer, yellow-headed blackbirds, kingbirds, meadowlarks and several species of hawks and owls can be seen near the roadside. Coyotes, jackrabbits and a variety of smaller mammals are all residents of the area. The **Columbia National Wildlife Refuge** and **Potholes Reservoir**, near Moses Lake, and the **Winchester Waterway**, near George, are all extremely rich in bird and animal life.

The Grand Coulee Dam, brightly lit for a nighttime tour.

No visitor should leave central or eastern Washington without seeing their fair share of wheat-fields. Although the chief wheat producing area of the state is in the Palouse Hills of southeastern Washington, large crops are also grown in central Washington on the beautiful plateau above and to the east of the Columbia River.

US 2 traverses this plateau in an almost unbroken straight line between Orondo and Coulee City – a drive of only 60 miles (95 km). A few farmhouses and cars momentarily interrupt the view of flat golden wheatfields lying beneath the intensely blue sky, recalling the lines every schoolchild learns – "O beautiful, for spacious skies, for amber waves of grain…" from the song *America the Beautiful*.

On the banks of the Columbia River at the junction of US Highways 97 and 2 sits the town of **Wenatchee**, the gateway to central Washington and British Columbia. Its many motels and restaurants attest to its convenience and its popularity as a convention center.

Apple capital of the world: It is proudest, however, of its claim to be the apple capital of the world. Apple trees are everywhere – even clinging to narrow ledges on steep hillsides. Dry air, long hot days and cool nights, ample water supply, and excellent soils make ideal growing conditions for the crisp Delicious apples that have made Wenatchee and its environs famous.

A drive past the perfumed orchards in spring is a delight to the senses; and in late summer and fall the trees, laden with their red and golden fruit, are a wondrous sight. During the harvest season, beginning in early September, roadside stands open for business along nearly every single road leading from Wenatchee, and a few are open all year long. Most vendors sell their own fruit.

US 2 on both sides of the Columbia River offers many opportunities to browse and choose from the Red and Golden Delicious or more exotic varieties available – Greenings, Winter Bananas, Gravensteins and Pippins. Tree ripened cherries, apricots, peaches and

Left, farmlands near Enumclaw. Right, Tumwater Canyon and the Wenatchee River near Leavenworth.

nectarines can also be found in season, usually starting early in July.

Ohme Gardens, 4 miles (6 km) north of Wenatchee on State 97 overlooking the Columbia River, makes a pleasant stop. Begun in 1929 by the Ohme family of Wenatchee, its 9 acres (4 hectares) have been transformed into an alpine meadow, with firs, heathers, mosses, alpine flowers and pools of water.

Nearby **Cashmere**, to the west, and **Leavenworth**, at the mouth of the Tumwater Canyon (both on US 2), have adopted an artificial identity. Cashmere has created an old-fashioned Main Street with post lantern street lamps and covered walkways. An unsuspecting visitor might be startled at the first glance of Leavenworth. Once a prosperous railroad and logging center, it fell into decline when both industries left. To attract tourists and regain some measure of prosperity, the town now presents itself as a Bavarian village. Much of the architecture in the center of town has been modified to resemble alpine chalets, with geranium-filled window boxes, and baskets of brightly colored flowers hang from eaves throughout the town.

Kittitas County: Scenic State Highway 970 in **Cle Elum**, just east of the Cascades, winds through the sleepy looking **Teanaway River Valley**, some of the prettiest country in the state. **Hidden Valley Guest Ranch**, the state's oldest dude ranch, lies deep within the sunwashed valley. Here guests sleep in rustic cabins, and hike and ride horses along trails with splendid views. The Teanaway Valley is one of the few remaining areas where many species of native wildflowers are undisturbed by man; visitors come to see the demure yellow bell and the more commonly seen but no less beautiful balsamroot, camas lilies and wild iris that burst forth in splashes of blue and gold in the spring.

Ellensburg is the geographic center of the state and the seat of Kittitas County. Cattle and horse ranching, and corn and grain production are major occupations in this area. The city is home to **Central Washington University**, and State 10 passes its tree-lined campus as it heads toward **Vantage**.

Turn-of-the-century buildings in the downtown district lend a certain authentic charm to the city, and a visit to the **Olmstead Place**, with its 19th-century log cabin and farm buildings, gives the visitor an idea of how the early settlers lived. The Ellensburg Rodeo, held each year on Labor Day weekend, has been an institution since 1923, drawing visitors from far and wide.

From Ellensburg to Vantage, Interstate 90 passes large cattle and horse ranches in the flat Kittitas Valley, their houses framed by cotton-woods and lilacs, and then threads through unoccupied sagebrush country, **Gingko Petrified Forest State Park**, located just outside of Vantage, has shaded picnic grounds and several trails leading up the steeply inclined hills to partially excavated petrified trees – good reason to stop for a visit. Two and a half miles (4 km) down the highway the park interpretive center recounts the complex geological history of the area and presents many fascinating exhibitions and specimens of petrified trees. The gingko is known today only in cultivation, and petrified gingko is found nowhere else in the world. The Visitors' Center is perched on a bluff high above the Columbia River with splendid views of the river and basalt cliffs.

The Yakima Valley: Leaving Ellensburg for **Yakima** and south central Washington, the traveler has two choices. Interstate Highway 82 climbs Manashtash and Umtanum ridges and extends for miles with panoramic views of sagebrush plains dotted with wildflowers in spring and early summer. Or take State 821, known as the Yakima Canyon Road, along the Yakima River. Wild rose bushes perfume the roadside in June, and narrow groves of green trees by the river stand in sharp contrast to the dry brown hills.

The Yakima Valley is one of the richest and most productive agricultural regions in the United States. Three hundred days of sunshine per year, fertile volcanic soil, hot days and cool nights during the growing season make it a prime area for growing a wide variety of crops. With the support of the federal government for the Yakima Project in the early 20th century, the valley and its agricultural production have grown steadily; it is now the leading producer of apples and hops in the country. Large quantities of cherries, pears, grapes, peaches, mint, corn and other garden produce are also grown, and livestock and dairy industries thrive in this area. Roadside stands, orchards and U-Pick farms during the summer offer a wide array of sun-ripened fruits and vegetables at reasonable prices.

The city of Yakima is the commercial center of the valley and a popular convention site. The **Yakima Valley Museum** features exhibitions pertaining to the Yakima Indians and the white settlers of the valley but is best known for its wonderful collection of horse-drawn carriages and wagons, including a Conestoga wagon and a real surrey with a fringe on top.

The **Yakima Nation Cultural Center** is farther south on State 22 just outside of **Toppenish**. The museum presents interpretive materials related to the large population of Yakima Indians still in the area and also has a theater and a library. **Toppenish National Wildlife Refuge**, about 3 miles (5 km) south of the town on US 97, is an excellent area for birds all year long.

From Toppenish, State 220 leads to **Fort Simcoe Historical State Park**. The restored military fort is located on what is now the **Yakima Indian Reservation** and during its history has also served as an Indian agency and a school.

At Goldendale, **Goldendale Observatory State Park** has a 24½-inch (62-cm) reflecting telescope, one of the largest in the world available for public use, and a large Celestron telescope with a special filter for looking at the sun. After a stop here the traveler can continue on to the **Maryhill Museum of Art**, 2 miles (3½ km) west of US 97 on State 14. The museum houses an eclectic collection: Rodin bronzes, early Indian artifacts, various personal possessions of Queen Marie of Rumania (a friend of the museum's founder), and a variety of other objects.

The village of Leavenworth has adopted a Bavarian look.

INLAND WASHINGTON

The story of the "Inland Empire" goes back to the words of the Reverend George H. Atkinson of Oregon City, who, after traveling through what was in 1898 virtual wilderness, pronounced the Walla Walla and Palouse region to be "a great Inland Empire."

Remote and inaccessible: Lewis and Clark bypassed the southern edge of the region in 1805, as they found the Columbia River and transcontinental access to the Pacific Ocean for the United States. Later territorial immigrants also passed by, along the Oregon Trail; to them, Eastern Washington seemed remote and inaccessible. It was the fascination with the profits to be gained from the fur trade with Native American tribes which first inspired white men to investigate the land north of the junction of the Snake and Columbia rivers.

During the next century, Eastern Washington was settled by traders, missionaries, miners, farmers and homesteaders. The region had its share of Indian wars, boom towns and fast-growing immigrant centers. Early agricultural development of the Walla Walla area spread north into the Palouse Hills and west from the Spokane River area into the dry farming region on the eastern edge of the scablands of the Columbia Basin. The new cities of Spokane and Walla Walla were soon competing for dominance with Seattle, Tacoma and Port Angeles.

Cattle and sheep ranching were major concerns of the early settlers, mainly because they felt that the surface soil of the **Palouse Hills** (later identified as loess, "windblown" dust from the Cascade Range) was basically non-arable. But it was discovered – and no one is quite sure by whom or exactly when – that the loess was actually only a few feet deep, and rich fertile soil lay beneath its surface as deep as 150 feet (45 meters) to a lava base. This discovery and the innovation of crop rotation turned the Palouse Hills and the lands west of Spokane into veritable gardens of wheat

and the southern Palouse and Walla Walla regions into fields for peas.

The Inland Empire's geography ranges from the sparsely populated, ruggedly mountainous Asotin in the southeast corner past the lushness of the Walla Walla Valley and the fertile Palouse Hills to the east. It extends through rolling dry-farm wheatfields in the west and northwest, to the lakes, trees and small farms of Spokane and northeast Washington.

Throughout the entire area, there is little evidence of human habitation before the turn of the century. Some old houses remain, mostly in Spokane and Walla Walla, where old homes and some of the buildings of Whitman College (founded in 1865 as memorial to Marcus Whitman and the missionary movement) stand as reminders of the stable and settled prosperity of the late 19th century. Evidence of the passionate struggle for land, and of the trading days, is gone; it has been replaced by cement or stone markers or imitation frontier settlements for tourists.

The absence of history is not, however, something that residents grieve over. After all, settlement and development happened almost hand in glove in the Inland Empire. The land went from wilderness to civilization in no more than a wink of historical time's eye. The people of the Inland Empire are proud of the man-made beauties of their region. The spring colors of the Palouse Hills or Big Bend's sea of golden wheat are as inspiring as the results of the river front/downtown renovation Spokane business leaders effected for the World's Fair Expo '74. Inland Empire dwellers are also proud of the hydro-electric wonders harnessing the power of the Columbia River and the gourmet restaurants in towns and cities all the way from Sandpoint, Idaho, in the north to Walla Walla in the south.

Spokane: To the casual visitor, contemporary **Spokane** (urban/suburban population over 325,000) may seem to be the American Dream made reality. At the very heart of the city is lovely 100-acre (40-hectare) **Riverfront Park**, covering the islands in the Spokane River and highlighting the spectacular falls. Directly south of the park, 10 blocks of Spokane's leading department stores, specialty shops and restaurants are connected by a latticework of covered, street-spanning skywalks. Spokane's business is conducted either in beautiful new buildings or in carefully restored older ones. Understandably, many residents prefer to shop in the city's pleasant downtown area rather than in the suburban malls.

Spokane looks like a city that was planned and then created to be "livable" – clean, safe, pretty, friendly and middle-class. There is no evidence remaining of the roughness and intense competition of the frontier in Spokane.

Yet as recently as 1972, evidence of the historical process sprawled over the center of Spokane. A tangled complex of railroad tracks, yards and stations covered what is now Riverfront Park; there were no skywalks, and transients or unemployed railroad workers huddled at night in alleys on a "skid road" now lined with chic shops.

A new look for the city: Back in 1910, when the railroad and mining barons of the Inland Empire discovered that they had created a real city in Spokane, they hired the famous Olmsted brothers of New York to design a system of parks and scenic roadways for the city. They followed most of the Olmsted's advice (prime examples are the still-existing **Manito Park** and **Rockwood Boulevard**) but one idea they ruled out was the creation of a "Gorge Park," which would have reclaimed the riverfront from their own rail yards. The access and convenience was too important economically to sacrifice the land to the city's beautification.

The next 60 years saw the decline of the power of the rail and mining interests that had made Spokane. Economic changes at last made it possible – and profitable – to reclaim the riverfront and give Spokane a new face for the World's Fair Expo '74.

One remnant that survived the city's face-lift is the clocktower of the **Great Northern Railroad Station**, built in

A historical interpretation of Spokane Falls.

188

1902. The massive station is now gone, but the clocktower still stands in Riverfront Park, a monolithic reminder of the turbulent railroad days and the dynasties that created fortunes, built the city and made it the center of the Inland Empire. The old clocktower stands as a mute, historic marker of the last days of the west.

Today Spokane is noted for its medical and educational facilities, for its variety of consumer goods and entertainment. It is an immaculate and efficient "service station" for the vast area of farms, ranches, lumber and mining towns between the Columbia River and the Rocky Mountains.

There are, to be sure, the parks and houses that the new-rich of the Inland Empire of the turn of the century built to celebrate their wealth. The 1876 **William Kirkman House** in Walla Walla and the 1880 **James Perkins House** in Colfax are well-preserved examples. **Browne's Addition** (just west of downtown Spokane), for instance, has many old mansions.

Yet old mansions have a way of becoming museums, or being converted into modern gourmet restaurants. The elegant home built in 1898 by Coeur d'Alene mining czar Patrick Clark, on Second Avenue in Brown's Addition, may be visited for a fine meal.

The Inland Empire has become more tourist-conscious recently, and local information may be obtained in any of the larger towns.

The traveler might take Interstate Highway 90, for instance, east to Spokane for a good view of the dry wheat land and scab-rock of the **Big Bend Country**. Big Bend, reminiscent of the American Southwest in places, extends from about 20 miles (32 km) east of the town of **Moses Lake** all the way to the forests around Spokane.

Heading south on US Highway 195 from Spokane to **Clarkson** will take travelers through the Palouse Hills and down the famous **Clarkston Hill** to the Snake River. From the **Colfax** fork of US 195, State Highways 26 and 127 and US 12 branch off and lead through the

Spokane's modern Riverfront Park.

back country of the Palouse, rich with its wheat and cattle ranches.

Through the Idaho Panhandle: US 95 north from **Lewiston**, Idaho, will take the traveler through the lake country of the Idaho Panhandle, past brilliantly clear **Lake Coeur d'Alene** with its pretty 109-mile (175-km) shoreline. Farther north is **Sandpoint**, Idaho, and **Lake Pend Oreille**, one of the largest lakes in the United States. Pend Oreille is famous for Kamloops trout as well as 13 other varieties of game fish.

Heading east at the junction of US 95 onto I-90 leads around the top of Lake Coeur d'Alene, through the **Fourth of July Canyon** in the Coeur d'Alene mountains, and the historic mining towns of **Wallace** and **Kellogg**, Idaho. US 2 northeast from Spokane goes through the pristine wooded lands, lakes and small farms of northeast Washington and joins US 95 at Sandpoint. US 2 west from Spokane heads through the rolling dry farm wheatlands and leads to **Grand Coulee Dam**.

Just off US 395 (heading south) State 28 west of **Kettle Falls** leads past Grand Coulee Dam's massive back-up lake, **Lake Roosevelt**. Continue further past the Colville and Spokane Indian reservations, and again pass through farm land and into the irrigated land of the **Columbia Basin Project**.

The Tri-Cities: US 395 leads south all the way to the Tri-Cities of **Richland**, **Kennewick** and **Pasco**. The Tri-Cities are strictly a modern phenomena, a group of what had been small towns clustered together along the Columbia River just at its junction with the Snake.

Pasco was claimed by settler David Thompson in 1811 and founded as a railroad town in 1880, and Kennewick was founded in 1892. Yet the area remained relatively quiet until the 1940s, shadowed by the growth of Spokane as a railroad center.

Then, in 1943, the Federal Government created the **Hanford Atomic Works** at Richland, and brought 60,000 workers into a town of 250 people. The eventual expansion of atomic energy work and research at the plants, combined with the development of irrigated land, soon rocketed the population of the three towns to 80,000 people. But the area has now plunged into the economic doldrums with the closure of the Hanford atomic facility.

The Inland Empire features natural lands – and sporting opportunities – in abundance. There are more than 200 lakes in the region, 76 of them within an hour or two of Spokane. Nearby lakes range from tiny **Fish Lake** and **Liberty Lake**, barely outside the city limits, to the huge and beautiful **Coeur d'Alene**, **Pend Oreille** and **Priest Lakes** in the nearby state of Idaho.

Spring, summer and fall offer boating, fishing, river rafting and swimming at a myriad of locations. Winter is the time to take in skiing – on **Mount Spokane**, in western Idaho's mountains, or the Blue Mountains south of Walla Walla. Climbing and hiking are year-round possibilities in the many wilderness areas. There are tour boats available on the larger lakes, as well as seaplane excursions.

Restaurants and eateries: Prior to the regional modernizations of Expo '74, dining in the inland Washington region was strictly American fare. Beef and potatoes reigned supreme, with a smattering of fish straight from local streams and into the frying pans, so to speak. Menus invariably featured Texas-style barbecue and homemade pie for dessert. A few of these places became well-known locally: steaks by the ounce and rocky mountain oysters became specialties of the Oasis (on the Oregon/Washington border south of Walla Walla), and regionally famous grilled burgers were the order of the day at Spokane's Park Inn Tavern.

As dining habits became more enlightened and tastebuds more educated, these restaurants were joined by places like Patsy Clark's (in the old Clark Mansion) in Spokane and The Golden Horse (featuring Mandarin cuisine) in Walla Walla. Even smaller towns like Richland and Dayton became increasingly cosmopolitan. The Patit Creek in Dayton, for instance, has a clientele that comes far and wide to sample its French (and very good) fare.

Right, desert landscape and sand dunes near Wallula Gap.

THE COLUMBIA RIVER GORGE

The Columbia Gorge, a geological wonder resulting from the fires and floods of past eons, allows the Columbia River passage through the Cascade Mountain range east of Portland along the northern edge of Mount Hood.

As the Columbia approaches this breach, the river has gained most of its tributary force, broadening out for the final stretch of its 1,234-mile (1,985-km) journey down from Canadian headwaters to the Pacific. The Columbia is so massive that it discharges more water than any other US river, excepting only the Mississippi.

A drive through the gorge along the 24-mile (38-km) **Scenic Highway 30** on the Oregon side of the river presents compelling vistas, intriguing waterfalls and engaging walks. Beyond the east end of the Scenic Highway rests Bonneville Dam, where you can watch migrating salmon and other species of fish swim upriver, clearly visible a few feet away. Beyond Bonneville, at **Cascade Locks**, the human story of the gorge can be studied in the **Cascade Locks Museum**. At the locks, you can board a paddlewheel steamer for a water-level view of the gorge. Ending the trip, a tour of Hood River introduces the traveler to the rural pear- and apple-growing valley that stretches south toward the symmetrical white beauty of Mount Hood.

The climate along the gorge is often mild or warm, bathed in warm air from eastern Oregon. In summer, swimming and sunbathing are popular along the beachfront state parks, such as Benson State Park, near Multnomah Falls. October is the fall foliage month for deciduous trees, such as aspen.

As you leave Portland, heading east, look for the signs that announce the Scenic Highway. This is the old and beautiful road that rides the rim of the Columbia Gorge. The more modern Interstate 84 is unquestionably more efficient and faster, situated at water

Preceding pages: Beacon Rock overlooks Columbia River Gorge. Below, early train along the gorge.

level, but the scenic road is of far greater interest to the leisurely sightseer.

The scenic road turns inland along the Sandy River at **Troutdale**. **Lewis and Clark State Park**, along the Sandy River, is a favorite for dip netting silver smelt in spring, sunbathing in summer, and steelhead fishing in winter. Walk the nature trail to see specimens of the plants that the explorers reported to an amazed audience back East.

Viewing the gorge: The road climbs to **Corbett** and beyond to the first striking vista, at **Women's Forum Park**. Here you can see the broad Columbia, the mountains and Vista House at Crown Point, the next major stop. At the park, you'll see a sign honoring Sam Hill, Roadbuilder. Hill was instrumental in building the road, in 1913–15. As you drive along, note the quality of the stone workmanship and the care with which the roadbed was created.

Seven hundred feet (210 meters) above the river is **Vista House** at Crown Point, offering a superlative view over the gorge. Vista House was built as a memorial to Oregon's pioneers and is open to the public for tours most days. Crown Point's panorama illustrates the observations of geologists, who believe that the gorge was formed by a long series of uplifts, glaciers and volcanic activity. The most recent episodes were a cluster of disastrous floods, perhaps 40 in all, which completed the present shape of the 12,000-year-old gorge.

A side road from the scenic highway takes you to **Larch Mountain**, a favorite weekend picnic and hiking retreat for Portlanders. Larch Mountain reaches an elevation of 4,058 feet (1,240 meters), offering excellent views. Trails and picnic tables await you at the end of a winding road. From **Sherrard Point**, at the end of the trail, hikers enjoy satisfying views of the Columbia River, Mount Hood and Portland.

Into waterfall terrain: East from Crown Point, the road leads into a terrain appreciated by connoisseurs of waterfalls. There are 11 major waterfalls in as many miles (18 km). **Latourell** is first: a trail leads to a footbridge at the base of the falls. **Shepherd's Dell**, a mile (2 km) beyond Latourell, is reached by a stone trail leading to the falls. **Bridal Veil**, the next falls, is below the roadway, so only a hike makes it accessible. Then comes **Wahkeena**, a tumble of waterfalls. The name of the site is taken from an Indian word for "most beautiful."

The greatest of the waterfalls is **Multnomah**, a star attraction of the Columbia Gorge. Park in the ample lot at the base of the falls, where the scenic roadway and I-84 lie proximate to each other, and walk to the falls, allowing time to absorb its beauty. Consider a walk to the top of the falls, as well as the view from the bridge opposite. At 620 feet (190 meters), Multnomah is the fourth highest waterfall in the United States. The nature center at the base of Multnomah Falls alerts you to the region's geology and flora. The restored **Multnomah Falls Lodge**, an establishment dating from the period of the original road, is open for breakfast, lunch and dinner.

Along the road, you pass both Oregon state parks and National Forest

Multnomah Falls.

Service lands. Both are interlaced with myriad hiking and walking trails. Picnic places are numerous and overnight camping is possible at some of these parks, such as Ainsworth, just east of Multnomah Falls.

Stop at the state parks for brochures on the trails or buy one of the area guidebooks, available at the Multnomah Falls gift shop, if you want a thorough list of trails. The Forest Service also supplies excellent maps; ask for their brochure *Forest Trails of the Columbia Gorge*. If you want to stretch your legs on a section of the Pacific Crest trail, that long walk between Canada and Mexico, the Oregon section begins west of Cascade Locks.

East from Multnomah Falls, **Ainsworth State Park**, set above the river over a landscape of steep forested cliffs, is a recommended overnight stop if you are camping, or as a picnic site if you make a day trip. The philosophy of the Oregon state park system is to create campgrounds with a managed, manicured look, as opposed to the rustic appearance of National Park and US Forest Service campgrounds.

Driving east from Multnomah with waterfalls in mind, **Oneonta** is next, accessible by a watery, adventuresome route. To see the falls, you must walk up the narrow bed of Oneonta Creek. However, there are more falls to come for those who favor dry feet. **Horsetail Falls** trail takes you underneath the spray. **Elowah Falls** has short hikes to both its lower and upper falls.

Bonneville Dam: After Elowah, the main falls are behind you and the river-taming **Bonneville Dam** looms ahead. Named after a 19th-century explorer, Captain Benjamin de Bonneville, the project was started in 1933 and completed in 1939. The 1,450-foot (440-meter) dam was the first major hydroelectric project located on the mighty Columbia River, and the cornerstone of electrical power generation in the Pacific Northwest.

Protection of the fishery, especially for salmon, was an important economic and environmental concern when the

Punchbowl Falls on Eagle Creek.

196

dam was built. Elaborate ladders were arranged to allow the fish to migrate past the dam. With an eye for public support, the US Corps of Engineers, which built the dam, eventually included a handsome visitors' center to tell the story of Bonneville's construction and let the public witness the migration of fish. Bonneville Dam and Multnomah Falls are the two most popular stops for travelers along the Columbia Gorge.

Both outdoor and indoor fish viewing at Bonneville are impressive throughout the year. Outdoors, you can watch as salmon rest in the troughs and hurl themselves up ladders. You can also see ships ply their way gingerly through the 500-foot (150-meter) navigation locks. Indoors, through underwater viewing windows, you can see large chinook salmon and the smaller salmon species in their perennial migration to the small feeder streams where they were born. There they will lay their eggs and die, becoming food for the eagles and bears. Besides salmon, you may see eel and steelhead fighting the current.

At Bonneville Dam, another fascinating stop is the **Oregon State Fish Hatchery**, where you can gaze into pools blackened by fingerling salmon. Watch the feeder cast pellets of food on the water, provoking an instant eruption of fish seeking nourishment. In other ponds, you can observe up close trophy-size trout or even a behemoth sturgeon. Such fish stimulate the dreams of angling Oregonians, even as they strip the ice from the ferrules of their rods with frost-bitten fingers during winter expeditions.

On the history trail: East from Bonneville is **Eagle Creek**, one of the Gorge's better known trails. Extensive fossil beds have been uncovered near here. A well-maintained and very beautiful trail climbs through green forests to **Metlako** and **Punchbowl** waterfalls.

At **Cascade Locks Marine Park**, a National Historical Site, a traveler comprehends the human story of the Columbia and gets a water-level view of the gorge. The museum, once the lock tender's residence, has many early day photos of the steamboats, railroads and

Mount Hood from Lost Lake.

portaging operations at the locks. Nearby is the Northwest's first steam locomotive, the Pony Engine.

According to archaeological evidence, Native Americans thrived here for over 9,000 years, surviving on the rich salmon fishery. Native legends held that the gods constructed a huge stone bridge over the waters west of the present-day locks. Today, a man-made bridge, called the **Bridge of the Gods**, links Oregon and Washington west of the locks. Built in 1926, it was raised in 1938 to provide clearance over the rising waters behind Bonneville Dam. At the locks, if you walk west, you will still find Natives exercising their rights to fish for salmon with dip nets along the river.

Explorers, fur trappers and traders, and finally the overland settlers, made use of the Columbia as transportation. Settlers traveling west on the Columbia River in the 19th century risked the treacherous Cascades rapids here. Numerous hapless parties, near the end of their long trek west, lost all their earthly goods, including their homesteading tools and seeds, to the river. The locks were built in 1896, taming the rapids and allowing safe river passage. Each year in September, the community of Cascade Locks celebrates the historical past with its Portage Days, complete with a salmon bake.

On the river: The Columbia Gorge Sternwheeler moors in Cascade Locks from Memorial Day to September, offering daily river excursions and a romantic link to the riverboats of the past. In summer, the 2-hour nostalgic boat ride, enhanced by a narrated commentary on history and nature, leaves three times a day, daily from mid-June to late September. Dinner and brunch trips require reservations.

Beyond Cascade Locks is the economically important river town of **Hood River**, with a road turning south to apple and pear country and the white crown of Mount Hood. (The name is believed to have come from an adventurous British admiral, Samuel Hood.)

Traditionally, like so many Oregon small towns, Hood River grows an amazing array of flowers. Petunias, dahlias,

roses, forsythia and other flowering shrubs, and mature shade trees flower in profusion in almost every yard. Vegetable gardens complement the setting in the suburban areas and rural edges of the community.

Hood River is the gateway to **Mount Hood**, and at 11,235 feet (3,420 meters), the reigning monarch of the Oregon Cascades. From Portland, the snowy, serene crest of the mountain is a subtle presence on clear days. Mount Hood and the Cascades are a source of inspiration and wilderness meditation today, but to the early explorers pushing west, they were formidable obstacles.

Since 1973, these steep slopes have been turned to advantage by skiers at "Oregon's Hall of the Mountain King," **Timberline Lodge**. Artwork inside echoes the pioneer past in the state's pre-eminent wilderness retreat.

At the town of Hood River, stop in at the travel information center at **Port Marina Park** (exit 64 off I-84). The center has an interesting relief map that shows the terrain of this part of the state.

Tree-lined trails are commonplace.

198

One of the most lovely views in the region is from **Panorama Point**. A quarter mile (0.5 km) south on State Highway 35, turn onto Eastside Road, then drive 2.5 miles (4 km); this is a viewpoint for the Hood River Valley and Mount Hood.

Fruit farming: Hood River is the urban focus for the lumbering and pear growing industries of the Hood River Valley. Oregon leads the country in lumber production, and you can see vigorous lumbering just south of the city at **Elkhorn**. You'll also see well-tended fruit farms. Hood River hosts a Blossom Festival in April and the harvest is in full operation from June through September. Anjou pears and apples (of several varieties) are the main crops here, and are sold along the roadway. The pears must be taken home for aging before eating.

The first white settler at this eastern end of the Columbia River Gorge was Nathaniel Coe, who staked his claim in 1854 and promptly planted fruit trees. Since the turn of the century, fruit production and timber have vied with each other as major industries here. However, fruit agriculture has its risks. From 1890 until 1920, Hood River was world famous for its apples. Then, in 1921, a disastrous freeze killed thousands of the trees. Many farmers replanted with hardier pear trees rather than apples. Hood River County is now the leading producer of Anjou pears in the world.

West of Hood River, the restored **Columbia Gorge Hotel**, a 1921 creation on a bluff overlooking the river, is a recommended lodging or dining stop for tourists. Originally built by timber and tourism baron Simon Benson to encourage travel along the Columbia, the hotel is noted for its elegant dining, handsomely appointed rooms, and its own 207-foot (63-meter) waterfall.

In 1986, Congress passed a bill establishing the Columbia River Gorge scenic area. Various factions came up with differing views, but on one point everyone who has traveled up the gorge, walked its paths and gazed at its streaming, misty waterfalls agrees: this is one of the world's natural treasures.

Farmlands near the Columbia River.

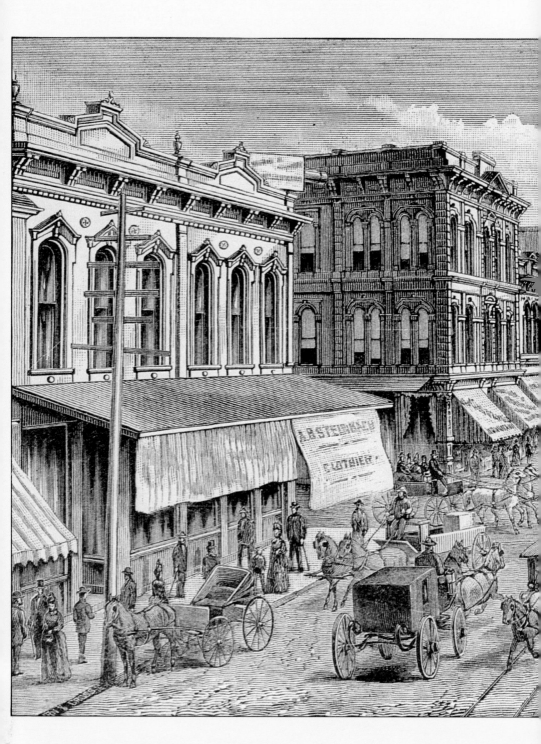

PORTL

REGON.

PORTLAND, OREGON

Although it is home to around 450,000 people and the largest city in Oregon, in many ways Portland is just an overgrown small town. Like the rest of the state, for years Portland had a reputation as a solid, attractive, maybe a bit stodgy, but overall comfortable city. It featured regularly, then as now, on "Most Livable City in the US" lists.

Portland's sleepy, somewhat backwater image is changing. The city has been discovered, among others, by high-technology industries, young urban professionals and a range of international residents. That discovery has caused its share of schizophrenia, forcing the city to decide how big it wants to get, what kind of development it wants to encourage and just how much change it can tolerate while still preserving its peaceful character.

Despite its rapid growth, Portland is still an open, safe and friendly place.

Like other major cities, Portland saw an increase in crime and gang activity in the 1980s and 1990s, but out-of-towners are often struck by the city's pedestrian-friendly downtown area. Blocks are half as long as those in other large towns; parks, fountains and public art seem to dot every street corner.

Portland's livability is rooted in a philosophy that values its environment. Examples are everywhere. A large percentage of the population recycles its household and business waste. Commuters walk, jog and bike to work. Mass transit is popular. The Friends of Trees organization provides low-cost trees for residents to plant in city-owned curbside parkways.

Portland was the first US city to develop a comprehensive – and controversial – energy plan and an ordinance to protect the solar access of buildings designed to use solar energy. A continuing project, the Willamette Greenway, preserves open space along the Willamette (pronounced Wi-lam-it) River, which flows through Portland.

Preceding pages: Portland, 1887. Below, city skyline and the Willamette River.

The city created **Tom McCall Waterfront Park** by taking out a highway and replacing it with green space and fountains along the river. There are height restrictions on downtown buildings to ensure egalitarian views. And residents often spend weekends in the mountains, the desert or at the ocean, all within a three-hour drive of the city.

This premium on protecting and enjoying the city's environment springs from the fact that it is a pretty place, worth saving and savoring. Portland's setting and its temperament are intimately interwoven. Its city limits extend north to the Columbia River, just across from the state of Washington; east into the rich volcanic and alluvial soils where farms once flourished; south into the countrywide-famous and highly productive Willamette Valley; and west over the backbone of the Tualatin Mountains (also known as the West Hills) into the Tualatin Valley.

Rivers and mountains: Two rivers define the city: the mighty Columbia to the north and the Willamette, which bisects the city roughly east and west. The junction of these two rivers made Portland, as its name implies, a natural harbor. The **Port of Portland** is the most active in the Pacific Northwest in wholesale trade and auto imports. Primary products are wheat, logs, lumber and yellow corn. Once filled with pollutants, the Willamette is now fairly clean; city dwellers often fish and boat on it. Until the mid-1970s the city nestled comfortably into the natural confines of the Willamette Valley flood plain – previous residents long ago diked and walled the river – but now the city sprawls into former farmland to the east, the south and the west.

In addition to its rivers, Portland enjoys one of the more dramatic backdrops among US cities. Its western ridge rises 1,200 feet (370 meters), then drops again into the Tualatin Valley, only to climb again in about 25 miles (40 km) into the purple-blue-green undulations of the Coast Range mountains. On the city's east side Mount Scott and Mount Tabor, both extinct volcanoes, bump up out of the plain.

And beyond them, often visible from the city, lie the Cascade Mountains – Rainier, Adams and St Helens in Washington; Hood and Jefferson in Oregon. St Helens, the fabled and explosive volcano which has erupted several times since May 1980, twice blanketed Portland in inches of lung-scarring, gritty ash. If you drive 45 minutes north of Portland and cross the Columbia River into Castle Rock near Vancouver, Washington, you can visit the **Mount St Helens National Historic Monument**. In the Visitor's Center there is a walk-through model of the volcano with a slide presentation and exhibits. Farther east at the end of Highway 504 you can observe the aftermath of the destruction at first hand.

Mount St Helens sits flat-topped and snow-capped, about 50 miles (80 km) north of the city. Its conical (and volcanic) cousins jut dramatically, almost in single file, usually showing at least some snow, reminders that they, too, may blow. Yet the Cascades lure city dwellers to explore their glaciers, snowfields,

Downtown Portland

West Burnside St.

S.W. Ash St.
U.S. Bank Plaza
S.W. Oak St.
S.W. Pine St.
New Market Theater

S.W. 12th Ave.
S.W. 11th Ave.
O'Bryant Sq.
S.W. Stark St.
S.W. 10th Ave.
S.W. 9th Ave.
S.W. Washington
S.W. Alder St.
Bishop's House
Old Town District

S.W. Morrison St.
Ave.
St.
S.W. Taylor St.
Yamhill
St.
S.W. Salmon
Pioneer Courthouse & Square
St.
S.W. Park Ave.
S.W. Broadway
S.W. 6th Ave.
4th
St.
S.W. 3rd
St.
S.W. 2nd Ave.
S.W. 1st Ave.
S.W. Front Ave.
Morrison Bridge
Park

S.W.
Art Museum
Main
Multnomah County Courthouse
Willamette Center
Visitor Info-Center
Waterfront
Willamette River

Oregon Historical Society
S.W.
S.W. 5th Ave.
City Hall
Madison St.
Jefferson St.
S.W. Columbia
S.W. Clay St.
State Office Building
St.
Benjamin Franklin Center
S.W. Market St.
Madison St.
S.W. Mill St.
Civic Auditorium
Portland State University
Portland Center
Hawthorne Bridge

thigh-testing switchback trails, crystalline waters (Portland's water, among the purest in the US, flows from the slopes of Mount Hood), and flower-covered meadows. On a cold, clear winter morning, a warm summer afternoon or a moody early-spring day, when just its broad base pokes out beneath a thick gray cloud bank, Mount Hood dominates the Portland skyline. In many ways, Hood is Portland's mountain.

A temperate climate: Portland's temperate (don't say rainy!) climate also contributes to its character. And no, it isn't always wet. Perhaps the annual fluctuations can best be likened to a moderate monsoon, without the torrents. Despite its reputation, the city averages only 38 inches (1 meter) of moisture a year, roughly the same as New York City, but it comes in prolonged – sometimes longer than two weeks nonstop – drizzles from November to May. After that the skies clear and the city basks in the sun until October, when a gorgeous Indian summer often gives a breather before winter sets in for the season.

Winters are mild, with average temperatures of 39–46°F (4–8°C), with occasional freezes, snow and ice storms. Yet some residents insist that the rain is "dry," eschewing the umbrellas and foul-weather gear visitors and newcomers always seem to require. Construction goes on, people continue to walk to work and weekend campers tough it out despite the downpour.

Perhaps a few sun-needing transplants will pack up and pull out after a winter or two, but others weather it out. The much-loved Oregon Ungreeting Cards' main character, Hugh Wetshoe, intones, "Oregonians don't tan in the summer – they rust!" and "Last summer 10,000 Oregonians fell off their bicycles… and drowned!"

Yet there are pluses to a temperate winter climate. Snow shoveling is a little-known art. Pipes rarely freeze. Outdoor mobility is mostly unaffected. Even in December and January, heather and Japanese cherry flowers color the city. Camellias bloom in February and the first crocus pops up promptly on

A tug pulls logs down the Willamette.

February 1. Soon after this event, the city's lawns and parks explode in an almost fluorescent show of impossibly colored azaleas and rhododendrons, flowering plums, dogwood and bulbs by the gross.

Summer blows in roughly in late May. Midsummer daytime temperatures are rarely too hot, while nights are mostly cool, providing for good sleeping. It may not rain again for three months, and everyone piles outside, to backyards, parks or wilderness. Nearby U-Pick fruit and vegetable farms and orchards thrive. In mid-September things cool down and deciduous trees paint Portland red, orange, yellow and brown. And everyone gets ready for the return of the wet.

From casual to sophisticated: Portland's growth surge began in the mid-1970s; from 1970 to 1980, the population rose 20 percent, making it the thirty-second largest metropolitan area in the country. This coincided with the please-visit-Oregon-but-don't-stay-here era, in which former Governor Tom McCall tried to preserve Oregon from the kind of environmental destruction which other similarly desirable parts of the country had suffered.

In the 1970s, Portland was still thoroughly unpretentious and, in fact, nicely dull. Taco Bell was considered an ethnic restaurant. Downtown workers dressed "northwest casual" – corduroy slacks or skirts, sweaters, jogging shoes and hiking boots, rain-repellent parkas, beards, low-maintenance cosmetics and knapsacks. But all of that has been changing. Now the city has a more sophisticated feel, though the older, more environmentally rooted values still, for the most part, remain.

Some of Portland's mayors were instrumental in this transformation. From 1972 to 1979, Neil Goldschmidt restructured the city. Young, energetic and blessed with far-sighted vision, Goldschmidt had watched the flight to the suburbs and sluggish growth killing the downtown area. Using a master plan, he molded an embryonic Portland, programmed for neighborhood preservation, downtown revitalization and in-

dustrial growth. Then in 1979 President Jimmy Carter appointed him Secretary of Transportation and he moved to Washington, DC. Much of his dream was implemented during the term of Frank Ivancie, his successor, whose term also reflected the early 1980s preoccupation with law and order, and the need for economic growth at all costs.

Signs of the "improved" Portland sprouted everywhere. Close to two dozen buildings were renovated or newly constructed, including a dozen used for high-rise housing, office space, shops and restaurants. Several hotels have been completed, including one with more than 500 rooms. Pioneer Place, an office development with hotel and retail facitlites, includes a Saks Fifth Avenue store. And a performing arts center draws international talent and appreciative audiences to its facilities.

More than a dozen theater groups sprang up to meet the artistic demand. Tri-Met, the city's mass transit agency, completed the **Transit Mall**, which routed all bus traffic through down-

town, and **MAX** (Metropolitan Area Express) the agency's light rail system, began operation. High-tech firms such as Tektronix, Wacker Siltronics and Intel moved in and were successful. So did Nike International, the respected, high-profile designer and manufacturer of athletic equipment.

An influx of immigrants, many of them from Southeast Asia, now enliven the city's cultural base and give Portland a reputation among specialists for fine Asian foods; it's now easy to find restaurants featuring Egyptian, Szechuan, Lebanese, Irish, German, Haitian, Filipino, Italian, Vietnamese, French and Thai cuisine, as well as the excellent offerings the Pacific Northwest has always enjoyed: seafood, wine, fruits, nuts and vegetables.

This new Portland was inherited in 1985 by Ivancie's out-of-the-blue successor, Bud Clark, a tavern owner, neighborhood activist and philosopher whose successful campaign slogan was "Whoop! Whoop!" Colorful, iconoclastic, enthusiastic, casual, accessible and

Band at the annual Rose Festival Parade.

savvy, Clark greeted visitors in *leder–hosen* and rode his bike to his office in City Hall. Clark's influence made Portland a place which enjoys itself. Under him, Goldschmidt's plan for growth continued, shaped by Clark's human-scale agenda, favoring neighborhoods, small business, senior citizens and minorities, as well as limited large industry. All of this has continued into the 1990s, and is set to be the prevailing philosophical agenda well into the next century.

One thing which soon becomes apparent to any visitor is that there are two almost-distinct geopolitical Portlands. As mentioned previously, the Willamette River divides the city into east and west. For some residents that's almost a physical barrier, and they rarely leave their own side of town.

The west side is hilly, densely populated, commercial and home of the downtown core, transportation center and the city's largest park. The east side is mostly flat, residential and industrial: to some it's the "other side of the tracks." Yet many businesses have arisen in this part of town, including the **Convention Center**, the Lloyd's Center and fun, trendy Broadway shops. These have gentrified what 20 years ago was the working-class area of Portland.

Downtown Portland: The downtown area is an easy city center to traverse on foot or by bus, though not so easy by car. Bus travel in the **Free Fare Zone** is (obviously) free, and kiosks with closed-circuit television and free telephone information help locate routes. The city is colorful all year round. These hues take their shades from the flower planters, weather-proof banners and sculpture on the Transit Mall (Southwest Fifth and Sixth avenues), to sidewalk proselytizers, outdoor cafés, an abundance of refreshing fountains, public squares and tucked-away parks, riverfront activity and views of Portland's extraordinary surroundings.

Portland's architecture merits special mention. Many buildings from the late 1800s and early 1900s have been farily recently renovated and are included in fun and informed architectural walking tours. Soaring office structures, not really "skyscrapers," except by Oregonians' standards, record more than 20 years of architectural trends – from Mies van der Rohe glass boxes to the award-winning neoclassical **Portland Building** designed by Michael Graves. This once architecturally unnoticed city has deservedly gained international recognition in recent years.

Retail buildings also reflect this trend: to preserve the best of the old and to add quality to the new. The **New Market Theater** and **Galleria** were, until 1983, nondescript older buildings. Along these lines, brothers Bill and Sam Naito altered the city's retail scene more than anyone else. In the early 1970s, they began financing the restoration of the **Old Town** district on the northern edge of downtown and the Galleria, as well as building the **McCormick Pier** apartment complex (featuring solar-heated water) on the Willamette.

Another outstanding feature of downtown Portland sprawls along its western edge: over 5,300 acres (2,150 hectares) of contiguous parks, including **Forest**

Downtown flower vendor.

Park, at 4,683 acres (1,900 hectares), the largest wilderness area within the confines of a US city. The 214-acre (87-hectare) **Hoyt Arboretum** offers public tours and lectures about its extensive collection of trees and shrubs, as well as its wheelchair-accessible **Bristlecone Pine Trail**. Year round, visitors enjoy the serenity and subtle beauty of the **Japanese Garden**, a haven for contemplation amid the city rush. The **Washington Park International Rose Test Garden** sports more than 400 varieties of roses of every imaginable color and fragrance. They bloom from May to October and peak in June and July, ready for the **Rose Festival** in June.

Washington Park Zoo offers wildlife from around the world. Visitors to the **World Forestry Center** will learn about trees and lumber, so vital to the economy of the Pacific Northwest. In summer a large **outdoor amphitheater** echoes with musical and theatrical performances. As if that weren't enough, over 50 miles (80 km) of trails wind through Hoyt Arboretum and Forest Park: paths for joggers, hikers, picnickers and solace-seekers. Deer are common here, as are springs and clear creeks, wildflowers and dense woods.

Other important landmarks in the downtown Portland area include the **Arlene Schnitzer Performing Arts Center**, the **Portland Art Museum** and **Forecourt Fountain,** whose architect began a city tradition by wading into the fountain during its dedication. At **Pioneer Square**, the 25-foot (8-meter) **Weather Machine** celebrates Oregon's wet weather. Every day at noon it sprays out a misty cloud, then one of three weather creatures rises out of the mist to forecast the coming weather.

Powell's Bookstore (the largest new and used bookstore in the US) is worth a visit, as is **Portland State University**. The **Blitz-Weinhard brewery** offers free tours and tastings of popular Portland-style beers. Portland has more microbreweries and brew pubs than any other US city, and the extent of brews on offer has been compared to those available in Belgian towns or Munich. So if you acquire a taste for Oregon ale, you might try McMenamins' Ruby Ale (made with raspberries) or a Bridgeport Blue Heron Ale. Most Portland establishments of note have at least one microbrew on tap.

Southwest Portland: South of downtown is what's called – of course – Southwest Portland, broken into various neighborhoods of varying character and charm. Local associations nearest the city's center have helped preserve some of the Victorian-era mill housing endangered when 1960s "urban renewal" cleared thousands of homes to make way for freeways and new apartment buildings.

Much of the southwest quadrant is hilly, spilling up and over the **West Hills**. For a magnificent trip on a clear day, take the Scenic Drive which meanders throughout Portland. In the southwest it weaves through wooded hills, past showcase homes and old estates, to the **Council Crest Viewpoint**, the highest spot in Portland.

The viewpoint gives irresistible 360-degree vistas of the Cascade Mountains

Entryway of an Irving Street rowhouse.

range, from Rainier to Jefferson; the Willamette Valley; the Coast Range; Columbia River; and Portland itself. Farther west lies much of the suburban sprawl and still-developing "High Tech Corridor" in the areas of **Tigard**, **Beaverton** and **Hillsboro**.

Notable southwest landmarks include **Washington**, **Duniway** and **Terwilliger Parks**, with their bike/jog/exercise paths; the **Water Tower** located at **John's Landing** shopping area, and **Lewis and Clark College**.

Northwest Portland: Extending north of downtown is Northwest Portland, Oregon's melting pot: combining the densest and most diversified population area in the state, featuring heavy industry, near-wilderness and truck farms. The area adjacent to downtown, from Northwest 21st to 25th avenues and north of Burnside Avenue to Pettygrove Street, offers prime city walking, with lots of enticing shops and restaurants, multicolored San Francisco-styled restored Victorian homes, and the offices of book publishers and filmmakers.

At the northern end of the northwest quadrant, past the heavily industrial riverfront, is **Sauvie Island**, a city treasure. Pastoral and protected, the 20-mile long by 5-mile wide (32-km by 8-km) island houses dozens of U-Pick farms (especially good for strawberries, raspberries and pumpkins) and friendly roadside produce stands.

The East Side: To reach Portland's East Side, cross the Willamette River on one of the city's bridges, two of which have tenders – people employed to raise the bridges for river traffic. The tenders enjoy a romanticized life, and are regularly profiled in the local media. When a bridge goes up in Portland, commuters will pile out of their cars to watch the show rather than snooze, complain or yawn. The bridges also allow downtown workers to park on the less congested east side and enjoy a walk over the river to their jobs.

To get a sense of the role of the river in shaping Portland's character, take a morning or evening walk on the **Burnside, Morrison** or **Hawthorne**

The Japanese Tea Garden, Washington Park.

Bridges. Early in the morning, lean racing sculls will skim by, quietly powered by one or more rowers. Waterfowl will flap overhead, fish will jump, morning light will pinken the West Hills and bounce blindingly off high-rise windows and the sun will rise slowly from behind Mount Hood.

Sunset walks are usually more noisy and less contemplative, but evening colors are the reward with deepening shades of pink and red on the Cascades. Nighthawks will chatter and, in summer, boats will cruise by, some with water skiers attached.

The sparkling glass pyramid on the riverfront of the East Side sits on top of the **Oregon Museum of Science and Industry** (OMSI). If you want to experience the force of tornadoes or earthquakes, or beam a message into outer space, **OMSI**'s interactive exhibits are definitely for you.

Inside OMSI are two theaters. The **Murdoch Sky Theater** is a planetarium with a laser show. The **OMNIMAX Theater** has a five-story tall projection screen and 16,000-watt sound system that are guaranteed to alter your reality. OMSI also has a riverfront restaurant with an excellent view of both the river and the Portland skyline.

From the very early 1900s until the 1960s, with a peak in the 1930s, 1940s and 1950s, the old **Produce Row** flourished along the river on the southeast side of town. Here, vendors, many of them Italian immigrants, sold and distributed local fresh fruits, vegetables, meats and eggs, much of it produce from their own farms. This tradition has now been replaced by a 10-block, wide strip of light industry and wholesale warehouses, which blends into residential neighborhoods, the prime low-rent areas closest to downtown.

Traditionally, it has been senior citizens, students and minorities who have made up the inner-southeast population, but now a fairly stylish community has moved in, especially along **Hawthorne Boulevard**. This group has brought with it some of the best restaurants and crafts, antiques and clothing

stores in the city. The **Sellwood** neighborhood farther south is similar.

Southeast landmarks include **Mount Tabor** and **Mount Scott**, the **Scenic Drive**, **Reed College** and the **Crystal Springs Rhododendron Garden**. **Leach Botanical Park**, formerly a private estate, is now a city-owned park; **Oaks Bottom** and **Ross Island** natural areas are scenic necessities. Nearby is the Westmoreland neighborhood with its **Stars Antique Mall**.

The Northeast: The northeast of Portland is mostly residential with pockets of light industry. The **Irvington** neighborhood is particularly colorful in spring, when pink dogwood and other flowering trees and shrubs are in bloom.

Northeast Portland is the home of **Portland International Airport**, the **Lloyd Center** (the first covered shopping mall in the United States), **Memorial Coliseum** (home of the Portland Trailblazers basketball team until 1995) and **Holliday Market**.

North Portland is actually a geographical extension of the northeast, but it is considered a separate entity because it was formed from the annexed communities of **St Johns**, **Linnton** and others. It resembles the northeast in its mix of residential and light industrial sections, and is the site of yet another spur of the Scenic Drive, the Port of Portland's **Rivergate** complex and major docks, the **University of Portland** and **Portland Meadows Racetrack**.

Jantzen Beach/Hayden Island, the houseboat and commercial development at the Oregon end of the Interstate 5 bridge over the Columbia River, is also worth noting.

East along the Columbia's banks lie many of the city's **yacht clubs**. Sailing from these moorages (some boats can be rented) is not for the faint-hearted. It requires tricky tacking in strong winds and currents, as well as quick maneuvers away from tremendous ocean cargo carriers. However, intimate contact with the powerful and folkloric river and the spectacular views of Mount Hood, which dominates the eastern horizon, make this adventure well worthwhile.

A sea of joggers compete in the Cascade Run-Off.

THE OREGON COAST

The 400-mile (643-km) Oregon Coast is one of the world's most spectacular parks, owned by the people of Oregon. Legislative action in 1913 and in 1967 set aside the coastline for "free and uninterrupted use" by the public. Billboards are controlled, making the appearance unlike the southern California coast, for example. Oswald West, the governor who defended the public coastline early in the century, tapped a progressive strain in Oregonians that remains alive today.

This rugged coast offers unusual diversity to the traveler. One superlative element that distinguishes it is the 32,000-acre (12,950-hectare) Oregon Dunes National Recreation Area, consisting of huge sand dunes located between Florence and Coos Bay. Miles of monumental sand dunes remind one of the equally expansive sand dunes of Death Valley in California.

In addition to the dunes, the Oregon Coast offers forests, seashore, beachcombing, tidepooling, camping and fishing. There are over 60 state parks along US Highway 101, including some that preserve virgin vestiges of the state's impressive coniferous forests. Everywhere, the parks beckon the traveler to leave the car and actively enjoy the beach, the trails, the hillsides and the fresh and invigorating air.

Behind the coast rise the cliffs and headlands of the Coast Range of mountains, which increase in elevation as they stretch south, paralleling the Cascade Range.

Sunny summers and stormy winters: Due to the maritime influence, the Oregon Coast climate remains mild year-round. Summer is warm and sunny; often the pleasant autumn weather provides an Indian summer of exceptional color. In winter, slashing storms attack the coast. Appreciators of storms watch these tactics from snug coastal houses, warmed by wood-stove fires. Beachcombers rise early the following day to inspect the treasures deposited by the tossing surf.

Coast US 101 runs from Astoria to Brookings, the full length of the Oregon Coast. From the major towns of the Willamette Valley arteries lead west to the coast, or US 30 links Portland with Astoria at the coast's northern edge. The Sunset Highway, US 26, connects Portland with Seaside, the closest portion of the coast and a major coastal resort area.

Fishing and logging have traditionally been the livelihoods that supported settlers along the coast. Now visitors to the Oregon Coast amount to a major state industry, and tourism ranks as a "catch" edging out fishing.

Well-kept wilderness: To orient yourself to the coast, start at **Fort Stevens State Park** and work your way south. **Fort Stevens**, originally a Civil War fort, becomes a moderate-sized town in summer when its 605 campsites are filled. If this is your introduction to Oregon's state parks, you will learn that they appear manicured and well-groomed – an image of nature fully under control. There is a substantial

Preceding pages: a cresting wave at Cape Kiwanda, near Pacific City. Below, Astoria Tower.

biking and walking trail network at Fort Stevens. Four miles (6 km) of shoreline at the park offer surf fishing, clam digging and material for sand castling. Fort Stevens, which guarded the mouth of the Columbia River, had the distinction of being one of the few US mainland installations fired on by the Japanese in World War II. A Japanese submarine did little damage, but caused a stir by shelling Battery Russell. An interpretive center tells the story of the fort going back to the Civil War.

Along the water's edge at Fort Stevens, almost buried in sand, lies the forlorn wreck of the four-masted, iron-hulled British schooner, *Peter Iredale*, which ran aground in 1906. The wreck forcefully emphasizes the importance of lighthouses along this treacherous coast. A parade of ships has met an unfortunate fate against this stretch of rugged rocks and cliffs.

A maritime heritage: Just inland from Fort Stevens, along the Columbia River, lies the town of **Astoria**. Astoria has always had a maritime orientation, so it's fitting that it hosts the **Columbia River Maritime Museum** charting the Columbia River and general maritime history. Be sure to visit this museum along the Astoria waterfront to learn of the whaling, sealing and fishing activities that were so prominent in Oregon's past. The exhibitions on salmon fishing are instructive, and they include gill nets used by Native Americans and small boats rowed by solitary fishermen onto the open seas.

Besides exhibitions on the discovery and development of the Columbia, there are displays about larger patterns of seagoing exploration, trade and warfare. The museum's assemblage of model ships includes a replica of the battleship *Oregon*. The largest artifact at the museum, docked along the river, is the lightship *Columbia*, which served as a visual aid for ships crossing the Columbia bar from 1950–80.

While exploring in Astoria, you'll see sport fishing and commercial fishing boat traffic on the river. Fish canning operations flourish here. Large ships

Bridge spans the Columbia River at Astoria.

leave with agricultural and forest products, bound mainly for Asia. Among the agricultural products shipped out of Astoria are wheat, apples, pears, peaches and berries. Pleasure boating is also prominent, especially during the August Astoria Regatta.

Easy passage for large commercial boats became a severe problem after the 1980 eruption of Mount St Helens. The volcano, which lies to the northeast, deposited so much debris from its volcanic mudflows into the Columbia River that all shipping ground to a virtual standstill until the river could be dredged. The 4-mile (6-km) **Trans Columbia Bridge** connects Astoria with Megler, Washington.

For a panoramic view of the area, drive to a hilltop in Astoria, called **Coxcomb Hill**, to see the **Astoria Column**, which is 125 feet (37 meters) high. At the top of the column, a long frieze tells the story of the discovery of the Columbia and the founding of Astoria. The Astoria column was constructed in 1926 to commemorate events connected with the discovery, exploration and settlement of the Northwest. An observation platform, 166 steps up from the bottom, enables you to see the surrounding mountains, river and ocean.

As you drive the hilly streets of Astoria, you'll note the well-kept Victorian houses that generations of prosperous seafaring families have built and maintained. (For a map listing the choicest Victorians to drive or walk by, stop at the local Chamber of Commerce on the port docks.) Most of the prominent homes are on Grand and Franklin avenues. Queen of these is the Flavel Mansion, also known as the "house with the red roof." The mansion is now a **Clatsop County Historical Society Museum** with exhibits on the native inhabitants of the region and the contribution of different ethnic groups, such as the Chinese. Local families, many of them of Scandinavian descent, also celebrate their roots at a Midsummer Scandinavian Festival.

Fort Clatsop National Memorial, in honor of the expedition by Lewis and

Sunset at Bandon Beach.

Clark and located on the Lewis and Clark River, is worth visiting to immerse yourself in the rugged, self-sufficient world of the early explorers. Here, the party spent the winter of 1805–6, which they recorded as "wet and disagreeable," with only 12 days of sunshine. A replica of the original stockade has been created.

In the fort, details of daily life are enacted, from the skinning of a beaver to the forging of a musket ball. Among the exhibits is a 32-foot (10-meter) dugout canoe of the type the party used on the rivers. An informative film also brings the expedition alive. Meriwether Lewis and William Clark's journals provided the first comprehensive report on the region, fueling the imagination of trappers and settlers.

Popular vacation spots: Moving south, **Seaside** is a prominent resort and convention area that is often visited by Portland residents. It presents a lively ambience with a beach boardwalk. At a salt cairn here, comrades of Lewis and Clark boiled seawater down to get salt so that they could season food on the long trip homeward in 1806.

Cannon Beach, south from Seaside, received its unusual name from a cannon that washed ashore here in 1846 after the US Navy schooner *Shark* wrecked while attempting to leave the Columbia River. Cannon Beach is an artistic counterpart of Seaside. Sculptors and artists fill the galleries with their art and join thousands of vacationers on the beach each summer for a Sand Castle Building Contest. Cannon Beach has become a coastal cultural milieu, with Portland State University sponsoring the Haystack Program in the Arts, an extensive summer program of classes in music, photography, writing and other arts. Theatrical performances are presented at the **Coaster Theater**. Among several interesting stores is the **Fair Winds**, which specializes in old nautical artifacts, including marine paintings and prints. At Cannon Beach, a large offshore monolith and bird sanctuary called **Haystack Rock** provides enough shelter to allow small boats to be launched directly into the ocean.

South of Cannon Beach stands **Neahkahnie Mountain**, a high, forested headland with a wildflower-bordered trail leading to panoramic views of the coastline. South of Neahkahnie is the quiet village of Manzanita, and then Nehalem, a river town noted for its antique shops and good fishing.

Tasting wine and cheese: Past Nehalem turn briefly inland, following the road signs to **Mohler**, and visit Patrick McCoy's **Nehalem Bay Winery**, an example of Oregon wine production. The winery produces a Gewurtztraminer, a Pinot Noir, and a blackberry dessert wine. Linger for a self-guided tour of the winery and a look at the art gallery upstairs.

Other Oregon wine-tasting opportunities along the coast are at Lincoln City and at Bandon. At Seaside, stop at the **Airlie Tasting Room** at Spindrift Wine and Cheese, featuring Airlie Vineyards' Pinot Noir, Chardonnay, Reisling and Gewurtztraminer. At Lincoln City is the **Oak Knoll** tasting room. South, at Bandon, **Bjelland Vineyards** also has a

The rocky coast near Arch Rock.

tasting room. These tasting rooms are for wineries whose production facilities and vineyards are found farther inland.

Nehalem Bay and **Tillamook**, to the south, are prime picnic areas, at sites such as **Nehalem Bay State Park** or the **Three Capes Loop Road** west of Tillamook. Consider stocking up in the small town of **Garibaldi** – with bread at the **Bay Front Bakery** and with Dungeness crab or shrimp at **Phil and Joe's Crab** or **Smith's Pacific Shrimp**.

At Tillamook, two impressive cheese-making operations are worth a stop to fill out the picnic basket. The **Blue Heron Cheese Company** offers tastings of their Brie and Camembert cheeses, ranging from day-old Camembert used as a breakfast cheese to garlic-flavored varieties. They also produce a mild blue cheese, called Camemblue. Blue Heron also sells local wine. Nehalem Pinot Noir with Blue Heron Brie or Camembert make an excellent picnic duo. Cheese-making is a highly developed art in Oregon, and may be a consolation for the incessant rain. Dairies account for 25 percent of all farm income in the Tillamook area.

The second major cheese maker here is the **Tillamook County Creamery**, one of the largest cheese plants in the West. (The cheese plant is easily recognized, as on its lawn rests the replica of a large sailing ship, the *Morning Star*, built originally in 1854 to carry local produce and trade goods to west coast markets.) Tillamook Creamery produces a well-known cheddar sold under the Tillamook label. You can take a tour, taste cheese, and watch it being made from an observation area in the cheese factory. A visit to the cheesemaking museum is part of the tour.

Tillamook area history can be perused at length at the **Pioneer Museum** in Tillamook at Second and Pacific Avenue. Nature, the Native Americans and the pioneers are well-portrayed here. Of special interest are the wildlife displays and a mineral room featuring the rocks of Oregon.

Tall forests by the sea: West of Tillamook, the scenic Three Capes Loop

Fields of yellow lupine at Cape Sebastian.

takes you to three jutting promontories (Cape Meares, Cape Lookout and Cape Kiwanda). Here the tall forests come right down to the pounding surf. At **Cape Kiwanda** salmon may be purchased fresh from the boats. There is a lighthouse, built in 1890, at **Cape Meares**. Along this route you'll see a huge Sitka spruce tree, with multiple trunks, known as the Octopus Tree. **Cape Lookout** has a pleasant, year-round campground and an attractive beach to stroll along.

Almost all the rivers emptying into the Pacific along the Oregon Coast offer good trout, steelhead and salmon fishing. Along the coastal beaches you'll also see people with long suction tubes probing for succulent clams. In the spring, at **Yachats**, you may witness silver smelt coming in to spawn on the volcanic sand. The locals, aware of the smelt lifecycle, will be waiting with dip nets to harvest their allowed 25 pounds (10 kg) per person per day.

Southward, **Lincoln City** is the start of a well-publicized "Twenty Miracle Miles" strip of coastal property. Here the "ma and pa" establishments typical of coastal Oregon give way to larger corporate ventures, capable of convention-size gatherings. Among the noted resorts, the most famous is award-winning **Salishan Lodge**, built tastefully of native stone, rough-sawn fir and cedar, and set on 700 acres (280 hectares) of forest reserve with views of the ocean.

Lincoln City has several art galleries, plus opportunities to visit the artisans. Two popular galleries are **Ryan Gallery** and **Rickert Art Center**. At **Alder House II**, a half mile east of US 101 on Immonen Road, there's a glassblowing studio where owner Buzz Williams works in the traditional method, making each piece individually. **Mossy Creek Pottery and Gallery**, also on Immonen Road, emphasizes limited production of fine handmade pottery. In the adjacent gallery are handiworks crafted by owner Bob Richardson and several of his colleagues.

South from Lincoln City, **Cape Foulweather** is a headland notable for

Driftwood, Oregon Sand Dunes National Recreation Area near Florence.

its scenery. Towering 450 feet (135 meters) above the waves, Cape Foulweather offers the highest coastal vista in Oregon. (Captain James Cook named the cape in 1778.) **The Lookout**, a gift shop at the crest of Foulweather, sells a range of wood, shell and stone mementos from Oregon.

At **Newport**, stop in at the Oregon State University's **Marine Science Center** on Yaquina Bay. The center is a good place to study the natural history of the Oregon Coast and includes excellent exhibits explaining estuaries, the most productive and scarce natural areas on the earth. Estuaries occur only where rivers and streams enter the ocean: in the mix of fresh and salt water abundant vegetation and wildlife, including the young of many species of fish, can flourish. In the adjacent bookstore you can find an excellent selection of books about the flora and fauna of Oregon. The Marine Science Center has a major responsibility to study any adverse effects on the state fisheries, which have a dockside value of $60–70 million per year. The center includes a hands-on exhibition where children can touch friendly sea creatures.

Within walking distance of the Marine Science Center is the new **Oregon Coast Aquarium**, which opened in 1992. One of Oregon's top attractions, it features indoor and outdoor exhibits, showcasing Pacific marine life.

Seafood in abundance: Newport is the hub of the Dungeness crab and shrimp fishery. Salmon fishing and oyster farming aquaculture are also major businesses. Restaurants specialize in the local seafood. Newport Beach is also popular with agate hunters, who scour the shore. The April–May Sea Faring Festival attracts many visitors.

Yaquina Bay's lighthouse, built in 1871, overlooks a beach of jagged rocks and abundant driftwood, testifying to the currents and tides that made boating treacherous and a lighthouse advisable. The lighthouse includes a museum authentically refurnished with period artifacts celebrating the role of lighthouses along the Oregon Coast.

South of Newport is an Oregonian artistic effort that shouldn't be missed – chainsaw art. At an establishment called **Sea Gulch** you can see one of the largest collections of chainsaw carvings.

The **Heceta Lighthouse and Point**, 12 miles (20 km) north of **Florence**, is a scenic and rugged part of the coast. One major delight in the area is **Sea Lion Caves**, a natural wonder along the coast. The site is the only year-round home on the mainland for wild sea lions. An elevator takes you down to where the mammals can be viewed in the 1,500-foot (500-meter) cavern. Clusters of large sea lion bulls, the more docile females, and their young disport themselves within close view.

The town of Florence is noted for its rhododendrons, which flower here most profusely in May in time for the Rhododendron Festival celebrations. Along the waterfront, on Bay Street, the town's oldest buildings have been restored in recent years; now the area is a thriving district of shops and restaurants.

Dramatic dunes: Moving south from Florence, you enter an unexpected ter-

Arago Lighthouse, near Charleston.

rain where sand dunes replace the forested slopes and rocky shore. Between Florence and Coos Bay you'll witness 41 miles (66 km) of dunes. Orient yourself to the **Dunes National Recreation Area**, created in 1972, by stopping at the park service office in Florence (855 Highway Avenue) or at the overlook 10 miles (16 km) north of Reedsport which offers an excellent orientation. Viewing decks on three levels give you various perspectives on the dunes and the local vegetation, and a pleasant 1-mile (1½-km) trail leads down to the ocean.

At over 500 feet (150 meters) high, especially in the southern part of the dune territory, these dunes are higher than those of Africa's Sahara Desert. How the dunes came to be is an intriguing geologic tale. Although most of the coastal mountains of Oregon are basaltic, the stretch just behind the dunes is sandstone, which has eroded easily, producing the dunes' loose sand. Scientists believe that most of the dune creation has occurred in the last 10–15,000 years, both from erosion and from sediment

transported to the shore by rivers and streams. Ocean currents have distributed the sand along the shore, where wave action pushed the sand up on the beaches. When the tide is out, the dry sand is picked up by wind and deposited farther inland, forming dunes. Behind the dunes, most notably in the **Jessie Honeyman Memorial State Park**, are several freshwater streams and lakes populated by trout and bass.

A walk through the dunes offers an opportunity for solitude and aesthetic pleasure. Examine the sensuous sandy shapes, or look for the battering effects the constant chisel of blowing sand makes on logs and rocks. Where vegetation has grasped a foothold on the dunes, you'll find spring wildflowers amidst the silvery green beach grass. Swans, loons, hawks and ducks are plentiful.

Visitors to the dunes should be prepared for wind. Carry a wind-breaking jacket with layers of warm clothes underneath. The wind blows steadily from the northwest from April to September and from the southwest in winter. For a

Garibaldi Harbor at Tillamook Bay.

detailed hiking map of the area, check with the ranger at the Dunes headquarters in Florence. If you are thinking of camping, the national forest or national park service camps at the Dunes have an appealing rusticity.

Legacy of a lumber baron: South of the dunes, **Coos Bay** boasts one of Oregon's most attractive state parks, called **Shore Acres**. This floral landscape, including an oriental garden, was originally groomed for lumber baron Louis J. Simpson, one of the coast's most colorful historical personalities. Simpson played a substantial role in Oregon in the first decades of this century, including a run for the governorship. He was the son of the legendary Captain Asa M. Simpson, a New Englander who founded the Oregon lumbering and shipbuilding empire that still bears his name. It is said that Asa Simpson never insured his ships, but took the risks, which fortunately didn't ruin him. His son, Louis, came to Oregon in 1899 at age 22. Louis bought 320 acres (130 hectares) at Cape Arago and built a fashionable New England-style house, lavishly inlaid with native myrtle-wood, which now commands a high price even in small amounts. The house, built on a bluff 100 feet (30 meters) above the surf, was Simpson's gift to his bride and included Tiffany chandeliers and Persian carpets in the living room overlooking the sea.

By 1915, Simpson had 200 acres (80 hectares) of formal gardens cultivated around the house. To the native rhododendrons and azaleas, Simpson added plants from the regions where his ships sailed. He reached the apex of his career in 1918. In that year he ran for the governorship, but lost. Unfortunately, Louis Simpson's personal and business fortunes proved less secure than his father's. His wife died in 1920, and the house burned down a year later. A cluster of business ventures failed in the 1920s. Finally, in 1934, he deeded to the state the 134 acres (54 hectares) that form the park.

Coos Bay is the largest natural harbor on the west coast between Puget Sound and San Francisco. To Oregonians, Coos Bay is synonymous with lumber. The town calls itself the "world's largest lumber shipping port." (The state of Oregon leads the country in lumber production, but the 1980s was the most depressed decade in the history of the industry.) At Coos Bay you'll see freighters exporting lumber products, mainly to Japan. A tour of the **Weyerhauser Lumber Mill** shows how jets of water rip the bark off trees, exposing the wood. Giant saws quickly slice the trees into finished lumber. Aside from the lumber fleet, Coos Bay also supports a fishing fleet that ranges wide over the ocean and sport fishermen in smaller boats dream of catching striped bass.

A natural sanctuary: Founded in 1854 by J.C. Tolman of the Coos Bay Company, the town of Coos Bay preserves its interest in the past in a museum and several historical homes, which can be toured. Stop in at the Chamber of Commerce, 502 E. Central Avenue, for a self-guided map.

Coos Bay's conservation effort centers on the **South Slough Sanctuary**, a 4,300-acre (1,740-hectare) preserve of

Cape Foulweather, north of Newport.

fresh and salt water marsh set aside by the state of Oregon in 1974. Free guided trail walks are available on Fridays in summer, with rangers interpreting the varied life forms, ranging from oceanic waterfowl to a fir forest.

At Coos Bay, you also enter myrtle-wood country. This distinctive local hardwood is fashioned into dishes, jewelry and other decorative mementos. At the **House of Myrtlewood** factory in Coos Bay you can see myrtlewood logs sawn into slabs. Skilled artisans with lathes turn the wood into bowls, goblets and other products.

Though tidepool exploring opportunities are excellent all along the coast, **Cape Arago**, west of Coos Bay and south of Shore Acres State Park, is a particularly outstanding area. Of the three major coves here, **North Cove** is the largest, with numerous pools and channels among boulders and bedrock. Algae grow luxuriously.

Intertidal animals, including anemones, are abundant. **Middle Cove**, which is accessible by a steep but well-con-structed trail, is the smallest and most exposed of the coves. Purple sea urchins are numerous here. **South Cove** is the final cove, also accessible by a steep trail. Sharp, vertical cliffs give way to bedrock and large boulders. Large bull kelp quiet the subtidal flow. Watch for chitons, starfish and crab.

Beacons in the night: At Cape Arago, stop also for a look at the lighthouse. The names behind all these landmarks on the Oregon Coast have their stories. When Captain James Cook, the English navigator, first saw Cape Arago on March 12; 1778, he named it after the saint of the day, as was his custom, and it became Cape Gregory.

This sufficed as a name until 1850, when citizens sought to honor the great German Baron Alexander von Humboldt, the biologist, explorer and statesman who had described much of the flora and terrain of this wild region. Since the bay at Eureka, California, had already been named Humboldt Bay, local citizens came up with the name of Humboldt's friend, the distinguished

Ecola State Park, near Cannon Beach.

French physicist, Dominique Francois Jean Arago.

South of Coos Bay, you enter berry country. **Bandon** is Oregon's cranberry capital, with 900 acres (364 hectares) under cultivation. Coinciding with the harvest is a September Cranberry Festival. Bandon also boasts a prominent cheese company, the **Coquille Valley Dairy Co-op**, which produces – under the Bandon label – a variety of flavored cheeses (onion, garlic, jalapeno and smoked). The cheese plant includes a viewing window and a narrated slide show. Bandon also has a restored Old Town with cafes and shops selling everything from pottery to sticky candy.

South of Bandon, the Oregon Coast reaches its westernmost point at **Cape Blanco**. The Cape was first noted in the records of Spanish explorer Martin de Aguilar in January 1603. Cape Blanco's brick lighthouse, built in 1870, has been continuously in use and is open for inspection. The black sand at Cape Blanco is strikingly unlike the tan sand of the rest of the coast.

Port Orford, the most westerly city in the contiguous United States, is a friendly and unpretentious port town, thriving on fishing and lumber. Citizens of the town have made a determined effort to preserve its small-town 19th-century aura. Stop in at the Chamber of Commerce for a walking tour map of the oceanfront district.

Sightsee the ocean and the rivers: All along the Oregon Coast, you can watch the migration of gray whales south in December–January and again north in March–April. **Port Orford Wayside State Park** is one of the best places.

Gold Beach, at the mouth of the Rogue River, is the departure point for jet boat trips up this intriguing waterway, one of the best steelhead fishing streams in Oregon. The Rogue is also one of 10 designated "Wild and Scenic Rivers" in the United States. Guides on the jet boat trips are often competent naturalists and historians of the area. The jet boats, which can skim along on 6 inches (15 cm) of water, go 32 miles (50 km) up the river from Gold Beach to Agness (the "short trip") or 104 miles (165 km) to Paradise and the notorious rapids of Blossom Bar (the "long trip").

Brookings, just north of the California border, prospers with unloading and processing facilities for salmon, tuna, shrimp, crab and rock fish. Brookings is also the nation's major producer of Easter lilies and daffodils. Outstanding displays of azaleas can be seen in the **Azalea State Park** east of US 101. An Azalea Festival in May coincides with the major blossoming time. One other intriguing annual festival here is a Driftwood Show in April when connoisseur beachcombers congregate. The entire southern third of the Oregon Coast is a bonanza for driftwood collectors and kelp kickers. **Harris Beach State Park** and **Samuel H. Boardman State Park** are choice locations for such pursuits.

After encountering the multiple pleasures of the Oregon Coast, it's easy to comprehend why Oregonians feel so protective about it. They're proud of its wild splendor and enjoy sharing it with visitors; they only ask appreciation and careful use in return.

<u>Left</u>, kite flying near Lincoln City. <u>Right</u>, stony outcrop at Bandon Beach.

WILLAMETTE RIVER VALLEY

When people from outside the Northwest picture Oregon, they might imagine a chlorophyll commonwealth whose tolerance for new ideas and different lifestyles seems as fresh as the air in this rain-forested retreat. Of course, not all of Oregon today brings to mind the frontier, but in much of the lower **Willamette Valley**, the region settled in the wake of the Oregon Trail (circa 1840), one can still conjure the bygone era. Within minutes of Oregon's second and third largest cities, Eugene (pop. 113,000) and Salem (108,000), there is enough of the unspoiled physical landscape, pastoral charm and pioneer spirit to fulfill even the most romantic of preconceptions.

Tall timbers, undulating hillocks of green, and water, water everywhere surround the flood plain of the Willamette River here. The Cascade Mountains to the east and the Coast Range to the west further define the southern part of the valley. From the time the Oregon Trail pioneers marched upon the stage in this natural amphitheater, to the present, the southern Willamette's allure has been both constant and diverse. Today there are major cities where there had once been only the one-horse towns of Salem, Corvallis and Eugene. The campfires are gone now and the flickering lights in the forest in these places have become larger and more defined.

Those lights in the forest shone perhaps most brightly in the 1970s, when several "Quality of Life" surveys touted Eugene among the best American cities in which to live. Similarly, Cottage Grove in 1970 was one of a select group of highly rated "All-American" cities, and Salem rated the same accolade in 1961 and 1983. While such assessments are somewhat dated and highly subjective, a city and a region equidistant from some of the grandest mountain and coastal scenery must have a special appeal, survey or no survey.

Then, too, there are the dense evergreen forests which made the lower Willamette Valley the timber capital of the world, and the rich soil here that moved the pioneers to exclaim that "the crops never fail west of the Cascades." This impressive landscape takes on a special character thanks in part to the covered bridges, historic buildings and old homes that date from the days of the Oregon Trail.

Salem – capital ideas: The State Capitol building at **Salem** is a good place to get a historic and panoramic perspective on all of the aforementioned and to orient oneself to this Emerald Empire. As you approach the building you are greeted by the sculpted marble visages of Lewis and Clark as well as the wagon trains of the Oregon Trail pioneers. Inside the capitol, ornate panels in the rotunda show wagon trails along the Willamette and Columbia Rivers.

Those who climb the 121-step spiral stairway to the capitol dome are rewarded with a fine view of Salem and the valley, as well as Mount Hood and other Cascade Peaks over 40 miles (64 km) away. This view of the Willamette countryside against a snowcapped mountain backdrop is definitely something to savor.

The ecotopian outlook: Atop the capitol stands the gold-plated statue of a bearded, axe-wielding pioneer. This is a fitting symbol of a state whose trailblazing has not been confined to the wagon train's westward migration. Such controversial legislation as the "bottle bill" which mandated the recycling of aluminum and glass containers for deposit were enacted in these halls.

Oregon lawmakers eloquently stated their priorities when they mandated the cleanup of the Willamette River in the early 1970s. Since Jason Lee founded a Methodist mission on the Willamette in 1834, the valley's fortunes have been tied to the river. The pioneers and the Calapooya Indians drew salmon and steelhead from Willamette waters, and steamboats brought the produce of valley farms to Portland en route to the goldfields of California. In the modern era, 20 municipalities and more than 600 industrial plants chose to locate their premises on the Willamette.

Predictably, the water quality suffered, eventually becoming so poor that former Governor Tom McCall termed the waterway "an open sewer." Then came the state directives compelling industry to finance $50 million worth of pollution control and cleanup.

In the wake of this legislation, salmon and steelhead could be seen spawning in great numbers for the first time in over 40 years. In addition, many Willamette Valley towns have been able to develop riverside park and recreation areas from monies allocated under the river cleanup provisions.

This same kind of progressive outlook and environmentalism has prompted many commentators and columnists to brand state lawmakers as "ecotopian." This adjective synthesizing the words ecological and utopia was popularized by Ernest Callenbach's 1973 futuristic fantasy about the secession of Oregon from the United States based on environmental imperatives.

In any case, expectations of a "laidback" ecotopian capital are initially put to rest in downtown Salem by the spit-and-polish facade of its administrative buildings and the no-nonsense demeanor of the people who work in them. In fact, the ominous presence of Salem's State Mental Hospital was a backdrop for the film version of Oregon novelist Ken Kesey's book, *One Flew Over the Cuckoo's Nest*. The State Penitentiary and Xerox-copy drabness of the state office buildings compound the superficial impression that legislation, and little else, goes on here.

The hard edge of Salem is softened considerably, however, by a stroll through the many oases of greenery within city limits as well as exposure to the charm of preserved pioneer heritage. The tree-shaded campus of **Willamette University** (established 1842), the oldest in the west, and the landscaped grounds of the **Civic Center** featuring statues and sculptures seem worlds away from the nearby halls of bureaucracy.

Just south of the downtown area on Mission Street is **Bush Park**, which

<u>Preceding</u> <u>pages</u>: a pioneer-era cabin. <u>Below</u>, a settlement along the Columbia River.

features a Victorian gas-lit mansion with some original furnishings and an art museum with monthly exhibitions by Pacific Northwest artists.

Down from the **Bush House** on Mission Street is the elegant **Deepwood Estate**. Here, 4 acres (2 hectares) of cultivated formal gardens and natural wildflower displays offer another escape from the affairs of state.

Southeast of the capitol are the second- and third-oldest buildings in the Northwest, Jason Lee's house and parsonage. They are part of the **Mission Mill Village** complex, which has a working mill that spins yarn on antique equipment. Water power from the Willamette meant Salem's woolen and flour mills developed early. Later an iron works and lumber mills made the city flourish.

Up Highway 22: The past and present come together downtown at the **Reed Opera House**, the hub of Salem's cultural and social life during the Victorian era. Today, specialty shops thrive amid an atmosphere evocative of a "gussied-up" dance hall.

Proximity to great escapes abound outside of the Salem metropolitan area as well. One of the premier attractions is **Silver Falls State Park**, 26 miles (40 km) east of town via State Highways 22 and 214. Here in Oregon's largest state park, a variety of waterfalls decorate two densely forested canyons. This park is near the old mill town of **Silverton** and offers a swimming area, miles of horse and bike trails, a campground and a nature interpretive center. The 8-mile (13-km) trail to the various falls is a treat during fall foliage season and in winter when the east winds transform the gossamer-like flumes into ice sculptures. Half of the 14 falls are over 100 feet (30 meters) high, with the swirling mists of **South Falls** topping off the group at 177 feet (54 meters). Aside from having the largest concentration of waterfalls in the US, the park affords the opportunity to follow a trail which takes you behind many of the falls.

State 22 then threads through the foothills past stands of Douglas-fir the size of redwoods, numerous reservoirs, and

Left, the State Capitol building is topped by a gilded pioneer. Right, Deady Hall, University of Oregon at Eugene.

sparkling rivers and lakes well suited for fishing or water sports. There is also hiking and skiing in nearby National Forest and Recreation Areas.

The highway follows the North Santiam River, and offers a distant view of the second highest peak in the Cascades, **Mount Jefferson** (10,495 feet/ 3,200 meters). This peak can be seen by taking the spur road past **Detroit** up the Breitenbush River in the **Ollalie Scenic Area**. From this region of lava buttes, alpine meadows and lakes, the perpetually snow-clad slope of the mountains appears above thousands of planted Christmas trees.

Also in the area is **Breitenbush Hot Springs**, a retreat and conference center maintained by a spiritual community. This is a place for those for whom a contemplative experience transcends what might be called primitive facilities.

South from Salem: South of Salem, the fields of strawberries, sugar beets and grass seed seem endless. In addition to other such staples as beans, broccoli and cherries, regional specialties such as filberts (hazelnuts), peppermint and the early ripening Pinot Noir and Chardonnay grapes flourish here. The agricultural richness of the region is on display at the Oregon State Fair (late August) at the **Exposition Center** in northeast Salem. One of the largest farm cooperatives in the state, Agripac, located in Salem, Eugene and Woodburn, distributes the harvest throughout the United States, Asia and Mexico.

Crops are nurtured by the mild climate and by the blessing of what is usually a gentle but persistent rain. *The Washington Post*'s Joel Garreau described the typical October through April weather conditions here as a "difficult-to-define balance that is moister than mist but drier than drizzle." Unappetizing as this might sound, locals are quick to point out that the Willamette Valley's 46-inch (120-cm) average yearly rainfall does not appreciably exceed the totals reached in New York or Miami. The rainbows in the intermittent spring sunshine here alleviate the grayness endured through the winter.

A covered bridge over the McKenzie River.

The main route connecting the Willamette Valley cities, Interstate 5, avoids the congestion of in-town, stop-start traffic. Old State 99 parallels I-5 but runs through the small towns closer to the Willamette River.

These routes are distinguished by year-round greenery, a profusion of hawks perched on fenceposts, sheep in the pastures, and daffodils that chart a springtime yellow brick road through the Emerald Empire.

Houses, heritage and hospitality: While the black billows from smokestacks on I-5 in Millersbury temporarily interrupt this springtime reverie, once you leave the interstate a whole neighborhood of elegant 19th-century buildings brings back a more genteel era in **Albany**.

The 100-block central neighborhood features architectural styles including Carpenter Gothic, Italianate, Queen Anne and Stick Eastlake. The latter motifs reflect the era of affluence between 1850 and 1900 when the Willamette River and the railroad were used to export timber and produce at great profit. More than 350 historic buildings still exist between Elm and Jefferson avenues. Albany also boasts a number of historic covered bridges.

A little northeast of Albany, the pioneer era is similarly recreated by half-a-dozen covered bridges near Scio. In addition, the **Buena Vista Ferry Service** across the Willamette River, dating back to 1851, is just a short drive north of the city.

The 19th century is also alive and well just south of Albany in **Brownsville**. Nestled at the base of the Cascade foothills along the banks of the Calapooya River, this town's main street displays turn-of-the-century structures whose plaques tell something of their histories. The great arched doorways and tall windows of these buildings seem much more imposing after the ramshackle mill town encountered on the drive into town from Interstate 5.

The stage is set on Main Street. On the left side of the street is the **Moyer House**, a mansion built in the Italian villa style so popular in the 1870s, replete with

Mount Hood provides a backdrop for neatly kept orchards.

Palladian windows, ornate cornices, balconied porches and a third-story cupola. This house and the nearby pioneer museum recall the era when Brownsville was the county seat. The Moyer House is open Saturdays and Sundays year-round. A guide is on hand to answer questions but the rococo antique furnishings do the talking well enough to make the 20th century seem far away.

The past comes even more alive at the Linn County Pioneer Picnic, Oregon's oldest celebration, which takes place the third weekend in June. Other seasonal activities abound in the region, such as Lebanon's Strawberry Festival in early June and Albany's timber carnival on the Fourth of July.

The latter event sees modern-day Paul Bunyans compete in an Olympics of Logging. Lebanon's 8-foot (2-meters) high, 3,000-pound (1,360-kg) strawberry shortcake seems made-to-order for what surely must be a rash of lumberjack appetites in the area.

Friendly **Sweet Home**, a town east of these festival sites, feels as familiar as its name. This hamlet is combed by rock-hounds for petrified wood, red jasper agates and geodes.

As the last vestige of citified comfort before the mountains, it is also a gateway to State 20, the South Santiam Highway. The route goes up over **Santiam Pass** through the **Willamette National Forest** en route to central Oregon. This national forest is the American lumber industry's major source of softwood timber and merges the foothills east of the valley with the snowcapped cinder cones of the Cascade Range.

For the most part, State 20 follows the south fork of the river in the manner of the old Native American trails and pioneer wagon roads a century before. Initially, however, the road goes by Lebanon and Sweet Home continuing on past two dams, a lake and the middle Santiam River. The profusion of picnic areas and campgrounds near boating, trout fishing and swimming sites can create traffic bottlenecks on weekends. Farther down State 20 traffic thins out

Farm animals surround a peaceful pond.

when the road begins to run alongside the South Santiam River.

A nice place to stop along the route for a cold drink of water on a summer day is **Cascadia State Park**. The cold soda (sulfurous) water pumped from Soda Creek here might be a prelude to a half-mile hike to a cave with Native petroglyphs believed to be 8,000 years old. As the highway climbs, roadside vistas of old-growth fir, lava formations and canyons usher the motorist up into alpine scenery. Eventually, the high peaks of the Cascades become visible from lava fields in the area of Santiam Pass. This conduit between the Willamette Valley and central Oregon is also the home of **Hoodoo Bowl**, a popular ski area.

Moo U: From the heart of the Cascades, it's only a little over an hour to **Corvallis**, which is Latin for "heart of the valley." This town's population is dominated by people connected with Oregon's oldest state-supported university. Specializing in teaching agriculture and engineering, **Oregon State** is affectionately referred to as "Moo U." Should this moniker conjure the image of Corvallis residents as hayseeds who just got down off the tractor, a surprise is in store. A sophisticated high-tech community has grown up here recently due in great part to the presence of Hewlett Packard. The granddaddy of Silicon Valley computer outfits, this California-based concern came to Corvallis to recruit from a school renowned for technical education.

In addition, this clean quiet community is located one hour away from the best indoor and outdoor recreation Oregon has to offer. Whether the aim is big city culture in Portland or Eugene or world-class skiing and wilderness activities in the Cascades, on what might be the most efficient and picturesque coastal access road in the state, smooth flowing traffic arteries extend from the "heart of the valley" in a way which seems too good to be true.

In town, take in the **Horner Museum** at the bottom of **Gill Coliseum** located prominently on Western Boulevard and

Orchards near Pay's Creek.

26th Street off I-5. Apart from the antiques, fossils and stuffed Oregon fauna, the history pamphlets can supply the traveler with useful background information. Of the local 19th-century architectural landmarks, the nearby **Benton County Courthouse** is the finest.

A few miles west from Corvallis on State 34 lies **Philomath**, a small lumber town nudging the Coast Range. An almost unending succession of cloud masses are brought here by the prevailing westerlies off the Pacific Ocean, so much so that Philomath is thought by many to be the cloudiest place in the Willamette Valley. Rain or shine, it's hard to ignore the 1865 Georgian Brick structure that houses the **Benton County Historical Museum** here.

Not far from Philomath is the highest mountain in the Coast Range (4,097 feet/1,250 meters), **Mary's Peak**. A drive to the top is strongly recommended; from there, the Pacific Ocean can be seen to the west, and the Cascade peaks are often clearly visible to the east.

Those who don't mind a scenic, albeit much slower, alternative to heading south on I-5 might consider the Alsea-Alpine Road. This paved-over logging road winds through the tall timbers of the Coast Range. A mile south off State 34 in Alsea is a road marked "Alsea Falls/South Fork Road/Monroe." The road follows the green **Alsea River** much of the way, eventually coming to **Alsea Falls**, a small picturesque cascade where the lucky visitor in spring or fall can see salmon and steelhead battle the whitewater in their zeal to spawn.

This road continues down past clearcut slopes outside once active logging towns into farming country. The route ends up on State 99W south of Corvallis near the **William L. Finley National Wildlife Refuge**, a major nesting area for migratory waterfowl.

Eugene: Salem might be the capital and Portland the largest city in the state, but in many respects it is **Eugene** that is the jewel of the Emerald Empire. Eugene's garden-like setting with recreation from sea level to ski level and a cultural mix that befits the city's state-of-the-art concert hall makes this city something special – so special that many of the 118,000-plus people in this grown-up college and mill town endure the inconvenience of competing for employment in a very tight job market, just to live here.

While economic cycles fluctuate, the landscape architecture, historic buildings and cultural life at the **University of Oregon** exemplify the unending charm of Eugene. A feeling of timelessness pervades the campus area thanks to stately fir and spruce, as well as several species of redwoods in front of the school's first building, **Deady Hall**.

While the campus landscape exudes a gentle presence, the contemporary influences of the university on the Eugene community are often far reaching and dynamic. In addition to the college employing the largest work force in the city, the U of O's **Hayward Field** is the birthplace of Eugene's reputation as "Tracktown USA."

This is where Bill Bowerman popularized the jogging regimen which swept the country early in the 1970s and has kept Americans on their toes, so to speak, ever since. Hayward Field is also a frequent site of the Olympic Trials. World-class athlete Mary Decker Slaney calls Eugene home, and the city might well have the most joggers per capita anywhere in the country.

The **Prefontaine Trail** and the bike path straddling the Willamette River make this a runner's paradise. The same can be said for bicyclists and enthusiasts of water sports. Thousands take advantage of the bike lanes that encircle the city and the many points from which to embark on raft, canoe or kayak trips along the Willamette and McKenzie rivers. These venues, together with many pedestrian thoroughfares, make the car seem less pervasive than elsewhere in the west.

Perhaps the nicest place for a walk in all of Eugene is at **Hendricks Park** during the springtime blossoming of the rhododendrons. Located on Summit Drive a mile from campus, the 20 acres (8 hectares) also support camellias, azaleas and other plants that blossom from late March into early June.

Down by the river at the **Owen Municipal Rose Garden** on Jefferson Street, another floral fantasia is in full swing in the second and third weeks of June. In the center of the garden stands an impressive cherry tree that was planted in 1847, a year after Eugene Skinner filed the plan for the city.

Nearby **Skinner's Butte** offers a fine view of the Eugene skyline with the Coast Range visible on a clear day. About 6 miles (10 km) down Willamette Street is the **Spencer's Butte Trailhead**, also named after a pioneer. A magnificent perspective of the Coast and Cascade ranges rewards those who make the steep but beautiful hike of about a mile.

Hearty appetites stimulated by these jaunts can be sated by the many good restaurants here which run the gamut from health food to haute cuisine. In the shadow of the campus are scores of ethnic eateries, which are always cheap and cheerful and popular with students on a budget.

On High Street, a restored grain mill and warehouse known as the **Fifth Street Public Market** offers a choice of restaurants amid boutiques selling the wares of local craftspeople. Whether it be freshly squeezed juice or a middle eastern pocket sandwich, the market's variety and informality offer a bite-sized slice of Eugene life.

Festive occasions: The same sort of ambience prevails out of doors at the **Saturday Market**. This weekly event features entertainment and runs from April through late November on Oak and Eighth streets.

There are other seasonal festivals in and around Eugene. For those who like the ferris wheel, home-baked pies, or a look at prized bulls, there is the **Lane County Fair** in mid-August. In nearby Veneta during early July, there's the Old Oregon Country Faire, a Renaissance bacchanal in a mossy glade. The latter is also a paean to the lingering countercultural presence in the region.

Twenty miles south (32 km) in **Cottage Grove**, Bohemia Mining Days in mid-July recalls the late 19th-century gold strikes of James Bohemia Johnson.

The nearby Bohemia foothills have several of the old covered bridges.

Of all the seasonal events in the region, there is one that draws worldwide recognition. In late June and early July, at the Oregon Bach Festival, an international array of celebrated musicians perform master-works in Eugene's **Hult Center**. This hall is considered one of the finest cultural facilities in the west and features talents which have ranged from Ella Fitzgerald to the New York Philharmonic Orchestra.

Sea level to ski level: A year-round delight is coastal access State 126. Take this road past **Fern Ridge Reservoir** to **Veneta** and **Elmira**. Isolated farms and several small towns break up the dense **Siuslaw National Forest** en route to **Florence,** where golfers enjoy the award-winning Sandpines Golf Course. A small historic river town on the highway, **Mapleton**, is where well over 100 inches (250 cm) of rain fall a year.

The gateway to 126 is Eugene's sister city, **Springfield**. The McKenzie River drive through the foothills has covered bridges, excellent fishing and a topnotch public golf course, **Tokatee**. As the road climbs higher, lava fields and the snowcapped **Three Sisters** come into view. Lakes and waterfalls, as well as superlative trails and campsites dot the route and spur roads.

In summer, the turnoff for the Old McKenzie Highway, State 242, leads to a slower but more scenic entry to the Cascades. Atop McKenzie Pass, is a cluster of peaks from the **Dee Wright Observatory** which rests on extensive lava flows.

State 58 can be picked up out of **Goshen**, 7 miles (10 km) east of Eugene off I-5. The route sparkles with recreational reservoirs and lakes en route to **Willamette Pass**. The pass itself features skiing about an hour from Eugene. In addition, there is the presence of 286-foot (87-meter) high **Salt Creek Falls** located on the pass above the highway and the town of **Oakridge**. Seeing the Willamette River headwaters here can create the feeling of being close to the hand that sculpted the Emerald Empire in the valley below.

Right, alder trees.

THE ROGUE RIVER

Light plays tricks on the mind in southwestern Oregon. In winter, when moisture-laden weather fronts roll in from the Pacific Ocean, fog is a constant companion. It drapes the hillsides with a translucent blanket, painting the landscape like a movie scene shot deliberately out of focus. Viewed from a high vantage point in any season, the succession of deeply carved, mysterious valleys seem to roll away toward the horizon and disappear into infinity.

No wonder, then, that this is a land where the Bigfoot legend lives on. This hairy, oversized humanoid – sometimes known by its Native American name of Sasquatch – has reportedly been sighted in many remote areas of the Northwest, but the possibility of an encounter in a fog-bound canyon in southwestern Oregon seems palpable enough to reach out and touch. Where light plays tricks, anything seems possible.

But the true lure of this region is the range of outdoor activities that can be sampled and enjoyed during almost any season of the year. Whitewater rafting at its finest, wilderness hikes through forested canyons, superb fishing for salmon and steelhead, or a simple driving tour of historical sites through breathtaking countryside – the **Rogue Country** offers all of these in abundance to the traveler who dares to venture off the interstate highway and explore the opportunities.

But don't miss the easily accessible surprises just off US Interstate 5 on the way to southwestern Oregon. At Winston, 7 miles (11 km) south of Roseburg, the **Wildlife Safari** provides an unforgettable stop, especially for children. Exotic animals from Africa, Asia, and South America roam the 600-acre (242-hectare) park while visitors view the wildlife from their cars. The cheetah compound, home to the largest collection of these rare African cats in North America, is not to be missed. From a distance, safari fans should be able to spot the elephant family splashing away at the pond, or perhaps a couple of lazy tigers yawning in the shade. Be prepared also for the monkey that suddenly shows up at your windscreen!

Continuing south on US I-5, consider a stop for lunch or dinner at the **Wolf Creek Tavern**, 20 miles (32 km) north of **Grants Pass**. An old stagecoach stop built in the 1870s, the tavern has been restored by the state of Oregon and now serves a wide selection of carefully prepared· meals, many featuring locally grown foods. The crab bisque soup is a highlight. Overnight rooms are also available for the traveler who enjoys the atmosphere of a bygone era, but demands modern conveniences such as individual bathrooms.

Just 11 miles (18 km) south of Wolf Creek, take the Merlin exit off US I-5 for a pleasant drive that serves as an introduction to the **Rogue River**. The Merlin-Galice Road parallels the river in the section known as **Hellgate Canyon**. The paved road extends to **Grave Creek**, the start of the wild section of the Rogue. A mostly paved, sometimes

gravel road completes a loop from Grave Creek back to Wolf Creek or it backtracks toward Grants Pass via the Merlin-Galice Road.

Even this short driving tour gives a hint of the powerful attraction that the Rouge exerts on those who come to know the river. Its steep canyon walls, which average 3,000 feet (900 meters) high, contain an exciting combination of challenging whitewater, lively fishing action, historic sites and back-country charm.

The Rogue River begins at Boundary Springs on the north side of **Crater Lake National Park**. It gathers volume from tributaries as it flows through a broad valley that holds the cities of Medford and Grants Pass, then plunges into a steep canyon at Hellgate, cuts through the Oregon Coast Range and enters the Pacific Ocean at Gold Beach, over 100 miles (160 km) by air from its source. After it leaves the road at Grave Creek, the river becomes a whitewater enthusiast's dream, dropping through a series of spine-tingling rapids separated by quiet, even-flowing sections which are ideal for lying back and gawking at the spectacular scenery which slides by on every side.

Dangerous falls and channels: At **Raine Falls**, just downstream from Grave Creek, the river encounters a band of highly erosion-resistant rock that causes the entire flow to drop 12 feet (4 meters) straight down. All boats, unless piloted by those with a death wish, must be lined down a fish ladder on the side of the falls. At **Mule Creek Canyon** the river cuts through the heart of the Oregon Coast Range, producing a narrow channel with shear volcanic walls and suck holes such as the **Coffeepot**.

Downstream is a rock garden called **Blossom Bar** that had never been navigated safely in a boat until pioneer boatman Glen Wooldridge blasted out a channel with dynamite.

In 1925, Zane Grey hired a local guide named Claude Bardon to take his party and their wooden boats on a float trip down the Rogue River – a trip that most local people considered suicidal. Bardon

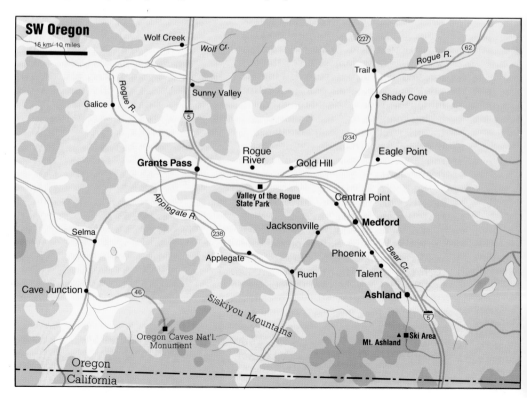

managed to get the party through safely, although one boat was lost and several were damaged. Grey's party was probably the first to run the river for sport, but his description of the trip makes it clear that the river was far more than he had bargained for.

Grey and his party were not the first to encounter the Rogue Canyon, however. Native peoples enjoyed the plentiful fishing and hunting there for centuries. White settlers first came in the 1850s in search of gold. The Rogue River Indian Wars were fought in 1855–6 and some of the famous battlefields are now campsites for whitewater rafters. Gold mining peaked around 1885 and many of the large pieces of equipment used in lode mining can now be seen rusting peacefully along the river. Between 1850 and 1961 an estimated $70 million worth of gold was extracted from southwestern Oregon.

Most "gold" today comes into the area in the form of recreational business. The Rogue was designated a federal Wild and Scenic Waterway in 1968 and the resulting publicity changed the river from the quiet canyon that Zane Grey knew to a bustling haven for river rafters and fishermen. When whitewater rafting began to take off in popularity in the late 1970s, the federal agencies that manage the river canyon imposed a strict limit on the number of river parties which could enter the wild section of the river (which begins at Grave Creek). This permit system is still in force during the busy summer months.

Since permits for private parties of rafters are distributed by lottery drawn before the season begins, the visitor who wants to float the river has to learn to work with the system. The best option is to take a float trip with a guide, whose permit quota is separate from the private party permits. Guides are licensed by the state and, in addition to their expertise at running whitewater, they provide excellent meals, current fishing information and knowledge of the natural and human history of the river. A complete list of local guides and the services they offer is available

A covered bridge near Chitwood.

from the Grants Pass Visitors' and Convention Bureau at 1501 N.E. Sixth Street.

For those with an urge to tackle the river without assistance, the section of the Rogue from Grants Pass down to Grave Creek can be floated without a permit at any time of year. This river section is designated "recreational" (the wild section is downstream) and since it is paralleled most of the way by a road, many services are available. Several outfitters run this section in jet boats which have the advantage of running upstream, then motoring back downstream to the original point of departure. The **Galice Store** rents both rafts and inflatable kayaks on a day basis.

The inflatable kayaks, called orange torpedoes by some, have been the rage on the Rogue in recent years because they allow much more freedom, maneuverability and thrills than a simple raft. They also assure that the occupant will be soaked to the skin after the first serious rapid, so unless the trip is attempted during summer weather, it is advisable to wear a wet suit.

Prime fishing and hiking: During almost every month of the year some large salmon or steelhead (the ocean-going form of rainbow trout) will be ascending the Rogue to their spawning grounds in the upper river. The prime fishing season is September and October, when most whitewater rafters have abandoned the river. Then anglers in their high-sided McKenzie River boats will vie for the best fishing spots. Once again, a guided trip with a professional fishing guide is the best bet for an inexperienced first-time angler.

One of the finest ways to experience the wild Rogue River canyon is to hike the **Rogue River Trail**. No permit is required for the trail, which runs between Grave Creek and Foster Bar – 40 miles (64 km) in all. The river trail is well-constructed, has moderate grades, and is generally snow-free all year long. Best hiking seasons are spring and fall, when it is not too crowded or too hot. Carry water to avoid drinking contaminated water from the river or tributary streams, and look out for rattlesnakes, **Forest tract invites exploration.**

242

which love to sunbathe along the trail.

Whether boating or hiking, the mid-summer months can be a crowded time in the Rogue Canyon; it's best to have alternative plans in mind if solitude is what you seek. The **Illinois River**, a tributary of the Rogue which joins it at Agness, is actually a more challenging whitewater river and also has a hiking trail which parallels its course. Expert skills are needed for rafting or kayaking on the Illinois and the water is often too low for safe boating after the month of June, but its canyon is far more pristine than the Rogue's.

The **Kalmiopsis Wilderness** is a good alternative for hikers who want to get away from the crowds. This wilderness is home to several species of rare plants and is bisected by steep canyons, one of which holds the headwaters of the **Chetco River**. The Kalmiopsis Wilderness and Illinois River are both accessible by road from the village of **Selma**, 25 miles (40 km) south of Grants Pass on US Highway 199.

Grants Pass serves as the hub and supply center for a variety of recreational activities in southwestern Oregon. Its restored historic downtown area also houses some shops worth visiting between outdoor adventures. Antique and collectable shops line G Street and at Sixth and First streets is a popular **Factory Outlet** center, selling T-shirts, jackets and other athletic wear at reasonable prices.

Next stop on US I-5 after leaving Grants Pass is the little community of **Rogue River**. Besides the distinction of annually hosting the Rooster Crow festival in late June, Rogue River is also the starting point for a self-guided tour of covered bridges in the area. Inquire at the Grants Pass Visitors' and Convention Bureau for the exact route.

The shop with the most special identity in Grants Pass is **Blind George's** newsstand on G Street near Sixth. Blind George's is the place to pick up an out-of-town newspaper as well as sample a slice of life from the vanished era when the newsstand was the vital nerve center of every small town in America.

Old buildings in the Rogue River Valley, in the shadow of Mount McLaughlin.

OREGON CAVES NATIONAL MONUMENT

No one will ever confuse **Oregon Caves National Monument** with the big attractions of the National Park Service – Yellowstone Park, the Grand Canyon or even nearby Crater Lake. By comparison, Oregon Caves is low-key, off the beaten path and lightly visited.

But therein lies much of its charm. Oregon Caves offers a pleasant side trip in a unique mountain setting, an adventure for those who enjoy a physical challenge, as well as a glimpse of the powerful forces that formed the Siskiyou Mountains. In the parlance of the local miners, it's a diamond in the rough.

Oregon Caves is located in the far southwestern corner of Oregon, just north of the California border. **Cave Junction**, the nearest town with services and accommodations, can be reached on US Highway 199 by traveling either 50 miles (80 km) south from Grants Pass or 76 miles (122 km) north from Crescent City, California. Oregon State Highway 46 leads to Oregon Caves from Cave Junction and is a paved, two-lane highway. However, it's narrow and twisting for the last few of its 20 miles (32 km), and in winter it would be wise to check conditions in Cave Junction before attempting the drive. Towing a trailer to the monument is not recommended at any time of the year.

The cave is tucked at the head of an isolated, wooded canyon. (Although the monument is known as Oregon Caves, only one cave, with many connected passages and rooms, has been found.) Its remoteness from population centers and elevation at 4,020 feet (1,226 meters) account for the cave's rather late discovery in 1874 by a local deerhunter, Elijah Davidson.

Elijah followed his dog through the brushy cave entrance in pursuit of a bear. When his supply of matches ran out, he was forced to navigate back to the outside world by following the noise of a stream (now named the **River Styx**) through pitch darkness. Modern cave

Left, basalt formations. Right, a rock-climber clings to stone with finesse.

244

visitors get a taste of Elijah's predicament when their guide dowses the cave's lighting system, momentarily engulfing would-be spelunkers in a state of sensory deprivation that's hard to match above ground.

All visitors wishing to see Oregon Caves must enter on a guided, 75-minute tour provided by the Oregon Caves Company. Before entering the cave, the guide will explain that visitors should dress warmly – the temperature inside the cave is almost always 41°F (5°C) no matter what the outside temperature may read – and to bring a flash attachment along with your camera. Carrying your own flashlight for better views of the cave's recesses is also a good idea. The tour itself is somewhat strenuous and not recommended for anyone with heart, breathing or walking difficulties. Children under 4 years of age are not permitted in the cave.

The geologic history of the Oregon Caves has been described as a play with three acts. Act One began 200 million years ago when the area was a seabed. Layers of mud, lime and lava were compressed into solid marble and then folded and uplifted by earth forces. The intense heat and pressure caused the marble to be shot through with thin cracks.

In Act Two, water charged with weak carbonic acid from the soil seeped down into the marble and dissolved it along the fractures. During this time the fractures became passages and larger rooms filled with water.

In Act Three, which is continuing, the water drained out of the passages but continued to drip and trickle into the cave, coating the walls and floor with a mineral called calcite. Where the water dripped, it formed stalactites (reaching down from the ceiling) and stalagmites (reaching up from the floor). Whenever stalactites and stalagmites met, a column was formed. Water that flowed with more volume either formed decorations, called flowstone, in the shape of frozen waterfalls or fell in rippled sheets called draperies.

Cathedral-like formations: As the tour progresses, examples of all these formations can be seen in the marble. The **Banana Grove** flowstone draperies resemble clusters of fruits. The **Grand Column** is the junction of a stalactite and a stalagmite, forming the largest column in the cave. **Joaquin Miller's Chapel**, named after a regionally well-known poet who visited the cave in the early days and aided in having it designated a national monument, has a pleasingly arrayed range of dripstone formations worthy of any cathedral. The **Ghost Room** is the largest in the cave – about 250 feet (76 meters) in length.

The Oregon Caves tour exits at a spot 200 feet (61 meters) higher than the entrance and most visitors walk down the mountainside to the cave entrance on a steep, 0.3 mile (0.5 km) path. However, a short hike uphill on the same trail will connect with several nature trails ranging from the 0.7 mile (1.2 km) **Cliff Nature Trail** loop to the 3-mile (5-km) **Big Tree Trail** loop. Besides providing some truly spectacular views of the surrounding Siskiyou Mountains on a clear day, the trails wind through stands of huge Douglas-fir trees as well as majestic stands of Port Orford cedar and incense cedar trees.

Oregon Caves visitors who wish to linger a while may stay at the **Oregon Caves Chateau**, a rustic 6-story lodge which offers comfortable accommodations with striking vistas of the surrounding forest. The chateau offers a range of wonders, from a huge double fireplace in native marble to the grand dining room with linen tablecloths, big picture windows and a brook that runs right through it. The chateau is only open from March through early October and it is wise to book ahead.

On the return trip to Cave Junction, consider a stop at the **Siskiyou Vineyards**. Located on Oregon 46 just 6 miles (10 km) from Cave Junction, this winery features some fine white wines which may be sampled in the tasting room. If you have a taste for smoked sausages you must include a visit to **Taylor Sausages**, three blocks off US 199 on Watkins Street near the Oregon Caves junction, where retail sales are made to the public in the middle of the production room.

SOUTHERN OREGON

Unless you've been to Ashland or Jacksonville, you might think of culture in southern Oregon as a traveling medicine show and jug band or a bakeoff at the grange hall. Nonetheless, a leading Shakespeare festival, as well as one of pioneer America's preeminent National Historical Landmarks, graces the logging and orchard country of the Rogue River Valley.

Shakespeare under the stars in Ashland is a midsummer night's dream for hundreds of thousands of theater goers who flock to this southern Oregon town during the festival's peak season. In addition to enactments of the Bard's works, the Oregon Shakespeare Festival also features a number of modern theatrical presentations.

The influx during summer is augmented by the Peter Britt Music Festival in nearby Jacksonville. This event brings together in concert an international array of top musicians. If the flurry of summer activity in the region doesn't have you thinking that all the world's a stage here, then tarry a while amidst the restored buildings of the mid-19th-century gold rush town of Jacksonville.

Lest one gathers from this description of cultural activities that all of southern Oregon is the Athens of the northwest, a larger perspective on the area south from Grants Pass is in order. The pattern of settlement in this section of the state is an amalgam of small logging towns and larger supply centers for the timber mills, pear orchards, dairy farms and cattle ranches which provide the economic sustenance of the southland.

Outside Medford, the region's population center and economic vortex, people who once enjoyed country life are now lamenting rural suburbs intruding on their piece of the American dream. Despite this recent growth, most of southern Oregon is still the kind of place where the names of country music stars such as luminaries Johnny Cash and Merle Haggard elicit more recognition from the average person than thespians along the likes of John Gielgud and Vanessa Redgrave.

It is precisely this "off-Broadway" ambience that gives the region's cultural potpourri a unique flavor. Small-town friendliness coexists with world-class theatrical productions, musical entertainment and one of the nation's definitive historical restorations.

Culture in the hinterlands: Surprisingly, Ashland's and Jacksonville's reputations as cultural meccas go back to the days of the frontier. Shortly after the gold strikes which created Jacksonville in 1851, vaudeville acts played the saloons and dance halls which proliferated in the boom town. Jacksonville was the first and only town in the region until the mill town of Ashland was created the following year. The Chautauqua Movement, a religious group dedicated to bringing culture to the Philistine hinterlands, sent lecturers, actors and wandering minstrels to these growing population centers.

It was in a theater built by Ashland's

Preceding pages: ponderosa pines. Left, miners hoping to find riches. Below, a courthouse window in Jacksonville.

Chautauqua group that Angus Bowmer, an English professor at the local college, decided to celebrate a 1935 Independence Day weekend by presenting *As You Like It.* The first sets featured bedsheets donated by local housewives. Boxing matches were held at intermissions to ensure profits. Fifty years later, it's hard to believe that a Shakespeare festival drawing some 300,000 people a year sprang from such humble beginnings. The tradition of "stay four days see four plays," which grew with the festival, transformed Ashland into a combination tourist town and art colony. The visible outgrowths include a Tudor-style McDonald's, a large permanent population of thespians, artists and craftspeople, and what are perhaps the highest prices of any city in the state.

Ashland – past and present: Of all the points of interest in Oregon, **Ashland** is the most blessed by its geography. The city is located 22 miles (35 km) north of the nation's most populated state, California, as well as being equidistant from San Francisco and Seattle.

The growth of tourism was envisioned here a decade before the Shakespeare Festival and the restoration of Jacksonville by a man named Jesse Winburne. After making a fortune from advertising on the subways in New York, Winburne retired to Ashland. Retirement was postponed as he became obsessed with the town's potential as a resort. He planned a spa centered on the local **Lithia Springs** mineral waters, which were supposed to be similar to the venerated waters of Saratoga Springs, New York. To create a similar retreat in Ashland, he developed a walking trail through **Lithia Park** which housed the source of the waters. **Winburne Way**, a beautiful tree-shaded trail, goes along Ashland Creek through the 99-acre (40-hectare) tract to the base of the Siskiyou Mountains. He also piped Lithia Springs water to the **Plaza Fountains** on Main Street in the center of town. Although his spa never got off the ground, due to the Depression, Winburne's efforts set the stage for festival tourism.

Two blocks down Main Street from

Jacksonville church.

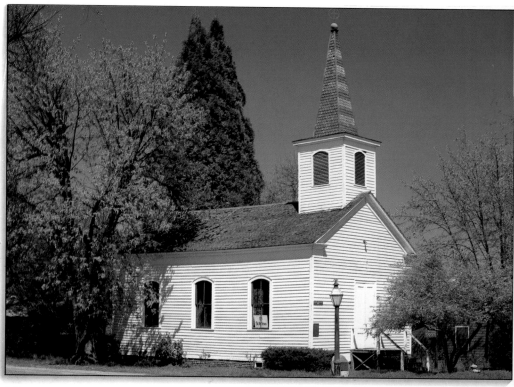

250

the plaza and the entrance to the park, the Lithia Springs Hotel (now called the **Mark Antony**) stands as the culmination of the Winburne legacy. The nine-story building was once the tallest structure between San Francisco and Seattle and today is a National Historical Landmark as well as serving as a first rate hostelry.

Shakespeare under the stars: Up the street from the Mark Antony is the Tony Award-winning **Oregon Shakespeare Festival.** Established in 1935, it is among the oldest and largest regional theater companies in the United States. The festival presents an eight-month season of 11 plays in repertory in three theaters: an outdoor Elizabethan Theatre (which has 1,200 seats), the versatile and gracious Angus Bowmer Theatre (with 600 seats) and the intimate Black Swan (the smallest, with 140 seats).

In the **Elizabethan Theatre**, modeled after the 17th-century Fortune Theatre of Shakespeare's London, the festival presents a three-play repertory by Shakespeare and his contemporaries from June through early October. Built on the site of the old Chautauqua Theater established in 1893, it is the oldest existing full-scale Elizabethan stage in the western hemisphere.

In the **Angus Bowmer Theatre**, named for the festival's founder, OSF presents five plays in repertory by Shakespeare, and by classic and contemporary playwrights from mid-February through October. The **Black Swan** focuses on the work of contemporary playwrights from a different stage.

Prior to every performance on the Elizabethan stage, the festival musicians and dancers present a **Green Show** of Renaissance music and dance. The show has three programs, one for each of the outdoor plays.

The festival also offers backstage tours, lectures, concerts, play readings and much more. The **Exhibit Center** – a museum of festival history, costumes, props and set pieces – is a popular attraction. Tickets and information are available at the courtyard box office located on South Pioneer Street.

Ashland's outdoor Shakespearean Theatre.

Ashland hospitality: And after the performance? In addition to the variety of restaurants and places to have a drink, many connoisseurs of the good life retire to one of the 60 or so bed-and-breakfast places in the Ashland area. For information on any of them, stop by the chamber of commerce visitor's center at 110 E. Main Street. A guest house by the name of the **Chanticleer Inn** rules the roost here with such amenities as a glass of sherry by a crackling fire to warm up those returning from a chilly night at the Elizabethan Theatre.

Restaurants on Ashland's Main Street run the gamut from the gourmet offerings at **Chateaulin** to old-fashioned soda fountain concoctions. This can be washed down with a swig of Lithia Springs water at the Plaza Fountains. Foul-tasting as it may be, Ashland's acerbic answer to Perrier is a fitting beverage to toast the spirits of Angus Bowmer and Jesse Winburne.

The spirit of the Bard is paid homage in the form of playbills in shop and restaurant windows, evident signs of a regional theatrical obsession. Ranging from the Shakespearean parodies staged by an offshoot company of festival performers to the western melodramas put on in several surrounding communities, the curtain never seems to fall here.

A new addition to Ashland's cultural palate is the **Pacific Northwest Museum of Natural History**, which features impressive recreations of Northwest regions and is dedicated to promoting awareness and preservation of the natural world.

The stagecoach road: Even Ashland's closest neighbor has a stagestruck name, although **Talent** bears little resemblance to her sister city. Located 3 miles (5 km) north of Ashland on State Highway 99, Talent's proximity to the surrounding pear orchards explains the large population of farmworkers here. With many fruit pickers of Mexican descent, a number of good inexpensive Mexican restaurants have grown up in the area. **La Burrita**, in Phoenix, is one such establishment and it enjoys special local acclaim for its ability to stretch a dollar.

Rushing creek through Lithia Park, Ashland.

The pear orchards and the through traffic off State 99 explain the Harry and David, Jackson and Perkins complex just north of Talent in the Bear Creek section of Medford. In addition to **Jackson and Perkins'** rose display garden, a commercial greenhouse selling the world's largest selection of roses is featured. **Harry and David's Bear Creek** stores purvey such regional delicacies as Rogue Valley cheddar cheese, their own brand of excellent herbal tea and gift packs of the jumbo pears that made them famous as well as reduced price "reject" fruit.

Jacksonville: Close by the Bear Creek complex on State 99 is a historical detour, where South Stage Road heads northwest toward the town of **Jacksonville**. The fancy homes and elaborate gold scales in the bank on California Street shows that this was not merely some distant outpost on the frontier.

In fact, this is one town whose streets were almost literally paved with gold. Jacksonville was built over an area covering some of the first strikes and much of the town was actually dug up by locals during the Great Depression. When 25,000 dollars' worth of ore was extracted from the corner of California and Third streets, there began serious talk of razing some buildings.

Fortunately, preservationists prevailed, even though many structures were ripe for the wrecker's ball. An architectural deterioration paralleled the decline in the town's fortunes, precipitated by the shortlived gold rush and the railroad's decision to bypass Jacksonville in favor of Medford in 1883. The decline culminated in 1927 when the county seat was moved to Medford. About a decade later and at about the same time that a similar effort was undertaken in Williamsburg, Virginia, the local citizens began a movement to restore many of Jacksonville's historic buildings. In 1967, Jacksonville was selected as the nation's fifth National Historical Landmark.

Take in Jacksonville's brief historical moment in the sun by visiting the **Jacksonville Museum** on North Fifth

Winter farm scene.

Street. While in the museum, pick up either the US Bank walking tour pamphlet and map or a similar publication put out by the Southern Oregon Historical Society. These can help plan and provide information for a post-museum foray through Jacksonville's restoration area to the cemetery a few miles northwest of town.

The Jacksonville Museum is housed in a towering brick building beneath a white cupola which served as the Jackson County Courthouse from 1884 to 1927. Begin your visit on the second floor. Here dioramas and artifacts trace the prehistory of the Takelma Indians, whose lands were invaded in 1851 when James Poole and James Cluggage discovered gold in Rich Gulch. Follow the exhibits evoking the early days of prospectors, homesteaders, gamblers and frontier justice.

Much of the museum's first floor is dedicated to Peter Britt, Jacksonville's Renaissance man of the last century. This Swiss immigrant settled here in 1852 and distinguished himself as a painter, photographer, vintner and horticulturist. The preservation of Jacksonville history owes a lot to the photographs by Britt, whose studio and parlor are recreated here, replete with period furniture and paintings.

A music festival: Oregon's oldest music and arts festival is named for Britt and is set in the gardens of his estate. Although his home and the first photography studio west of the Rockies were destroyed by a disastrous fire, the flowers and trees he planted have lived on as a backdrop to many years of cultural presentations here.

The **Peter Britt Music Festival** attracts top names in bluegrass, jazz, classical music and varied forms of dance from June through August. A gently sloping hillside on the estate forms a natural amphitheater with surprisingly good acoustics. The outdoor pavilion is located off State 238 on a bluff overlooking the town. Southern Oregon's summers are mild and quite dry, but you should nonetheless bring a wrap if you hope to attend an evening performance. In addition, a pillow or blanket can make sitting on the lawns and benches here more comfortable.

Should the excitement of the festival intrude on one's historical reverie, the mood can quickly be reestablished a stone's throw from the Britt Gardens. The dilapidated **Chinese Quarters** on West Main between First and South Oregon streets, and the first gold claim, **Rich Gulch**, located off Oak and Applegate streets, are haunting reminders of southern Oregon's heritage.

Perhaps for some, the long bar of California Street's **Bella Union** restaurant and saloon backed by a wall mural depicting a street scene from Jacksonville's golden era, better evokes the sound of miners' boots clumping into the boom town.

Of the 80 marked historical sites in this, the most preserved town in America, it might well be the **Pioneer Cemetery** where the echoes of the past ring most true. The white tombstones dating back to 1859 make the cemetery an historical locale with the closest connection to pioneer Jacksonville.

Left, a ride through the forest. **Right**, the McKenzie River.

BEND AND CENTRAL OREGON

Central Oregon is a region which defies concise description. In the middle of it all, near Bend and Sisters, there are cowboys and loggers as well as pant-suited tourists and sophisticated jet-setters in an après-ski atmosphere. To the south, a lunar landscape is evoked by the most varied array of volcanic features in the United States outside Hawaii. On the prairies an hour and a half north of Bend, a handful of ghost towns are broken up by an Indian Reservation operating a luxury hotel within its tribal bailiwick. The more one moves in an easterly direction, the more rapidly a semi-arid desert replaces alpine scenery. In addition to cattle ranches, wheat fields, and small plots worked by hard-rock farmers, this is where the deer and the antelope play. Above it all, the snowcapped Cascades on the western horizon make the whole region into a surrealistic dreamscape.

The 25 miles (40 km) between Bend and Sisters, the first major towns encountered east of the Cascades, showcase this mountain range in a memorable way. A half dozen white peaks appear in rapid succession, rising up sharply above the flat brown prairie in the foreground. The contrast is all the more dramatic because the traveler going east has just left behind the shimmering lakes, greenery and tall timbers on the western side of the mountains belonging to the **Willamette** and **Deschutes national forests**.

These centers for skiing, hiking, whitewater rafting and fishing are the major reason why Bend and its environs have achieved the highest rate of population increase in Oregon. Elaborate resort complexes and leisure-oriented communities have grown up here, and the cold clear winters and hot but not humid summers complement year-round recreation.

Bend in the river: However, the beginnings and early growth of the Bend area were due to very different circumstances.

Preceding pages: Shaniko is now a ghost town. Below, a sawmill at the height of production.

258

In the mid-1840s, when the town was known as Farewell Bend, it was a cut-off point on a pioneer trail which paralleled the Deschutes River. From a mere bend in the river, the area grew rapidly as a result of federal land giveaways to homesteaders from 1850 until the early 20th century.

It wasn't until the leisure boom of the last two decades, however, that this area became a major tourist destination. During this period, Camp Abbott, a military base with 270 people, was transformed into the leisure community of **Sunriver**. Located 20 miles (32 km) south of Bend, close to the ski lifts on Mount Bachelor and rafting on the Deschutes, the complex now has 5,000 residents. In addition, two Robert Trent Jones golf courses, pools, tennis courts and other facilities grace this playground which also has its own airstrip.

Riding the crest of the same wave, the **Inn at the Seventh Mountain** closer to town is another resort dedicated to roughing it in style. **Black Butte Ranch**, just east of McKenzie Pass, has also grown with the leisure boom. The presence of the ranch and similar establishments are also responsible for the herd of gift shops in the nearby cowtown-turned resort village of Sisters.

The federal government wisely created wilderness areas near these tourist meccas so as to spare the delicate forest ecosystems the fate of other loved-to-death paradises.

Mount Jefferson wilderness: The **Mount Jefferson Wilderness Area** is the most popular preserve of its type in Oregon. A large part of its allure is the powerful presence of Mount Jefferson itself. The second highest of the Oregon Cascades draws visitors because its height (10,495 feet/3,200 meters) and central location make it visible from a greater locus of points in the state than any other single peak in the range. With symmetrical contours reminiscent of Mount Fujiyama in Japan, the peak is a beacon to its surrounding wilderness.

The Jefferson Wilderness is easily accessible from either side of the Cascades via a network of interconnecting

mountain passes, but it is eventually reached by US Highway 22. Off this highway, **Whitewater Road 1044**, 12 miles (19 km) east of Detroit, offers access to the most direct hiking trail to higher elevations in the park. The trailhead of an easy 5-mile (8-km) route up Whitewater Creek can be found by driving this 8-mile (13-km) dirt road. Once on the trail, most people avoid picking flowers except perhaps for some small-scale foraging. But remember, while a few handfuls of wild strawberries and red huckleberries might abate hunger pangs built up during hiking, the bear, deer and other full-time denizens of the forest also rely on this part of the food chain. At any rate, there is more than ample food for the soul thanks to spectacular perspectives of Jefferson's snowy summit. At about 5,000 feet (1,525 meters) below the crest, alpine meadows full of purple and yellow lupine and red Indian Paintbrush are broken up by a cluster of lakes. This high plateau, known as **Jefferson Park**, usually has wildflowers in bloom in late July or early August.

For those with a notion to escape to a wilder version of the primeval forest, the **Mount Washington Wilderness** spans the area between the Santiam and McKenzie Highway. The jagged boulders and rough landscape left from earlier lava flows give this wilderness a stark appearance. Even the mountain itself is a metaphor of ruggedness. One look at 7,800-foot (2,375-meter) Mount Washington will explain why it is the supreme challenge to Cascade alpinists.

Hikers enjoy the 16 miles (26 km) of the **Pacific Crest Trail** that goes through here. This trail stretches from Canada to Mexico and connects all the Cascade wilderness systems. Entry points to the Pacific Crest Trail and its offshoots are at the Big Lake Campground south of US 20 and from atop McKenzie Pass on State Highway 242. The trailhead on the pass starts near the **Dee Wright Observatory**, a vantage point from which 11 Cascade Peaks are visible.

Peaks and volcano cones: Similarly, these peaks and the wilderness they define uplift many modern Cascade

explorers. And why not? The **Three Sisters Wilderness**, encompassing more land area than any other wildlands in the Oregon Cascades, sits in the shadow of an immense set of triplet volcano cones which form the most aesthetically pleasing group in the range.

Although a feast for the eye, the Sisters' 10,000-foot (3,050-meter) plus elevation and its conical shape fill many scientists with dread. They remember the recent eruption of a similarly contoured and supposedly dormant Cascade volcano, Mount St Helens.

Despite dire predictions, an eruption seems remote in the peace of the surrounding Three Sisters Wilderness. After the snow melts at high elevations during August and early September, an eden of wildflowers is born in the meadows as if to greet the incursion of hikers and mountaineers. The South Sister is the most popular ascent. Fishermen flock to some 300 lakes here.

While the Three Sisters Wilderness can be entered via State 242 on McKenzie Pass, it's often best to enter the

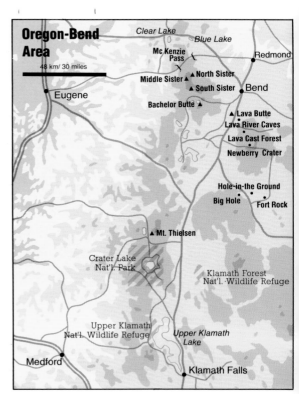

preserve from the drier eastern slope of the Cascades. You can obtain a wilderness permit, required for overnight backcountry hiking and camping, at the Bend Chamber of Commerce Visitor Information Center at the north end of Highway 97. About 20 miles (32 km) southwest of Bend, there are trailheads near the Cascade Lakes Highway – **Sparks, Elk, Lava** and **Cultus Lakes** – into the Three Sisters Wilderness. Farther south from these trailheads on the Cascade Lakes Highway, it's possible to enter the **Diamond Peak Wilderness**, another white jewel in the chain. Pan-fried rainbow trout from **Diamond Lake** here have helped thaw out many a Cascade explorer on a chilly morning. All four wildernesses drape the crest of the Cascades which divide the pine forests of central Oregon from the fir trees on the western side of the range. These wildlands are under the jurisdiction of the Willamette and Deschutes National Forest Service.

See and ski: While hikers and mountaineers can't wait for the snow to melt,

cross-country and downhill skiers enjoy seven months of topnotch conditions. The hub of most of this November to June activity is 9,060-foot (2,760-meter) **Mount Bachelor**. Riding the chairlift that goes almost to the summit offers what is perhaps the most all-encompassing view of the Cascades to be had from terra firma. As for skiing, it suffices to know that the slopes here were chosen as a training site for the US Olympic Team.

Only 20 miles (32 km) from Bend to the northeast and Sun River to the southeast, Bachelor's emergence in the last 20 years has transformed the region more than any other single outlet of recreation. **Bend**, with almost 18,000 people, is now the largest city east of the Cascades. Augmenting this growth, new industries are locating here because of such advantages as skiing and other fun in the annual 260 days of sun.

Nonetheless, European visitors expecting to see Swiss-style ski chalets in the shadow of the mountains are in for a disappointment. Architecturally and

culturally, Bend is still very much the pioneer settlement that lumber and cattle built. Ramshackle white-framed New England colonial homes predominate city residential areas. Downtown, the only relief from the honky-tonk ambience of the main drag is **Mirror Pond**, which provides habitat for a dozen species of waterfowl as well as otter, mink and beaver. Nearby **Pilot Butte** offers a drive to a lookout point on the Cascades to the west. If one can somehow forget the mountains when looking out from atop the butte, the grazing land and sagebrush desert surrounding Bend's beehive of activity recall an oil boom town on the Texas prairies after a lucky strike. The major difference is that this version of "Marlboro Country" puts more of a premium on slopes of white powder than barrels of black gold.

Up US Highway 97: Even though the ocher plains and snowcapped lava buttes may not yield oil bonanzas, other treasures from mother earth's womb abound in central Oregon. Just north of Bend, 2½ miles (4 km) west of US 97 is **Petersen's Rock Gardens**, where the earth's bounty is served up in intriguing ways. Petrified wood, agate, jasper, geode-like thunder eggs, malachite, lava and obsidian from an 85-mile (137-km) radius of the gardens have been molded here into a variety of statues and fairytale castles. A geology museum features a remarkable collection of crystals as well as local gemstones and fossils. Free-roaming peacocks, chickens, antique farm machinery and snowy alpine vistas add to the charm of a Danish immigrant farmer's flight of fancy.

As one moves north on US 97 drab town-sites coexist incongruously with Cascade panoramas west of the highway. **Redmond**, considered a sister city to Bend, typifies the other settlements here which still are what they were at their inception – supply centers of material necessities to farmers, explorers, and other travelers. To tarry too long in these refueling stops is to miss starry night skies unobscured by city lights and the diverse wildlife roaming the surrounding plains and forests.

An old schoolhouse in Shaniko.

Northeast of Redmond on State 26, the outskirts of **Prineville** provide rock hunting at Priday's agate ranch and birdwatching at the **Crooked River Grasslands**. In addition to eagles, horned owl and red-tailed hawk here, there is also a herd of more than a hundred antelope. Close by, the **Ochoco National Forest** offers hiking, and area waterways are a paradise for fishing and boating. Near the entrance of the National Forest, **Steins Pillar**, a giant basalt thumb protruding up out of an eroded hillside, is a local geological oddity of some interest.

Smith Rocks and Crooked River: Another hard to miss rock pile is the **Smith Rocks** located east of US 97, 22 miles (35 km) north of Bend. The 500-foot (152-meter) high jagged red escarpments stand in the middle of the parched prairies east of the highway in **Terrabone**. Here, non-hikers can enjoy the spectacle of rock climbers dangling on the rock walls above the **Crooked River**.

Back on US 97, the river can be viewed in another dramatic setting. Eight miles (13 km) north of Redmond, the **Ogden Scenic Wayside** overlooks a 400-foot (122-meter) canyon. A 300-foot (90-meter) high bridge is suspended over the Crooked River which flows through the basalt chasm. This viewpoint is named for a Hudson's Bay Company official who led a beaver trapping expedition here in 1825.

The Crooked River eventually comes together with the Deschutes and Metolius Rivers at **Lake Billy Chinook** west of US 97 below Madras. **Cove Palisades State Park** sits near the mouth of the Crooked River, in a region whose towering cliffs have prompted locals to wishfully declare it "The Grand Canyon of Oregon." Nonetheless, the multicolored exposed strata depict the mineral pages of Oregon's geologic past. Park personnel here can elucidate this 7 million-year-old story as well as direct the visitor to Native American petroglyphs dating back several millennia.

Ghost towns and sacred grounds: State 26 goes northwest of Madras into the **Warm Springs Indian Reservation**. Four million dollars were given to these native Americans as compensation for government interference with their traditional fishing grounds. They have used this money to create **Kah-Nee-Ta**, a luxury resort. Mineral hot springs and sun almost every day of the year make the resort's setting at the bottom of a canyon ideal. Tribal cultural events, golf, tennis, horseback riding as well as the only Olympic-sized pool east of the Cascades add to the allure.

The arrow-shaped hotel is staffed by members of the Warm Springs tribe who have contributed to the decor with Indian rugs and pottery as well as lending a traditional touch to the food. These dishes include fresh salmon cooked outside on wooden planks and bird-in-clay, for which a mallet is provided to break the clay coating around a game hen stewing in its own juices. Also on the reservation is the **Warm Springs Museum**, which opened in early 1993 and tells the story of the Pacific Northwest Native Americans.

The reservation is not the only different culture to be seen north of Bend.

Cross-country skiing at Mount Bachelor.

Shaniko, a ghost town on US 97, is a throwback to the turn of the century when this town was the self-proclaimed "wool capital of the world." Founded in 1876 by August Scherneckaw (the Natives pronounced it Shaniko), the town enjoyed its golden decade following the establishment of a railroad terminus in 1900. Thereafter, the gaiety of a boom town reigned against a backdrop of garish hotels, crowded saloons and bawdy houses.

Over the years museums grew up depicting the glory that was Shaniko's, as did the excesses of tourism. While the city hall, the wagons, the schoolhouse, the homesteaders' cabins and the Shaniko Hotel were either originally here or were "faithfully restored," this is not the case with some other sites in town. The cemetery and the church exemplify attempts to create an imaginary but marketable past.

Indian guru in Antelope Town: About 30 miles (48 km) northeast of Madras just east of US 97 is the site of a controversial international news story. Nothing in the history of the little ghost town of **Antelope** could have foretold such notoriety. It all began in 1981 when the residents of Antelope got some new neighbors. The 100-sq. mile (260-sq. km) **Big Muddy Ranch**, 20 miles (32 km) east of town, was bought by the red-garbed followers of Indian guru Bhagwan Sri Rajneesh.

As time went on, Antelope's population of retirees and ranchers raised eyebrows over reports of everything from the commune's unconventional attitudes to sex, to their alleged plans to take over the town. Meanwhile, thousands of followers from all over the world poured into **Rancho Rajneesh**. Today the ranch has been sold, and it may soon be developed. The site isn't marked and it is hard to find without local help – which may not be forthcoming as residents would just as soon forget this chapter of the town's history.

With the media's inflammatory reports about goings-on here, visitors should be aware that the mere mention of Rajneesh in Oregon will elicit a heated discussion. The atmosphere of conflict was once immediately evident by the sight of gun-toting Rajneesh Peace Force members in town, as well as a half dozen car checkpoints on the windy 18-mile (30-km) dirt road to the ranch. Once at the ranch, however, this initial suspicion gave way to friendliness, except that one could not move about freely in non-designated areas.

During the Bhagwan's hey-day the Chamber of Commerce offered a tour which concentrated on the agricultural transformation being worked by the commune. Many Rajneeshees put in 12-hour days, seven days a week using the latest agricultural technology and reclamation techniques to carpet this dry valley with fruit orchards, rows of vegetables, fields of grain, and herds of livestock. In addition, there was a fleet of DC-3 planes at the airstrip, clothing boutiques, restaurants, discotheques, a meditation school, a hotel and a vast auditorium where the Bhagwan spoke. The guru drove through "downtown" Rajneeshpuram each afternoon in one of his large retinue of Rolls-Royces.

Below, a camp in the Three Sisters Wilderness. Right, Lower Proxy Falls.

LAVA AND LAKE COUNTRY, OREGON

Although it comprises some 40 percent of the state, most Oregonians think of the Oregon Lava and Lake Country as "a whole lot of nothing." Not that there aren't some popular areas around the fringes of this area of the Pacific Northwest, which is bounded on the north by the Ochoco and Strawberry mountains and on the west by the Cascade Range. Here there are clear mountain lakes and cool forests, water and greenery – the kind of scenery that chambers of commerce like to describe. But the majority of Oregon's southeast corner is high desert country, 20,000 sq. miles (52,000 sq. km) of sand, sage and rimrock where rainfall rarely exceeds 10 inches (25 cm) per year. Few travelers ever get to see this part of the Pacific Northwest.

The high desert is Oregon's "forgotten corner." History books have us believe that no one ever came here but those who were hopelessly lost or permanently unbalanced. The wheels of the great immigrant wagon trains of the 1840s bypassed the desert, following the ruts of the Oregon Trail across the Blue Mountains to the Columbia River.

The few explorers and settlers who did pass through the region, it is said, took one good look at the place and moved on. Homesteaders made a brief attempt to "settle up" the desert in the early 1900s. Beaten by the unyielding landscape, they soon retired to more forgiving lands across the mountains. Towns sprung up overnight and just as quickly vanished. History, they tell us, evaded the desert. Anyone who believes that is in for a surprise.

Records of the past: The oldest records of civilization in Oregon were found, not on the coast or in the Willamette Valley, but in the desert. Artifacts discovered near Fort Rock date back 9,000 years. Geologic records recall an even more distant past. Marine fossils 225 million years old can still be found along Beaver and Grindstone creeks. Modern man has left his mark as well – Native

<u>Preceding pages</u>: Painted Hills in snow. <u>Below</u>, petroglyphs speak of earlier inhabitants.

268

American, miner, homesteader and stockman, there is a good deal of history in the desert and plenty of life, if you know where to look.

Oregon's desert counties contain numerous species of flora and fauna, including some 90 mammals, more than 200 birds, a dozen reptiles, hundreds of insects and thousands of plants. There is a 9,000-acre (3,640-hectare) forest of ponderosa pine east of the Christmas Lake Valley. It shouldn't be able to survive there, but it does. There are mountains, lakes and wildlife refuges. Above all, there is space.

A visit to the **High Desert Museum** provides a fascinating introduction to Oregon's Lava and Lake Country. Located 7 miles (11 km) south of Bend on US Highway 97, the museum offers natural and cultural history exhibits, nature trails, living wildlife displays, a forestry learning center and a full spectrum of guided tours.

Oregon's Lava and Lake Country offers myriad attractions for the traveler, but it takes a little work to find some of them. Paved roads are few, and many gravel and dirt roads are impassable to all but four-wheel-drive vehicles for much of the year.

If you are careful to check locally for road conditions, however, the small roads are the best way to see the country. Remember to carry water and to pay close attention to your gas gauge – towns are few and far between here. With a little planning and care, you can enjoy a visit to an area which retains more of the flavor of "The Old West" than any other in Oregon.

Lava lands: More than 200 million years ago, a shallow sea covered most of the Oregon interior – now a plateau with an average elevation of 4,000 feet (1,200 meters). As the millennia passed, the sea floor steadily rose. Sixty million years ago, moisture-laden winds swept off the Pacific, unimpeded by mountains. They nurtured a tropical forest where primitive rhinos and crocodiles prowled vast swamplands, and tiny four-toed horses roamed through groves of palm, fig and cinnamon.

The rise of massive shield volcanoes along the site of today's Cascade Range forever altered the Oregon interior. Eruptions blanketed the forests in lava and volcanic ash to depths of hundreds of feet, entombing in the process a fossil record of prehistoric life that can still be read today. As the mountains rose, they created a rain shadow. Moisture from the Pacific no longer reached central Oregon. The high desert was born.

At **Lava Lands Visitors' Center**, on US 97, a short drive south of Bend, dramatic dioramas vividly recreate the violent formation of the Cascade peaks. The building sits at the eastern edge of a huge lava flow which emanated from **Lava Butte**, a massive cinder cone that dominates the local landscape. Two interpretive trails begin at the Visitors' Center, leading the traveler across the lava beds and through the pine forest on its borders. A road winds to the top of Lava Butte, a vantage point that provides magnificent views of the Cascade peaks to the west. Another interpretive trail around the butte's crater and a large community of friendly ground squirrels

A fossilized leaf.

are additional attractions of the Lava Butte viewpoint.

Lava Cast Forest: The **Lava Lands** area of central Oregon encompasses more than 4,400 sq. miles (11,400 sq. km). It boasts what is perhaps the most varied display of outstanding volcanic features to be found anywhere on the North American continent. The **Lava Cast Forest** is one of the area's most unusual attractions. More than 6,000 years ago, this was the site of a thriving ponderosa pine forest, until volcanic eruptions from nearby Mount Newberry poured a succession of lava flows through the area. In the process, lava "casts" of the trees were preserved when the wood burned or rotted away leaving molds of the trees behind.

Lava caves and "tubes" are among the many other fascinating volcanic features of Lava Lands. The most impressive is found at **Lava River Cave State Park** on US 97. This tube, 1 mile (1½ km) long, was created when a river of lava began to cool. A hard crust formed while molten material continued to flow underneath the surface, finally draining away and leaving behind the huge tube visible today. In places, it is 69 feet (18 meters) high and 50 feet (15 meters) wide. The tube was discovered by local rancher Leander Dillman, who utilized the cave's year-round temperature of 40°F (4°C) as a natural refrigerator to store beef and venison. The cave can be explored using lanterns rented at the park's visitors' center.

Natural refrigeration in ice caves: Lava caves provided numerous benefits to early day settlers. For many years, **Arnold Ice Cave** was the main source of ice for citizens of Bend. Other caves were used to shelter livestock in hard weather, and not a few concealed stills during Prohibition.

Wind Cave is named for the strong breezes created by temperature differences between the cavern's interior and the open air. It is called a "breather" cave because it "inhales" on cold winter days and "exhales" in hot weather. At times, the winds pouring from the cave can be heard from a considerable distance and are capable of lifting debris into the air. **Lavacicle Cave** is known for the unusual formations created when heat from a forest fire melted the walls of a lava tube.

All of these caverns are located in the **Deschutes National Forest**, east of US 97 and north of Newberry Crater. Most are closed in winter due to the hazard posed by falling ice. A few, such as Lavacicle Cave, are accessible only on guided tours.

Like the Lava Cast Forest, the lava tubes and caves of this area were created by lava flows from nearby **Newberry Crater**. Ancient Mount Newberry once towered 10,000 feet (3,050 meters) above the surrounding plain. Over the course of thousands of years, the mountain's peak slowly collapsed, forming a crater graced today by two beautiful lakes. Both **Paulina** and **East lakes** are renowned for their trout fishing. Interestingly, there were no fish in these lakes until the white man came to central Oregon. Trout were carried in on horseback from nearby La Pine in 1910.

A paved road leads from US 97 to Newberry Crater, allowing the traveler access by auto during the summer months and by snowmobile, snowshoes or skis during winter. Miles of trails wind through the crater and around its rim. Perhaps most interesting is the **Trail of Glass**, which skirts the edge of a massive flow of obsidian (also called "volcanic glass"). Other trails provide spectacular views of the Cascades and the high desert to the west. From **Paulina Peak**, four states (Oregon, Washington, California and Nevada) can be seen on a clear day. The peak, the lakes and several other geographic and man-made features of central Oregon were named after a Paiute chief. Despite his record as a notorious raider and cattle thief, Chief Paulina is still respected today for his skills as a military tactician. His numerous hairsbreadth escapes earned him the nickname "Bullet-proof."

Cascade Lakes Highway: The crossroads at the town of La Pine provide the southern access to the **Cascade Lakes Highway**, part of a 100-mile (160-km) paved loop called the **Century Drive**. The highway travels through some of the most popular recreation areas in central Oregon. Here, in the shadow of the Cascade peaks, volcanic activity created a series of pristine lakes and a paradise for the photographer, hiker and sportsman.

Davis Lake, at the southernmost point of the highway, offers some of its most unusual scenery. Its northern end is completely blocked by a huge lava dam, which was responsible for the lake's creation. There is no visible outlet for its waters, which flow for 4 miles (6 km) through underground lava channels before emerging at **Wickiup Reservoir**. **Lava Lake**, the source of the Deschutes River, also has no visible outlet during much of the year.

Wildlife is abundant in the Cascade lake country. Most notable is the osprey population at **Crane Prairie Reservoir**, the site of the first osprey management area in the United States. When the Deschutes River was dammed at Crane Prairie in the 1930s to provide irrigation water for ranches to the east, the lodgepole pine forest was not cut down but simply flooded. The result was a forest of dead trees (or "snags") surrounded by water. Inadvertently, a prime habitat for osprey had been created. Today, the birds nest in the snags and dive for fish in the waters of the reservoir. This unusual scenery can be explored at close range in canoes or powerboats rented from the **Crane Prairie Resort**. Great blue herons and sandhill cranes nest near the reservoir, and bald eagles can often be seen soaring overhead. During the fall migration, thousands of waterfowl create a magnificent display.

The lakes of this region, as well as the waters of the **Deschutes River**, provide some of the best fishing in all the Pacific Northwest. There are 11 species of cold water game fish, including trout, Atlantic salmon and Kokanee. Waterfowl and deer hunting are popular here as well. For travelers interested in an extended stay in the Cascade lake country, there are numerous campgrounds along the highway, often near trailheads which provide access to the wilderness areas in the high mountain country. **Elk Lake**

Obsidian lava flow from Newberry Crater.

Lodge and **Cultus Lake Resort** offer rustic overnight accommodations, restaurants and boat landings for canoeists, windsurfers and sailors.

A large portion of the Cascade Lakes Highway is only open in summer, with the higher elevations usually not plowed until mid-June. During the winter months, the road serves as a trail for snowmobiles and cross-country skiers.

Klamath country: US 97 is the major north–south route through the Oregon interior. Moving south from Bend, it closely follows the course of a wagon road used by the pioneers. A worthwhile stop on the route is **Collier Memorial State Park**. Here an open-air museum of logging history and equipment tells the traveler of one of eastern Oregon's most important industries.

The town of **Klamath Falls** is the second largest in Oregon east of the Cascades. The community boasts that it receives 290 days of sunshine each year. If that statistic alone is not enough to entice the visitor, there are numerous parks and three fine museums in town.

The **Klamath County Museum** features exhibits devoted to local history, logging and military conflicts. The **Baldwin Museum** is a restored turn-of-the-century hotel which once played host to US Presidents Theodore Roosevelt, William Howard Taft and Woodrow Wilson. History of a different kind is preserved at the **Favell Museum of Western Art and Indian Artifacts**. In addition to works of some of America's most renowned Western artists, the museum can claim the largest collection of Native American arrowheads in the western United States.

The **Klamath Basin National Wildlife Refuges** are this region's best known attraction. The complex consists of six separate parcels which include open water, marshes, meadows, forests, grasslands, rocky cliffs and agricultural lands. Before the arrival of the white man, the basin was dominated by about 185,000 acres (74,860 hectares) of shallow lakes and marshland. Less than 25 percent of those wetlands remain today, the majority having been drained and converted to farmland. It is estimated that the basin once attracted peak concentrations of 6 million waterfowl back in early pioneer times. Although these numbers have been drastically reduced, the present fall peak of nearly 1 million ducks and geese provides what must surely be one of the most awe-inspiring wildlife displays in the nation. The best viewing is at **Lower Klamath** and **Tule Lake** refuges located just over the California border to the south. The Klamath Basin is also known as the winter home of the largest concentration of bald eagles in the 48 contiguous states.

On the California border: **Lava Beds National Monument** is a California attraction with strong ties to Oregon history as the site of the Modoc Indian War of 1872–3. (The ancestral home of the Modocs was in the area now occupied by the southern units of the wildlife refuge.) In the 1860s, the US government responded to pressure from settlers and moved the tribe north, where they were to share lands with the Klamaths in Oregon. The two tribes were unable to live together in harmony

Modern-day gold miners with a sluice box.

and so the Modocs attempted to return to their homeland on the Lost River (near the Oregon–California border). Their journey began at Modoc Point on Upper Klamath Lake. In November of 1872, the US Army decided to return the tribe to the Klamath Reservation by force. Led by Modoc Chief Kientpoos, also known as "Captain Jack," the Modocs retreated to the lava beds south of Tule Lake. There they held off 600 soldiers for nearly five months, even though the entire Modoc fighting force numbered less than 60.

Captain Jack's Stronghold Historic Trail is best enjoyed with the aid of a self-guiding tour book. It vividly recreates the struggle of the Modocs, who lost their tribal identity despite great courage against insurmountable odds. The monument's lava beds are honeycombed with caves, which make for fascinating explorations for the modern day traveler.

Blue Bucket Mine: In 1825, Peter Skene Ogden made the first recorded exploration of the Oregon interior, searching for fur trading possibilities for the Hudson's Bay Company. For over 40 years, few people followed except for an occasional wagon train searching for a short cut to bypass the grueling route of the Oregon Trail across the Blue Mountains to the northeast. Most famous of these was the Meek cutoff party – the "Lost Wagon Train" of 1843.

During the journey, children were sent to fetch water in a blue bucket, and yellow metal was discovered in the bottom of the pail. A few of the larger pieces were flattened out on wagon wheels and used as sinkers for fishing. When gold was discovered at Sutter's Creek in California three years later, members of the Meek party realized what that "yellow metal" had been. Although a half dozen diaries of the journey had been kept, the route of the train proved impossible to retrace. The "Blue Bucket Mine" was never found and remains one of the most enduring legends of the Oregon desert to this day.

Miners searching for the fabled mine were about the only folks in the desert

Prospectors of the Gold Rush era.

until the 1860s. In 1856, the Commander of the US Army's Department of the Pacific issued an order forbidding immigrants to locate east of the Cascades due to the presence of hostile Natives. But the lure of gold drew a steady stream of hardy souls to the desert despite the risk. "Gold trails" were established through the rugged terrain; towns and trading posts followed. The order forbidding settlement was soon rescinded.

Dramatic change came to the desert after 1862, when the Homestead Law was passed. Under this law, any US citizen could acquire 160 acres (64 hectares) of public land for only $1.25 per acre. And by living on the property for five years, the homesteader could acquire the title absolutely free. Later the acreage was doubled and then doubled again. Dozens of towns appeared in the high desert.

Heart of the desert: Most of the new residents were lured to the area by unscrupulous "land locaters" who claimed that the desert would soon bloom into a veritable Garden of Eden. Their sales pitch proved "irresistible to bank clerks, school teachers and others who believed in fairies" according to E.R. Jackman, author of *The Oregon Desert*. Most were ill-prepared to cope with the life that awaited them.

Only three of the towns once numerous on US 20 between Bend and Burns survive today. Life here wasn't always so peaceful. Around the turn of the century, this was the site of range wars – violent conflicts between cattlemen and sheepherders. The cattlemen claimed that sheep were ruining the range by trampling and overgrazing the native grasses.

During the winter of 1903–4, vigilante groups such as the Crook County Sheep Shooters Association were responsible for the slaughter of over 10,000 sheep. The range wars came to an end when the US government established a permit system controlling the use of range lands. This is still range country today, and motorists on US 20 sometimes have to share the right of way with herds of livestock.

Engine in Veterans' Park, Klamath Falls.

274

The business of William Brown: Just east of the town of **Hampton** is the site of William Walter Brown's **Gap Ranch**. A few abandoned buildings are all that remains of a spread that once covered 38,000 acres (15,380 hectares). Brown was a colorful figure who had an unusual way of doing business. He was apt to write a check on anything that was handy, be it a label from a can of tomatoes or a board from a packing crate. Too busy to attend to his general store in person, he left a cigar box on the counter so that his customers could pay for their purchases. Since most of his merchandise wasn't priced, some mighty good deals were struck in his absence. He is reputed to have made and lost several fortunes. A few miles farther east is **Glass Butte**, a popular area due to its large deposits of obsidian.

Fort Rock: State Highway 31 follows the approximate course taken by Captain John Fremont's expedition of 1843, which was mounted in the hope of finding an alternative route from Columbia to California. The highway didn't pan out as a major artery, but it does pass by numerous points of interest to modern travelers. **Fort Rock State Park** is the site of **Fort Rock Cave**. It was here that artifacts dating back 9,000 years were discovered, including sandals woven in the manner of the ancient Greeks (unlike the products of any known Native American culture). Little is known of the lifestyle or appearance of the cave's inhabitants, but it is known that their abode was sculpted by the waves of one of the huge inland lakes that once lapped against the rimrock of the high desert.

The dry beds of **Fossil** and **Silver** lakes have long been favorite haunts of fossil hunters and archeologists. Millions of years ago, camels and elephants roamed these shores; bison, deer and antelope followed. The abundance of game and wildfowl drew bands of nomadic Natives to the ancient lake country, and more Native artifacts have been found here than in any other part of Oregon. This is a fine area for exploring volcanic features as well. **Devil's Garden**, **Four Craters** and **Crack in the Ground** are all popular spots for photographers, hikers and rock-hounds.

Lost Forest and Summer Lakes: The **Lost Forest** is a few miles east of the town of Christmas Valley. This area has long attracted the attention of foresters and ecologists. Somehow a 9,000-acre (3,640-hectare) forest of ponderosa pine has managed to survive here where annual rainfall is less than 10 inches (25 cm). Elsewhere, 14 inches (35 cm) is thought to be the minimum needed to support such growth. It may have survived due to a layer of compacted volcanic ash below the sandy soil.

Not all of the high desert's ancestral lakes have dried up completely. **Summer Lake** is the site of a wildlife refuge that attracts thousands of migrating waterfowl, including a large contingent of snow geese. **Abert Lake**, farther to the south, attracts its share of birds as well. The spring months bring the height of the wildlife display to both lakes. A string of small *playas* (seasonal lakes) called the **Warner Lakes** provide yet another desert oasis for migrating birds at the foot of **Hart Mountain**. A display

Migrating geese seek wildlife refuge area.

of native desert plants and the **Hart Mountain National Antelope Refuge** are other noteworthy attractions of this rugged 3,600-foot (1,100-meter) escarpment. Members of Oregon's largest antelope herd are best viewed during the summer months.

Lakeview, at an elevation of 4,800 feet (1,460 meters), bills itself as "the highest town in Oregon." The **Schmink Memorial Museum** houses a collection of furnishings and other pioneer memorabilia. "**Old Perpetual**," the state's only continuously spouting geyser, is found just north of town. More active forms of recreation can be enjoyed at the **Warner Mountain Ski Area** or the **Gearheart Mountain Wilderness**, located within easy driving distance of Lakeview.

At the southeast corner: Probably the least known area of the state, the region encompassed by Harney and Malheur counties offers some of Oregon's grandest scenery. Dominating the landscape is **Steens Mountain**, a massive fault block rising from the desert floor. From its western base to the 9,700-foot (2,960-meter) summit is a gently sloping 23 miles (37 km). But from there east to the Alvord Desert nearly a mile lower in elevation is a distance of only 3 miles (5 km). This is one of the best known fault blocks in the Americas, if not the world.

Malheur National Wildlife Refuge: The **Malheur National Wildlife Refuge** is one of America's largest. Eagles, hawks, cranes, herons, egrets, bitterns, swans, ducks and geese, and a multitude of song birds contribute to a count of more than 250 species. A variety of mammals can also be seen, including deer, coyote, muskrat, beaver and weasel. An established auto tour route through the **Blitzen Valley** may well be the best place for wildlife photography in the entire state.

The **Frenchglen Hotel**, at the tour route's southern terminus, is a worthy attraction as well. This small (8-room) hotel is an impressive state historic site, which was once a stopping point for stagecoaches. Outstanding home-cooked meals are served family style. Reservations are usually required, so call ahead in advance.

To the east of Steens Mountain is the **Alvord Desert**. Hot springs are found at the edges of this vast expanse of hard packed sand, which is sometimes turned into a shallow lake by snowmelt from Steens Mountain. Still farther to the east is **Jordon Valley**. This has been the center of a Basque sheepherding community for many years. The town of **Basque**, named after the French-Spanish region, is noted for its colorful buildings and the **Pelota Frontone**, a traditional Basque handball court.

The nearby **Owyhee Mountains** provide what some call the finest wilderness hiking in the Northwest. It is undoubtedly a land of magnificent scenery. **Lake Owyhee** is the most popular recreation area in the southeast corner of Oregon. Scenic tours through such areas as **Leslie Gulch** and **Succor Creek** provide views of brilliantly colored rock, which are said to rival those at Bryce Canyon in Utah.

Ontario, the eastern gateway to Oregon on Interstate 84, is the largest community in this region.

Below, cactus on a wall of basalt. Right, ranger-led hikers investigate the lakeshore.

JOHN DAY FOSSIL BEDS

US Highway 26 heads east from Ontario to the town of **John Day**. This community still retains some of its frontier atmosphere, as large herds of livestock are still driven right down its main street on their way to spring pastures. Atmosphere of a different kind can be experienced at the **Kam Wah Chung & Co. Museum**. This building has been restored to look as it might have in the early 1900s, when it served as the economic, social and religious center of a thriving Chinese community whose members were drawn to the area by its once numerous gold mines.

The focal point of John Day's gold rush was **Canyon City**, located just south of John Day on US 395. As of 1980, this was a town of some 600 residents, but in its heyday in the 1860s Canyon City had a population in excess of 10,000. Gold mining activity died out almost completely in the 1940s. It has seen something of a renaissance in recent years thanks to the rise in gold prices. An excellent presentation of the town's history can be found at the **Herman and Eliza Oliver Historical Museum**, which features an excellent display of mining apparatus and pioneer relics like the Joaquin Miller Cabin and the Greenhorn City Jail.

Antelopes in Bear Valley: Continuing south from Canyon City on US 395, the traveler passes through **Bear Valley,** where herds of antelope can often be observed during the winter months. To the east is the **Strawberry Mountain Wilderness**. This region of rugged peaks and high mountain lakes includes samples of five of the seven major life zones found in the United States. For a glimpse of days gone by, return to the Bend area by way of the winding state road that joins US 395 between Canyon City and Seneca. In the town of **Paulina**, a dance hall still has a sign by the front door requesting that patrons check their guns before entering. Abandoned homesteads along the route attest to the harshness of the climate. (Peter Skene Ogden's

1825 party were forced to eat their horses to survive while wintering along the upper Crooked River.)

The major route to the Bend area follows the valley of the John Day River. US 26 passes through fertile farmland and near country very popular among Oregon's deer hunters.

The **John Day Fossil Beds National Monument** is a park where you can spend the day hiking to a breathtaking overlook and never see another soul, even though it is a holiday weekend and you are never more than 2 miles (3 km) from the nearest road. It is a park where rangers still have time to give you the personal attention that can mean the difference between a mediocre visit and a memorable one. It is a park where you can enjoy beautiful scenery and a world famous scientific resource – in peace.

The fossil assemblages of John Day country were brought to the attention of the scientific community by Thomas Condon, a Methodist pastor from Fort Dallas on the Columbia River. In 1870, Condon shipped a collection of his finds to the Smithsonian Institute in Washington, DC, a substantial portion of which were "missing links" in the known chain of evolution. His discoveries were eagerly received.

During the next 30 years, many of the world's most eminent paleontologists either traveled to the region to add to their collections or hired others to do so for them. Although the frequency of major expeditions declined after the turn of the century, amateur fossil collecting continued unabated. The State of Oregon began buying up some of the most outstanding beds during the 1930s, and in 1974 the US Congress authorized the creation of the National Monument.

John Day Fossil Beds consists of three widely scattered "units" – Sheep Rock, Painted Hills and Clarno – encompassing more than 14,000 acres (5,660 hectares), and includes the former state parks and surrounding land. Fossil records unearthed here, new and old, are still studied today in museums and universities all over the world. They reveal the region's surprising past, records of a time when the high desert was the floor

Left, Painted Hills of the John Day Fossil Beds National Monument.

of an ancient sea framed by tropical forests no human saw.

Responsibility for preserving and interpreting the fossil resource rests with the National Park Service. Preservation is a fairly straightforward task. Random collection of fossil material is no longer permitted, although scientific and educational research continue under a permit system. The second phase of the Park Service's responsibility is more problematic. How can the fossils of the high desert and the history they reveal be brought to life for the casual visitor?

The answer is a unique combination of museum, laboratory and outdoor school developed by a talented staff with a contagious enthusiasm for the subject. A former park ranger, Kim Sikoryak, had a personal theory that "everyone was a dinosaur freak when they were 10 years old, so it's easy to entice them back into the wonderful world of prehistoric beasts." The park's obscurity doesn't hurt it either, because visitors get a "one-at-a-time, custom visit" according to Sikoryak.

The best place to begin your journey in "Oregon's time machine" is at the **Sheep Rock Visitor's Center**, open year-round, but closed on weekends from late November through February. An intriguing variety of exhibits awaits you. One room of the house has been set aside to show what the interior might have looked like 60 years ago, complete with original furnishings and portraits of the Cant family on the walls. Outside in the orchard, farm implements reflect the house's historical function. This is a park that does not want to be a government outpost isolated from the rest of the world, but a cultural asset that represents the character and values of the community of which it is a part.

Of course the visitors' center's primary role is to introduce the public to the fossil resource. During the summer months staff members present museum talks and trail hikes and are always ready to answer questions and alert visitors to sights of particular interest. Displays of fossils unearthed at the monument are supplemented by paintings of

Desert landscape of the John Day Fossil Beds.

"paleobiomes," depicting the landscape as it might have appeared millions of years ago.

More fossil replicas: The next stop is **Blue Basin** and the **Island In Time Trail**. A short hike takes you into a canyon with 400-foot (120-meter) badland exposures composed of 29-million-year-old claystone of the upper John Day formation.

Fossil replicas are installed along the trail in much the same positions in which they were discovered. Nearby paintings recreate the Oregon of the late Oligocene geologic epoch. Fossil finds of the *oreodont* were most numerous here. This small herd animal about the size of a sheep vanished millions of years ago. Other finds include the remains of a saber-toothed cat and a tiny three-toed form of the horse called *Miohippus*.

After exploring Blue Basin's intricate maze of canyons and washes, you may want to hike up the overlook trail. Here, exposures of ancient formations are visible in all directions, some blue-green like those of Blue Basin, others deep red, signaling the presence of clays that are still more ancient.

The lower, and therefore older, John Day Formation preserves fossil records reaching back 37 million years. They are best viewed at the **Painted Hills** unit near Mitchell on US 26. Here you will find the most spectacular scenery in the monument. The overlook trail provides a sweeping view of the brilliantly colored hills, while the trail at **Painted Cove** provides a closer look.

The strata of the John Day formation tell of a land in transition. The deposits are a remnant of an epoch in which widely scattered volcanic activity showered ash across a verdant landscape to depths of up to 1,000 feet (300 meters). Paleobotantists can trace the changes in vegetation through the fossil records preserved in the ash. The fossils of the upper John Day Formation indicate a climate much wetter than today's in which oak, beech, birch and similar species flourished. The lower John Day formations speak of a still wetter climate. These changes occurred as the ancestral Cascade Mountains rose to the west, creating a rain shadow which precipitated the development of the current high desert climate.

The **Clarno Unit** of the monument is located just east of the town of Antelope. Here the pillars and palisades of the Clarno formation rise above a small valley. These fossil beds preserve the limbs, leaves, seeds and nuts of plants that grew here 35 to 50 million years ago. Their remains indicate a near-tropical climate similar to that of contemporary India. The Clarno Unit also features an interpretive trail. The highlight of the walk is the chance to view numerous leaf fossils. Each leaf tooth and vein is visible even after millions of years.

The John Day Fossil Beds have yielded a succession of animal and plant fossils extending over a period of 40 million years. They are the only ones on earth that do so. Some day the traffic jams of other parks may also appear at John Day Fossil Beds. But for now the monument provides the visitor with a chance to travel quietly down the corridors of time.

A lava tube shows volcanic forces at work.

NORTHEAST OREGON

To most people, Northeast Oregon is pretty much *terra incognita*. They may have heard of the Pendleton Round-Up or Hell's Canyon on the Snake River, but for the most part it's dismissed as desert, just something to be gotten through on the way between Portland and Boise or Salt Lake City.

Northeast Oregon is a lot more than that. This four-county corner of the state has more mountains than desert; little streams and big rivers; wilderness areas; national forests; wildlife refuges; Hell's Canyon National Recreation area; Forest Service campgrounds and state parks. It's an outdoor enthusiast's paradise: horse and backpacking; camping; float trips down the Grande Ronde and Snake Rivers; jet boat trips through Hell's Canyon; hunting and fishing; downhill and cross-country skiing in winter; and some spectacular scenery.

Northeast Oregon is also working country, with an economy based mostly on agriculture, cattle and logging. That means it's periodically depressed – when the housing market is bad and the mills shut down or cut back, or when beef prices are low, its unemployment rate soars, and many mill hands and loggers are forced to leave the region.

On the Old Oregon Trail: Northeast Oregon is also part of one of the most interesting and exciting eras of American history: the Old Oregon Trail practically bisects it. Wagon trains by the hundreds came through this area on the next-to-last leg of their journey west – one of the biggest mass migrations ever, starting in the early 1840s with the first large-scale trains. Interstate 84, the main east–west highway in this latitude, parallels the Oregon Trail and, though you don't catch many glimpses of the ruts worn by the wagons, there are monuments, markers and roadside signs recounting the events of those days.

Start with **Farewell Bend State Park**, on the Snake River, just north of the Baker County line. This is where the wagon trains left the Snake for the Columbia River, northwest over the Blue Mountains, one of the most rugged parts of the trip. The park features camping, boating, fishing and swimming.

Along the back road to the little town of **Huntington** (population 522), north of Farewell Bend, the visitor can see some remnants of the Old Oregon Trail, including a small iron cross that marks the spot where Natives killed a number of immigrants in 1860. Huntington itself has a wild history. It's rather quiet now, but it was a hell-raiser in the last part of the 19th century; a stagecoach station and later a railroad center, it had its share of saloons, gunfighters and Chinese opium dens.

Boom towns and ghost towns: So did **Baker City** (population 9,100), 45 miles (72 km) farther north. Now it's a cattle and logging town, but before and after the turn of the century it was the supply and transportation center of a widespread gold rush. In 1890 its 6,600 residents made it bigger than Spokane or Boise. Baker City boomed as it dealt with gold-mining towns like Bourne,

Sumpter and Granite, west of the city, and Cornucopia and Copperfield to the east. These are ghost towns now, and there isn't much left of them except sagging buildings and some abandoned equipment, like a big dredge at Sumpter which is being restored and opened to the public in 1995. There's a restored narrow-gauge railroad that travels the Sumpter Valley through rugged country, as its predecessor did 80 years ago.

The Bureau of Land Management operates an impressive $11 million **National Historic Oregon Trail Interpretive Center** in Baker City. Completed in 1992, the center focuses on life along the trail and is open daily, drawing 300,000 visitors annually.

Baker City is also the gateway to the southern end of Hell's Canyon, the deepest gorge in North America. To get to the gorge, take State Highway 86 for 70 miles (112 km) through Richland (population 175), Halfway (population 350), and Copperfield (population zero) to the Snake at Oxbow Dam.

Around the turn of the century, in the gold rush era, **Copperfield** was probably the champion tough town: saloons, dance halls, whorehouses, gambling dens. **Oxbow Dam** was being constructed then, and rivalries between the dam roughnecks and the railroad workers were frequent and fierce. Rocks, beer bottles, fists, brawls and riots were a way of life, all this encouraged by rival saloons. There were no jails or police, and the Baker County sheriff was unable to maintain order. The governor, in faraway Salem, threatened the town with martial law, which got him a promise of execution if he showed his face in Copperfield. He didn't.

What he did do was send his secretary, Miss Fern Hobbs, all 5' 3" and 104 pounds (47 kg) of her, to demand the resignations of town officials. She was received graciously, and the town was so bemused by her arrival that residents failed to notice that she was accompanied by the warden of the state penitentiary, his chief of guards, and five burly members of the state militia. When the town officials refused the demands of

Hell's Canyon and the Snake River, from Hat Point.

Miss Hobbs for their resignations, she produced an order from the governor imposing martial law – and her escorts made it stick. A few months later, the town burned to the ground and was never rebuilt. Arson was suspected, and not for the first time.

At the southern end of its grand canyon, the Snake River has been tamed by three dams, of which Oxbow is the middle one. To the south, upstream, is **Brownlee Dam**, which can be crossed to get to Idaho; downstream is **Hell's Canyon Dam**, a starting point for float trips through the steep walls of the gorge itself. Reservoirs behind the dams provide boating and other water recreation, but it's in Hell's Canyon that the spectacular scenery lies.

Created in 1975, **Hell's Canyon National Recreation Area** (NRA) is more than 650,000 acres (263,000 hectares) of some of the roughest country in the world. Within the NRA are the 190,000 acres (76,900 hectares) of **Hell's Canyon Wilderness**, rising to the Seven Devils mountain range on the Idaho

side of the river and to rimrock, grassy benches, and timbered ridges on the Oregon side. Bisecting both the NRA and the Wilderness, thousands of feet below the rims, is the **Snake River**. Designated a Wild and Scenic River, it rushes through its incredible gorge at twice the volume of the Colorado. Rapids follow rapids with terrifying frequency, so that the river seems to be mostly whitewater. From the rim this power is hard to see. The immensity of the view and the depth of the gorge are overwhelming, and the river seems lost at the floor of the canyon. But on the river itself the power is clear: this is not a trip for amateurs.

How deep?: For almost 40 miles (64 km), the canyon depth averages more than 5,500 feet (1,680 meters), and for some 15 miles (24 km) the average is more than 6,000 feet (1,830 meters). One point on the Idaho rim is more than 7,800 feet (2,380 meters) above the river. And how narrow? Rim to rim, the canyon averages 10 miles (16 km), and sometimes considerably less – in one

A buck near a winter stream.

spot less than 5 feet (8 meters). And at the canyon floor there are places where the bleak walls rise almost vertically, no more than 200 feet (60 meters) apart.

On the river, there are float trips, mostly starting below Hell's Canyon Dam, and jet boat trips, starting far downstream at Lewiston, Idaho, or Clarkston, Washington. In the Wilderness, motorized vehicles are prohibited, so the visitor must go on foot or horseback. In the Recreation Area formerly treacherous roads have been improved but check with the NRA if you're driving a recreational vehicle.

Just below Hell's Canyon Dam is a new visitor's center, operated by the US Forest Service from May through October. The center offers a stunning view of the canyon as well as information.

Hell's Canyon NRA can also be entered from its northern end, through Wallowa County, the most northeasterly part of Oregon. For details, contact Hell's Canyon NRA Headquarters (tel: 503-426-4978) in Enterprise.

To return from a side-trip to the Old Oregon Trail from Hell's Canyon, start again at Baker City, on I-84. The highway travels through the Powder River Valley with the Elkhorn Mountains standing at 9,000 feet (2,750 meters) in the west and the Wallowas towering even higher in the east.

About 20 miles (32 km) north of Baker is the little town of **North Powder** (population 416), which is the turn-off to **Anthony Lakes**. With a base elevation of 7,100 feet (2,164 km), this is one of the highest ski areas in the Northwest, offering both a chairlift and poma and miles of cross-country terrain. Its altitude and 10-foot (3-meter) annual snowfall give Anthony Lakes some of the best skiing in the area.

Continuing northwest, I-84 crosses over into the Grande Ronde Valley and Union County. **LaGrande** is a lumbermill and railroad town, and the home of Eastern Oregon State College. From here, the Oregon Trail immigrant wagons left the relatively easy valleys and started up into the Blue Mountains on their way to the Columbia River.

A deep desert gorge with an inviting road.

This was one of the hardest parts of the entire western migration and one wonders how the wagons made it.

Perhaps the most rewarding side-trip in this corner of the state starts at LaGrande. Turn northeast on State 82, through **Imbler** and **Elgin**, and on to Wallowa County, one of the most remote and beautiful parts of the state.

Remote and scenic Wallowa: From Elgin, State 204 leads northwest 21 miles (34 km) to the other major ski area in this part of the state, **Spout Springs**, in the Blue Mountains. State 82 continues northeast up over Minam Summit, down the twisting Minam Grade, and into Wallowa County, the "Switzerland of America," "Gateway to Hell's Canyon," and "Oregon's best-kept secret," as it is variously called. Wallowa County is not on the way from anywhere to anywhere else. If you're there, it's because you were headed there.

There's a mythic quality to Wallowa County. Slightly larger than life, it is the only place in the state where a 10,000-foot (3,050-meter) alpine environment – the High Wallowas – lies less than 50 straight-line miles (80 km) from a sub-tropical one – the sun-baked floor of Hell's Canyon, about 1,300 feet (400 meters) above sea level.

State 82 follows the canyon of the Wallowa River up onto the floor of the Wallowa Valley, past the farming towns of **Wallowa** and **Lostine** to **Enterprise** (population 2,015), the county seat. It is here that the first close and unobstructed view of the High Wallowas appears.

The view continues during the 6-mile (10-km) drive to the picturesque town of **Joseph**, and on to the very head of the valley, where **Wallowa Lake** lies, a true jewel nestled among the steep slopes of the mountains. Wallowa Lake, of glacial origin, is 4 miles (6 km) long and about a mile (2 km) wide, and its sides are textbook examples of lateral and terminal moraines, a geologist's delight. **Wallowa Lake State Park**, at the head of the lake, is one of the largest and busiest in the state system.

Back in the heart of the mountain range is **Eagle Cap Wilderness Area**,

Hiking in the Eagle Cap Wilderness.

300,000 acres (121,500 hectares) of high, wild and beautiful country, touching Baker and Union counties as well as Wallowa. There are more than 50 lakes in the wilderness, most of them accessible by Forest Service trails. The lakes are stocked with brook and rainbow trout, and steelhead and chinook are common in area rivers.

The Eagle Cap ecology is fragile, so the Forest Service enforces some rules concerning usage: camp no closer than 200 feet (60 meters) from lake shores, practice "no trace" camping (meaning haul out your own trash), and hobble or picket horses instead of tying them to trees and shrubs. For maps or wilderness-use permit information, contact the Eagle Cap Ranger District Headquarters in Enterprise.

Home of the Nez Perce: The Wallowa Valley was once the home of Chief Joseph's band of Nez Perce. The treaty-breaking eviction of the tribe to a reservation near Lapwai, Idaho, was one of the contributing causes of the Nez Perce War (1877). During this war, Joseph and the other Nez Perce leaders conducted a 1,700-mile (2,736-km) retreat with women, children, old people, cattle and thousands of horses from near Lapwai to the Bear Paw Mountains near the Canadian border in Montana, fighting almost all the way. This military miracle took place mostly through hostile country, with the Nez Perce chased by and constantly out-maneuvering and out-fighting soldiers, settlers and Natives until they were trapped less than 50 miles (80 km) from safety in Canada.

The end of the war at the Bear Paws gave rise to Chief Joseph's famous surrender speech, that ended with these moving words: "Hear me, my chiefs! I am tired. My heart is sick and sad. From where the sun now stands I will fight no more forever."

A lot goes on in Wallowa County: **Chief Joseph Days**, a rodeo and parade event participated in by Nez Perce Natives from the reservation at Lapwai (late July in Joseph); Hell's Canyon Mule Days (early September, Enterprise); a balloon festival (mid-June, Enterprise); and a 3-day **Alpenfest** (mid to late September, head of Wallowa Lake).

Joseph has recently become an artists' community and houses four bronze foundries as well as a number of fine galleries. There are two museums in town. **Nez Perce Crossing**, a museum owned by artist Dave Manuel, is full of Indian and western memorabilia. The **Wallowa County Museum**, dedicated to area history, is housed in what was once a bank, and is the site of one of the most Wallowa-Countyish stories around. In 1896, an out-of-town dude recruited some local talent and robbed the bank, though not without some trouble. The citizens responded with gunfire, and when the smoke cleared one man was dead and another wounded. The wounded man, one of the local boys, did his time in the state penitentiary and came back to become a vice-president of the bank that succeeded the one he'd robbed. The topper is that the local newspaper, located in the back of the bank building, was in the middle of a press run that drowned out the noise of the robbery; the newsmen were the last to learn of it.

Views from a cable tramcar: At the head of Wallowa Lake is a unique attraction – a cable tramway with four-person cars that carry passengers 3,700 feet (1,130 meters) from the head of the lake to the 8,200-foot (2,500-meter) top of **Mount Howard** in about 15 minutes. Wildlife can often be seen on the way up, and there are walking trails around the top of the mountain that provide a series of stunning views; back into the Eagle Cap Wilderness, down to the lake below and out over the valley to the Blue Mountains beyond, and the Seven Devils mountain range just on the other side of Hell's Canyon to the east. On a really good day, you can see the Bitteroot Mountains in Montana.

To reach the wild and scenic north end of Hell's Canyon, take the Imnaha Highway 30 miles (48 km) east out of Joseph to the little hamlet of **Imnaha**. From here there are several options. A rutted dirt road leads 24 miles (38 km) to **Hat Point**, one of the most spectacular overlooks above Hell's Canyon, more than a mile above the river. Or there is a road down to the river itself, at **Dug Bar**. The same road gives access to the **Nee-Me-Poo Recreational Trail** down to the same point on the river. This trail, 4 miles (6 km), follows the route the Nez Perce Indians took when they left their valley forever. These roads are seasonal, so check before trying them.

This is hot country in the summer, and there is no water along the trail. The visitor should carry his own – a good idea anywhere in the canyon. Also, this is rattlesnake habitat, so hikers should be watchful and carry snakebite kits.

The Grande Ronde River: Back in LaGrande, the Old Oregon Trail heads northwest again, parallel to I-84. The highway leaves the **Grande Ronde Valley** abruptly, and starts up into the Blue Mountains. For a time, the road follows the scenic Grande Ronde River. This stretch of the river is a good short trip for beginners, though there's a hazard about halfway down: two rifle ranges. (Floaters should either shout out and let shooters know they're there or raise a white flag as they pass.)

Up over the Blue Mountains, the road leads past **Meacham** (along Ladd Canyon, southeast of LaGrande) and then to **Emigrant Springs State Park**. Here the wagons rested before starting the precarious descent. Just past the park the road starts across the **Umatilla Indian Reservation** and continues, steep and winding, down into the flatlands.

Pendleton is the home of the Blue Mountain Community College and the Pendleton Woolen Mills, and there is a variety of water sports behind **McNary Dam** on the Columbia River. Tourists come to see the resorted underground city which Chinese immigrants built beneath the streets of Pendleton in the late 1800s. But the big event is the **Pendleton Round-Up**, begun in 1910 as a cowboy convention and now one of the major rodeos in the West. *Happy Canyon*, the night show that's an integral part of the rodeo, came into existence a few years later, and now draws enormous crowds of its own. It's a pageant and extravaganza that portrays the settlement of the West in song and action.

Golden wheatfields near Pendleton.

OLYMPIC NATIONAL PARK

No other region in North America combines the natural whimsy, gentle wildness and variety of ecologies to be found in **Olympic National Park**. The 1,400-sq.-mile (3,625-sq.-km) wilderness – or mostly wilderness – contains an archetypal temperate-zone rain forest, the last wilderness ocean beaches in the conterminous United States, and alpine mountains so spectacular as to be compared with the European Alps.

The park's three distinct ecologies serve as three different park experiences, all within a day's drive. One of them – the park's Ocean Strip – is, however, geographically separated from the main park.

It wasn't until 1889 that an exploring party sponsored by the *Seattle Press* newspaper crossed the Olympic Mountains, probably the first men to penetrate the Olympic ranges. Even Indian tribes of the Olympic Peninsula had bestowed the region's high country with enough legends and mystery to discourage travel into the mountains.

The early Northwest logging industry saw choice opportunity in the lowland rain forests, however, and timber fellers were cutting their way through them like gophers in carrot patches until concerned naturalists lobbied to preserve the heart of the Olympic Peninsula in the Olympic Forest Reserve in 1897. This became Olympic National Monument in 1909, and Olympic National Park in 1938.

Few parks in America have had a more bitterly contested history. Disputes between conservationists and the logging industry have changed park boundaries like lines on a sales chart. From an original size of 615,000 acres (248,884 hectares), it dwindled to 300,000 acres (121,407 hectares) in 1915, then grew by degrees to its present size of 922,000 acres (373,133 hectares). Attempts by developers to build a road along the park's Ocean Strip occur about as regularly as spring thaw, and assaults on big chunks of the rain forest are as predictable as leap year. Boundary disputes, road contracts and issues of land use in and around the park are not calmly discussed or even negotiated – they are plea bargained.

Meanwhile, Olympic's park status protects the fragile rain forests, eight wildflower species found nowhere else, five world-record trees, the continent's largest Roosevelt elk population, and much, much more.

Olympic's summer climate is mild; winters are moist, but not severe. There are no dangerous reptiles or insects. The only bothersome plants are the nettle, which is not common, and devil's club, a long-thorned shrub that is easy to recognize and avoid.

Many almost-level trails proceed for miles through primeval forests; others climb into the high country; along the coastal strip walkers use the beaches and headlands for a trail system. Throughout the park, even in the high country during summer, the climate is mild in comparison to the North Cascades. The Pacific Ocean's Japanese Current brings warm air to the Olympic Peninsula, along with rain.

Walkers should always be prepared with raingear – ponchos or waterproof outer clothing, and a tent with rain fly. In all, for backpackers there are 600 miles (900 km) of trails. Roads enter the park, but none traverse it.

The rain forests: Moisture laden North Pacific trade winds sweep eastward across the Pacific for 2,000 miles (3,220 km) before smacking into the Olympic Mountains where they cool and deposit rainfall beneath the tumult. Between 150 and 200 inches (380 and 500 cm) fall annually into the **Bogachiel**, **Hoh**, **Queets** and **Quinault Valleys**, the west-facing river valleys of the park. Hoh, Queets and Quinault are three of the major rain forest valleys which may be driven into. Because of its size and Park Service Interpretive Center, the Hoh is the most popular. For accommodations, the **Lake Quinault Lodge** is a stylish old resort hotel in the heart of the Quinault Valley.

Summer weather in the rain forests is often sunny, but even on the soggiest midwinter day an intriguingly cheerful ambience prevails. Colonnades of virgin spruce and hemlock rise to form an evergreen lattice above; under them, vine maples spiral from pillowy forest-floor coverings of club moss. Huckleberry, fern, oxalis, vanilla leaf, bedstraw, bunchberry, twisted stalk and skunk cabbage grow in shady glades between gnarled nurse logs and upended tree roots. The moss-mantled trees and shrubs, and small, delicate greens, along with rare liverworts, lichens and fungi, make up the rain forest.

The Olympic Mountains: To walk in the Olympics for an afternoon or a week is to walk through some of the world's loveliest mountains. They are not lean or long like the Cascade Range across Puget Sound to the east, but a cluster of lofty canyons, flowered ridges and glaciated peaks. The highest is **Mount Olympus** standing at 7,980 feet (2,430 meters) – high enough, icy enough, and rugged enough to challenge even world-class climbers.

An annual snowfall of more than 400 feet (120 meters) supports some 50 active glaciers in the Olympic Mountains. Much of the park's trail system weaves through and over the high country, past dozens of glacial lakes. From late June through August there is a perpetual springtime gaiety in these mountains. Within yards of trailheads, blacktail deer graze belly-deep in avalanche lilies, marmots scurry from rock to rock, and insects hum in the wildflowers. With luck you may see some of the park's resident mountain goats. Black bears are common.

The most popular high country trail approaches are from the Hoh Valley and the Soleduck Valley. The trails between them join a system that converges at **High Divide**, close to **Seven Lakes Basin**, a huge amphitheater-like, glacier-carved valley punctuated by crystal-clear ponds. It's usually crowded with backpackers and fishermen in summer, and even hearty day-walkers who hike the 14-mile (23-km) round trip from **Soleduck Hot Springs**.

Less crowded are the trails that begin

Visitors' Center with view of Hurricane Ridge.

from low-elevation access roads at other points – in the **Elwha Valley** (longest river drainage in the park), the **Dosewallips** area, along the North Fork of the Skokomish, and the Quinault and Queets rain forest valleys.

Hurricane Ridge, at an elevation of 5,200 feet (1,585 meters), is one of the most popular destinations in the park. It is reached by a 17-mile (24-km) drive from Port Angeles over winding, paved roadway. At the top are plenty of parking, a Visitors' Center, and views of stunning beauty. From Hurricane Ridge one looks straight across into the soul of the Olympic Mountains. From here too one can walk through flowery meadows while deer, for which Hurricane Ridge is famous, step nonchalantly from your path. For the deer-watching alone, this is a wonderful place to bring children.

The Ocean Strip: The Ocean Strip of Olympic National Park is, in small scale, what most of the Pacific shoreline once looked like from Canada to Mexico. Flotsam piles high on beaches where it will; outgoing tides sweep other beaches clean of all but fine-grained sand. Mists hover over forested headlands, while now and then elk, bears, skunks and wildcats emerge from the forests to walk along the beaches.

US Highway 101 runs along 11 miles (18 km) of the strip, where you can explore beaches just 100 yards (90 meters) from your car. A popular overnight destination in the park along US 101 is the 58-unit **Kalaloch Lodge**, sited on a long, sandy beach which is well-known for its surf fishing, clamming and beach-combing.

North of **Ruby Beach** – famous for its offshore seastacks – to the mouth of the **Hoh River**, and on to the small towns of **La Push** and **Cape Alava**, the beaches are roadless and usually empty.

Where headlands block your path from beach to beach, muddy but marked trails offer passage over most; a few must be rounded at low tide. And along the 30 miles (48 km) of wilderness waterfront, Pacific waves roll in as they have for millennia, slowly carving and reshaping this edge of the continent.

The chalet in Enchanted Valley.

NORTH CASCADES NATIONAL PARK

Moist forests and rivers through sharp valleys; arid golden rolling hills; volcanoes streamed in glaciers and dusted with ash; wildflower meadows; sawtoothed peaks. **North Cascades National Park** is part of the Cascade Mountain range, actually a jigsaw puzzle of many very different parks, forests and wilderness areas. Blended into one green blur on most maps, the Cascades are more than the lush forests of evergreens most people imagine them to be. As the snowmelt begins, each area begins its own individual cycle.

One might categorize the area into North Cascades, Alpine Lakes and South Cascades but even these three categories are much too broad to describe in a few short words. Begin with the North Cascades and head south.

First take a map and orient yourself with the area. The North Cascades extend from north of US Highway 2 to the Canadian border. **North Cascades National Park** comprises all the **Mount Baker National Forest**, **Wenatchee National Forest**, part of the **Okanogan National Forest**, and a section of **Snoqualmie National Forest**. **Glacier Peak Wilderness** and **Pasayten Wilderness** adjoin the park on its southern and eastern sides respectively.

Mount Baker National Park and Pasayten Wilderness are the northernmost sections of this area. The Pasayten Wilderness of arid valleys has gentle hills and vast rolling meadows. The open spaces tend toward long stretches of barren views, but during the spring delicate flowers add a special touch to the otherwise empty landscape. Mount Baker National Park in the northwest extremity of the Cascades contrasts dramatically with the open, rolling hills of its neighbor.

Mount Baker, 10,780 feet (3,285 meters), itself is one of the glacier-covered Cascade volcanoes. The trail along **Heliotrope Ridge** through forests to flowery moraines offers views of the frozen rapids of Coleman Glacier.

The hike to **Kulsan Cabin**, the base camp for summit seekers, is a rewarding day trip, but danger lurks just above the camp. (Only the experienced climber should venture farther onto the crevassed glacier.) Mount Baker is a spectacular and mammoth mountain. Ridge trails to the north offer full views of it.

Hiking possibilities: There are endless numbers of possible hikes through the North Cascades, each with its own special attraction. Harvey Manning, writing in *The North Cascades National Park*, describes a moment during one hike that he took: "Tight switchbacks mounted a lava scarp, the brown-dusty cliffs dotted with tiny red strawberries – delicious sweet and damp…An interlude of squealing joy amid misery past and misery present."

Manning has written a number of hiking guides to the Cascade and Olympic mountains. The hikes described range from short walks along **Ross Lake** (a national recreation area) to bushwacking along rivers, following ridges and summitting peaks. Lowland trails are recommended in the early summer months, not only for the wildflowers, but also because of the amount of snow still in the highlands. Peaks and high ridges are most accessible from mid-July through August. Regardless of where and when you hike, unless you are just going on a short stroll, prepare for weather changes, especially wet ones.

The cliffs, glaciers and gorges of North Cascades National Park are bordered on the eastern edge by the arid hills of the Okanogan National Forest. In the center of the horseshoe-shaped forest are the tourist towns of **Winthrop** and **Twisp**. Cross-country ski meccas in the winter, they turn into RV and airstream trailer display areas in the summer. The tame hills cater to the vacation whims of traveling folk. Again, be prepared for weather changes.

Yet the drastic changes in weather and mood can be rewarding. As Manning described: "There are fogs and fogs. Yesterday's fog had been dark and close, a world-destroyer. Today's fog offered hope the sun might still exist… We stayed long into the afternoon, nearly to evening, and lingered down, stopping for the lupine perfume, the yellow heather – white heather – red heather, the goat wool, the andesite slabs, the gaudy blocks of schist."

Wide wilderness areas: On the southern side of North Cascades National Park sits Glacier Peak Wilderness. This is the heart of the entire North Cascades, with 10,540-foot (3,210-meter) **Glacier Peak** as its centerpiece. Glaciers end in ice blue lakes, and meadows blanket small corners between broken spires.

Glacier Peak Wilderness and Alpine Lakes Wilderness are perhaps Washington's two most impressive wilderness areas and ideal hiking spots for the outdoor enthusiast. Heading north of Seattle and east on US 2, **Mount Index** welcomes you to this spectacular region as you begin to head up **Stevens Pass**. Mount Index, a stark presence above US 2, stands out against the green hills surrounding it. There is a short hike to the base, but it goes literally straight up the side of the mountain; hikers pull on tangled roots to get up the cliff.

South of US 2 begins the Alpine Lakes Wilderness Area. A steep hike up **Icicle Creek**, outside Leavenworth on the eastern side of the pass, brings you to **Snow Lakes** at the base of the massive **Mount Temple**. Another steep ascent brings you over a saddle within sight of the splintered crags of the **Stuart Range** and the innumerable **Enchantment Lakes**. Because of the amount of snow, the best hiking is from July through mid-November.

Parties that want to stay overnight or longer in dedicated lands must obtain a back-country permit. This is not intended to discourage hikers but to limit the number of people who trample certain delicate trails each year. Permits can be obtained at the Forest and Parks Service Stations at the major entry roads to the parks.

Snoqualmie Pass, although not as lofty as its North Cascade neighbors, offers equally magnificent wooded ridges and alpine lakes. The paths are peopled on the weekend since it is an easy getaway from Seattle.

Liberty Bell Mountain.

MOUNT RAINIER NATIONAL PARK

The white presence of **Mount Rainier** is so familiar to Seattleites that they simply call it "The Mountain." The Indians called it *Tahoma*, "the mountain that was God." There is always a new perspective of the mountain to wonder at – as the seasons progress, as the light changes, as the cloud cover alters. For the vista collector, hiker, camper, or climber in summer, for the skier in winter, Mount Rainier has much to offer. Its snowy top, crumpled glaciers and lacy waterfalls are clearly visible; enticing, enchanting. Mount Rainier receives high and deserved praise as an arctic island in a temperate zone. The mountain is not only high; it also rises abruptly from the surrounding landscape, assuming a majestic appearance. And for these many virtues, Mount Rainier has been established a National Park.

Mount Rainier National Park is accessible year-round from Seattle, only 70 miles (110 km) away. The drive takes about three hours, on narrow scenic roads that invite lingering. A weekend auto tour from Seattle can get you to Mount Rainier and back, leaving plenty of time to hike and look around. A network of roads encompasses the park, as well as an elaborate 305-mile (490-km) trail system. Both make much of Mount Rainier easily explorable in a day's hike. (Call ahead, in all months but July and August, to check if the high roads circling the park are open.)

Fire and ice: Mount Rainier's compelling natural history is a geologic story. Both volcanic fire and glacial ice have contributed to the mountain's formation. Geologists estimate that volcanic activity enabled Mount Rainier (part of the Cascades Range) to reach a height of 16,000 feet (5,300 meters) about 75,000 years ago. Glaciers later stripped 2,000 feet (650 meters) off its top. Rainier's present height of 14,410 feet (4,800 meters) makes it the tallest volcanic mountain in the lower 48 states. Twenty-six glaciers grind away at the sides of the mountain: Mount Rainier is host to the single largest glacier system in the continental United States.

At the park entrance near **Longmire**, you'll see the results of 1974's massive natural mudflows at **Kautz Creek**. The landscape is mute testimony to the danger when warm rains – or volcanic activity – cause rapid glacial melt. (Mount Rainier's last volcanic eruption occurred around 500–600 years ago. Its considerable cataclysmic power is now considered dormant.)

The Mount Rainier area was first settled by the Longmire family in the 1880s. An interpretive center at Longmire and the short Shadow Trail there acquaint you with the Longmires, who developed the area by extolling the presumed healthful properties of local mineral waters for drinking and bathing. (It is worth noting, if you don't feel youthful enough for a mountain hike, that James Longmire arrived here in 1883, at age 63, and promptly climbed the mountain.)

On a clear day at Mount Rainier National Park the main attraction is the white, symmetrical beauty of the mountain. Yet there can also be long periods of cloud cover. Mount Rainier's weather is variable, changing by the minute, so come prepared for the wet and cold. Snow may fall at the higher elevations in any month of the year.

Deeper in the park from Longmire, **Paradise** is a highly-visited area which is accessible all-year round and has excellent audio-visual introductions to the region. One display shows the climbing gear that mountaineer Jim Whittaker used for his historic Mount Everest ascent on May 1, 1963; his party prepared for Everest on Mount Rainier.

From the Paradise vista point you'll see stunning views of the nearby Cascade Range relatives of Mount Rainier, including Mount St Helens. Also at Paradise you can hike, ski or snowshoe to an overlook of the **Nisqually Glacier**. A full-service rental facility at Longmire can outfit you with winter cross-country or snowshoeing gear.

Serious climbing parties depart from Paradise for **Camp Muir** at 10,000 feet (3,300 meters) and then the assault on the summit. Ranger-led ascents in summer take three days; contact the Park Service if you wish to participate.

In addition to Paradise, three other park entrance points with visitors' centers orient you to the mountain. They are open only during the brief summer season. At the southeast corner of the park, the **Ohanapecosh Visitors' Center** can acquaint you with the trout-filled river of the same name, open only to fly fishing. On the east side of the park the **Sunrise Visitors' Center**, which is accessible along a high road at the upper line of vegetation, emphasizes geologic history. Here you can see the **Emmons Glacier**, and get a good view of technical climbers ascending the mountain. Summer wildflowers here are exquisite.

The least-visited part of the park is at the northwest corner, reached through the **Carbon River** entrance. There is good camping, hiking and fishing in this area at **Mowich Lake**.

Rainier's rain-shadow: Mount Rainier towers over the other mountains along the spine of the Cascades. With the lesser peaks at its shoulder, "The Mountain" helps force the incoming ocean air to drop moisture on the west face of the mountain. Rainier's influence on Washington's climate is clearly visible: the western part of the state is wet; the east, in the rain-shadow of the Cascades, relatively dry.

In winter, Mount Rainier receives heavy snowfalls. The greatest snowfall ever recorded anywhere fell here at the Paradise ranger station in 1972 (the snowpack reached 94 feet or 29 meters). The months with the least rain are July and August, but Mount Rainier can be wet even then.

Mount Rainier National Park invites walking, and the trails here are varied in their demands. Some are gentle, while others are arduous technical climbs. The park is a good place to hike on the Pacific Crest Trail, which stretches from Mexico to Canada through some of the West's most magnificent country. The trail cuts through the park, and is most accessible during the brief summer months between snow cover.

Paradise Inn under new snow.

CRATER LAKE NATIONAL PARK

A visitor's first view of **Crater Lake** tends to remain firmly etched in the memory. After climbing gradually up a fir and hemlock-edged road, beyond the 6,000-foot (2,000-meter) level, you suddenly come to the top of a rim where, entirely unexpectedly, a huge, blue oval stretches below you. The bowl of this extraordinary mountain-top lake is 5 miles (8 km) across and 4,000 feet (1,300 meters) deep – of which nearly 2,000 feet (650 meters) is water. This natural gem, the deepest lake in the United States, is preserved in Oregon's **Crater Lake National Park**.

The blue of the lake has inspired awe in visitors since the first white men recorded their impressions in the 1850s. Everyone reaches for the vocabulary adequate to describe it: cobalt blue, azure, aquamarine, indigo, turquoise, sapphire or cerulean.

Crater Lake's water is exceptionally clear, so clear that sun penetration causes moss to grow in the lake at 400-foot (130-meter) depths. The lake has no inlet or outlet, few suspended particles, and very little organic matter; it is this clarity that actually causes Crater Lake's extraordinary blue appearance.

Sinnott Memorial Overlook, near Rim Village at the south end of the lake, is a good starting point for viewing Crater Lake. With the help of a Park Service Ranger, you can begin to unravel the wondrous geologic story of Crater Lake's origin.

The creation of Crater Lake: The forces that created Crater Lake were eons in building but momentarily cataclysmic in their expression. For nearly a half million years, geologists believe, layer upon layer of volcanic material built up the dome of a mountain, called **Mount Mazama**, at the site of Crater Lake. Finally, the great forces of earth heat came to the surface almost 7,000 years ago and a great volcanic blast occurred, blackening the skies with pumice and ash as far away as modern Wyoming.

Similar volcanic events have taken place on Mazama's sister Cascade Range peaks, Lassen Peak in California (1921) and Mount St Helens in Washington (1980). Yet the magnitude of Mazama's devastation dwarfed the more recent Mount St Helens' explosion, geologists have concluded.

To comprehend the drama, geologists have measured ashfall in the surrounding area and fingerprinted the types of lava rock in the vicinity. The most recent estimate is that an amazing 42.5 cubic miles (180 cubic km) of ash and rock erupted from the volcano or gushed out in avalanches of molten material. The ash blew in a northeasterly direction as far as Saskatchewan, and steaming rivers of lava and mud rushed as far as 40 miles (60 km) at ferocious speed down the canyons around the mountain.

After Mazama's initial explosion, the walls of the volcano collapsed in on the center, creating a basin, or caldera. (*Caldera* is a Spanish word for cauldron.) Over centuries, the caldera gradually gathered rainwater and snowmelt, forming Crater Lake.

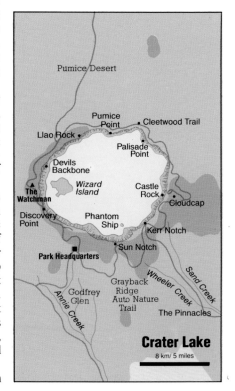

Crater Lake
8 km/ 5 miles

Preceding pages: Crater Lake and Wizard Island. Left, The Pinnacles, Crater Lake National Park.

Early Native Americans in the region witnessed the explosion, and some died as a result of it. In 1938, an archaeology team from the University of Oregon uncovered a dry lake bed Native habitat buried in pumice some 70 miles (110 km) northeast of Crater Lake at a place now called **Fort Rock**. At the site they discovered artifacts, including 75 pairs of charred sandals, which were carbon-dated to the time of the explosion. Mud, burned red by the heat of the pumice, was found between the twisted rope soles of the sandals, further linking these artifacts to the explosion.

The eruption of Mazama remained alive in the oral tradition of local Native Americans over thousands of years. In the 19th century, local Klamath and Modoc tribes considered Crater Lake a taboo place: they never went near it. In their legends were elaborate explanations of the explosion. One variation can be savored, while driving the lake's rim, as you stop at a lookout called **Skell Head**. Klamath mythology held that a battle occurred between Skell, god of the world above, who lived in Mount Shasta, and Llao, evil god of the lower world. Llao had entered the world above and been enthralled by a maiden. He invited her to come and live with him in the lower world where she would enjoy eternal life, but she found him distasteful and rebuffed him. Llao became furious and attacked the people of her world. Their protector, Skell, came to the rescue and beheaded Llao's mountain, ridding the world of this demon forever. The beheading was, of course, the eruption of Mount Mazama.

Understanding Crater Lake's geologic forces at work is an ongoing study. Scientists come to the lake each summer for further measuring and testing. Mapping the bottom of the lake and monitoring the water quality and water properties are current pursuits.

From Deep Blue Lake to National Park: As the white man explored the West, the absence of abundant fur-bearing animals and the lack of good farming land in the Crater Lake region caused the impressive lake to remain undiscovered

A display shows the unique formation of Wizard Island.

WIZARD ISLAND

until relatively late. Not until an errant gold miner stumbled across it did the lake become known. John Wesley Hillman, searching for an entity called the "Lost Cabin Mine," had the honor of the first recorded look at the lake in 1853. He called the cavity, somewhat literally, Deep Blue Lake. Soldiers from Fort Klamath later hung a more regal moniker on the body of water, calling it Lake Majesty. The words Crater Lake first appeared in 1869 in a Jacksonville, Oregon, newspaper article about the lake by one Jim Sutton. In 1874 the pioneering photographer, Peter Britt, lugged his camera equipment up the side of the mountain to take the first reproducible image of the lake.

William G. Steel, who, with his family, came to Oregon from Kansas as a boy, so appreciated the beauty of the lake that he lobbied for 49 years to have it designated a National Park. Steel almost single-handedly created the park, just as John Muir is credited with arousing the legislative passions that formed Yosemite National Park. Thanks to his

The lake from Mount Scott.

efforts, the bill establishing Crater Lake, Oregon's only National Park, finally became law on May 22, 1902.

Steel's main achievement while serving as guardian and, during one period, superintendent of the park, was the building of the **Rim Drive** in 1918. The new roadway gave the public access to this national treasure, as the age of the automobile dawned.

Around the lake's rim: Make your own survey of Crater Lake by meandering around Rim Drive. **Wizard Island**, the largest of the lake's intriguing islands, is a small volcanic dome of cinders that built up in the western corner of the lake. The best view of Wizard Island is from a turnoff called **The Watchman**.

The Phantom Ship, a small island near Rim Village, was given its fanciful name by early explorers. If seen under a certain misty light, the Phantom Ship can appear to be sailing out at you from Samuel Coleridge's poem *The Rime of the Ancient Mariner*.

The **Godfrey Glen Nature Trail** near Rim Village offers a good interpretation

of the volcanic presence. The trail circles the rim of a steep-walled canyon for about a mile. Interaction of powerful and perennial natural forces – volcanism, erosion and weather – are the main stories here. Later land erosion has created a spired, sculpted effect, both here and at a site southeast of the lake called **The Pinnacles**.

A good place to enjoy the flora and fauna of the Crater Lake region is the **Castle Crest Wildflower Trail**, a 4-mile (6-km) loop through forests and meadows where trees and many colorful wildflowers are identified. The Shasta red fir, the dominant tree here, is easily identified by the snowflake pattern its needles create. Mountain hemlock, noted for its drooping top, and lodgepole pine are also numerous.

The **Annie Creek Trail** interprets the role of water and its effect on plant and animal life. One of the delights of Annie Creek is a common bird called the water ouzel, or dipper, that dives into the creek and walks across the bottom looking for an insect snack. Mule deer, black-tailed deer, an occasional brown bear, numerous foxes and bobcats, rabbits, pikas, marmots and elk are among the other inhabitants of the park.

Crater Lake Lodge at Rim Village on the south side of the lake was renovated not long ago, while the nearby 40-room **Mazama Village** is open from May to October.

Camping is popular at the 198-site **Mazama Campground**, near the Annie Springs entrance. This campground fills quickly, on a first-come basis. There are an additional 900 available campsites in the National Forest areas within 40 miles (65 km) of Annie Springs.

The Park Service maintains a vigorous program of interpretive nature talks, campfire talks and ranger-led hikes. One of the unusual and popular interpretive walks is a nightly star-gazing outing.

Bicyclists find the ride around the lake invigorating, especially when they are pedaling against the prevailing winds, which flow east to west. Runners converge here every August for a marathon race called the Rim Run.

One of the nicest ways to see the lake is by a concessionaire-operated boat that leaves from the north side of the lake at **Cleetwood Cove**. Tickets for this 2-hour ride, crossing the surface of a water-filled volcano, are sold at the cove. Between early July and Labor Day, the boat trip operates daily.

One option during the boat tour is a stop at Wizard Island, where you can get off and remain on the island until the boat arrives with the next tour. While on Wizard Island, walk to the top of the volcanic mound to see the miniature cone. Ardent fishermen often visit the island in search of the 30–35 inch (76–90 cm) trout that can be found in the lake. Fish thrive in relative safety in the middle of the lakes because anglers have access to the lakeshore only at Cleetwood Cove and Wizard Island; private boats are not allowed.

Midway up the mountain is the region's only gasoline and service station. At Rim Village, you'll find the Park Service Interpretive Center, a small grocery and camping supply store, a gift shop and cafeteria.

Below, the Phantom Ship formation. **Right**, the deep, deep blue of Crater Lake.

310

INSIGHT GUIDES
Travel Tips

Bicrell

FOR THOSE
WITH MORE THAN
A PASSING INTEREST
IN TIME...

Before you put your name down for a Patek Philippe watch *fig. 1,* there are a few basic things you might like to know, without knowing exactly whom to ask. In addressing such issues as accuracy, reliability and value for money, we would like to demonstrate why the watch we will make for you will be quite unlike any other watch currently produced.

"Punctuality", Louis XVIII was fond of saying, "is the politeness of kings."

We believe that in the matter of punctuality, we can rise to the occasion by making you a mechanical timepiece that will keep its rendezvous with the Gregorian calendar at the end of every century, omitting the leap-years in 2100, 2200 and 2300 and recording them in 2000 and 2400 *fig. 2.* Nevertheless, such a watch does need the occasional adjustment. Every 3333 years and 122 days you should remember to set it forward one day to the true time of the celestial clock. We suspect, however, that you are simply content to observe the politeness of kings. Be assured, therefore, that when you order your watch, we will be exploring for you the physical—if not the metaphysical— limits of precision.

Does everything have to depend on how much?

Consider, if you will, the motives of collectors who set record prices at auction to acquire a Patek Philippe. They may be paying for rarity, for looks or for micromechanical ingenuity. But we believe that behind each $500,000-plus

bid is the conviction that a Patek Philippe, even if 50 years old or older, can be expected to work perfectly for future generations.
In case your ambitions to own a Patek Philippe are somewhat discouraged by the scale of the sacrifice involved, may we hasten to point out that the watch we will make for you today will certainly be a technical improvement on the Pateks bought at auction? In keeping with our tradition of inventing new mechanical solutions for greater reliability and better time-keeping, we will bring to your watch innovations *fig. 3* inconceivable to our watch-makers who created the supreme wristwatches of 50 years ago *fig. 4.* At the same time, we will of course do our utmost to avoid placing undue strain on your financial resources.

Can it really be mine?

May we turn your thoughts to the day you take delivery of your watch? Sealed within its case is your watchmaker's tribute to the mysterious process of time. He has decorated each wheel with a chamfer carved into its hub and polished into a shining circle. Delicate ribbing flows over the plates and bridges of gold and rare alloys. Millimetric surfaces are bevelled and burnished to exactitudes measured in microns. Rubies are transformed into jewels that triumph over friction. And after many months—or even years—of work, your watchmaker stamps a small badge into the mainbridge of your watch. The Geneva Seal—the highest possible attestation of fine watchmaking *fig. 5.*

Looks that speak of inner grace *fig. 6.*

When you order your watch, you will no doubt like its outward appearance to reflect the harmony and elegance of the movement within. You may therefore find it helpful to know that we are uniquely able to cater for any special decorative needs you might like to express. For example, our engravers will delight in conjuring a subtle play of light and shadow on the gold case-back of one of our rare pocket-watches *fig. 7.* If you bring us your favourite picture, our enamellers will reproduce it in a brilliant miniature of hair-breadth detail *fig. 8.* The perfect execution of a double hob-nail pattern on the bezel of a wristwatch is the pride of our casemakers and the satisfaction of our designers, while our chainsmiths will weave for you a rich brocade in gold *figs. 9 & 10.* May we also recommend the artistry of our goldsmiths and the experience of our lapidaries in the selection and setting of the finest gemstones? *figs. 11 & 12.*

How to enjoy your watch before you own it.

As you will appreciate, the very nature of our watches imposes a limit on the number we can make available. (The four Calibre 89 time-pieces we are now making will take up to nine years to complete). We cannot therefore promise instant gratification, but while you look forward to the day on which you take delivery of your Patek Philippe *fig. 13,* you will have the pleasure of reflecting that time is a universal and everlasting commodity, freely available to be enjoyed by all.

Should you require information on any particular Patek Philippe watch, or even on watchmaking in general, we would be delighted to reply to your letter of enquiry. And if you send us

fig. 1: The classic face of Patek Philippe.

fig. 4: Complicated wristwatches circa 1930 (left) and 1990. The golden age of watchmaking will always be with us.

fig. 6: Your pleasure in owning a Patek Philippe is the purpose of those who made it for you.

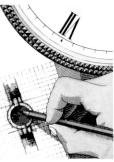

fig. 9: Harmony of design is executed in a work of simplicity and perfection in a lady's Calatrava wristwatch.

fig. 10: The chainsmith's hands impart strength and delicacy to a tracery of gold.

fig. 2: One of the 33 complications of the Calibre 89 astronomical clock-watch is a satellite wheel that completes one revolution every 400 years.

fig. 5: The Geneva Seal is awarded only to watches which achieve the standards of horological purity laid down in the laws of Geneva. These rules define the supreme quality of watchmaking.

fig. 7: Arabesques come to life on a gold case-back.

fig. 11: Circles in gold: symbols of perfection in the making.

fig. 3: Recognized as the most advanced mechanical regulating device to date, Patek Philippe's Gyromax balance wheel demonstrates the equivalence of simplicity and precision.

fig. 8: An artist working six hours a day takes about four months to complete a miniature in enamel on the case of a pocket-watch.

fig. 12: The test of a master lapidary is his ability to express the splendour of precious gemstones.

✠
PATEK PHILIPPE
GENEVE

fig. 13: The discreet sign of those who value their time.

your card marked "book catalogue" we shall post you a catalogue of our publications. Patek Philippe, 41 rue du Rhône, 1204 Geneva, Switzerland, Tel. +41 22/310 03 66.

INSIGHT GUIDES

COLORSET NUMBERS

North America

160	Alaska
173	American Southwest
184I	Atlanta
227	Boston
275	California
180	California, Northern
161	California, Southern
237	Canada
184C	Chicago
184	Crossing America
243	Florida
240	Hawaii
275A	Los Angeles
243A	Miami
237B	Montreal
184G	National Parks of America: East
184H	National Parks of America: West
269	Native America
100	New England
184E	New Orleans
184F	New York City
133	New York State
147	Pacific Northwest
184B	Philadelphia
172	Rockies
275B	San Francisco
184D	Seattle
	Southern States of America
186	Texas
237A	Vancouver
184C	Washington DC

Latin America and The Caribbean

150	Amazon Wildlife
260	Argentina
188	Bahamas
292	Barbados
251	Belize
217	Bermuda
127	Brazil
260A	Buenos Aires
162	Caribbean
151	Chile
281	Costa Rica
282	Cuba
118	Ecuador
213	Jamaica
285	Mexico
285A	Mexico City
249	Peru
156	Puerto Rico
127A	Rio de Janeiro
116	South America
139	Trinidad & Tobago
198	Venezuela

Europe

155	Alsace
158A	Amsterdam
167A	Athens
263	Austria
107	Baltic States
219B	Barcelona
1187	Bay of Naples
109	Belgium
135A	Berlin
178	Brittany
109A	Brussels
144A	Budapest
213	Burgundy
122	Catalonia
141	Channel Islands
135E	Cologne
119	Continental Europe
189	Corsica
291	Côte d'Azur
165	Crete
226	Cyprus
114	Czech/Slovak Reps
238	Denmark
135B	Dresden
142B	Dublin
135F	Düsseldorf
149	Eastern Europe
148A	Edinburgh
123	Finland
209B	Florence
154	France
135C	Frankfurt
135	Germany
148B	Glasgow
279	Gran Canaria
124	Great Britain
167	Greece
166	Greek Islands
135G	Hamburg
144	Hungary
256	Iceland
142	Ireland
209	Italy
202A	Lisbon
258	Loire Valley
124A	London
201	Madeira
219A	Madrid
157	Mallorca & Ibiza
117	Malta
101A	Moscow
135D	Munich
158	Netherlands
111	Normandy
120	Norway
124B	Oxford
154A	Paris
115	Poland
202	Portugal
114A	Prague
153	Provence
177	Rhine
209A	Rome
101	Russia
130	Sardinia
148	Scotland
261	Sicily
264	South Tyrol
219	Spain
220	Spain, Southern
101B	St. Petersburg
170	Sweden
232	Switzerland
112	Tenerife
210	Tuscany
174	Umbria
209C	Venice
263A	Vienna
267	Wales
183	Waterways of Europe

Middle East and Africa

268A	Cairo
204	East African Wildlife
268	Egypt
208	Gambia & Senegal
252	Israel
236A	Istanbul
252A	Jerusalem-Tel Aviv
214	Jordan
270	Kenya
235	Morocco
259	Namibia
265	Nile, The
257	South Africa
113	Tunisia
236	Turkey
171	Turkish Coast
215	Yemen

Asia/Pacific

287	Asia, East
207	Asia, South
262	Asia, South East
194	Asian Wildlife, Southeast
272	Australia
206	Bali Baru
246A	Bangkok
234A	Beijing
247B	Calcutta
234	China
247A	Delhi, Jaipur, Agra
169	Great Barrier Reef
196	Hong Kong
247	India
212	India, South
128	Indian Wildlife
143	Indonesia
278	Japan
266	Java
203A	Kathmandu
300	Korea
145	Malaysia
218	Marine Life in the South China Sea
272B	Melbourne
211	Myanmar
203	Nepal
293	New Zealand
205	Pakistan
222	Philippines
250	Rajasthan
159	Singapore
105	Sri Lanka
272	Sydney
175	Taiwan
246	Thailand
278A	Tokyo
255	Vietnam
193	Western Himalaya

Getting Acquainted

The Place 314
Time Zones 314
Climate 314
The People 314
The Economy 314

Planning the Trip

What to Bring 314
Entry Regulations 314
Currency 314
Public Holidays 315
Getting There 315

Practical Tips

Emergencies 315
Weights and Measures 316
Business Hours 316
Tipping 316
Media 316
Postal Services 317
Tourist Information 317
Consulates 317

Getting Around

Public Transportation 317
Private Transportation 317
Car Rental 318

Where to Stay

Washington Hotels & Motels ... 318
Oregon Hotels & Motels 318
Bed and Breakfast 319
Youth Hostels 319

Eating Out

Where to Eat in Washington 319
Where to Eat in Oregon 319
Drinking Notes 320

Attractions

Museums 320
Art Galleries 320
Theaters 320
Movies 321
Libraries 321
Tourist Attractions 321
Tours 322

Festivals and Events

A Portland Calendar 323
A Seattle Calendar 324
Nightlife 324

Shopping

Sales Tax 325
Shopping Areas 325

Sports & Leisure

Participant Sports 325
Spectator Sports 325

Language

General 325
In the Airport 325
In Print 326
In Hotels 326

Further Reading

General 326
Other Insight Guides 326

Art/Photo Credits 327
Index 328

Getting Acquainted

The Place

The Pacific Northwest comprises the most northwesterly states in the US: Oregon (south of Washington) and Washington (on the Canadian border).

Oregon covers 96,185 sq miles (249,117 sq km) and has a population of 2,600,000. The state capital is Salem, and its largest city is Portland (population 437,000). Washington covers 66,500 sq miles (172,000 sq km) and has a population of just over four million. Its capital is Olympia and its largest city is Seattle, with a metropolitan population of more than 250,000.

The Pacific Northwest is part of the Pacific Rim and, as such, travelers will find it much more oriented toward Asia and the Pacific than Europe.

Time Zones

The Pacific Northwest runs on Pacific Time, which is two hours behind Chicago, three hours behind New York City, and eight hours behind GMT. On the first Sunday in April, the clock is moved ahead one hour for Daylight Savings Time. On the last Sunday in October, it is moved back one hour to return to Standard Time. For the local time, tel: (206) 976-1616 in Seattle or (503) 976-8463 in Portland.

When it is noon Standard Time in Seattle it is:
10am in Hawaii.
2pm in Chicago.
3pm in New York and Montreal.
8pm in London.
6am (the next day) in Sydney.

Climate

The Cascade mountain range creates two distinct climate patterns in the Pacific Northwest. Moisture-laden clouds move inland from the Pacific Ocean, releasing precipitation mainly in the western half of the region. This range also poses a barrier to prevailing westerly winds, leaving the eastern area dry and, in some areas, extremely arid.

The western region enjoys a generally mild climate. In winter, maximum daily temperatures average 45°F (7°C), rarely falling below 25°F (4°C). From October through April, Seattle and Portland get 80 percent of their annual rainfall. Summer produces pleasantly warm days and very little precipitation. Maximum daily temperatures average around 70°F (21°C).

East of the mountains, average temperatures are higher in summer and lower in winter than in the west, but seldom above 90°F (33°C) or lower than 20°F (-6.6°C).

Winter brings snow to higher elevations, to the delight of skiers. Large accumulations of snow are rare at lower levels. For information on the weather, tel: (206) 526-6087 in Seattle or (503) 236-7575 in Portland.

The People

The area has a rich mix of cultures – both Washington and Oregon have large Scandinavian and Asian populations. People are for the most part friendly, outgoing and willing to help. Most people do not speak a foreign language, so visitors should have a basic understanding of English.

Translating services and interpreters can be hired in Seattle. Call Documents International, tel: (206) 285-9598, or Washington Academy of Languages, tel: (206) 682-4463.

The Economy

The Pacific Northwest derives its economic strength from a variety of sources, including aerospace, shipping, agriculture, commercial fisheries, tourism and forest resources.

Commercial forest lands support a major share of the region's economy, producing a third of the nation's softwood timber harvest.

Foreign tourists annually spend $3.5 billion enjoying the region's various recreational opportunities.

Planning the Trip

What to Bring
What to Wear

Residents of the Pacific Northwest are quite casual, so informal clothing is fine for most daytime activities. The cities (and mountains) are best explored on foot, so be sure to bring comfortable walking shoes.

A light raincoat, collapsible umbrella and sweater are good companions. For trips to the mountains, you should put on several layers of clothing (including a warm coat and hat).

The Northwest is home to several makers of outdoor apparel. Travelers who need to purchase such gear will find a good selection from which to choose. Recreational Equipment Incorporated (REI) is a good bet and is located in both Seattle and Portland, tel: 1-800-426-4840.

Electricity

The US generally uses 110-volt alternating current. Foreign visitors with electrical appliances may need a convertor and adaptor plug.

Entry Regulations
Visas & Passports

Canadian citizens entering the US do not need a visa. Most British citizens will not need a visa for visits of 90 days or less if their carrier participates in no-visa travel and they have an onward ticket. Britons visiting the US may visit Mexico, Canada, Bermuda or the Caribbean Islands and return to the US without a visa. Visitors from other countries require a visa. Any questions should be directed to the nearest American Embassy or Consulate.

Currency

American-dollar travelers' checks are the safest form of currency. When lost or stolen, most can be replaced and they can be used as cash in most stores, restaurants and hotels. Banks will generally cash large amounts of travelers' checks.

The most frequently used paper currency comes in $1, $5, $10 and $20 denominations. US coins are the penny (1¢), the nickel (5¢), the dime (10¢) and the quarter (25¢). Less widespread are the 50¢ piece and the Susan B. Anthony dollar piece.

Foreign currency exchange is available at major Seattle and Portland banks and at some major downtown hotels. In Seattle, American Express, 600 Stewart, tel: (206) 444-8622, exchanges currency Monday to Friday 9am–5pm. Currency may also be exchanged at Sea-Tac airport. The exchange rates for major currencies can be found in the daily newspapers or tel: (206) 243-1231.

Public Holidays

January 1: **New Year's Day**
January 15: **Martin Luther King's Birthday**
3rd Monday in February: **Presidents' Day**
Last Monday in May: **Memorial Day**
July 4: **Independence Day**
1st Monday in September: **Labor Day**
1st Tuesday in November: **Election Day**
November 11: **Veterans' Day**
4th Thursday in November: **Thanksgiving**
December 25: **Christmas Day**

Getting There

By Air

Most major commercial carriers have services to Seattle-Tacoma International Airport (Sea-Tac) and Portland International Airport.

Most airlines have both local and toll-free telephone numbers for information and reservations. Look under "Airline Companies" in the *Yellow Pages*, or call 1-800-555-1212 for toll-free telephone number information.

Domestic carriers serving Seattle include Alaska, America West, American, Continental, Delta, Hawaiian, Northwest, United and US Air. Several local commuter airlines serve Seattle.

Seattle is also served by international carriers: Aeroflot, Air BC, British Airways, Air Canada, Japan Airlines, Korean Air, Mexicana, Northwest, Scandinavian, TWA, and others.

Domestic airlines serving Portland include Alaska, America West, American, Continental, Delta, Hawaiian, Northwest, TWA, United, United Express and US Air.

By Boat

The Washington State Ferry system, the largest in the country, serves the Puget Sound area, linking Seattle with the Olympic Peninsula via Bremerton and Bainbridge Island. It also provides service from Anacortes, 90 miles (145 km) northwest of Seattle, through the San Juan Islands to Victoria, on British Columbia's Vancouver Island.

The Victoria Clipper operates passenger-only ferries between Seattle and Victoria with three daily departures. Reservations are necessary. A new Victoria Line car ferry departs from Pier 48 daily at 1pm in the summer. For ferry information, tel: 1-800-542-7052.

The following companies offer boat services in Seattle.
Alaska Ferries (Bellingham), tel: 1-800-642-0066.
Black Ball Ferry, tel: (206) 622-2222.
Gray Line Water Sightseeing, tel: (206) 626-5208.
Victoria Clipper, tel: (206) 448-5000.
Washington State Ferries, tel: (206) 464-6400.

By Train

Amtrak, tel: (212) 582-6875, runs US-wide train services. The *Empire Builder* runs from Chicago to Seattle, Portland and Vancouver, BC, tel: 1-800-USA-RAIL. The *Pioneer* runs from Salt Lake City. The *Coast Starlight* runs from Los Angeles. Seattle's Amtrak station is at Third Ave and S. Jackson St. Portland's station is on NW Broadway near the Broadway Bridge and the central bus terminal.

By Road

Major land routes through the Pacific Northwest are Interstate 5 from Canada to Mexico, Interstate 90 linking Seattle with Boston, and Interstate 84 from Portland to Salt Lake City. Federal and state highways are well maintained and policed, and they have refreshment areas and service stations at regular intervals. All highways are free, but there are occasional bridge tolls.

By Bus

Transcontinental bus lines providing services throughout Seattle and the Pacific Northwest include Greyhound, Cascade Trailways and Gray Line.

Several bus companies link Sea-Tac airport to downtown Seattle and major hotels. Among these are Gray Line Airport Express, tel: (206) 624-5077; Shuttle Express, tel: (206) 626-6088; and Metro Transit. Look under "Bus Lines" in the yellow pages for more telephone information.

For road transport in Seattle, contact:
Community Transit, tel: (206) 778-2185.
Greyhound, Eighth Ave and Stewart St, tel: (206) 628-5526.
Metro King County Transit, tel: (206) 553-3000.
Monorail, Fourth Ave and Pine St and Seattle Center.
Trailways, 1936 Westlake Ave, tel: (206) 728-5955.

For road transport in Portland, contact:
Greyhound, 550 NW Sixth Ave, tel: 1-800-231-2222.

Practical Tips

Emergencies

Security and Crime

In the Pacific Northwest personal crimes are relatively few. It is safe to walk the streets day and night in most areas, although simple caution is always advised. Ask a hotel concierge or local shopkeeper about specific areas to avoid at night.

Lock your car, and never leave luggage, cameras or other valuables in view – lock them in the glove compartment or in the trunk. Never leave money or jewelry in your hotel room, even for a short time. Use the hotel's safe deposit service. Carry only the cash you need, using travelers' checks whenever possible.

Medical Services

Medical care in the Pacific Northwest is excellent, particularly in Seattle and Portland. However, healthcare is very expensive in the US – be sure you are covered by medical insurance while traveling. An ambulance costs around $200, emergency-room treatment costs a minimum of $50, and a hospital bed costs at least $300 per night.

For medical emergencies, call 911. The front desk of your hotel can reach a doctor 24 hours a day. Most hospitals have 24-hour emergency rooms.

Certain drugs have to be prescribed by a doctor and purchased through a pharmacy. Check the *Yellow Pages* under "Pharmacies" or ask your hotel concierge for nearby pharmacies.

Below is a listing of major hospitals in the Seattle and Portland areas and places for non-urgent medical care.

SEATTLE HOSPITALS

Children's Hospital and Medical Center, 4800 Sand Point Way NE, tel: (206) 526-2000.
Harborview Medical Center, 325 Ninth Ave, tel: (206) 223-3000.
Providence Medical Center, 500 17th Ave, tel: (206) 320-2000.
Swedish Hospital, 747 Broadway Ave, tel: (206) 386-6000.
University of Washington Medical Center, 1959 NE Pacific St, tel: (206) 548-3300.
University of Washington Hospital Interpretation Services, tel: (206) 548 4425.
Virginia Mason Hospital, 925 Seneca St, tel: (206) 624-1144.

OTHER SEATTLE SERVICES

King County Medical Society, tel: (206) 621-9393 (physician referral).
Seattle-King County Dental Society, tel: (206) 443-7607 (dentist referral).
Coast Guard emergencies, tel: (206) 217-6000.
Crisis clinic, tel: (206) 461-3222.
FBI, tel: (206) 622-0460.
Poison Control, tel: (206) 526-2121.

PORTLAND HOSPITALS

Emanuel Hospital, 2801 N. Gantenbein, tel: (503) 280-3200.
Good Samaritan, 1015 NW 22nd Ave, tel: (503) 229-7711.
Providence Medical Center, 4805 NE Glisan, tel: (503) 230-1111.

OTHER PORTLAND SERVICES

Multnomah County Dental Service, tel: (503) 223-4731.
Multnomah County Medical Referral Service, tel: (503) 222-0156.
Crisis Intervention, tel: (503) 223-6161.

Weights & Measures

The US is not on the metric system, so visitors should carry a chart to convert miles to kilometers, pounds to kilograms, ounces to grams and yards to meters. A conversion chart for clothing and shoe sizes is also helpful.

Business Hours

Businesses and banks are generally open 9am–5pm Monday to Friday, and closed on Saturday, Sunday and public holidays. Certain banks open for limited hours on Saturday. Many government agencies close for holidays (*see* "Public Holidays"). Local banks and businesses may also be closed.

Tipping

Tips are an appreciation for good service, and they should reflect the quality of service rendered.

The accepted rate for porters at the airport is 50 cents per bag or suitcase, similarly for hotel bellboys and porters. A doorperson should be tipped if he or she unloads or parks your car. It is not necessary to tip chambermaids unless you stay several days.

In restaurants, tip 15–20 percent of the total bill. Unlike some other countries, a service charge is not included in the bill unless you are with a large party. Tipping is not usually necessary in cafeterias.

Taxi drivers, barbers, hairdressers, bartenders, etc. should be tipped 10–15 percent.

Media

Newspapers

The major daily newspapers in Seattle are the morning *Seattle Post-Intelligencer*, tel: (206) 448-8000, and the afternoon *Seattle Times*, tel: (206) 464-2000. On Sunday, the two combine into one large edition. Friday tabloid sections in both papers are useful guides to events.

Seattle Weekly, a tabloid newsmagazine, prints a summary of many of the week's events, including visual arts, theater, music and film.

Foreign language newspapers include the Japanese daily *North American Post*, the *Seattle Chinese Post*, and the *Hispanic News*.

For Portland activities, check the daily *Oregonian*, tel: (503) 221-8240, and the free weekly *Willamette Week*, tel: (503) 243-2122.

For a list of stores selling out-of-town newspapers and periodicals in Seattle and Portland, look in the *Yellow Pages* under "News Dealers."

Seattle's main library at Fourth Ave and Madison St, is a good place to browse newspapers.

Radio

Most US radios pick up AM and FM. FM has fewer commercials and a better range of programs. Popular stations in the Seattle area include:

AM
570	KVI, popular music, sports
710	KIRO, news, sports
880	KIXI, hits from '40s, '50s and '60s
1000	KOMO, adult contemporary, news
1090	KING, news, talk shows
1300	KMPS, country

FM
88.5	KPLU, Public Radio
90.3	KCMY, alternative, worldbeat, international artists
92.5	KLSY, soft rock
94.1	KMPS, country
102.5	KZOK, classic rock
103.7	KMTT, popular and soft rock
107.7	KNDD, alternative rock

Television

In addition to the national networks and cable-TV options, many towns have their own local TV station. Listings appear in the daily newspapers. Around Seattle, the major stations are:

Channel	
4	KOMO, ABC
5	KING, NBC
7	KIRO, CBS
9	KCTS, PBS
11	KSTW, Independent, Tacoma
13	KCPQ, Independent, Tacoma
22	KTZZ, Independent

The Portland-area major stations are:

Channel		
	2	KATU, ABC
	6	KOIN, CBS
	8	KGW, NBC
	10	KOPB, PBS
	12	KPTV, Independent

Postal Services

Post offices generally open 8.30am–5pm Monday to Friday. However, hours can vary between big-city branches and those in smaller towns, so call or check with your hotel personnel.

Stamps may be purchased at the post office and from vending machines in hotels, stores, airports and bus and train stations.

If you don't know where you'll be staying in a particular town, you may receive mail simply by having it addressed to you, care of General Delivery at the main post office of that town, where it will be held for you.

Be sure to include a five-digit zip code (at least) for all addresses within the US. Information about zip codes may be obtained from any post office. An overnight delivery service, Express Mail, is provided by the post office and some private companies – look in the *Yellow Pages* under "Delivery Service."

SEATTLE

US Post Office, Main Branch, 301 Union St, tel: (206) 442-6340.
US Post Office, 415 First Ave N, tel: (206) 284-0750.

PORTLAND

US Post Office; Main Branch, tel: (503) 294-2300.

Tourist Information

Both Washington and Oregon have travel information centers throughout the state, providing extensive information. Visitors can get information prior to their visit by calling Tourist Information in Washington, tel: (206) 753-5600, or Oregon, tel: (503) 378-3451.

In Seattle, the best source of information on attractions, activities, accommodations and restaurants is the Seattle-King County Convention and Visitors' Bureau in the Washington State Convention Center between Eighth and Ninth avenues and Pike and Union streets, tel: (206) 461-5840. Entrance is on Union St. Hours are 8.30am–5pm, Monday to Friday, with Saturday opening in summer. The bureau also has an information center at Sea-Tac Airport, open daily 9.30am–7.30pm.

Alternatively, you may call **Travelers' Aid**, tel: (206) 461-3888.

In Portland, the best source of information is the **Portland/Oregon Visitors' Association**, 26 SW Salmon St, tel: (503) 222-2223. Hours are 8.30am–5pm Monday to Friday, 9am–3pm Saturday.

For information in other cities, consult the Chamber of Commerce or Convention and Visitors' Bureau.

State Tourism Agencies

Oregon Tourism Division, 775 Summer St NE, Salem 97310, tel: (503) 986 0000 or 1-800-547-7842.
Washington State Tourism Office, General Administration Building, Olympia 98504, tel: (360) 586-2088 or (360) 753-5600.

Consulates

Foreign consulates in the Pacific Northwest are located in Seattle, including the UK, Canadian and New Zealand representatives.

Getting Around

Public Transportation

By Bus/Metro

Both Seattle and Portland have excellent bus services. Most bus lines operate weekdays, weekends and holidays, serving all major hotels, shopping areas and other points of interest. Buses are free in specially designated downtown areas. You must have the exact fare when boarding a bus. Monthly passes are available. Metro also provides a "Ride Free Area" in the downtown core bordered by the I-5 freeway to the east, the waterfront to the west, Jackson St to the south and Battery St to the north.

Portland – Tri-Met, tel: (503) 238-RIDE
Seattle – Metro, tel: (306) 553-3000

By Taxi

In Portland and Seattle, there are taxi stands at major hotels, the bus depot, train station, airport and some street corners. Taxi cabs are regulated in both cities.

SEATTLE

Farwest Taxi, tel: (206) 622-1717.
Gray Top Cab, tel: (206) 622-4800.
Yellow Cab, tel: (206) 622-6500.

PORTLAND

Broadway Cab, tel: (503) 227-1234.
Radio Cab, tel: (503) 227-1212.

Private Transportation

Driving Advice

The official national speed limit is 55 mph (88 kph). On Interstate highways outside of populated areas, individual states may opt for 65 mph (104 kph). Most city speed limits are 25–35 mph (40–56 kph).

A right turn is permitted on a red light, but drivers must come to a complete stop before proceeding.

In addition to street signs advising no-parking hours and special tow-away zones, the color of the curb often governs the kind of parking permitted. Red curbs mean no parking at all.

Yellow curbs indicate limited stops (usually for trucks only). White curbs are limited to short-term stopping for passenger pick-up only. It is not advisable to ignore any of these signs. Police will summon tow trucks for vehicles found illegally parked.

In Seattle, parking is often a problem on steep hills. Turn your front wheels into the curb, so that the tire is resting on the curb at an angle that would keep the car from rolling downhill unexpectedly. Be sure to set the emergency brake.

Pedestrians always have the right of way. In Seattle, jaywalking is prohibited and carries a stiff penalty for violators.

Although legal except on freeways, picking up hitchhikers is potentially dangerous.

For information on the condition of mountain roads in winter, tel: (206) 434-7277 in Seattle or (503) 889-3999 in Portland.

A wide selection of rental cars is available in the Pacific Northwest. Rental offices are in most cities and all major airports. A major credit card is required, and the driver must be over 25 years and have a valid driver's license. Local rental companies sometimes offer less expensive rates. Be sure to check insurance provisions before signing anything.

Below are some car rental agencies that can be contacted while in the US.

Avis	1-800-831-2847.
Budget	1-800-527-0700.
Hertz	1-800-654-3131.
National	tel: 1-800-227-7368.

Where To Stay

Washington Hotels & Motels

SEA-TAC AIRPORT

Best Western Airport Executel, 20717 Pacific Hwy S, tel: (206) 878-1814.
Holiday Inn Sea-Tac, 17338 Pacific Hwy S, tel: (206) 248-1000.
Seattle Airport Hilton, 17620 Pacific Hwy S, tel: (206) 244-4800.

SEATTLE DOWNTOWN

Alexis Hotel, First and Madison Sts, tel: (206) 624-4844.
American Youth Hostels, tel: (206) 281-7306.
Chambered Nautilus, 5005 22nd Ave. NE, tel: (206) 522-2536.
The Edgewater Inn, 2411 Alaskan Way, tel: (206) 728-7000.
Four Seasons Olympic, 411 University St, tel: (206) 621-1700.
Inn at the Market, First Ave. and Pine St, Pike Place Market, tel: (206) 443-3600.
Mayflower Park Hotel, Fourth Ave. and Olive Way, tel: (206) 623-8700.
Roosevelt Hotel, 1531 Seventh Ave, tel: (206) 621-1200.
Stouffer Renaissance Hotel, 515 Madison St, tel: (206) 583-0300.
Sorrento Hotel, 900 Madison St, tel: (206) 622-6400.
Warwick, Fourth Ave. and Lenora St, tel: (206) 443-4300.

West Coast Vance, 620 Stewart St, tel: (206) 441-4200.
Westin, 1900 Fifth Ave, tel: (206) 728-1000.

BELLEVUE

Bellevue Hilton Hotel, 100 112th Ave. NE, tel: (206) 455-3330.
Best Western Bellevue Inn, 11211 Main St, tel: (206) 455-5240.
Hyatt Regency, 900 Bellevue Way NE, tel: (206) 462-1234.
Red Lion Inn-Bellevue, 300 112th Ave. SE, tel: (206) 455-1300.

BELLINGHAM

The Castle B&B, 1103 15th St, tel: (360) 676-0974.
Best Western Lakeway Inn, 714 Lakeway Drive, tel: (360) 671-1011.
Ramada Inn, 215 Samish Way, tel: (360) 734-8830.

LA CONNER

La Conner Country Inn, Second and Morris Sts, tel: (360) 466-3101.
Whispering Firs, 1957 Kanako, tel: (360) 678-6707.

EVERETT

Cypress Inn, 12619 Fourth Ave. W, tel: (206) 347-9099.
Howard Johnson Plaza Hotel, 3105 Pine St, tel: (206) 339-3333.

OLYMPIA

Harbinger Inn, 1136 East Bay Drive, tel: (360) 754-0389.
Holiday Inn Select, 2300 Evergreen Park Drive, tel: (360) 943-4000.

OLYMPIC PENINSULA

F.W. Hastings House Old Consulate Inn, 313 Walker St, Port Townsend, tel: (360) 385-6753
James House, 1238 Washington St, Port Townsend, tel: (360) 385-1238.
Kalaloch Lodge, Hwy 101, Kalaloch, tel: (360) 962-2271.
Lake Quinault Lodge, S. Shore Rd, Lake Quinault, tel: 1-800-562-6672.
Resort at Port Ludlow, 9483 Oak Bay Rd, Port Ludlow, tel: (360) 437-2222.

ORCAS ISLAND

Kangaroo House, North Beach Road, tel: (360) 376-2175.
Rosario Resort, Eastsound, tel: (360) 376-2222.

SAN JUAN ISLAND

Inns at Friday Harbor, 680 Spring St, Friday Harbor, tel (360) 378-4000.
Olympic Lights B&B, 4531-A Cattle Point Road, Friday Harbor, tel: (360) 378-3186.
Roche Harbor Resort, Roche Harbor, tel: (360) 378-2155.

WHIDBEY ISLAND

Captain Whidbey Inn, 2072 W. Captain Whidbey Inn Road, Coupeville, tel: (360) 678-4097.
The Cruperville Inn, PO Box 370, Cruperville, tel: (360) 678-6668.

SPOKANE

Cavanaugh's Inn at the Park, 303 NW River Drive, tel: 1-800-THE-INNS.
Holiday Inn Express, 110 E. Fourth Ave, tel: (206) 328-8505 or 1-800-465-4329.
Red Lion Motor Inn, 1100 Sullivan Road N, tel: (509) 924-9000.
Red Lion City Center, 322 N. Spokane Falls Court, tel: (509) 455-9600.

EASTERN WASHINGTON

Campbell's Lodge, Chelan, tel: (509) 682-2561.

WASHINGTON CASCADES

Mazama Country Inn, Mazama, tel: (509) 996-2681.
Mountain Home Lodge, Mountain Home Road, Leavenworth, tel: (509) 548-7077.
Sun Mountain Lodge, Winthrop, tel: (509) 996-2211.

Oregon Hotels & Motels

PORTLAND AIRPORT

Holiday Inn-Airport, 8439 NE Columbia Blvd, tel: (503) 256-5000.
Imperial Hotel, 400 SW Broadway. Tel: (503) 228-7221 or (800) 452-2323.
Sheraton Inn-Portland Airport, 8235 NE Airport Way, tel: (503) 281-2500.
Shilo Inn, 11707 NE Airport Way, tel: (503) 252-7500.

PORTLAND DOWNTOWN

Heathman Hotel, SW Salmon at Broadway Sts, tel: (503) 241-4100.
Hotel Vintage Plaza, 422 SW Broadway, tel: (503) 228-1212.
Imperial Hotel, 400 SW Broadway, tel: (503) 228-7221 or (800) 452-2323.
Mallory Hotel, 729 SW 15th Ave, tel: (503) 223-6311.

Portland Hilton Hotel, 921 SW Sixth Ave, tel: (503) 226-1611.
Portland Marriott Hotel, 1401 SW Front Ave, tel: (503) 226-7600.
Red Lion Hotel, 310 SW Lincoln, tel: (503) 221-0450.
West Coast Benson, 309 SW Broadway, tel: (503) 228-2000.

ASHLAND AREA

Ashland Hills Inn, 2525 Ashland St, tel: (503) 482-8310.
The Ashland Hostel, 150 N. Main St, tel: (503) 482-9217.
Chanticleer Bed & Breakfast Inn, 120 Gresham St, tel: (503) 482-1919.
Pine Meadow Inn, 1000 Crow Road, Merlin, tel: (503) 471-6277.

EASTERN OREGON

Sunriver Lodge, Hwy 97 south of Bend, tel: (503) 593-1221 or 1-800-547-3922.
Inn of the Seventh Mountain, 18575 Century Drive, tel: (503) 382-8711.

EUGENE

Best Western Greentree Motel, 1759 Franklin Blvd, tel: (503) 485-2727.
Eugene Hilton, 66 E. Sixth Ave, tel: (503) 342-2000.

OREGON CASCADES

Black Butte Ranch, Sisters, tel: (503) 595-6211.
Columbia Gorge Hotel, 4000 W. Cliff Drive, Hood River, tel: (503) 386-5566 or 1-800-345-1921.
Crater Lake Lodge, Crater Lake, tel: (503) 594-2511.
Oregon Caves Chateau, Oregon Caves, tel: (503) 592-3400.
Timberline Lodge, Timberline, tel: (503) 231-7979 or 1-800-547-1406.

OREGON COAST

Best Western Inn of The Beachcomber, 1250 S. Hwy 101, Gold Beach, tel: (503) 247-6691.
Driftwood Shores Resort, 88416 First Ave, Florence, tel: (503) 997-8263.
Hotel Newport, 3019 N. Coast Hwy, tel: 1-800-547-3310.
House on the Hill, Oceanside, tel: (503) 842-6030.
Inn at Otter Crest, 301 Otter Crest Loop, Otter Rock, tel: (503) 765-2111.
Johnson House, 216 Maple St, Florence, tel: (503) 997-8000.
Salishan Lodge, Gleneden Beach, tel: 1-800-452-2300.

Hallmark Resort, 1400 S. Hemlock, Cannon Beach, tel: (503) 436-1566.

Bed & Breakfast

Greater Northwest B&B Information Services covers Southern BC, Washington and Oregon.

SEATTLE

Pacific Bed & Breakfast Agency, tel: (206) 784-0539.
Seattle Bed & Breakfast Association, PO Box 95853, tel: (206) 547-1020.

PORTLAND

Northwest Bed & Breakfast, 610 SW Broadway, tel: (503) 243-7616.

Youth Hostels

Portland International Hostel, 3031 SE Hawthorne Blvd, tel: (503) 236-3380.
Seattle International Hostel, 84 Union, tel: (206) 622-5443.

Eating Out

Where to Eat in Washington

SEATTLE

Elliott's, Pier 56, tel: (206) 623-4340.
Il Bistro, Pike Place Market, tel: (206) 682-3049.
Kokeb, 926 12th Ave, tel: (206) 322-0485.
Labuznik, 1924 First Ave, tel: (206) 441-8899.
Leschi Lake Cafe, 102 Lakeside Ave. S, tel: (206) 328-2233.
Mikado, 514 S. Jackson St, tel: (206) 622-5206.
Ray's Boathouse, 6049 Seaview Ave. NW, tel: (206) 789-3770.
Rover's, 2808 East Madison St, tel: (206) 325-7442.
Saleh al Lago, 6804 E. Green Lake Way N, tel: (206) 524-4044.
Serafina, 2043 Eastlake Ave. E, tel: (206) 325-0807.
Trattoria Mitchelli, 84 Yesler Way, tel: (206) 623-3883.
Union Bay Cafe, 3505 NE 45 St, tel: (206) 527-8364.

BELLEVUE

Andre's Gourmet Cuisine, 14125 NE 20th St, tel: (206) 747-6551.
Azalea's Fountain Court, 22 103rd NE, tel: (206) 451-0426.
Domani, 604 Bellevue Way NE, tel: (206) 454-4405.
Spazzo, 10655 NE Fourth St, tel: (206) 454-8255.

ISSAQUAH

LaCosta, 240 NW Gilman Blvd, tel: (206) 392-8980.
Mandarin Garden, 40 E. Sunset Way, tel: (206) 392-9476.

TACOMA

Grazie, 2301 N. 30th Ave, tel: (206) 627-0231.
The Lobster Shop South, 4013 Ruston Way, tel: (206) 759-2165.

OFF THE BEATEN PATH

The Virginia Restaurant, 808 N Cascade Hway, Winthrop, tel: (509) 996-2536.
Duck Soup Inn, Friday Harbor, San Juan Island, tel: (360) 378-4878.
The Herbfarm, 32804 Issaquah-Fall City Rd, Fall City, tel: (206) 784-2222.
The Oyster Bar, Chuckanut Dr, south of Bellingham, tel: (360) 766-6185.
The Three Crabs, north of Sequim on the Olympic Peninsula, tel: (360) 683-4264.

Where to Eat in Oregon

PORTLAND

Alexis, 215 W. Burnside St, tel: (503) 224-8577.
Atwater's, 111 SW 5th Ave, tel: (503) 275-3600.
Bijou Cafe, 132 SW Third Ave, tel: (503) 222-3187.
Bread and Ink, 3610 SE Hawthorne Blvd, tel: (503) 239-4756.
Couch Street Fish House, 105 NW Third, tel: (503) 223-6173.
Dan and Louis' Oyster Bar, 208 SW Ankeny St, tel: (503) 227-5906.
Elizabeth's, 3135 NE Broadway, Portland, tel: (503) 281-8337.
Fong Chong, 301 NW 4th Ave, tel: (503) 220-0235.
Genoa, 2832 SE Belmont St, tel: (503) 238-1464.
Heathman Bakery & Pub, 901 SW Salmon St, tel: (503) 227-5700.
Indigine, 3723 SE Division St, tel: (503) 238-1470.

Jake's Famous Crawfish, 401 SW 12th Ave, tel: (503) 226-1419.
L'Auberge, 2601 NW Vaughn St, tel: (503) 223-3302.
Ron Paul, 1441 NE Broadway, tel: (503) 284-5347.
Yen Ching, 1135 SW Washington, tel: (503) 222-1455.
Zefiro, 500 NW 21st, tel: (503) 226-3394.

OFF THE BEATEN PATH

Cafe Xenon, 898 Pearl St, Eugene, tel: (503) 343-3005.
Chanterelle, 207 E. Fifth Ave, Eugene, tel: (503) 484-4065.
Jacksonville Inn Dinner House, 175 E. California St, Jacksonville, tel: (503) 899-1900.
Pine Tavern Restaurant, 967 NW Brooks, Bend, tel: (503) 382-5581.

Drinking Notes

You must be 21 to buy or consume alcohol. Liquor is sold by state stores (closed Sunday and holidays) and licensed venues (until 2am in Washington, 2.30am in Oregon). Packaged wine or beer is sold in grocery stores.

DRINKING IN WASHINGTON

Washington Wine Commission, PO Box 61217, Seattle, WA 98121, tel: (206) 728-2252. Free list of Washington wineries.
Yakima Valley Wine Growers Association, PO Box 39, Grandview, WA 98930, tel: (509) 786-2163. Free touring map.
Hoodsport Winery, US 101, just north of Hoodsport, tel: (360) 877-9894. Open daily 9am–6pm.
Rainier Brewery, 3100 Airport Way S, Seattle, tel: (206) 622-6606. Open Monday to Saturday 1–6pm.

DRINKING IN OREGON

Oregon Winegrowers Association, 1200 NW Front Ave, Suite 400, Portland, OR 97209, tel: (503) 228-8403. Send for brochure on six regions that hold most of Oregon's wineries.
Blitz-Weinhard Brewing Co, 1133 Westburnside, Portland, OR 97209, tel: (503) 222-4351. Home of the famous Henry Weinhard's beer. Tours on Thursday and Friday.
Portland is the Pacific Northwest's hub for micro-breweries, check the *Yellow Pages* for listings.

Attractions

Museums

SEATTLE

Museum of Flight, 9404 E. Marginal Way S, tel: (206) 764-5720. Exhibits trace the history of aviation with special emphasis on Northwest contributions. Stunning new wing displays dozens of aircraft, some suspended from the ceiling. Open 10am–5pm daily, until 9pm on Thursday. Admission fee.
Museum of History and Industry, 2700 24th Ave. E, tel: (206) 324-1125. Exhibits on the history of Seattle, King County and the Pacific Northwest. Open 10am–5pm daily. Admission fee charged.
Burke Museum, NE 45th and 17th NE, tel: (206) 543-5590. Exhibits on geology, natural history, archaeology and anthropology which illuminate the region's prehistoric and native past. Open 10am–5pm. Admission free.
Wing Luke Asian Museum, 407 Seventh Ave. S, tel: (206) 623-5124. Exhibitions on the cultural heritage of Asians in the Pacific Northwest. Tuesday to Friday 11am–4.30pm, Saturday and Sunday noon–4pm. Admission fee charged. Thursday free.

Other museums you can visit are:
Bellevue Art Museum, 301 Bellevue Square, tel: (206) 454-6021.
Frye Art Museum, 704 Terry Ave, tel: (206) 622-9250.
Henry Art Gallery, 15th Ave. NE and NE 41st St, tel: (206) 543-2280.
Nordic Heritage Museum, 3014 NW 67th St, tel: (206) 789-5707.
Seattle Art Museum, First Ave. and University St, tel: (206) 654-3100.
Seattle Asian Art Museum, Volunteer Park on Capitol Hill at 14th East and East Prospect, tel: (206) 654-3100.

PORTLAND

Oregon Historical Society, 1200 SW Park Ave, tel: (503) 222-1741. Headquarters of the Oregon Historical Society. One of the finest collections of western pioneer and Indian artifacts in the US, including gear and journals from the Lewis and Clark expedition. Open Tuesday to Saturday, 10am–5pm, Sunday noon–5pm. Free.
Oregon Museum of Science and Industry (OMSI), 1945 SE Water Ave, tel: (503) 797-4000. By the Washington Park Zoo. Diversified science education center and one of the best fun-to-learn-in museums in the US. Omnimax, laser and Sky Theater shows daily. Science store. Open daily. Admission fee charged.

Other museums worth a visit include:
American Advertising Museum, 9 NW Second Ave, tel: (503) 226-0000.
Portland Art Museum, 1219 SW Park Ave, tel: (503) 226-2811.
Oregon Maritime Center & Museum, 113 SW Front Ave, tel: (503) 224-7724.

Art Galleries

SEATTLE

Bailey/Nelson, 2001 Western, tel: (206) 448-7340.
COCA, 65 Cedar St, tel: (206) 728-1980.
Davidson Galleries, 313 Occidental Ave. S, tel: (206) 624-7684.
Foster/White Gallery, 311 1/2 Occidental Ave. S, tel: (206) 622-2833.
Francine Seders Gallery, 6701 Greenwood Ave. N, tel: (206) 782-0355.
MIA Gallery, 536 1st Ave. S, tel: (206) 467-8283.

PORTLAND

Contemporary Crafts, 3934 SW Corbett St, tel: (503) 223-2654.
Gango Gallery, 205 SW First St, tel: (503) 222-3850.
Photographic Image Gallery, 208 SW 1st Ave, tel: (503) 224-3543.
Quintana's Gallery, 139 NW Second Ave, tel: (503) 223-1729.

Theaters

SEATTLE

A Contemporary Theater, Union and 7th St, tel: (206) 285-5110.
Empty Space Theater, 3509 Fremont N, tel: (206) 547-7500.
Intiman Theater, Seattle Center Playhouse, tel: (206) 626-0782.
Seattle Repertory Theater, 155 Mercer St, tel: (206) 443-2210.

Portland Center for the Performing Arts, SW Broadway and Main, tel: (503) 796-9293.

Portland Civic Theater, 1515 SW Morrison, tel: (503) 248-4345.

Portland Repertory Theater, 25 SW Salmon, tel: (503) 224-4491.

Movies

The Northwest cinema scene is quite sophisticated. Producers often preview new films in Seattle, and more than one "unreleasable" film has found an enthusiastic audience here.

First-run movies, fresh from Hollywood, are those screened for the first time. Most American theaters show exclusively first-runs. Many theaters offer afternoon matinees at reduced prices. Check the newspapers for current offerings and show times.

Seattle has several theaters that screen foreign films (subtitled for US audiences). These include: **Guild 45th**, 2115 N. 45th, tel: (206) 633-3353, the **Harvard Exit** and its companion **Top of the Exit**, 807 E. Roy St, tel: (206) 323-8986 and the **Metro Cinemas**, 4500 Ninth NE, tel: (206) 633-0055. The **Varsity**, 4329 University Way NE, tel: (206) 632-3131, specializes in repertory offerings of classics, oldies and foreign films. The **Seattle Art Museum**, tel: (206) 654-3100, often features art films or the work of a single director or actor.

In Portland, a highlight of the cinema scene is the **Northwest Film and Video Center**, 1219 SW Park Ave, tel: (503) 221-1156. The center shows 300 unusual contemporary and classic films each year.

The **Roseway Theater**, 7229 NE Sandy Blvd, tel: (503) 287-8119 is a leading revival house.

Libraries

Libraries can be found in just about any Washington or Oregon town with a population of a few thousand. Larger cities have library systems, built on a main branch that offers major collections and special services.

Neighborhood branches around the city offer smaller reading collections and limited reference services. State library systems offer services to the blind, deaf and physically handicapped.

Use of all libraries is free. Although non-residents cannot borrow books, they can use reference materials and read daily newspapers and foreign-language periodicals in the building. Ask the librarian if you need assistance.

SEATTLE

Public Library, Main Branch, tel: (206) 386-INFO for quick information.

PORTLAND

Multnomah County Central Library, tel: (503) 248-5123.

Tourist Attractions

SEATTLE

Aquarium, Pier 59 at Waterfront Park, tel: (206) 386-4320. Seattle's Aquarium is a $5.4-million complex, featuring 14,500 sea mammals and seashore creatures and some 5,500 kinds of trees and shrubs from temperate climates throughout the world in its 200 acres (80 hectares). It is open 10am–7pm during the summer and 10am–5pm the rest of the year. Admission fee charged.

Washington Park Arboretum, tel: (206) 543-8800. Huge wooded park with vast array of plant families. An authentic Japanese Garden and traditional tea house is located at the south end of the grounds. Open March through November. Admission fee to Japanese Garden. Arboretum is free and open year round.

Chittenden Locks, tel: (206) 783-7059. The Hiram M. Chittenden Locks make the transition from saltwater Puget Sound to freshwater Lake Union, raising and lowering sea vessels of all shapes and sizes from the lake to the Sound. Visitors in the underwater viewing room can see salmon fighting their way up the fish ladder. Open to the public 7am–9pm. Admission free.

Fisherman's Terminal, 1735 West Thurman St, on Salmon Bay. The busiest terminal of its kind in the North Pacific. Walk out on the piers and see hundreds of commercial fishing boats and stroll the new public plaza featuring interpretive panels that detail the development of the local fishing industry. Several excellent seafood restaurants are nearby. Admission free.

International District, home for many

of the city's Asian communities, located at the southern end of downtown Seattle. Highlights of the area are **Uwajimaya**, perhaps the largest Japanese retail store in the country, the **Wing Luke museum** and the **Nippon Kan Theater**. Reservations are needed for tours of the International District, tel: (206) 236-0657.

Northwest Trek Wildlife Park, Eatonville, tel: 1-800-433-8735. In the foothills of Mount Rainier, tram tours, animal exhibitions and nature trails allow visitors to explore this park's natural wonders. Call for visiting hours.

Pacific Science Center, 200 Second Ave. N, tel: (206) 443-2001. Six buildings full of science adventures for the whole family. Weekdays 10am–5pm, weekend 10am–6pm. Admission fee charged.

Pike Place Market, tel: (206) 682-7453. Overlooking Elliot Bay along Western Ave. between Virginia and Pike St. One of the premier food and crafts markets in the US. Allow several hours to wander by the fruit and vegetable stalls, fish markets, flower vendors, jewelry makers, bakers, butchers, delis and street musicians. Stalls open daily 9am–5pm.

Seattle Center, tel: (206) 684-8582. Site of the 1962 Seattle World's Fair. The Center's 74 acres (30 hectares) form a cultural hub for performing arts groups, including the Seattle Opera Company, the Seattle Symphony Orchestra, the Pacific Northwest Ballet, the Bagley Wright Theater, the Seattle Repertory Theater and the Intiman Theater. The Center also holds the Space Needle, Fun Forest amusement park; the Pacific Science Center; the Center House, with 50 shops and restaurants; the Northwest Craft Center; and the Coliseum and Key Arena which host trade shows, concerts and professional sports events, such as Seattle Sonics (basketball) games. You can reach the Center in 90 seconds on the monorail from Downtown.

The Space Needle, Seattle Center, tel: (206) 443-2111. Panoramic views of Puget Sound, the Olympic Mountains, the Cascade range and Mount Rainier from the 607-ft (152-meter) upper platform. A restaurant at the top turns one full circle each hour. Hours are 9am–midnight daily. Elevator fee charged except for restaurant patrons.

Woodland Park Zoo, 50th Ave. N. and

Fremont Ave, tel: (206) 684-4800. Award-winning zoo of innovative design simulating the natural habitats of many animals: the African Savannah for lions, hippos, giraffes, and zebra; the Nocturnal House teeming with exotic animal life; the gorilla habitat duplicating the lush lowlands; and the swamps and marshes favored by many waterfowl. Admission fee charged. Open daily 9.30am–sunset.

PORTLAND

The Weather Machine, Pioneer Courthouse Square. Designed by local artist Terence O'Donnell, a globe on a 25-foot column comes to life with a musical fanfare at noon each day. From a misty cloud, a weather creature emerges – a stylized sun for clear days; a dragon forecasting storms and a blue heron to signify drizzle, mist and transitional weather.

Mount St Helens National Volcanic Monument, just across the river east of Vancouver, at Castle Rock, Washington, tel: (206) 274-4158, is a Visitor Center where you can walk through a model of the mountain while viewing a slide presentation about the disastrous 1980 eruption. Open daily 9.15am–7pm.

Washington Park, 4001 SW Canyon Road. One of Portland's oldest, offers 145 acres (58 hectares) of views and walks. It is the home of the world-renowned **International Rose Test Gardens** and its 400 varieties of roses. Blooms are at their peak from June until September. The Park is crowned by a **Japanese Garden**, tel: (503) 223-4070, acclaimed as one of the most authentic Japanese gardens outside Japan. Winter hours are 10am–4pm; summer hours, 10am–6pm. Admission fee charged. Take the zoo railway from the Park into the **Washington Park Zoo**, tel: (503) 226-ROAR. The first elephant to be born in captivity in the western hemisphere in nearly half a century was born here in 1962. Open daily 9.30am–dusk. Admission fee charged.

World Forestry Center, 4033 SW Canyon Road, tel: (503) 228-1367. Slide shows and displays on forestry and wood, special weekend woodworking shows and demonstrations. Open daily 9am–5pm. Admission fee charged

---

Parks

National Forests and Parks outdoor recreation information is available about **Washington**, tel: (206) 902-3002, and **Oregon**, tel: (503) 594-2211.

The Pacific Northwest has four national parks – **Mount Rainier**, **Olympic** and **North Casades** in Washington, and **Crater Lake** in Oregon. National monuments include Oregon Caves and Mount St Helens. There are national recreation areas at Coulee Dam and Oregon Dunes. (*See relevant chapters.*) These, plus thousands of acres of national forest, provide abundant opportunities for outdoor recreation – mountains to climb, wilderness to hike, beaches to comb and lakes and streams to fish.

Olympic National Park, 600 East Park Ave, Port Angeles, WA 98362, tel: (360) 452-0330. Open all year-round, 24-hours. No entrance fee. Small camping charge.

North Cascades National Park, 800 State St, Sedro Wooley, WA 98284, tel: (360) 856-5700. Open all year-round, 24-hours. Roads are closed during winter. No entrance fee. Small camping charge.

Mount Rainier National Park, Tahoma Woods, Star Route, Ashford, WA 98304, tel: (206) 569-2211. Open daily, 24-hours. Closed from Memorial Day to winter. Small admission and camping charge.

Crater Lake National Park, PO Box 7, Crater Lake, OR 97604, tel: (503) 594-2111. Open in summer from noon to midnight, winter until dusk. Small admission and camping charge.

Tours

Gray Line, tel: 1-800-544-0739, has city tours as well as trips to Mount Rainier, Vancouver/Victoria, Mount Hood, the Columbia River Gorge, Mount St Helens and other scenic attractions in both Seattle and Portland.

Boeing Plant/Paine Air Field is the only commercial aviation plant that conducts tours. Visitors can observe the manufacture of 747s, 767s and 777s in various stages of assembly on a 1-hour tour including a 25-minute video presentation of Boeing's history. The tour is free, but space is limited. Call in advance, tel: (206) 342-4801.

Kingdome, tel: (206) 296-3663. Tours of this multi-million-dollar indoor stadium are available mid-April to mid-September. Admission fee charged.

Seattle Harbor Tours, tel: (206) 623-1445. Offers one-hour guided trips along Seattle's waterfront and shipyards from Pier 56 at Seneca St.

Tillicum Tours, tel: (206) 443-1244. Combines sightseeing harbor tours with trips to Blake Island for Indian-style salmon bake and traditional Native American dances.

Underground Tours, tel: (206) 682-4646. Offers five-block walking tours of Pioneer Square, including subterranean sidewalks and storefronts remaining from the 1889 fire.

PORTLAND

Self-guided walks. There are itineraries for several city walking tours. The Metropolitan Art Commission, tel: (503) 823-5111, and Art Media, 902 SW Yamhill, tel: (503) 223-3724, have brochures locating museums and art galleries. The Portland Development Commission, 1120 SW 5th St, tel: (503) 823-3200, has a map of historical and architectural sites.

Private guided walking tours are available, tel: (503) 227-5780.

Northwest Tours, tel: (503) 241-2844. One-day tours of Portland, the Wine Country, the Coast, Mount St Helens, Columbia Gorge and others.

Oregon Vineyard Tours, tel: (503) 786-0732. Guided tours of Oregon's award winning wineries, including transport, lunch, history and wine samples.

Rose City Riverboat Cruises, tel: (503) 234-6665. Includes dinner cruises, Sunday brunch, Portland harbor or Oregon City Falls tour.

Festivals & Events

The visitor seeking local festivals and events will find many from which to choose throughout the year, with the heaviest concentration from May to September. They include everything from Chinese New Year to the Wenatchee Apple Blossom Festival in Washington and from the Bach Festival to Pendleton Round-Up in Oregon.

State Tourism Offices in Oregon, tel: (503) 484-5307 or 1-800-547-5445, and Washington, tel: (206) 586-2088 or 1-800-544-1800, publish lists of annual festivals and events.

A Portland Calendar

JANUARY

Reel Music, tel: (503) 221-1156. Celebration of music on film by Portland Museum's Northwest Film Center.
All Oregon Products Show, Washington County Fairplex, Hillsboro, tel: (503) 648-1416.

FEBRUARY

Pacific Northwest Sportsmen's Show, Expo Center, tel: (503) 246-8291.
International Film Festival, Portland Art Museum Northwest Film Center, tel: (503) 221-1156.
Greater Portland International Auto Show, Oregon Convention Center, tel: 1-800-732-2914.

MARCH

Winter Games of Oregon, Mount Hood Meadows, Timberline, tel: (503) 520-1319.
America's Largest Antique & Collectible Show, Portland Expo Center, tel: (503) 282-0877. More than 1,300 booths of items.
Northwest Quilters Show, Portland State University, tel: (503) 222-1991.

APRIL

Spring Rhododendron Show, Jenkins Estate, Aloha, tel: (503) 642-3855.
Great Astoria Crab & Seafood Festival, Mooring Basin, Hammond, tel: (503) 325-6311. Wine tasting, food, arts and crafts, entertainment.
Hood River Blossom Festival, tel: 1-800-366-3530. Arts and crafts, antiques and rides on the Mount Hood Railroad.

MAY

Cinco de Mayo Festival, SW Front and Salmon, tel: (503) 823-4572. Arts and crafts, ethnic food, dancing.
Kite Festival & Salmon Bake, Rockaway Beach, tel: (503) 355-5108.

JUNE

Portland Rose Festival, tel: (503) 233-3333. Hot air balloons, rose show, Indy car races, visiting ships and the Grand Floral Parade in a month-long celebration.
High Wind Classic, Hood River, tel: 1-800-366-3530. Sailboard racing in the Columbia Gorge.
AeroFair, Portland-Troutdale airport, tel: (503) 669-7473. Airshow with plane and helicopter rides.
Native American Powwow, Delta Park, tel: (503) 630-5195. Ceremonial dancing, crafts and food.

JULY

Oregon Brewers' Festival, tel: (503) 241-7179. The largest US gathering of independent brewers with music, food and scores of beers to sample.
Waterfront Blues Festival, tel: (503) 282-2855.
Historical Pageant, Champoeg, tel: (503) 678-1649. Outdoor drama of Oregon's heritage.
Scottish Highland Games, Mount Hood Community College, Gresham, tel: (503) 293-8501.

AUGUST

The Bite...a Taste of Portland, tel: (503) 248-066. Wine and food specialties from local chefs accompanied by music from local and national bands.
Hood River Apple Jam, tel: (503) 387-7529. Music festival in the Columbia Gorge.
Homowa Festival for African Arts, Washington Park Rose Garde, tel: (503) 288-3025.

Oregon State Fair, Salem, tel: (503) 378-3247. Rodeo, carnival, horse-racing, games, product booths.

SEPTEMBER

Artquake, Pioneer Courthouse Sq, tel: (503) 227-2787. The state's largest celebration of visual, performing and literary arts.
Fall Kite Festival, Lincoln City, tel: 1-800-452-2151.
Indian Style Salmon Bake, Depoe Bay, tel: (503) 765-2889. Delectable salmon steaks baked on an open fire.
Oktoberfest Celebrations, various locations, tel: (503) 230-1056. German festivals with beer, food and music.

OCTOBER

Zooboo, Washington Park Zoo, tel: (503) 226-1561. Haunted train rides, a not-too-haunted house, face painting and games for the whole family.
Great Pumpkin Harvest Festival, Carver, tel: (503) 654-7777.
Portland Marathon, tel: (503) 226-1111.
Greek Festival, Holy Trinity Orthodox Church, tel: (503) 234-0468. Food, gifts and entertainment.

NOVEMBER

Meier & Frank Holiday Parade, downtown Portland, tel: (503) 203-9166. Premature arrival of Santa Claus in a parade featuring horse-drawn carriages, floats, bands and celebrities.
Wooden Toy Show, World Forestry Center, tel: (503) 228-1367. Toy makers converge for sale and display of their wares.

DECEMBER

Festival of Lights, tel: (503) 222-2223. Choral festival illuminated by 70,000 lights along with a brightly lit up zoo and 50 illuminated ships cruising the Willamette and Columbia rivers every evening.
Christmas at Fort Vancouver, tel: (206) 696-7655. Old England and the American West mingle styles at this National Historic Site.

JANUARY

Art Gallery Walks at Pioneer Square, tel: (206) 467-8283. Also runs other months.
International Boat Show, Kingdome, tel: (206) 634-0911.
Annual Gorge, Columbia Winery, tel: (206) 488-3460.
Washington Sportsmen's Show, Puyallup, tel: (206) 841-5045.

FEBRUARY

Spam Carving Contest, Pioneer Square, tel: (206) 682-4646.
Smile Day, Seattle Aquarium, tel: (206) 386-4320.
Valentine Sweethearts, Pike Place Market, tel: (206) 447-9994.
Green River Depression Era Glass Show, Kent, tel: (206) 852-5250.
Writers on Stage, Mercer Island, tel: (206) 236-3545.
Mozart Mania, Bainbridge Island, tel: 1-800-378-8569.
Northwest Flower and Garden Show, tel: (206) 461-5805.

MARCH

Penn Cove Mussel Festival, Coupeville, tel: 1-800-366-4097.
Kids' Arts Day, Kent, tel: (206) 853-3991.
Jazzin' the Square, Pioneer Square, tel: (206) 621-7379. Also runs other months.
Enological Society's International Wine Fair, tel: (206) 624-5587.

APRIL

Family Imagination Celebration, Seattle Center, tel: (206) 684-7200.
Skagit Valley Tulip Festival, Mount Vernon, tel: (206) 42-TULIP.

MAY

Parade of Boats opens the yachting season, tel: (206) 325-1000.
Northwest Folklife Festival, tel: (206) 461-5805.
Pike Place Market Festival, tel: (206) 447-9994.
Bicycle Sundays, Lake Washington Blvd, tel: (206) 684-7092. Runs through September.
International Children's Festival, Seattle Center, tel: (206) 684-7346.

JUNE

Summer Arts Festival, Mercer Island, tel: (206) 236-3545.
Chamber Music Festival, Lakeside School, tel: (206) 282-1807.
Arts and Crafts Fair, Fremont, tel: (206) 632-1285.
Mainly Mozart, University of Washington, tel: (206) 443-4740.

JULY

Seafair Festival, tel: (206) 728-0123. With parade and hydroplane race.
Bite of Seattle, tel: (206) 461-5805. Food festival.
Wooden Boat Festival, Lake Union, tel: (206) 382-2628.
Emerald City Marathon, tel: (206) 285-4847.

AUGUST

Bumbershoot Urban Art Festival, Seattle Center, tel: (206) 461-5905.
Washington Food and Wine Festival, Woodinville, tel: (206) 481-8300.
Jazz Festival, Gig Harbour, tel: (206) 627-1504.

SEPTEMBER

Native American Heritage Festival, Westlake Center, tel: (206) 467-1600.
Western Washington State Fair, Puyallup, tel: (206) 845-1771.
Ellensburg Rodeo, tel: 1-800-637-2444.

OCTOBER

Kitsap Color Classic, Cascade Bicycle Club, tel: (206) 776-6711.
Wild Mushroom Show, Bremerton, tel: (206) 377-8267.
Horsemanship/Trailbike Weekend, Miracle Ranch, tel: (206) 697-1212.
Pacific NW Vintage Fashion Market, Seattle Center, tel: (206) 531-4194.
Used Book Sale, Kirkland, tel: (206) 684-6605.
Electronic Media Expo, Bellevue, tel: (206) 967-1801.
Fall Community Carnival, Federal Way, tel: (206) 661-4050.
Lutefisk Dinner, Poulsbo, tel: (206) 779-2622.
Great NW Microbrewery Invitational, Seattle Center, tel: (206) 684-8582.

NOVEMBER

Coffee Fest – Seattle Style, State Convention Center, tel: (206) 232-2982.

Wholesale Heaven, Seattle Center, tel: (206) 885-5827.
Wearable Art Show, Vashon Island, tel: (206) 463-6217.
Kirkland Art Walk, tel: (206) 889-4627. Also runs other months.
Holiday Parade, Kent, tel: (206) 813-6976.
Pottery Show and Sculptors' Workshop, Edmonds, tel: (206) 745-0773.
Enchanted Forest Display, Rainier Square, tel: (206) 623-0340.

DECEMBER

Merchants' Holiday Open House, Vashon Island, tel: (206) 463-6217.
Parade of Boats, Port Orchard, tel: (206) 876-3505, and Poulsbo, tel: (206) 779-4848.
Holiday Fest, Silver Bay Herb Farm, tel: (206) 692-1340.
Christmas Ship Festival, Argosy Cruises, tel: (206) 623-1445.

Nightlife

SEATTLE

The Backstage, 2208 NW Market, tel: (206) 781-2805.
Central Tavern, 207 First Ave. S, tel: (206) 622-0209.
Comedy Underground, 222 S. Main St, tel: (206) 628-0303.
Crocodile Cafe, 2200 Second Ave, tel: (206) 441-5611.
Doc Maynard's, 610 First Ave, tel: (206) 682-4646.
Moe's Mo'roc'n Cafe, 925 E. Pike, tel: (206) 323-2373.
Murphy's Pub, 1928 N. 45th St, tel: (206) 634-2110.
DV8, 131 Taylor N, tel: (206) 448-0888.
Palomino, 1420 Fifth, tel: (206) 623-1300.
Rick's, 11332 Lake City Way NE, tel: (206) 362-4458.
Top of the Hilton, Sixth Ave. and University St, tel: (206) 624-0500.
Triangle Tavern, 3507 Fremont Pl. N, tel: (206) 632-0880.
Virginia Inn, 1937 First Ave, tel: (206) 728-1937.

PORTLAND

The Drum, 14601 SE Division, tel: (503) 760-1400.
Dublin Pub, 6821 SW Beaverton-Hillsdale Hwy, tel: (503) 297-2889.
Key Largo, 31 NW First St, tel: (503) 223-9919.

Lotus Room, 932 SW Third, tel: (503) 227-6185.
West Coast Benson Hotel, 309 SW Broadway, tel: (503) 228-2000.
White Eagle Cafe and Saloon, 836 N. Russell St, tel: (503) 282-6810.

Shopping

Sales Tax

Washington has a sales tax that is added to the price of retail goods. The minimum is 6.5 percent and municipalities can add an additional tax to this rate. In Seattle, for example, sales tax is 8.2 percent. Food, except in restaurants, is not taxed. Oregon has no sales tax.

Shopping Areas

SEATTLE

Bellevue Square, NE Eighth St and Bellevue Way, Bellevue, tel: (206) 454-8096.
The Bon Marche, Third Ave. and Pine St, tel: (206) 506-6000. Also branch stores.
Gilman Village, Issaquah, tel: (206) 392-6802.
Nordstrom, 1501 Fifth Ave, tel: (206) 628-2111. Also branch stores.
Northgate, 555 NE Northgate Way, tel: (206) 362-8786.
Pike Place Market, First Ave. and Pike St, tel: (206) 682-7453.
Pioneer Square, tel: (206) 623-1162.
Rainier Square, 1301 Fifth Ave, tel: (206) 628-5050.
Southcenter, I-5 and I-405, Tukwila, tel: (206) 246-7400.
Uwajimaya, 519 Sixth Ave. S, tel: (206) 624-6248.
Westlake Center, Fourth Ave. and Pine St, tel: (206) 467-1600.

PORTLAND

Clackamas Town Center, I-205 at Sunnyside Road, tel: (503) 653-6913.
Fred Meyer, Inc, 41 stores throughout Oregon.
The Galleria, 921 SW Morrison, tel: (503) 228-2748.
Jantzen Beach Center, 1405 Jantzen Beach Center, tel: (503) 289-5555.
Lloyd Center, NE 10th & Weidler, tel: (503) 282-2511.
New Market Village, 50 SW Second, tel: (503) 228-2392.
Nordstrom, 701 SW Broadway, tel: (503) 224-6666. Also branch stores.
Old Sellwood Antique Row, Sellwood Bridge and SE 13th, tel: (503) 233-7334.
Pioneer Place, 700 SW Fifth, tel: (503) 228-5800.
Washington Square, off Hwy 217 southwest of Portland, tel: (503) 639-8860.
The Water Tower at John's Landing, 5331 SW Macadam Ave, tel: (503) 228-9431.

Sports & Leisure

Participant

In the Pacific Northwest, sporting travelers can participate in golf, tennis, bicycling, rafting, fishing, boating, swimming, hiking and backpacking and downhill and cross-country skiing. Runners will find over 200 road races each summer throughout the Pacific Northwest. The Seattle Marathon runs in April, the Portland Marathon in September. Walkers can join a *volksmarch* just about any weekend of the year.

Portland

Bicycles can be rented at Bike Central, 835 SW Second Ave, tel: (503) 227-4439, and most bicycle stores have booklets about local routes. There is an **ice skating** rink in Lloyd Center, tel: (503) 288-6073. There is **skiing** two-hours drive from Portland at Mount Bachelor, tel: 1-800-800-8334, and at several other Oregon sites.

Spectator

For spectators there is the Seattle Mariners baseball team, the Portland Trailblazers and Seattle Supersonics basketball teams, the Seattle Seahawks football team and dog racing at Fairview Track in Portland.

Language

General

Most Northwesterners speak only English, and there are few multilingual signs, making it more difficult than Europe or Asia for non-English speaking travelers. One notable exception is Japanese because of the area's economic connection with Japan.

Seattle has a multilingual travel and reservation assistance and a language bank, both accessible by phone.

At the Airport

At Sea-Tac Airport, recorded verbal instructions on underground trains are in English and Japanese, and signs in airport shops are in the two languages. A Japanese information booth is staffed by people fluent in the language. Maps of the airport are available in English, French, German, Spanish, Japanese, Chinese and Korean.

The Port of Seattle and the United States Travel and Tourism Administration sponsor "Operation Welcome" to meet international flights at Sea-Tac. Administered by the Seattle-King County Convention and Visitors' Bureau, it provides interpreters in 21 languages to greet passengers.

Another service provided by the bureau, in cooperation with the YMCA's International Student Service, is meeting visiting students and helping them with connecting flights, phone calls, lodging and other services.

325

The Seattle-King County Convention and Visitors' Bureau distributes a Seattle brochure in French, Spanish, German, Japanese and English. The Portland/Oregon Visitors' Association puts out brochures in Japanese, German, Spanish, Chinese and French.

The *Seattle Guide*, a weekly visitor information publication, is printed both in English and Japanese. The *Pacific Companion* is a bimonthly Japanese tourist guide.

Most large hotels in Seattle and Portland offer multilingual concierge services or front desk staff who have information regarding city/airport transportation, currency exchange and other visitor services. At the Seattle Sheraton, for example, menus and welcome notes are in Japanese, and guests receive complimentary Japanese newspapers. Both the Sheraton and the Stouffer Madison serve Japanese breakfast.

Further Reading

All Over Oregon & Washington, by Frances Fuller Victor. John H. Carmany Co, 1872.

A Camper's Guide to Oregon and Washington, by Kiki Canniff. Ki2 Publications, Portland, 1995.

Great Northwest Nature Factbook, by Anne Saling. Alaska Northwest Books, Bothell, 1991.

A Guide to the Indian Tribes of the Pacific Northwest, by Robert H. Ruby and John A. Brown. University of Oklahoma, 1986.

The Hidden Northwest, by Robert Cantwell. Lippincott, 1978.

Hunting Mister Heartbreak: A Discovery of America, by Jonathan Raban. Edward Burlingame Books, 1990.

Kidding Around Seattle: A Young Person's Guide to the City, by Rick Steves. Square Press, Santa Fe, 1980.

The Last Wilderness, by Murray Morgan. Viking Press, 1955.

Mountaineering: The Freedom of the Hills, by Ed Peters. The Mountaineers, Seattle, 1982.

Mt St Helens, Lady With a Past, by Kenneth L. Holmes. Salem Press, 1980.

The Nordstrom Way, by Robert Spector & Patrick D. McCarthy. John Wiley & Sons, 1995.

Northwest Best Places, by Stephanie Irving and David Brewster. Sasquatch Books, Seattle, 1995.

The Northwest Green Book, by Jonathan King. Sasquatch Books, Seattle, 1991.

Northwest Passage, A Literary Anthology of the Pacific Northwest from Coyote Trails to Roadside Attractions, by Bruce Barcott. Sasquatch Press, Seattle, 1994.

Northwest Passage, The Great Columbia River, by William Dietrich. Simon & Schuster, New York, 1995.

Oregon Territory or Emigrants' Guide, by P.L. Edwards. The Herald, Liberty Mo, 1842.

Pacific Northwest Indian Wars, by Ray Hoard Glassley. Binford & Mort, 1953.

Pacific Northwest Restaurants, Including Seattle, Portland and Vancouver. Zagat Survey, New York, 1995.

Pacific Salmon and Steelhead Trout, by R.J. Childerhose. University of Washington Press, Seattle, 1981.

Puget Sound, by Murray Morgan. University of Washington Press, Seattle, 1979.

Red Man's America, by Ruth Murray Underhill. University of Chicago Press, 1971.

The San Juan Islands – Afoot and Afloat, by Marge and Ted Mueller. The Mountaineers, Seattle, 1995.

Sexless Oysters and Self-tipping Hats: 100 Years of Invention in the Pacific Northwest, by Adam Woog. Sasquatch Books, Seattle, 1991.

The Story of Seattle, by Roberta Frye Watt. Lowman & Hanford, 1932.

Surveyor of the Sea: Life and Voyages of Captain George Vancouver, by Bern Anderson. University of Washington Press, Seattle, 1960.

Taking the Kids to the Pacific Northwest, by Eileen Ogintz. Harper Collins West, 1995.

The Tourists' Northwest, by Ruth Kedzie Wood. Dodd, Mead & Co, 1916.

Vancouver's Voyage, Charting the Northwest Coast 1791–1795, by Robin Fisher. University of Washington Press, Seattle, 1992.

Walks and Hikes on the Beaches Around Puget Sound, by Harvey Manning and Penny Manning. The Mountaineers, Seattle, 1995.

Washington: A Bicentennial History, by Norman H. Clark. W.W. Norton, 1976.

Washington Trivia, by Patricia Callander Hedtke & John V. Hedtke. Rutledge Hill Press, 1991.

Women & Men on the Overland Trail, by John Mark Faragher. Yale University Press, 1979.

The widely-acclaimed Insight Guide series includes 190 titles covering every continent. There are also more than 100 Pocket Guides and 60 Compact Guides.

Insight Guides which highlight travel destinations in this region include *Insight Guide: Seattle* and *Insight Guide: Vancouver*.

A team of local writers and photographers provide honest, incisive text and vivid images to explain one of the fastest-growing cities in America.

This young, beautiful city isolated from the rest of Canada is both explained and explored by a team of local, and literate, residents.

Art/Photo Credits

All photography by Ed Cooper except:

George Baetjer 266/267, 269, 272, 275, 277, 280
Chris Bennion 66/67, 68, 69, 71
Bruce Bernstein Collection, Courtesy of the Princeton University Library 26, 27, 28L&R, 29, 30, 31, 34, 35, 36, 37, 38, 39, 41, 44, 45, 148/149, 155, 188, 194, 200/201, 229, 239, 248, 254, 258, 273
Elizabeth DeFato 57
Gail Denham 56, 263
Chuck Flaherty 91
Lee Foster 72, 210L, 214, 224, 311
Barbara F. Gundle 54, 205, 206, 207, 208, 211
David Jensen 244R, 253, 268, 276, 281, 284, 285, 287, 288
Gregory J. Lawler 204
Kuhn, Inc/Image Bank Cover
Marilyn McFarlane 73
Pat O'Hara 47, 128L, 289
Portland Oregon Visitors Association 202, 210R
Joel W. Rogers 1, 58/59, 60, 62, 63, 64, 65, 74/75, 76, 77, 78, 79, 80, 81, 109
Charles Seaborn 89
Tony Stone Worldwide 55, 106/107, 292/293

Maps Berndtson & Berndtson

Visual Consultant V. Barl

Index

A

Abbie Creek Trail 310
Aberdeen 158
Abert Lake 275
Agate Beach 157
agriculture 51, 174, 182
Ainsworth State Park 196
Alaska-Yukon Pacific Exposition
    (1909) 46
Albany 232
Alki Point, Seattle 119
Allen, Paul G. 62
Alsea River 235
Alvord Desert 276
American Legion Park 137
Anacortes 141
Antelope 264
Anthony Lakes 288
Anti-Alien Association 77
apple growing 175, 181, 198–9
Applegate, Jesse 36
Arlene Schnitzer Performing Arts
    Center, Portland 208
Arnold Ice Cave 270
Ashland 249–52
Astor, John Jacob 32, 80
Astoria 215
Astoria Column 216
Avalanche Warning Hotline 170
Azalea State Park 224

B

Bagley Wright Theater 116
Bainbridge Island 136
Baker City 285
Ballard, Seattle 122
Bandon 217
Bangor 138
Barkley, Charles 30
Barlow Road 37
Barlow, Sam 36, 77–8
baseball 117
basketball 117
Bavarian Nordic Club 170
beachwalking 87–8
Beacon Hill, Seattle 121
Bear Valley 279
bears 154, 165
Beaver Lake 177
"Beaver Money" 38
"Beaver State" (Oregon) 57
Bellevue 125
Bellevue Art Museum 126
Bellevue Community College 126

Bellevue Jazz Festial 126
Belltown, Seattle 114
Bend 258–9, 261–2
Benson State Park 194
Benton County Historical Museum 235
Boeing Field International, Seattle 122
Bhagwan Shree Rajneesh 57, 264
Big Bend Country 189
Big Muddy Ranch 264
bike routes (see cycling)
birds, birdwatching, birdwatchers 87,
    155, 157, 165, 180, 217
Blake Island 138
Blitz-Weinhard Brewery, Portland 208
Blossom Festival 199
Blue Basin 281
Blue Lake 176
Blue Mountains 20
Bonneville Dam 79, 194
Bohemia Mining Days 236
Bonaparte Lake 177
Bowerman Basin 158
Breitenbush Hot Springs 231
Bridge of the Gods 198
Bridgeport State Park 177
British influence, British trade 30,
    39, 40
Broadway Plaza, Tacoma 128
Broadway, Seattle 120
Brookings 224
Brownlee Dam 287
Brownsville 232
Buchanan, President James 40
Buena Vista Ferry Service 232
Burke-Gilman Trail 125

C

Cannon Beach 217
Canyon City 279
Cape Alava 162
Cape Araga State Park 91
Cape Arago 223
Cape Blanco 224
Cape Disappointment 152–3
Cape Flattery 163
Cape Foulweather 219
Cape Kiwanda 219
Cape Lookout 210
Cape Meares 219
Capitol Hill, Seattle 120
Captain Jack's Stronghold Historic
    Trail 273
Cascade Bicycle club 125
Cascade Locks 194, 198
Cascade Locks Marine Park 197
Cascade Locks Museum 194
Cascade Range (Cascade Mountains)
    20–1, 23, 77, 95–6, 194
Cascades Lakes Highway 270
Cascadia State Park 234
Cashmere 182
Castle Crest Wildflower Trail 310
Cave Junction 244
Cayuse Indians 80
Cayuse War 35
Cedarbrook Herb Farm 164
cedars 25–6

Celilo Falls 77
Centennial Exposition 42
Center House (Seattle) 115
Central Kitsap 138
Central Washington University 182
Century Drive 270
Charleston Lighthouse 91
Chateau Ste Michelle Winery 70, 125
Chetco River 243
Chetzemoka Park 134
Chief Joseph 290
Chief Joseph Dam 177
Chief Joseph Days 290
Children's Park (Seattle) 119
Chilly Hilly Bike Ride 137
Chinese 46, 49
Chinese Quarters (Jacksonville) 254
Chism Beach 126
Chittenden Lock (Seattle) 122
Christmas Lake Valley 269
"City of Roses" (Portland) 45
Civil War 46
Clallam County Museum 164
Clark, William 21, 25, 31–2, 35, 217
Clarke's Rhododendron Nursery 154
Clarkston Hills 189
Clarno Unit 281
Clatsop County Historical Society
    Museum 216
climate 22, 204
climbing 170–1
Coast Guard Lifeboat Station and Surf
    School 153
Coast Oyster Company 155
Coast Range 21
Coliseum (Seattle) 115
Collier Memorial State Park 272
Columbia 31
Columbia Basin Irrigation Project 175
Columbia Gorge 21, 194
Columbia National Wildlife
    Refuge 175, 180
Columbia Plateau 21
Columbia River 21, 36, 77–80,
    175, 194
Columbia River Maritime Museum 215
Columbia Seafirst Center 50, 111
Colville Indian Reservation 177
Colville National Forest 177
Commencement Bay (Tacoma) 128
Cook, Captain James 29–30
Coos Bay 91, 222, 223
Copeland, Aaron 23
Copperfield 281
Cornish College of the
    Arts (Seattle) 120
Corvallis 234
Coulee City 179
Coulee Dam National
    Recreation Area 178
coulees 174
Coupeville 140
Cove Palisades State Park 263
cranberries 154, 156–7
Crane Prairie Reservoir 271
Crater Lake 21
Crater Lake National Park 96, 240,
    307–10

Crooked River Grasslands 263
Crystal Mountain 169
cycling, bicyclists 64, 124, 143
Cyrus T. Walker Nursery and Forest
    Research Center 136

D

dams 78, 79
Davis Lake 270
Daybreak Star Indian
    Center (Seattle) 120
Deadman's Island 138
Deception Pass 140
Dee Wright Observatory 236, 260
Deeny Regrade (Seattle) 114
Deepwood Estate 230
Deer Harbor 143
Deschutes National Forest 258, 270
Deschutes River 271
Destruction Island 161
Devine, Robert S. 79
Diamond Peak Wildnerness 261
Dietrich, William 62, 78, 79
Discovery 165
Discovery Park (Seattle) 120
Douglas firs 23
Drake, Francis 28
Dry Falls 21, 179
Dumwamish Waterway (Seattle) 122
Dunes National Recreation Area 221
Dungeness National Wildlife Refuge 91
Dungeness Recreation Area 165
Dungeness Spit 165

E

Eagle Cap Wilderness Area 289
Eagle Creek 197
eagles 139, 141, 142, 144, 160,
    163, 272
East Lake 270
East Side (Portland) 209
Eastside Philharmonic Orchestra
    (Seattle) 126
Eastside (Seattle) 125
Eastside Youth Symphony 126
Eastsound 143
economy 49, 51
Edmonds 139
Elam 158
Eliott Bay 44, 45
elk 154, 297, 310
Ellensburg 182
Elliott Bay 119
Elliott Bay Bikeway (Seattle) 113
Emerald City (Seattle) 44, 109
Emigrant Springs State Park 291
Emmons Glacier 303
Enchantment Lakes 301
environmental issues 57, 63, 64, 79
Eugene 235
Everett 139
Evergreen Point Floating Bridge 125
"Evergreen State" (Washington) 57
Evergreen State College (Olympia) 139
Exhibition Hall (Seattle) 115
Exposition Center (Salem) 231

F

Farewell Bend State Park 285
Favell Museum of Western Art and
    Indian Artifacts 272
Fay Bainbridge State Park 137
Fern Ridge Reservoir 236
festivals 115, 134, 216, 220, 236
Fidalgo Island 141
Fillmore, President Millard 40
First Hill (Pill Hill), Seattle 121
Fish and Game Department 88
Fish Lake 190
Fisherman's Terminal 122
fishing 51, 80, 154, 163, 176,
    220, 258
Forest Park (Portland) 208
Fort Astoria 32
Fort Canby State Park 153
Fort Casey 140
Fort Clatsop National Memorial 216
Fort Flagler 135
Fort Okanogan Interpretive
    Center 177
Fort Simcoe Historical State Park 183
Fort Stevens 49, 214–15
Fort Stevens State Park 214
Fort Ward 137
Fort Worden 134
Fort Rock State Park 275
Fossil Lake 275
Foster Island Wildlife Sanctuary
    (Seattle) 124
Fourth of July Canyon 190
Freeland 140
Freeway Park 111
Fremont Drawbridge (Seattle) 122
Fremont (Seattle) 122
Frenchman Coulee 174
Friday Harbor 143
Frye Art Museum (Seattle) 121
furs, fur trade 28, 30, 32, 187, 198

G

galleries 117, 137
Gasworks Park (Seattle) 122
Gates, Bill 51, 62
Gearheart Mountain Wilderness 276
Gifford Pinchot National Forest 97
Gig Harbor 138
Gig Harbor Summer Arts Festival 138
Gingko Petrified Forest State Park
    174, 182
Glacier 169
Glacier Peak 301
Glacier Peak Wilderness 178, 300
Glass Butte 275
Godfrey Glen Nature Trail 309
Gold Beach 224
gold 37–9, 43–4, 273–4
Golden Hind 28
Goldendale Observatory
    State Park 183
golf 170
Gooseberry Point 144
Grand Coulee 21
Grand Coulee Dam 175, 190

Grande Ronde Valley 291
Grants Pass 57, 239
Grave Creek 239
Gray, Robert 30–1, 157
Grayland 157
Grayland Beach State Park 157
Grays Harbor 157
Great Depression 47
Great Northern Line 61
Great Northern Railroad 42
Grey, Zane 240–1
Guthrie, A. B. 23

H

Hanford Atomic Works 190
Hanford Nuclear Reservation 78–9
Harris Beach State Park 224
Hart Mountain National Antelope
    Refuge 276
Hat Point 290
Hayward Field (Eugene) 235
Heceta Lighthouse and Point 220
Hell's Canyon Dam 287
Hell's Canyon National Recreation
    Area (NRA) 287
Hellgate Canyon 239
Hendrick's Park (Eugene) 235
Henry Art Gallery (Seattle) 123
Herman and Eliza Oliver Historical
    Museum 279
herons 139, 141
Hidden Valley Guest Ranch (dude
    ranch) 182
High Desert Museum 269
high-technology industries 51
Hing Hay Park (Seattle) 119
Hispanics 55
Holden Village 178
Hole-In-The-Wall Rock 90
Holmes Harbor 140
Hood Canal 165
Hood Canal Bridge 135
Hood Head 135
Hood River 77, 198
Hoodoo Bowl 234
Hoquiam 158
House of Myrtlewood 223
Hoyt Arboretum (Portland) 208
Hudson's Bay Company 32, 34,
    36, 39, 77
Hurricane Ridge 299
Hwaco Heritage Museum 153
hydro-electricity 78, 175

I

Illinois River 243
immigration, immigrants 42, 61, 118,
    187, 206
Indian Island 135
Inn at the Seventh Mountain 259
Inspiration Point 138
International District (ID),
    Seattle 117–19
International Fountain
    Court (Seattle) 115
Intiman Theater 116

"Invisible Empire" 46
Irvington (Portland) 211
Islander Lopez Resort 142
Issaquah 126

J

Jacksonville 253–4
Japanese 77, 118–19, 215
Japanese Garden (Portland) 208
Japanese Garden (Seattle) 124
Jefferson County Historical
    Museum 133
Jefferson Park 260
Jefferson, President Thomas 22, 31
Jessie Honeyman Memorial
    State Park 221
John Day Fossil Beds National
    Monument 279
John Wayne Marina 165
Jordon Valley 276
Jacksonville Museum 253–4

K

Kah-Nee-Ta 263
Kalaloch 160
Kalmiopsis Wilderness 243
Kam Wah Chung & Co. Museum 279
kayaking, canoeing (also see
    whitewater) 171
Kelley, Hall Jackson 33–4
Kelsey Creek Park 126
Kettle Falls 190
Kingdome (Seattle) 117
Kirkland 126, 127
kite festivals 154
Klamath Basin and National Wildlife
    Refuge 272
Klamath Falls and Museum 272
Klamath Indians 308
Klamath Mountains 20
Klickitat Indians 21
Kobe Park (Seattle) 119
Kopachuck State Park 138
Ku Klux Klan 46–7

L

La Conner 144
La Tienda Folk Arts
    Gallery (Seattle) 124
LaGrande 288
Lake Bath 177
Lake Billy Chinook 263
Lake Chelan 178
Lake Coeur d'Alene 190
Lake Franklin D. Roosevelt 175, 190
Lake Pend Oreille 190
Lake Owyhee 276
Lake Ozette 162
Lake Quinault 160
Lake Washington 119
Lakeshore Park 178
Lakeside Park 178
Lane County Fair 236
LaPush 161
Larch Mountain 195

Lassen Peak 96
Lava Beds National Monument 272
Lava Butte 269
Lava Cast Forest 270
Lava Lake 271
Lava Lands 270
Lava Lands Visitors' Center 269
Lava River Cave State Park 270
Lavacicle Cave 270
Leadbetter Point 155
Leadbetter Point State Park Natural
    Area 155
Leavenworth 182
Lee, Jason 35, 228, 230
Legislative Building (Olympia)
Lenore Caves 180
Lenore Lake 180
Lewis and Clark Exposition (1905) 45
Lewis and Clark State Park 195
Lewis and Clark Interpretive
    Center 153
Lewis, Meriwether 21, 31–2, 35, 217
Liberty Bay Park 137
Liberty Bell Alpine tours 170
Lincoln City 217, 219
Liberty Lake 190
Linn County Pioneer Picnic 233
Lithia Springs and Park (Ashland) 250
logging (lumber) 42–3, 51, 222,
    233, 297
Lok, Michael 29
Long Beach Peninsula 153
Loomis Lake 154
Lopez 142
Louisiana Purchase 31
Lucerne 178
Lummi Indian Reservation 144
Lummi Indian Stomish 144
Lummi Island 144

M

Magnolia (Seattle) 119
Makah Indians 162
Makah Research and
    Cultural Center 163
Malheur National Wildlife Refuge 276
Manson 178
manufacturing companies 49
Marina Park (Kirkland) 127
marine life 85–91
Marrowstone Island 135
Marsh Island 124
Maryhill Museum of Art 183
McCall, Governor Tom 50, 205, 229
McCormick Pier (Portland) 207
McKenzie, Alexander 31
McLoughlin, Dr John 32, 34, 35, 77
Memorial Coliseum (Portland) 211
Mercer Island Floating Bridge 125
Methow River 177
Methow Valley 177
Methow Valley Ski Touring
    Association 170
Metro Transit System (Seattle) 113
micro-brewing 64
Microsoft 51, 62
Mission Mill Village 230

Mission Ridge (Wenatchee) 170
missionaries 35
Modoc Indians 308
Mohler 217
Moran State Park 142
Mount Bachelor 259, 261
Mount Baker 96, 169
Mount Baker National Forest 300
Mount Constitution 142
Mount Hood 21, 23, 77, 96, 169, 198
Mount Howard 290
Mount Index 301
Mount Jefferson 231
Mount Jefferson Wilderness Area 259
Mount Lakes 301
Mount Mazama 307
Mount Olympus 298
Mount Rainier 21, 23, 96, 169, 302
Mount Rainier National Park 302–3
Mount Shasta 96
Mount Spokane 190
Mount St Helens 21, 95–7, 169
Mount St Helens National Geological
    Area 97
Mount St Helens National Volcanic
    Monument 97, 203
Mount Temple 301
Mount Washington Wilderness 260
Mowich Lake 303
Mukilteo 139
Mulee Creek Canyon 240
Museum of Flight (Seattle) 122
Museum of History and Industry
    (Seattle) 124
Myrtle Edwards Park (Seattle) 112

N

Nahcotta 154
Naselle River 155
National Historic Oregon Trail
    Interpretive Center 286
National Motor Lifeboat School 80
National Oceanic and Atmospherics
    Administration 171
Native American artifacts 123, 129,
    272, 275
Native Americans 25–6, 35, 152, 187,
    215, 233 also see individual tribes
Naval Air Show (Whidbey) 141
Naval Air Station (Whidbey) 141
Neah Bay 162
Neahkahnie Mountain 217
Nee-Me-Poo Recreational Trail 291
Nehalem Bay State Park 218
New Market Theater and Galleria
    (Portland) 207
Newberry Crater 270
Newport Marine Science Center 220
Nez Perce Crossing 290
Nez Perce Indians 35, 177, 290
Nisqually Delta 139
Nisqually National Wildlife Refuge 91
Nordstrom's 64
North Cascades National Park 178,
    300–1
North Kitsap Peninsula 135
Northern Pacific Railroad 61

Northwest Company 31, 32
Northwest CyberArtists 62
Northwest Environment
    Watch (NEW) 64
Northwest Outdoor Center 149
Northwest Passage 28, 30

O

Oak Harbor 140
Oakridge 236
Ocean City State Park Marine
    Interpretive Center 159
Ocean Shores 159
Odlin County Park 142
Ogden Scenic Wayside 263
Ogden, Peter Skene 33, 273
Ohme Gardens 182
Okanogan County 170
Okanogan County Historical
    Museum 176
Okanogan Highlands 176
Okanogan National Forest 176, 300
Okanogan River Valley 176
Old Man House, Squamish 136
Old Perpetual (geyser) 276
Olga 143
Ollalie Scenic Area 231
Olmstead, Frederick Law 45
Olmsted, John 45
Olympia 138–9, 165
Olympic Mountains 23, 152, 298–9
Olympic National Park 164, 297–9
Olympic Peninsula 152
Ontario 276
Opera Association (Seattle) 115
Opera House (Seattle) 115
Orcas Island 142
Oregon Bach Festival 236
Oregon Caves National
    Monument 244–5
Oregon Coast 214–24
Oregon Coast Aquarium 220
Oregon Dunes National Recreation
    Area 91
Oregon Exchange Company 38
Oregon Museum of Science and
    Industry (OMSI), Portland 210
Oregon Shakespeare
    Festival 249–51
Oregon State Fair 231
Oregon State Fish Hatchery 197
Oregon Trail 228, 285–6, 288
Oregonian (newspaper) 22, 49
Owyhee Mountains 276
Oxbow Dam 281
oysters 154
Oysterville 154

P

Pabst Brewing Company 138, 139
Pacific County Courthouse 155
Pacific Crest Trail 260
Pacific Fur Company 32, 80
Pacific Northwest Arts and
    Crafts Fair 126
Pacific Northwest Ballet 115

Pacific Northwest Museum of Natural
    History 252
Pacific Ocean 22, 152
Pacific Rim 51
Padilla Bay National Estuarine
    Sanctuary 141
Painted Cave 281
Painted Hills Unit 281
Palouse Hills 187
PANACA Gallery (Bellevue) 126
Pantages Center (Tacoma) 128
Paradise 302
Park Lake 180
Pasayten Wilderness 300
Paulina 279
Paulina Lake 270
Pearl Harbor 49, 77
Pendleton 291
Pendleton Round-Up 291
Peter Britt Music Festival 254
Peter Kirk Building 127
Petersen's Rock Gardens 262
Philomath 235
Pierce, Governor 47
Pike Place Market (Seattle) 113, 114
Pioneer Building (Seattle) 116
Pioneer Cemetery (Jacksonville) 254
Pioneer Museum (Tillamook) 218
Pioneer Place Park (Seattle) 116
Pioneer Square (Portland) 208
Pioneer Square (Seattle) 116
Point Defiance Park (Tacoma) 129
Point of Arches 163
Point Wilson Lighthouse 134
pollution 79
Polson's Museum 158
ponderosa pine 23, 174
population 63
porpoises 89–90
Port Gamble 136
Port Marina Park 198
Port of Portland 203
Port Orford 224
Port Orford Wayside State Park 224
Port Townsend 133, 165
Portage Head 163
Portland 23, 42, 45, 202–11
Portland Art Museum 208
Portland Building 207
Portland Docks 78
Portland International Airport 211
Portland Meadows Racetrack 211
Portland State University 208
Potholes Reservoir 180
Poulsbo 137
Produce Row (Portland) 210
Puget Sound 30, 40, 42, 43, 133–41
Puget Sound Agricultural Company 36
Puget Sound Cooperative Colony 57
Puget, Peter 30

Q

Queen Ann Hill (Seattle) 120
Queets River 160
Quileute Days 161
Quileute Indian Reservation 90, 159
Quinault River 159

R

Raban, Jonathan 61
racism 46
Raft Island 138
rain forests 297
Raine Falls 240
Rainier Brewery (Seattle) 121
Rainier Tower (Seattle) 110
Rancho Rajneesh 264
Raymond 155
Redmond 262
Reed Opera House (Salem) 230
Remington, Frederick 23
restaurants (Seatte) 114, 118–19,
    129, 189, 190, 206, 236
Rialto Beach 162
RiverWatch 79
Roche Harbor 144
Rogue River 224, 239–43
Rogue River Trail 242
Roosevelt, President Franklin D. 49
Rosario Resort 143
Rose Festival (Portland) 208
Ross Lake 300
Royal Brougham Collection 117
Ruby Beach 161
Russian exploration 28, 31

S

Sacagawea 22
Salem 228–9
Salmon Bay (Seattle) 120, 122
salmon 80, 157, 196–7, 263
Salt Creek 164
Salt Creek Recreation Area 91
Samish Bay 144
Samuel H. Boardman State Park 224
San Juan Island 143
San Juan Island Historical society 143
San Juan Islands 141–4
Sand Point 162
sand dunes 220–2
Sanke River 287
Santiam Pass 233
Sauvie Island (Portland) 209
Scenic Highway 30 194
Sea Lion Caves 220
Sea to Ski Race 169
sea kayaking 148–9
sea lions 88–9
sea otters 29, 88, 141
seals 88–9
Seaside 217
Seattle 23, 42, 43–5, 109–27
Seattle Aquarium 112
Seattle Art Museum 112
Seattle Asian Art Museum 121
Seattle Center 109, 115
Seattle Center Playhouse 116
Seattle Hills 119–21
Seattle Opera 63
Seattle Symphony 63
Seattle Symphony Orchestra 115
Seattle Times 62
Seattle Tower 112
Seattle Youth Symphony 115

Seaview 153
Sehome Hill 144
Sekiu 162, 163
Sequim 164–5
Sequim Bay State Park 165
Seven Lakes Basin 298
Shaniko 264
Shark Reef Park 142
Shaw Island County Park 142
Sheep Rock Visitors' Center 280
Shi-Shi Beach 163
Shoalwater Indian Reservation 156
Shore Acres 222
Silver Lake 275
Silverdale 138
Silverton 230
Sinclair Inlet 138
Sinlahekin Wildlife Refuge 176
Sinnott Memorial Overlook 307
Siuslaw National Forest 236
Skagit River 144
Skagit Wildlife Recreational Area 144
Skell Head 308
Ski Acres Cross Country Center 170
skiing, ski areas and
    resorts 169–70, 258
slavery 40, 46
Smith Tower 50
Snake River 21
Snoqualmie National Forest 300
Snoqualmie Pass 169, 301
Snow Lakes 301
Soap Lake 180
Soleduck Hot Springs 298
"sourdoughs" 44
South Bend 155
South Falls 230
South Slough Sanctuary 222
Southeast Asians 55–6, 61
Space Needle (Seattle) 49, 115
Spalding, Henry H. 35
Spaniards, Spanish influence 28–9, 31
Spencer Spit State Park 142
Spencer's Butte Trailhead 236
Spokane 187–9
Spout Springs 289
Springfield 236
St Mark's Cathedral (Seattle) 120
Starbucks 64
Starwave Corp. 62
State Capital Museum (Olympia) 139
Steamboat Rocks State Park 179
Ste Chappelle Vineyards 70
Steel, William G. 309
Steens Mountain 276
Stehekin 178
Stehekin Valley 178
Stevens Pass 169
Straits of Juan de Fuca 30
Strawberry Mountain Wilderness 279
Striped Peak 164
Stuart Range 301
Summer Lake 275
Sun Lakes State Park 180
Sun Mountain Lodge 177
Sunriver 259
Suquamish 136
Suquamish Indians 136

Suquamish Museum 136
Sweet Home 233

T

Tacoma 42, 128–9
Tacoma Art Museum 128
Tacoma Dome 129
Taholah 159
Talent 252
Tatoosh Island 163
Teanaway River Valley 182
Teawhit Head 162
Twin Harbors State Park 157
The Dalles 36
The Pinnacles 310
The Phantom ship 309
theater 116 (also see Shakespeare
    Festival)
Thomas Burke Memorial Washington
    State Museum (Seattle) 123
Three Sisters Wilderness 260
Tillicum Village 138
Toke Point 156
Tokeland 156
Toppenish National Wildlife
    Refuge 183
tourism 51, 154
Trail of Glass 270
Trans Columbia Bridge 216
Tri-Cities 190
Twain, Mark 26
Twenty-five Mile Creek State Park 178
Twisp 300

U

Umatilla Indian Reservation 291
University Bookstore (Seattle) 123
University of Oregon (Eugene) 235
University of Portland 211
University of Washington (Seattle) 124
US Army Corp of Engineers 79
US Forest Service 79

V

Valerianos, Apostolos (Juan de Fuca)
    29–30
Vancouver, Captain George 30
Vantage 174
Vashon Island 138
Villard, Henry 42, 61
volcanoes, volcanic activity 20, 95–7
Volunteer Park (Seattle) 121

W

WahMee Club 118
Wallowa County Museum 290
Wallowa Lake State Park 289
Wallowa Mountains 20
War of 1812 32
Warm Springs Indian Reservation 263
Warner Lakes 275
Warner Mountain Ski Area 276
Washington Athletic Club (Seattle) 112
Washington Coast 152–65

Washington Mountains 168–71
Washington Mutual Tower 111
Washington Park
    Arboretum (Seattle) 124
Washington Park International Rose
    Test Garden (Portland) 208
Washington State Ferries 141, 146–7
Washington State Historical Society
    Museum 129
Washington Park Zoo (Portland) 208
Washington, President George 40
Water Street, Port Townsend 133
Waterfall Gardens (Seattle) 117
waterfalls 195–6
Waterfront Activity
    Center (Seattle) 124
Waterfront Park (Seattle) 112
Wenatchee 181
Wenatchee National Forest 300
West Hills (Portland) 208
Western Washington State
    University 144
Westhaven State Park 157
Westport 156
Westport Coast Guard Station 157
Weyerhauser Lumber Mill 222
whale museum, Friday Harbor 90
whales 88, 90, 143
Whidbey Island 140
whitewater rafting 171, 240–2, 258
Whitman, Marcus 35
Wickiup Reservoir 271
wildflowers 179, 182, 297, 298, 310
Wildlife Safari 239
wildlife 95, 129, 161, 165, 220, 310
    (also see individual wildlife refuges)
Willamette National Forest 233, 258
Willamette Pass 235
Willamette River 77, 228–33
Willamette River Valley 23, 36–7, 39,
    228–33
Willamette University 229
Willapa Bay 154
Willapa National Wildlife Refuge 154
William I. Finley National Wildlife
    Refuge 235
Willie Keil's Grave 156
Winchester Waterway 180
Wind Cave 270
wine, wine industry 68–73, 165, 245
Wing Luke Asian
    Museum (Seattle) 119
Winslow 136
Winthrop 177, 300
Wizard Island 309
Woodland Park Zoo (Seattle) 123
World Forestry Center (Portland) 208
World War II 47, 49, 77, 118, 215
World War I 47
World's Fair 109, 115, 187

Y

Yachats 219
Yakima 182
Yakima Indian Reservation 183
Yakima Nation Cultural Center 183
Yakima Valley Museum 183

A
B
C
D
E
F
G
H
I
J
a
b
c
d
e
f
g
h
j
k
l